W9-ADE-376

A DAY OF DEDICATION

By the Same Author

THE MODERN AGE

Editor of:

THE ESSENTIAL LINCOLN
(with Gerald E. Stearn)

THE ESSENTIAL JEFFERSON

SOCIALIST THOUGHT
(with Ronald Sanders)

Forthcoming:

THE JEFFERSONIAN AND HAMILTONIAN TRADITIONS
IN AMERICAN POLITICS

A Day of DEDICATION

The Essential Writings & Speeches of WOODROW WILSON

Edited, with an Introduction, by ALBERT FRIED

The Macmillan Company, New York
Collier-Macmillan Limited, London

First Printing

The Macmillan Company, New York
Collier-Macmillan Canada, Ltd., Toronto, Ontario

Library of Congress catalog card number: 65-22613

Printed in the United States of America

DESIGNED BY RONALD FARBER

To the Memory of
MY PARENTS

ACKNOWLEDGMENTS

I should like first of all to thank the Manuscript Division of the Library of Congress for enabling me to consult and use the Papers of Woodrow Wilson and the Ray Stannard Baker Collection; and Mr. John Wells Davidson for permitting me to excerpt generously from his fine work on Wilson's 1912 presidential campaign, *A Crossroads of Freedom* (New Haven, Yale University Press, 1956).

I was fortunate to have the help of several close friends. I am indebted to Irwin Shapiro, who took time out from his own writing to give me the benefit of his astute suggestions and advice; I hope I have learned something from him. Edith Firoozi's assistance throughout was indispensable; words will not convey my felt obligation to her. I am deeply grateful to Dr. David Golding for his penetrating criticisms. To Emily Bernstein and Shareen Blair I once again owe thanks for their help in preparing the manuscript.

CONTENTS

Six TREATY 1918–1919

Seven TRAGEDY 1919–1924

INTRODUCTION

WOODROW WILSON'S political career is unique in American history. With the exception of military heroes, the men who become President of the United States usually spend many years in political apprenticeship. Wilson was elected President less than three years after entering politics. And, what was even more improbable, he came directly from the academic world, where he had been a college teacher and president. Yet no one was less surprised than Wilson; he had long been preparing himself for a career in politics. His many articles and books on government give the impression of having been written by a statesman rather than a professor. He moved into political life with the deftness of a man who had finally found his calling.

Thomas Woodrow Wilson was born on December 28, 1856, in the small town of Staunton, Virginia. His father, Joseph Ruggles Wilson, had moved there from Ohio many years before to be a minister of a Presbyterian congregation. The family line on both sides was Scotch-Irish and militantly Calvinist. But Wilson's father was no typical Southern fundamentalist. By all accounts he was a scholarly and cultivated man. This was fortunate for young Wilson, who, until he went to college, received his education at home. No doubt he owed to his father the Calvinist virtues that were to distinguish his character throughout his life.

In 1875, after an unhappy year at a small Presbyterian college in North Carolina, Wilson came to Princeton, or, as it was then called, the College of New Jersey. There he worked out the basis of the political philosophy which he later elaborated in his numerous books. He was only a junior when he brought out his first essay, a long analysis of Bismarck, whose strong leadership and capacity to call forth the German nation's sense of duty he admired. A year later, he published what was probably his best piece of writing, "Cabinet Government in the United States," a long article on America's crisis of leadership since the Civil War. The reason for this crisis, he maintained, lay in the system of separation of powers which divided the responsibility of governing, and so gave rise to political divisiveness and obstructionism. Wilson advocated that the United States adopt a modified form of the British cabinet system under which members of Congress would be held to account for interfering with presidential power. In his later writings on political theory, Wilson expanded the ideas set forth in this short essay.

The road to politics, then as now, was through the law. After graduating from Princeton, Wilson took a law degree at the University of Virginia. He practiced in Atlanta, which by 1882 had become a representative community of the "New South"—the South that had left its defeat and demoralization behind and was wholeheartedly embracing the spirit of business enterprise. After less than two years of practice, Wilson had had enough of law. The crassness, the money-grubbing, the pettifoggery, repelled him. He wanted a profession in which he could think and work at leisure and yet live in comfort. He was willing to let politics wait. He decided on a college teaching career and accepted a fellowship to take an advanced degree at Johns Hopkins University in Baltimore.

Johns Hopkins was then the leading school of higher education in the country, the first to introduce a doctoral program on the German model. Wilson wrote his dissertation under a remarkable teacher, Herbert Baxter Adams, whose seminars attracted many of the best young scholars in the country. The dissertation, later published as *Congressional Government*, elaborated the theme of his senior essay. Having grown up in the era of Johnson, Grant, Hayes and Arthur, Wilson assumed that the President was the tool of Congress. The federal government, he wrote, "lacks strength because its powers are divided, lacks promptness because its authorities are multiplied, lacks wieldiness because its processes are roundabout, lacks efficiency because its responsibility is indistinct and its action without competent direction." Only a cabinet form of government could overcome these defects, he held, because it would fuse executive and legislative authority, thus making each responsible for the failings and the successes of the other.

Congressional Government was Wilson's most original book. Published in 1885, it is the only one of his works that has continued to be read down to the present. But its defects are prominent: it is rhetorical, oversimplified and highly moralistic. Moreover, it exaggerates the genius of Britain's politics and underrates the genius of America's. Wilson's own career was to be a decisive refutation of its thesis. A cabinet system of government would never have allowed a political outsider to climb to the summit of power.

Publication of his first book launched Wilson on a successful career as teacher and writer. He taught at Bryn Mawr and then at Wesleyan College, and in 1890 returned to Princeton as professor of jurisprudence and political economy. Between 1893 and 1902 he found time to bring out nine books, including a five-volume *History of the American People,* and thirty-five articles, most of them for popular magazines. By 1900 he was becoming well known in the East as a sober conservative, an ardent defender —at a time when insurgent movements were starting to challenge the status quo—of traditional authority and the unsullied virtues of free enterprise.

When the president of Princeton retired in 1902, the board of trustees at once selected Wilson to succeed him. Wilson soon proved that they had made a wise choice. He charged every cell in the university with his energy, and soon Princeton became the talk of the academic world.

His first project was to institute a revolutionary change in the mode of instructing undergraduates. He was convinced that learning from textbooks and lectures alone failed to elicit a mature intellectual response from college men. "The only way to instruct them," he said, "is to provide a certain number of men sufficiently qualified as instructors, as scholars, who will be companions and coaches and guides of the men's reading." Accordingly, he recommended that Princeton take on fifty preceptors who would coach and guide the men for an experimental period of three years. The trustees and faculty welcomed the bold idea. By 1905 he had raised enough money to get the preceptorial system under way. It was an immediate success. Within a short time, thanks also to an extensive reorganization of the curriculum, Princeton had become one of the leading universities in the country.

Wilson was acclaimed Princeton's greatest president by students, faculty, alumni, and trustees alike. But success only whetted his desire for fresh reforms. Two years after launching the preceptorships, he advanced another revolutionary proposal: that Princeton abolish its student fraternities, or eating clubs as they were called. Having grown outrageously exclusive and lavish over the years, these clubs obviously jeopardized the preceptorial system. Students could hardly be faithful to the spirit of freedom and democracy when they gave their first loyalties to rigidly hierarchical fraternities. He therefore proposed a "quad plan" to replace the clubs with "academic communities." The clubs were to be absorbed into four residential quadrangles, each housing a separate class, and each being more or less self-sufficient.

To Wilson's surprise the quad plan met opposition from the start. For most of the alumni, attendance at Princeton had more social than intellectual importance. They considered abolition of the eating clubs to be the equivalent of abolishing Princeton itself. Several important members of the faculty also opposed Wilson. They felt slighted because he had not consulted with them before getting the board of trustees to approve the quad plan. His chief enemy on the faculty was Andrew F. West, the powerful dean of the graduate school, a man as intractable and combative as Wilson. According to West, the quad plan threatened to kill "the Spirit of Princeton."

Most of the trustees, yielding to the alumni, sought to modify Wilson's plan by reforming, rather than removing, the clubs. In October of 1907 they voted to table the plan. Wilson refused to accept their decision. He appealed directly to the alumni—only to be rebuffed. The quad plan suffered final defeat early in 1908 when a faculty committee of Wilson's own friends issued a report agreeing with the trustees' recommendation that the clubs needed only to be reformed. The battle over the quad plan disclosed certain flaws in Wilson's qualities as a leader; he was averse to compromise, tended to turn conflict into a death-struggle, and regarded opponents as enemies.

A deeper and more consequential struggle immediately followed. This new controversy concerned the location of the graduate school. Again Wilson's chief adversary was Andrew West, dean of the school. Several years before, West had proposed that a new and expanded graduate school be located off campus, and he had already found a suitable site. Wilson demanded that the graduate school be located on campus and integrated with the rest of the university. He was supported by the trustees, who, at his insistence, stripped West of most of his power over the graduate school. But West was as resourceful as Wilson—and much better connected with rich alumni. In May, 1909, he informed Wilson that a Cincinnati soap magnate, William Cooper Procter, was offering Princeton $500,000 to help build a graduate school on the site chosen by West. The board of trustees did not take long to capitulate, and in October they overruled Wilson's objections and accepted the gift. Wilson was prepared to resign unless the board reversed its decision. The dispute dragged on through the fall and early winter. Finally, Procter withdrew his offer. Wilson was elated; the battle appeared to be his.

By this time the conflict had become known to the public. On February 3, 1910, *The New York Times* carried an editorial attributing Wilson's difficulties at Princeton, beginning with the quad plan, to his desire for democracy and his opposition to the entrenched aristocracy of wealth. The outcome, the *Times* predicted, "will decide the issue whether the American colleges shall henceforth fall short of their democratic mission." Neither the public nor anyone at Princeton knew that Wilson himself had furnished the *Times* with information for the editorial.

In an extraordinary speech on April 16, 1910, to the Pittsburgh alumni, Wilson made his point openly. Two days before, the trustees had nominated one of his opponents for membership on the board—an obvious slap in the face. In his speech, Wilson maintained that Princeton had failed to carry out its chief function, which was to attend to the needs of the "masses" rather than of the "classes." To be true to its calling in a democracy, the university must reflect the strength of the nation, which "comes from the great mass of the unknown, of the unrecognized men, whose powers are being developed by struggle." Wilson was clearly addressing himself not to the alumni or the trustees, but to the nation as a whole, to the "masses."

The graduate-school affair ended badly for Wilson. A sudden turn of events made his uncompromising position meaningless and assured West's triumph. On May 18, 1910, Isaac C. Wyman died, and left, in West's charge, an estate of several million dollars for the purpose of building a graduate school. The trustees accepted at once. Far from protesting, Wilson blandly announced that he no longer objected to construction of the school off campus. He resigned from Princeton in a curt ceremony on October 20, 1910, five weeks after his nomination as Democratic candidate for Governor of New Jersey.

Ever since William Jennings Bryan and the radical West had captured the Democratic party in 1896, Eastern conservatives had been casting about for a man who could lead the party back to the principles of Grover Cleveland. A number of these Eastern Democrats began to take notice of Wilson, whose work as president of Princeton and whose speeches and writings had already brought him to the public's attention. He especially impressed George Harvey of New York, the editor of *Harper's Weekly* and a friend of politicians and industrialists. As early as February, 1906, Harvey spoke of Wilson as a possible presidential candidate.

Wilson gave every appearance of being "safe." In the many speeches he made between 1907 and 1909, he argued that freedom meant economic individualism and that that government was best which governed least. His remarks to the Cleveland Chamber of Commerce in November, 1907, were typical: "We turn more and more with a sense of individual helplessness to the government, begging that it take care of us because we have forgotten how to take care of ourselves, begging that it will regulate our industries, scrutinize our economic undertakings, supervise our enterprises. . . . In such courses we are turning directly away from all the principles which have distinguished America and made her institutions the hope of all men who believe in liberty." On several occasions Wilson refused to share the same platform with Bryan. In 1908 he publicly described Bryan as "the most charming and lovable of men personally, but foolish and dangerous in his theoretical belief."

In early 1910, Harvey set about making Wilson Governor of New Jersey, the first step on the road to the White House. Harvey's shrewd eye perceived that the governorship of that state would easily fall to the Democrats—provided they chose the right candidate. The Republican party in New Jersey was split into progressive and "standpat" factions. During the long years of Republican rule, certain special interests, particularly the utilities and the railroads, had had things their own way. In no state did they exercise power more brazenly. Most of the corporate holding companies in the United States received their charters from New Jersey, and the state came to be known as "the mother of trusts." But shortly after the turn of the century an insurgent movement arose in the Republican party. Led by an extraordinary man, George L. Record, the New Idea, as the movement was called, plumped for strict regulation of railroads and utilities and for widespread political reforms. It hoped in this way to break the power held by the trusts and the political bosses who ran the state. Though progressivism grew in the Democratic party as well, its main strength lay in the Republican party, now hopelessly divided. There was no doubt that 1910 would be a Democratic year, the first in nearly two decades.

Harvey acted as intermediary between Wilson and the leaders of the New Jersey Democratic organization. They were in the market for a man such as Wilson appeared to be: known and trusted by the people, yet safe for the politicians. The boss most responsible for clearing the way to Wilson's nomination was James Smith, Jr., longtime head of the huge Essex County machine. Smith agreed to support Wilson on receiving his promise not to set up an organization of his own. Beyond that, Smith gave him considerable leeway "in the matter of measures and men." Harvey and Smith even convinced Wilson that he might become President. Democratic leaders in several states, they said, wanted Wilson to head off other potential candidates for the Presidency in 1912. All of this appealed to Wilson's vanity, which was equaled only by his naiveté. He asked himself why the bosses had chosen him and not another, and he came up with this answer: "These gentlemen recognized the fact that a new day had come in American politics, and that they would have to conduct themselves henceforth after a new fashion."

In the period between the announcement of his candidacy on July 15 and his nomination exactly two months later, Wilson underwent a sudden and surprising change in his political point of view. The Wilson who was the Democratic candidate for governor emerged as a completely committed progressive of the Bryan school. The high moral standards which lay at the heart of progressivism were congenial to Wilson's temperament; progressivism provided a much more suitable outlet for his deep passion for social duty and moral right than conservatism ever had. He began to see transcendent ideals as concrete issues. Wilson came into his own in the summer of 1910.

At first neither the bosses nor the progressives of New Jersey perceived the change. Progressive insurgents of both parties had vigorously opposed his candidacy. Having struggled for years against bossism, they knew why Wilson had been chosen. Organized labor, too, opposed Wilson. It felt a special grievance against a man who had often shown hostility to the very principle of unions. In the course of his campaign, however, he convinced labor that he was its friend; he even apologized for his ignorance of unions in the past.

Above all, he convinced progressives that he was on their side. In an important and unusual public exchange of letters with George L. Record, the leader of New Jersey progressivism, he removed once and for all any doubts about exactly where he stood. On October 19, 1910, Record put nineteen questions to Wilson dealing with every controversial issue in New Jersey politics. Wilson's reply six days later could have been written by Record himself, so completely did it accord with the progressive position. In short, he had abandoned his commitment to the Democratic machine. Harvey and his friends had placed Wilson on the road to the White House—but he would have fallen by the wayside had he not made the right choice at the first juncture.

The election results justified Wilson's most sanguine hopes.

He won by 50,000 votes; the Democrats swept the field, winning both houses in the legislature. Wilson's progressivism would now be put to the test.

It became clear to Wilson soon after his election that in order to regulate the special interests, he first had to smash the political machine which protected them. The struggle began when James Smith, Jr. decided to return to the United States Senate, where he had served a term many years before. Nothing could have stood in his way if Wilson had not intervened. For progressives it was especially important to keep Smith from the Senate—Senators traditionally controlled state governments by virtue of the vast quantity of federal patronage at their disposal. Wilson had no choice but to fight Smith to the bitter end. He knew full well that, if he lost, he could go no further in politics. But Smith proved no match for him. Riding the crest of his enormous popularity, Wilson won the backing of nearly every Democrat in the legislature except those from Smith's own bailiwick. On January 28, the legislature voted Smith's rival, James E. Martine, an old Bryan Democrat, into the Senate. Wilson was the unchallenged leader of the state.

In his first year as governor, Wilson put through more reforms than any governor in the history of New Jersey. Under his relentless prodding, the legislature of 1911 enacted his four major campaign promises. The most important of them was the direct primary law, which the political machines fought in New Jersey as in all other states. Under its terms the people, and not the party organization, were to select candidates for office. Both progressives and machine politicians believed that a direct primary law would completely destroy bossism. The Geran bill, as the direct primary bill was known, was stalled repeatedly in the legislature. But Wilson was as uncompromising then as he had been in every one of his previous conflicts. Again the opposition crumbled—and the Geran bill was passed.

Thereafter Wilson's program sailed easily through the legislature. This program consisted of a wide-ranging law to eliminate corrupt practice, requiring candidates to indicate their sources of contribution and to spend no more than a specified amount;

a public utilities law, as advanced as any in the country, establishing a three-man commission to regulate all public service industries in the state; and a workman's compensation law, for the first time forcing employers to help compensate workers injured on the job. According to George L. Record, the legislature of 1911 was the most impressive "ever known in the political history of this or any other state." Wilson properly received much of the credit for it. He had broken the machine, he had organized the progressive forces in both parties, and he had persuaded the legislature to adopt, with few reservations, his entire reform program.

Wilson looked ahead to the presidential election of 1912. His chances for the Presidency, or rather for the Democratic nomination, rested on his continued mastery of New Jersey politics. Rarely do presidential nominating conventions consider men, however attractive or whatever their virtues, who do not have the solid backing of a state organization. Wilson suffered a setback when the Republican party—still the majority party in the state—overwhelmingly won both houses of the legislature in the election of 1911. A majority of the 1912 legislature would have liked nothing more than to wreck his presidential chances. The contrast with the previous session was astonishing. Wilson vetoed forty-nine bills which he thought were intended to destroy the great work of the previous session, accompanying the vetoes with sharp verbal attacks. The Republicans charged that Wilson, using New Jersey as his footstool to the Presidency, was derelict in his duty as governor. Nevertheless Wilson was able to retain control over the Democratic party organization. He again decisively triumphed over the Smith machine when, in the primary election of May 28, 1912, almost every delegate to the coming Democratic convention was instructed to back him. Less than two years after his entry into politics, Wilson was a contender for the Democratic presidential nomination.

Soon after the extraordinarily successful legislative session of 1911, an organized movement to nominate Wilson was begun, its nucleus consisting of lesser-known Eastern and Southern progressive politicians. Early in 1912 Wilson traveled throughout the country on a well-publicized speaking tour in which he went out of his way to affirm his solidarity with Bryan and Bryan's ideals. Bryan knew, of course, of Wilson's former close relations with Eastern conservatives. But this made Wilson's progressivism all the more trustworthy. Wilson's former friends, especially George Harvey, tried hard, through devious means, to sow discord between the two men. The result, however, was to convince Bryan beyond question that Wilson was a true believer.

Wilson's campaign started well but came to a halt before the Democratic convention opened on June 25, 1912. Most state organizations refused to support a man who had demolished the New Jersey machine and, as a progressive, seemed to be hostile to all bosses. Actually, Wilson's camp never eschewed alliances with state machines. Wilson knew that such alliances were the only means for securing the votes of two-thirds of the convention, the amount then necessary for nomination. His difficulties arose not so much from his repudiation of the bosses' support as from the bosses' preference for a more reliable man.

They had found such a man in Champ Clark, a shrewd, moderately progressive cracker-barrel politician from Missouri, who had been Speaker of the House of Representatives since 1910. By June, Clark was far in the lead. A number of states in the deep South favored Representative Oscar Underwood of Alabama, chairman of the House Ways and Means Committee: tariff bills originated in this committee, and the deep South was indebted to Underwood for his attempts to win tariff reform. After more than a year of canvassing, Wilson appeared to have only enough votes to swing the nomination to another candidate, but not enough to win it himself.

The Baltimore convention of 1912 is one of the most famous in American political history. That Wilson, a fading possibility when it opened, was nominated testifies to the indeterminacy of American politics at that time. The convention lasted a week and went through forty-six ballots. On the first ballot, Clark had 440½ votes to Wilson's 342 and Underwood's 117½; 710 were necessary to win. On the tenth ballot, the New York delegation, headed by the notorious Boss Murphy, cast its votes for

Clark, whose total now rose to 556, a majority. Not since 1844 had a Democratic convention failed to nominate a candidate who gained a majority.

But Boss Murphy's sudden move was instrumental in losing the nomination for Clark. At the start of the convention, Bryan had dissociated himself from the Clark movement because it was supported by most of the machines, by William Randolph Hearst and, allegedly, by important Wall Street interests. But Bryan did not openly oppose Clark's nomination until Murphy made his announcement. He then threw his full support to Wilson who steadily gained strength at Clark's expense. Wilson reached a crisis on the forty-fifth ballot. By this time he had slightly more than 600 votes. Actually, he was in great danger, for the Illinois delegation, which had switched to Wilson on the forty-third ballot, would revert to Clark on the forty-sixth unless Wilson received further support. This came on the forty-sixth ballot, when Southern delegations, realizing that Clark would benefit from their continued support of Underwood, gave their votes to Wilson. The long struggle was over.

As its final act, the convention ratified a platform which summarized the progressive aims of the party. Important planks recommended exemption of labor unions from antitrust legislation, adoption of the constitutional amendments on income tax and on direct election of Senators, and opposition to a centralized banking system, controlled by Wall Street, as proposed by the Republicans. It was a tremendous triumph for Wilson as well as for the principles of Bryan.

Since 1896 the Republicans had dominated national affairs. A small conservative group in the Senate laid down national policy, especially on tariffs, for the party as a whole. Republican Presidents McKinley, Roosevelt and Taft carried out policies set by the congressional conservatives who controlled the party organization. Meanwhile, however, a revulsion against the trusts and the politicians allied with them swept the Republican North. Insurgency rose within the Republican party at the very moment when conservatism stood at the apogee of its power.

Robert La Follette of Wisconsin was among the first—and was

to prove the greatest—of the Republican insurgents. In the early 1890's, he challenged the Republican state organization, of which he had till then been a faithful member. He proposed the regulation of special interests, above all railroads, and the enactment of a direct primary law designed to destroy the old guard machine. After a long and courageous struggle, La Follette became governor of Wisconsin in 1901 and proceeded to carry out his promises, initiating a pattern of insurgency that was to be followed in other solid Republican states throughout the country. In Iowa, Kansas. Minnesota, the Dakotas, Oregon, Washington and California, insurgents captured the state government and went on to become United States Senators and Congressmen. In 1905, La Follette became the first of the insurgents to enter the Senate; by 1909 there were six, and in 1911 there were thirteen. These La Follette formed into a strong bloc which held the balance of power between the two parties.

While the Republican party seethed with rebellion, President Taft remained loyal to the conservative old guard. He committed blunders on the questions of tariff reform, conservation and railroad regulation which made him appear more conservative than he actually was. By 1912 he had completely alienated the now sizeable insurgent wing of his party. Theodore Roosevelt, who had chosen Taft to be his successor and had then become dissatisfied with his protégé, joined the insurgents within the party. Roosevelt and Taft were the two main contenders at the Republican nominating convention of June, 1912. When Taft won, thanks to the unanimous support of the still dominant old-guard machine, the progressives bolted the convention, formed their own party, and nominated Roosevelt for President. The platform of the Progressive party, "A Contract with the People," called for extensive political reforms, including the recall of judicial decisions and the introduction of a direct primary to choose presidential candidates. Above all, it proposed extensive economic reforms, including a national child labor law, minimum wages for working women, and a stricter regulation of trusts.

With the Republican party thus divided, only a miracle could prevent Wilson from becoming the next President. Even so, the campaign of 1912 proved to be one of the most significant in American history.

It was obvious from the start that Taft was out of the running, that the presidential race would be fought between Wilson and Roosevelt. Eugene Debs, the Socialist candidate, whose vote had been rising sharply since 1900, represented no immediate threat, though the long-run prospects for socialism alarmed both parties.

The main issue in the campaign was how the government should deal with monopolies. The issue grew especially acute after the depression of 1893, when Wall Street investment bankers formed immense industrial combinations. The Sherman Antitrust Act of 1890 proved altogether ineffective—except against labor unions. Theodore Roosevelt's reputation as a "trust-buster" rested on a few well-publicized cases but, during his administration, trustification continued without letup. Taft did better than Roosevelt in combating trusts, but the country in the meantime had moved further to the left. In 1912 the Democratic and Progressive parties, both responding to the country's impatient mood, promised drastic action to solve the trust problem.

Before the campaign, Wilson's knowledge of the problem was perfunctory. He had often delivered homilies on the evils of monopoly and on the need to locate and punish the responsible men rather than the impersonal corporation. Now Wilson had to take a definite stand. To what end should corporations be regulated? How should the regulating be carried out? To answer these questions, Wilson drew entirely upon the wisdom of Louis D. Brandeis, one of the remarkable reformers of the era. A deep sense of social justice had moved Brandeis to abandon his brilliantly successful career as a Boston corporation lawyer and to champion the public interest against the very clients whom he had once served. He thereafter advised the leading progressives of the country and achieved the distinction of being the arch-nemesis of the special interests.

In a long meeting with Wilson on August 28, 1912, and in subsequent conferences in the course of the campaign, Brandeis elaborated the economic philosophy in which Wilson conscientiously schooled himself. "We believe," Brandeis wrote Wilson on September 28, "that no methods of regulation ever have been or can be devised to remove the menace inherent in private monopoly and overweening commercial power." In the 1912 campaign, Wilson echoed Brandeis in calling for a "New Freedom" which would revivify American life—the freedom of unfettered competition between small entrepreneurs, regulated and protected by public commissions. According to the New Freedom, monopolies were evil and unjust in themselves and should be removed; where they were necessary they should be owned by the government. The task of government, then, was to liberate the energies of the people by guaranteeing their independence and liberty and equality of opportunity.

The difference between Wilson's New Freedom and Roosevelt's New Nationalism in 1912 was the difference between regulated competition and regulated monopoly. Roosevelt saw nothing intrinsically wrong in monopolies. The object was to make them good by regulating them. These concentrations of industry, Roosevelt thought, possessed a vast and beneficent power which a strong government could harness in the public interest. Generally speaking, the New Nationalism valued concentrations of power. Economic and social progress consisted in the cooperation between organized groups—farmers, labor, business—under the aegis of the federal government, representing society as a whole. Roosevelt regarded the New Freedom as a fantasy, an attempt to recall the lost world of Jefferson and Jackson. Wilson regarded the New Nationalism as paternalistic and alien to the American tradition of individualism and liberty.

Yet, despite the eagerness of each candidate to exploit his differences with the other, ideologically there was little to choose between them. Both were avowed progressives, both thundered against the special interests and the political bosses, and both believed that monopolies had to be severely dealt with if American democracy were to survive. Their differences over means were trivial and served most of all to disclose how deeply the country felt about the problem of monopolies. As events were to show, Roosevelt's acceptance of monopolies was more realistic than Wilson's desire to break them up. Once he was President, Wilson pragmatically adopted Roosevelt's standard of differentiating the bad ones from the good ones. Breaking the monopolies would have required a revolution, and Wilson was no revolutionist.

Wilson and the Democratic party won the 1912 election with

ease. Wilson received 435 electoral votes to Roosevelt's 88 and Taft's 8. For the first time in twenty years the Democrats controlled both Houses of Congress, but it was clear that Wilson had won because of the Republican split. He received far fewer votes than Roosevelt and Taft combined, and even fewer than Bryan had received in 1908. The important thing, however, was that Wilson and the New Freedom had won. He had promised a new era in American history: it came with a ferocity and in a form that no one could have predicted.

Since the Civil War, the intensively industrialized Northeast had directed the country's economic and political destiny. Under nearly continuous Republican rule, this section of the country had benefited most from the policies of the federal government: the high tariffs, the hard money, the extravagant giveaways of land and of natural resources. The New Freedom attempted to distribute the beneficence of government to the South and the West, to farmers, the lower middle classes and labor. A solid coalition of interests and classes was formed—a coalition which was to endure long beyond Wilson's administration.

His legislative program in 1913–1914 embraced the three major economic problems before the country: tariffs, banking, and monopolies. Tariff reform, the first order of business, threatened to upset the most cherished of all Republican traditions. Although the Tariff Law of 1909 had somewhat lowered the staggering rates established in 1897, this concession hardly satisfied Democratic and Republican progressives. So far as they were concerned, the mighty trusts, long nurtured by high tariffs, had been left untouched. Taft had upheld Republican tradition; in 1912, according to the progressives, he had betrayed the people by vetoing a tariff bill which would have drastically reduced rates.

Wilson asked for a law similar to the bill which Taft had vetoed. On April 8, 1913, he read his tariff message to Congress—the first time since John Adams that any President had personally addressed Congress. The administration proposed, in the Underwood bill, to continue protection for some industries while reducing or withdrawing protection from others. Goods produced by monopolies were left unprotected. A slightly graduated income tax, now legal under the Sixteenth Amendment, was added to the bill to make up for the expected loss of revenue. In final form, the Underwood Tariff of 1913 brought down average rates from 1909 by some 25 percent. Its passage was a triumph for Wilson, who proved that he could get along with his party in Congress and that he could put the ideals of the New Freedom into practical effect.

The Federal Reserve Act, passed in December, 1913, was the result of a long and complex battle that at several points threatened to disrupt the Democratic party. Since 1896 the party, under Bryan's direction, had been committed to changing the banking and currency system. Farmers and small businessmen needed easier access to cheaper money. The banking and currency system, they charged, was controlled by Eastern plutocrats who maintained a tight money policy, not only to get a high profit, but to destroy the independence of the people. Populists and progressives favored centralized government control over banking and currency. In time Eastern bankers, too, saw the need for centralization—under their own control. The Panic of 1907 made reform imperative. Accordingly, Congress in 1908 created a Commission of eighteen Congressmen, headed by arch-conservative Nelson Aldrich, to inquire into and report on the banking and currency practices in the United States and Europe. In January, 1912, the Commission recommended that Congress create a centralized banking and currency system—called a national reserve association and consisting of regional branches—to be solidly controlled by the banking community.

Wilson knew little about banking, but for political reasons alone he turned down the Aldrich Commission's recommendations. The task of drawing up fresh recommendations fell to Congressman Carter Glass of Virginia, a member of the House Banking Committee. Glass was a conservative. His chief quarrel with the Aldrich, or bankers', plan was that it would establish a too narrowly centralized system. Glass proposed instead a decentralized system of some twenty independent federal reserve banks, again under private control. The bankers gladly accepted Glass's proposals. Wilson also approved them and was prepared to back them as legislation. Then, in the late spring of 1913, Democratic progressives suddenly rebelled against the administration. To the radicals in the party, the Glass bill was rank betrayal. They could not allow the banking and currency apparatus to fall into the hands of private bankers.

Wilson then consulted Brandeis, who, siding with the progressives, advised that the government control the Federal Reserve Board which was to decide policy for branch reserve banks. Wilson adopted Brandeis's position, and it was written into the bill. Also written into the bill, over tremendous opposition from bankers, were provisions allowing reserve banks to discount agricultural notes, a boon to farmers seeking cheaper credit. In late December, the Glass-Owen, or Federal Reserve, Act was signed into law. In six months it had evolved from a patently conservative to a patently progressive instrument of control over the nation's credit and currency.

But there was an epilogue to the Federal Reserve Act. Wilson nominated bankers and businessmen to represent the government on the Federal Reserve Board. This about-face surprised everyone, bankers and businessmen as well as progressives. Wilson's behavior was inexplicable, particularly his nomination of Thomas D. Jones, a good friend of his, to the Federal Reserve Board. Jones was a director of the notorious International Harvester trust, then under indictment for violating the Sherman Antitrust Act. Wilson defended his nomination on the ludicrous ground that Jones had joined the Harvester trust in order to reform it. But Jones, appearing before the Senate Banking Committee, which was considering his nomination, stated that he agreed with the policies of the trust and had no intention of reforming it. The Committee then forced Jones to withdraw. It approved the other appointees, however, and the Federal Reserve System remained safe for bankers.

The New Freedom's antitrust program consisted of two laws, the Clayton Antitrust Act and the Federal Trade Commission Act, both passed in the fall of 1914. In his special address of January, 1914, Wilson affirmed that the Sherman Act of 1890 had to be strengthened. He cautioned against exacerbating differences between government and business, now that tariff and banking laws had been enacted. And indeed the Clayton Act only slightly modified the Sherman Act. Though it prohibited price-fixing and interlocking directorates in large corporations, held officials responsible for the wrong-doings of their companies, and enabled the government to stop certain malpractices, the Clayton Act was hardly a serious threat to the amassed power of monopolies. In one respect it did embody a significant change. It allowed workers and farmers to organize without fear of illegally restraining trade. It also legalized strikes, picketing and boycotts by labor and made court injunctions against these practices more difficult to invoke. Nonetheless, Senator James Reed of Missouri did not exaggerate too much in describing the Clayton Act as "a sort of legislative apology to the trusts, delivered hat in hand, and accompanied by assurances that no discourtesy is intended."

The Federal Trade Commission Act was meant to be a powerful defender of small businessmen against monopolies. Brandeis thought so in drawing it up, and so did Wilson in approving it. The act established a Federal Trade Commission of three members who were to police all corporations other than banks and railroads by inquiring into and if necessary stopping monopolistic practices. The commission might have become an important force in American economic life had Wilson not defeated the intention of the law by selecting commissioners—as he had done in his appointments to the Federal Reserve Board—who were friendly to the interests they were charged to regulate.

Wilson's New Freedom had succeeded somewhat in restoring the principle of economic individualism, the spirit of competition which the Republicans had interred during their long tenure of office. Equality of opportunity was enlarged for small businessmen and farmers and labor, but not at the price of upsetting the structure of economic power. The reforms enacted after 1913 were moderate to begin with; Wilson removed whatever sting they had by executive appointments. The monopolies which he had execrated in his 1912 campaign learned by 1915 that they had nothing to fear from the New Freedom.

Wilson's policy toward Negroes contradicted the avowed purpose of the New Freedom. As a result of his policy the condition of the Negro reached its lowest point since Reconstruction. The Negro's condition had been deteriorating for many years in the South; by 1912 he was the victim of Jim Crow laws in every Southern community. Now, in order to appease the Southern Democratic hierarchs who dominated Congress, Wilson allowed Jim Crow to enter the federal government as well. With his knowledge, and despite the warnings of his liberal friends, the federal civil service was partially segregated in 1913. Wilson justified the practice on the ground that it worked to the advantage of Negro civil servants, who, of course, were not consulted. The injustice was compounded for having been perpetrated by a government which prided itself on being the champion of equal rights for all.

The New Freedom inaugurated a new foreign policy. To Wilson, a country's foreign policy reflected its internal policy. He shared with progressives generally the belief that a truly free and democratic country could not be an imperialist one. America had become imperialistic, had brandished the big stick, and had imposed dollar diplomacy; precisely, America had become monopolistic. To change one meant necessarily to change the other. But the gap between intentions and actions is wider in foreign than in domestic affairs, as Wilso soon discovered.

Wilson and Secretary of State Bryan set about helping to democratize the countries of Central America by withdrawing support from dictators, the helpmates of foreign imperialism. But for Wilson to effect such a change in these countries, it would have been necessary to revolutionize American foreign policy. Wilson was certainly not friendly to dictators and to American economic interests, but neither did he take positive steps to promote democracy in Latin America. As a result, when the old despotic regimes fell in such countries as Nicaragua, the Dominican Republic, and Haiti, it was chaos and not democracy that followed. Wilson sent soldiers to restore order—for the sake of order, not for the sake of democracy. In the end, the sole beneficiaries of Wilson's interventions were the very interests and the very despotisms which he opposed. He jettisoned dollar diplomacy, but he affirmed America's customary role as policeman of the Caribbean. Under Wilson, the United States directly intervened in more Latin American countries than she did under any other President. And the countries which came under the enforced tutelage of American democracy have remained the worst governed in this hemisphere.*

Wilson's policies toward Mexico pointed up the ambiguities of his New Diplomacy. The democratic ideals which he cherished had already struck roots in Mexican soil. Though few realized it at the time, Mexico was experiencing a full-blown revolution. In 1911 the corrupt and tyrannical regime of Porfirio Diaz had been overthrown by a coalition under Francisco Madero. Madero had taken the revolution seriously, threatening Mexico's ruling groups—the Church, the landed aristocracy, and foreign business interests—and paid for his zeal with his life. He was suddenly and treacherously assassinated by his chief general, Victoriano Huerta, who then led the country back to the conditions of the old regime. A parody of the Latin dictator—impulsive, cruel, and ruthless—Huerta was welcomed by the privileged interests both inside and outside of Mexico.

Wilson refused to recognize Huerta, whom he regarded as a "butcher." Moreover, a fresh revolutionary movement of anti-Huertists had arisen in the provinces. Calling themselves Constitutionalists, these followers of Madera were led by Venustiano Carranza, who in personal character and political philosophy proved to be Mexico's equivalent of Wilson. Wilson followed a policy of neutrality toward the contending factions until Huerta assumed unmitigated dictatorial power. Wilson thereupon actively supported the Carranza Constitutionalists and hoped to direct their movement for reform.

But by the spring of 1914 it had become apparent that American aid to Carranza would not topple Huerta. An incident then occurred which Wilson seized upon as the means for bringing Huerta to his knees; what ensued was a comic-opera sequence of events. On April 10, 1914, Huerta's forces captured the crew of the U.S.S. *Dolphin* in Tampico on the charge of aiding the Constitutionalist army which surrounded the city. Huerta immediately released the Americans and apologized as well. But a simple apology was not enough. The commander of the Amer-

* Trujillo was dictator of the Dominican Republic until his assassination in 1961. In 1965 the notorious Samozas still run Nicaragua. And Haiti, victimized by a succession of tyrants, groans under Duvalier.

ican fleet off Vera Cruz insisted, with Wilson's approval, that the Mexicans humble themselves before the American flag by firing a twenty-one-gun salute. Huerta refused to allow this unless American guns answered volley for volley. Outraged, Wilson went before Congress on April 20 and asked for special powers to punish the Mexican dictator. He had already ordered Vera Cruz occupied in order to prevent a shipment of German arms from reaching Huerta's army. Thus, under an absurd pretext and for the sake of "democracy," Wilson had ordered military intervention in Mexico.

The situation was embarrassing to Wilson and the government. Both factions in Mexico united to oppose the occupation of Vera Cruz, and progressives of both parties in the United States were hard put to reconcile Wilson's actions to his professed solidarity with the ideals of the Mexican Revolution. Confronted with these developments, Wilson eagerly accepted the offer of Argentina, Brazil, and Chile, the so-called ABC powers, to mediate the dispute. Thanks to their efforts, and to the success of Carranza's armies, Huerta was forced to flee on July 15, 1914. Several months later American troops left Vera Cruz.

This did not settle matters. There followed nearly three years of deepening antipathy between the two countries. Successive blunders of American policy brought them to the edge of war in the summer of 1916. It was not until March 13, 1917, that the United States gave *de jure* recognition to the Carranza government.

Four years before, Wilson had believed that he needed only to will a change in policy toward Mexico and it would be done: instead of supporting dictators and the special interests the United States would support the people and political democracy. But the Mexican Revolution was destined to take its own course; it was not to be guided—or contained—even by the best-intentioned outsider.

In the first year of Wilson's administration a great war was remote from the American consciousness. An aura of peace, progress and optimism enveloped the land. Secretary of State Bryan, whose whole political life had been dedicated to high ideals, inspired the government to negotiate treaties of conciliation with other countries. According to these treaties, international disputes were to go before a commission while the nations concerned "cooled off" for a year or so. The United States signed such "cooling-off" treaties with twenty-nine nations, including Britain and France. But the First World War turned the treaties into so many caricatures of American idealism.

Wilson sincerely and conscientiously attempted to maintain a policy of neutrality toward the two warring coalitions in Europe, but it was a static and defensive policy which had to yield to the logic of America's economic, political and military position. American prosperity came to depend on the purchases of goods and demand for credit made by the Allies, particularly Britain. At first, Wilson flatly refused loans to belligerents. By October, 1914, his order had been modified to permit a small loan to France. By early 1917, all restraints had been removed, and two and a half billion dollars had been loaned to the Allies. The United States had an enormous stake in Germany's defeat.

Politically, Britain enjoyed obvious advantages over Germany. The most important members of Wilson's circle of advisers, led by Colonel House and seconded by Robert Lansing, who later succeeded Bryan as Secretary of State, sympathized with Britain and the Allies. As the war progressed they found it increasingly simple or convenient to characterize it as a titanic struggle between democracy and autocracy. Eventually, they convinced Wilson that the United States and Britain together could someday ensure the peace of the world—something that Wilson was only too willing to believe.

Britain's military actions were more compatible with American interests than were Germany's. Though Britain's blockade of Germany was onerous enough to the United States, especially to the cotton-growing South, it did not hurt the United States as much as unrestricted submarine warfare, which was Germany's only retaliatory weapon. Britain's control of the seas enabled her to avoid the provocations inherent in submarine warfare. Britain's violation of international law guaranteeing freedom of the seas to neutral countries resulted in no loss of American life, while Germany's did. Wilson might have lessened Britain's advantage by preventing Americans from traveling in the war zone, but he insisted categorically on affirming their right to do so under international law.

Neutrality failed most of all because Germany blundered disastrously. The choice before Kaiser Wilhelm's regime was whether the risk of fighting the United States was worth the advantages of unlimited submarine warfare. Germany knew precisely the limits of American neutrality. The decision to defy America, when it came in the fall of 1916, was made by men—the dominant military groups—who underestimated America's military capacity and overestimated the effectiveness of submarine warfare. This miscalculation cost Germany the war.

On February 4, 1915, Germany declared her intention of conducting unlimited submarine warfare against neutral ships. Until then, America's main quarrel had been with Britain. To maintain her rigorous blockade of Germany, Britain issued increasingly extensive lists of contraband goods and then proceeded to search American vessels bound for Germany or Austria. But the quarrel was never allowed to get out of hand. At no point during the first years of the war did Wilson challenge Britain as sharply and as categorically as he challenged Germany. The British blockade rankled and even humiliated, but it took no lives and little property. That was the difference.

Wilson's tough line toward Germany—he asserted that he would hold Germany strictly accountable for violations of American neutrality—was resisted by Secretary of State Bryan, who, in his concern for peace, wanted Wilson to be as fair to the German point of view as to the British. Differences between Wilson and Bryan exploded following Germany's sinking of the British liner *Lusitania*, on May 7, 1915. Of the 1,198 lives lost, 124 were American. Nothing like this had ever happened before to the United States, and Wilson was under relentless pressure to end German violations of American neutral rights. Robert Lansing, then Counselor of the State Department, advised Wilson to break relations with Germany. Bryan, who reflected the beliefs of the large and militant pacifist groups in the country, advocated a milder protest. Wilson's position, defined in his first *Lusitania* note of May 13, stood roughly in between. He held the German government strictly accountable for the sinking and insisted that it give up unrestricted submarine warfare. His second *Lusitania* note—Germany having unsatisfactorily replied to the first—demanded an explicit pledge of forbearance. Bryan besought Wilson to soften this note, contending that Germany, in view of its disadvantages, was not unreasonable, and that the United States should try to negotiate rather than send angry notes. When Wilson refused to budge, Bryan resigned. With Lansing now Secretary of State the line stiffened further. The third *Lusitania* note was practically an ultimatum. It told Germany that the United States would consider another such act as "deliberately unfriendly"—a euphemism for the threat to end diplomatic relations.

The *Lusitania* notes at least brought the issue to a head: unless German submarines stopped the practice of sinking ships with Americans on board without prior warning, the United States would go to war. Wilson left it up to the Kaiser. That Germany had decided to retreat became evident with the next crisis, following the sinking on August 19, 1915, of the British steamer *Arabic*, in which two Americans died. Following an American protest, the German government pledged not to sink liners before warning them. Only this pledge deterred Wilson from severing relations between the two countries.

But the issue was far from settled. Germany had never admitted her guilt in sinking the *Lusitania.* To make matters worse, she announced on February 10, 1916, that despite the *Arabic* pledge, her submarines would sink armed merchantmen without warning. Germany had no choice, short of abandoning submarine warfare altogether, because the Allies had been arming their ships. A submarine which warned an armed vessel invited destruction. But Secretary of State Lansing insisted that Americans would remain free to travel on merchant ships, armed or not. Once again the two nations were involved in a crisis which might easily lead to war.

Matters came to a boil when the unarmed French steamer *Sussex* was sunk on March 24, 1916, and several Americans on board were injured. House and Lansing recommended that relations with Germany should be severed. But instead, on April 18, Wilson sent an ultimatum which virtually ordered Germany to abandon unrestricted submarine warfare. Once again the German government, fearful of American intervention, yielded to Wilson.

In a note of May 4 it promised that its submarines would observe the rule of visit and search before taking action. In effect this meant abandoning submarine warfare. Wilson gratefully accepted the *Sussex* pledge as the condition of peace between the two countries.

By the spring of 1916, then, neutrality seemed assured. Wilson's policy was proving successful. The country reaped the rewards of war while avoiding the liabilities. But Wilson's policy rested on the fragile premise that Germany would refrain from using her most potent retaliatory weapon even as she anxiously watched her enemies derive all the benefits from trade with the United States.

The sinking of the *Lusitania* brought home to America the reality of war. It also marked the point at which the character of Wilson's New Freedom changed. Before the spring of 1915, Wilson had repeatedly warned against the danger of militarism to American democracy. He had in mind a large and influential group of people, led by the truculent Theodore Roosevelt, who had been trumpeting for a large-scale program of military preparedness ever since the war in Europe began. The sinking of the *Lusitania* convinced Wilson that some start toward preparedness had to be made.

On November 4, 1915, Wilson delivered a famous speech in New York City outlining his own preparedness program to the nation. Several months before, he had received plans from the War and Navy departments for substantially enlarging the size of the armed forces, and these plans became the basis of his program. Wilson was surprised by the reception of his speech. Progressives reviled it as a fatal step down the road to autocracy. The preparedness advocates on the other hand thought Wilson's program at best a feeble start; Theodore Roosevelt felt Wilson was being typically pusillanimous. In January and February of 1916, in an attempt to drum up support for his faltering program, Wilson went on an intensive speaking tour of several Middle Atlantic and Midwestern States. But he failed to penetrate the thick layer of isolationism which clung to these regions, and he failed also to elicit a favorable response from the country at large. His program was moribund.

But with the *Sussex* affair, opposition to preparedness melted. Between June and September of 1916, Congress, at Wilson's urging, enlarged the army and navy, gave the government permission to mobilize certain industries in the event of emergency, and created a government board empowered to build up the nation's merchant marine. Many of the liberals who opposed these measures found satisfaction in the fact that preparedness was to be paid for by a steeply graded system of progressive taxation.

Entering his fourth year as President, Wilson had so far been a disappointment to progressives. His preparedness program and his hazardous neutrality policy had alienated the Bryan wing of the Democratic party. Progressives generally had come to regard the New Freedom as an attempt to restore the faded glories of laissez-faire liberalism. But after January, 1916, Wilson set out on a broad welfare-state program that recalled the promises of Theodore Roosevelt in 1912 and that anticipated the New Deal reforms after 1933. Had the war not interrupted there is no telling how far this second New Freedom might have carried. In any case, by the time of the presidential campaign of 1916, progressives were honoring Wilson as a champion of social justice and as a protector of the peace.

Wilson gave an augury of his new intentions in late January when he nominated Louis Brandeis to the Supreme Court. The Bar Association and other conservatives, shocked at Wilson's sudden impertinence, fought hard to keep Brandeis off the bench. Only after a four-month struggle did the Senate Judiciary Committee yield to Wilson's relentless pressure and finally consent to the nomination of Brandeis. Throughout 1916 Wilson applied the full power of his office in prodding Congress to adopt such liberal measures as a federal employees' compensation law; a child labor law (later nullified by the Supreme Court); a rural banking law providing farmers with cheap long-term credit; and a law granting near-autonomy to the Philippines.

Wilson gave the most striking evidence of his new direction in responding to the great railroad dispute of 1916. In early August the railroad unions called a strike—their demands for an eight-hour day and for time-and-a-half for overtime had been rejected by management, and a mediation board had failed to settle the dispute. Wilson could not permit the railroads to stop functioning just when preparedness was getting under way. After failing to get the two sides to agree, Wilson proposed—insisted might be more accurate—that the eight-hour demand be accepted, that the overtime demand be tabled, and that an impartial commission be established to investigate the industry. Labor accepted these proposals, but management rejected them. The unions then called a strike for September 4. On September 2, Congress passed the Adamson Act which embodied Wilson's original proposals. Satisfied that Wilson had definitively set the seal of progressivism on his administration, the men who had supported Theodore Roosevelt in 1912 did not hesitate to support Wilson in 1916.

Wilson was renominated by acclamation for the presidency as a progressive and as a man of peace. The Democratic party was united behind him. Bryan, magnanimous as ever, spoke glowingly of his leadership. Nevertheless the Republican party was expected to win because it was still the majority party—in 1912 Roosevelt and Taft together had received over a million votes more than Wilson—and because it had in Charles Evans Hughes a candidate of experience and integrity. Hughes had been a distinguished reform governor of New York before becoming a justice of the Supreme Court, from which position he had resigned to run for President.

Wilson won the election of 1916 because Hughes, whatever his qualities as a man, turned out to be a poor candidate. He equivocated on major issues while Wilson stood behind his controversial domestic and foreign policies. Hughes alienated large blocs of voters, especially foreign-born Americans, by criticizing Wilson's alleged appeasement of both Germany and Britain. Finally, Hughes blundered in California. To win California it was necessary for him to retain the loyalty of its large progressive Republican movement. Lacking political finesse—for he antagonized Hiram Johnson, the leader of California progressives—Hughes lost the state and thus the election.

The West backed Wilson overwhelmingly in the election. East of the Mississippi and above the Mason-Dixon line only two states, Ohio and New Hampshire, went to Wilson. West of the

Mississippi he won eighteen of the twenty-two states, almost all of them traditionally Republican. California was decisive. A switch of only 1,500 votes there—a fraction of the progressive Republicans who voted for Wilson—would have made Hughes President. But the narrow margin of Wilson's victory should not minimize his achievement. He overcame the normal Republican majority (he had a half million plurality over Hughes), he received almost three million votes more than he had in 1912, he carried a Democratic Congress with him, and he was backed by almost all the progressives and by a significant number of Socialists (whose 1912 vote was almost halved in 1916). What fresh assaults upon the special interests would progressivism have mounted had the war not come?

In the summer of 1916 Wilson decided that should he be re-elected he would try to bring an end to the World War. Actually the initiative for the peace effort came from the German government, which had concluded, during the military stalemate of 1916, that with Wilson's help a peace treaty might be secured which would be favorable to its interests. The German government also concluded that, should his effort fail, full-scale submarine warfare would be resumed as part of a comprehensive military assault on the Allies. Wilson realized that neutrality could not go on indefinitely, that the United States would be drawn into the war unless he did something to end it.

Immediately following his election, Wilson drafted a long note, a profound and eloquent plea for peace, asking the belligerents what they were fighting for. Their answers would, he hoped, serve as the basis for a peace conference. Neither House nor Lansing approved this draft in its original form. They argued that it placed the Allies in a disadvantageous position: what would the United States do, they asked, if Germany responded to Wilson's satisfaction, and the Allies did not? In fact Germany—without knowing what was in Wilson's mind—announced on December 12 that she was ready to negotiate a peace treaty. Encouraged, Wilson revised the note in accordance with the objections of House and Lansing. The original draft had said that American policies would be guided by the belligerents' replies and that there should be a peace conference; the official note of December 18 only requested that they state their war aims.

Chiefly interested in a peace which would lead once and for all to a system of world law and justice, Wilson entered into tentative negotiations with the German ambassador. To attain that end he was willing to help Germany in her negotiations—on condition that he be present at the prospective peace conference. The German government, however, wanted Wilson only to bring the conference together; it did not want him to participate in it. Nor did it take seriously what it regarded as Wilson's apocryphal hopes for world law and justice, though it was willing to humor him. But Wilson would not allow himself to be the catspaw of German interests. He saw through the German strategy, and his talk with the ambassador proved fruitless.

The last hope for peace dissolved when both sides officially answered Wilson's note of December 18. On January 12, 1917, the Allies asserted that their war aim was to destroy German hegemony over central and southern Europe. On January 31 Germany, having abandoned all hope, or pretense, of obtaining peace either with the Allies or with the United States, candidly replied that her war aim was to secure recognition of her privileged place in Europe and of her legitimate status as a colonial and maritime power. This was accompanied by the chilling announcement that unrestricted submarine warfare would begin the next day. The German government knew that this meant war with the United States, but it was confident that German submarines could knock Britain out of the war sooner than the United States could come to Britain's assistance. On February 3 Wilson responded by announcing that relations with Germany had been broken and that the United States would take appropriate measures against "actual overt acts." These acts were soon forthcoming.

In March, the Allies informed Wilson that they were on the verge of collapse and desperately needed American help. Russia was in the throes of a revolution which might lead to her withdrawal from the war. The German offensive against Allied and neutral shipping was taking a devastating toll (over 500,000 tons were sunk in March alone). On March 16 three American ships were sunk with heavy loss of life. This was the kind of overt act to which Wilson had referred on February 3. His advisers and cabinet unanimously agreed with him that Congress should be asked to declare war on Germany.

Wilson's war address to Congress on April 2 marked the point when progressivism ascended from a domestic to a world-wide crusade. German autocracy replaced the selfish interests as his *bête noir*. The war became a struggle of freedom against oppression, of the people against autocracy. The world was to be made "safe for democracy."

Had American soldiers not arrived in France by the spring of 1918, the massive German offensive would probably have crushed the depleted armies of France and Britain. Russia's departure from the war in March had released hundreds of thousands of German troops for combat in the west. To make matters worse France had had to shift precious reserves to Italy in the late fall of 1917. But by July, 1918, thanks to the presence of over a million American troops in France, the German offensive petered out. The initiative then passed to the Allies. The hundreds of thousands of fresh American troops thrown into the battle every month overwhelmed the German armies, worn and dispirited by four years of war. By November, the Allied and American armies were ready to invade Germany.

Like the countries of Europe, the United States mobilized all of the resources of society for total war. Under Wilson's direction the country was soon converted into a smoothly functioning war machine. Of the twenty-four million men who had registered, nearly three million were called up to fight. Only a few thousand resisted the draft, a surprisingly small number in view of the pacifist sentiment before 1917. Wilson skillfully administered a vast proliferation of federal agencies. The government took control of transportation and communication and rigorously supervised wages and working conditions as well as the production and distribution of goods. Never had the country displayed such uniformity of action and purpose.

Widespread political and intellectual repression accompanied the tide of patriotism which flooded America after 1917. Persons who spoke German invited suspicion, often censure. Skepticism toward the war, not to speak of outright criticism of it, was often a legal offense. Far from attempting to combat this destructive passion, the federal government, with Wilson's acquiescence, directed it into precise channels of action. The Espionage Act of 1917 and the Sedition Act of 1918 invested federal bureaucrats with full powers for punishing individuals whose opinions were suspect. Thousands were imprisoned, most of them socialists and anarchists.

Many progressives eagerly participated in this cruel orgy of "patriotism"; for example, the most ruthless hunter of "subversives," Attorney General A. Mitchell Palmer, had been a longtime Wilsonian progressive. The conduct of the country—of the government especially—during and immediately after the war was the most shameful episode of its kind since the days of the Alien and Sedition Acts of 1798.

What were America's war objectives? To Wilson the question was tantamount to asking what kind of peace the world would have after the war ended. This was not after all a conventional war, a struggle between equally predacious powers; it was a war to end all wars. From 1917 on Wilson's major utterances swelled with confidence that the war would bring democracy, and democracy would bring peace. Wilson imparted to the world the progressive ideals which had grown out of the American experience and which his own political life had exemplified. He regarded autocracy as lawlessness, and he conceived international law as a possibility only when the governments of the world truly represented their peoples. Wilson's war policy was consistent with this belief in the inseparability of democracy, law and peace. That policy, in brief, was: first, to encourage the German people to overthrow their autocratic regime; second, to assure establishment of a league of nations.

The Bolshevik Revolution in October (November by the Western calendar), 1917, gave special urgency to Wilson's liberal war policy. The Bolsheviks, too, affirmed the ideal of universal peace and of international law resting on democracy—although by democracy they meant revolutionary socialism, not liberalism. The Bolsheviks asserted that the war served the ruling classes of every capitalist country; they did not distinguish between the Allies and Germany, between "democracy" and "autocracy." Peoples everywhere, they cried, should overthrow their governments and make peace. The Allies feared Bolshevik precept and example. The weary masses of France and Britain might be persuaded to abandon the fight just when they were to be put to their severest test. Wilsonian idealism answered the Bolshevik challenge by asserting that the only basis of universal peace and justice lay in the defeat of autocratic Germany.

Wilson specified his war aims and laid down the guidelines for peace in his great Fourteen Points Address of January 8, 1918. Eight of the points (VI–XIII) defined the boundaries of states whose peoples had hitherto been denied self-government, in particular the Balkan peoples under Austro-Hungarian and Ottoman rule; they also made territorial adjustments in favor of aggrieved nations, and ordered the removal of foreign armies from self-governing states. The other six points dealt with profounder and more important questions. The first point affirmed the principle of open and fully publicized negotiations between states, so that no secret treaty could be foisted upon peoples by their governments. The second and third proclaimed the ideal of unimpeded commerce between nations. The fourth provided guarantees against arms competition. The fifth attempted to oblige the colonial powers to observe the right of self-determination. The fourteenth point, the copestone of the rest, announced that an "association of nations" would be created which would have the power to secure "political independence and territorial integrity to great and small states alike." Wilson's Fourteen Points (later supplemented by nine others), promising "peace without victory," shook the world to its foundations.

The Fourteen Points affected Germany even more profoundly than they did the democracies. Convinced by the fall of 1918 that it could not win the war, the German government asked for negotiations on the basis of their provisions. Wilson was amenable but the Allies were not. Having suffered and bled for four years, they could hardly be expected to consent to a peace without victory. Moreover, before America entered the war, they had made secret agreements (for example with Italy) which explicitly contradicted the Fourteen Points. The Germans knew of the rift between Wilson and the Allies and hoped to exploit it. But Wilson prevailed over both Germany and the Allies. After he refused to treat with the old regime in Germany, it was overthrown by a democratic revolution in early November. And, by threatening to sign a separate peace, he forced the Allies to accept the Fourteen Points as the basis for negotiation. At last, on November 11, 1918, the generals of both sides signed the armistice which ended the fighting. All eyes now turned to the peace conference and in particular to the great democrat, representing the strongest power on earth, who had laid down the conditions of peace for victors and vanquished alike.

Historians agree that Wilson made several errors of judgment before the peace negotiations began. On October 25, 1918, eleven days before the Congressional elections, he asked the people to prove their faith in his leadership by returning a Democratic Congress. In doing so he allowed his prestige to depend upon the election results. The Democrats had only a scant majority in the 65th Congress and, given the historic pattern of mid-term elections, the odds heavily favored their losing control of the 66th. As might have been predicted—for mid-term elections usually go against the party in power—the Republicans won both Houses and announced that the election had revealed the country's dissatisfaction with Wilson's leadership.

Wilson further alienated the party whose support he now needed by failing to take any important Republicans with him to the negotiating table. He could have included in his vast entourage such Republican *éminences grises* as Elihu Root or former President William Taft, both of whom were strong internationalists. Had such men shared responsibility for the treaty, the Republican Senate might have dealt with it more kindly. Finally, Wilson added to his difficulties by consenting to hold the negotiations in Versailles, where the pressure from the Allies, particularly from France, to compromise on vital matters was bound to be more intense than in a neutral country. All in all, however, historians would have paid little attention to these preliminary acts of imprudence had the fate of the Versailles peace treaty turned out differently.

Wilson's primary objective at the Versailles conference was to draw up and incorporate into the treaty a covenant establishing a league of nations. This ideal had been the focus of his hopes since 1916. It had been consummated in his Fourteen Points. Without a league, he thought, the treaty would be, like all treaties before it, an arrangement among victorious powers to divide the spoils of war. To assure adoption of the covenant Wilson needed the approval, first, of the other big powers—Britain, France, Italy and Japan—and, then, of two-thirds of the United States Senate. Wilson expected the Allies to offer serious obstacles; he never imagined that the Senate would offer insuperable ones.

Wilson arrived at Versailles in December, 1918, with a league of nations covenant which he, with the help of Colonel House, had drafted on the basis of earlier reports by British and American lawyers. Over European objections Wilson insisted that a league covenant be the first item of business at the conference and that it be woven into the fabric of the treaty; the Allies would have put aside the covenant until they had settled accounts with Germany. Wilson was in charge of the committee which drew up the final outline, based on his own earlier version, for the peace conference as a whole. After making further revisions, the conference adopted the League of Nations Covenant on April 28, 1919. This was a triumphant moment for Wilson. The war had not been fought in vain. Humanity, it appeared, had accepted the sacred gift of peace.

But Wilson paid a heavy price for his triumph. The powers at Versailles had no intention of yielding up their claims, ratified by years of suffering, to fulfill vague and distant Wilsonian ideals. France's Clemenceau, the "Tiger," summed up their thinking. "God," he said, "gave us the Ten Commandments and we broke them. Wilson gave us his Fourteen Points—we shall see." The European powers, France in particular, wanted heavy economic reparations from Germany; for four years the war had been fought on French soil. France also wanted to occupy German territory west of the Rhine as concrete protection against another German attack. But Wilson resisted these demands for reparations and territories—at one point he threatened to return to America—and succeeded in scaling them down considerably. Wilson also resisted Italy's demands for territory and so aroused deep Italian resentment against himself—and against the conference as a whole. Japan meanwhile pressed her claim to a large area in China, the Shantung province, which Germany had controlled before the war. Wilson saw little choice here but to compromise with Japan; it was important to bring the most formidable Asian power into the League; moreover, Britain had promised Japan Shantung in 1917. And so in one instance after another Wilson found himself compromising the principle of non-vindictive peace in order to realize the transcendent principle of a world order of free nations.

So far as Germany was concerned the treaty was a crime. Germany did not think peace had been achieved without victory. Her reparations were astronomical, all her colonies were taken away, part of her territory was and would be under occupation and, most bitter of all, a clause in the treaty accused her of exclusive guilt for the war. Wilson, she felt, had yielded to the wolves at Versailles and had reneged on the promises made in the Fourteen Points. But Germans hardly asked themselves what kind of treaty they would have imposed had they won the war. The Weimar Republic, whatever its virtues, was disastrously short of critical self-examination. Nonetheless, German democrats were right to complain that America had let them down when they needed help most. Hatred of democracy spawned on the discontent caused or aggravated by the treaty. In 1933 the German people threw out the democracy which they identified with "the shame of Versailles."

On July 10, 1919, two days after returning from Europe, Wilson presented the Versailles Treaty to the Senate. Though he knew the treaty was far from perfect he was satisfied that he had achieved his primary objective. The League of Nations Covenant was an inseparable part of the treaty which would have to be swallowed whole or not at all. Was it remotely conceivable that the Senate would not approve it? Wilson realized of course that the Covenant was the provocative feature. America's entry into the League would represent an extraordinary departure in her tradition and foreign policy. For over a hundred years America had been conscientiously isolationist. Her increasingly intimate relations with Europe after 1914 had been necessary and had ended with the cessation of war. Now the peace treaty would bind her to the countries of the world for the indefinite future.

Like any law, the Covenant was no stronger than its enforcement provision. For this reason Article x was the heart of the League. Article x stated that League members "would undertake to respect and preserve as against external aggression [their] territorial integrity and existing political independence" and that, should aggression or the possibility of aggression arise, the League Council would "advise upon the means by which the obligation shall be fulfilled." Article x, therefore, obliged each member state to help guarantee the others' external security. To Wilson this obligation fell most heavily upon the United States. For the United States was not only the strongest country in the world and therefore the best guarantor of order; she also represented the democratic hopes of mankind. American tutelage, Wilson believed, would ensure both order and freedom in the world. He would accept nothing less than full adherence to Article x of the Covenant.

While the country generally agreed with Wilson—most of the press and most organizations favored America's participation in a strong League—the Middle and Far West for the most part remained adamantly isolationist, distrusting any traffic other than commercial with the Old World. Also, several large groups of foreign-born Americans, mainly German and Irish, were dead set against the treaty—the Germans for obvious reasons and the Irish because nothing was done at Versailles to free Ireland from Britain. The most potent opposition to the League, however, came from Republican opponents of Wilson who, precisely because the public supported the League, hoped to wrest political capital from any embarrassment which they might cause him. The ghost of the presidential election of 1920 hovered constantly over the Senate chamber.

This group of Republican Senators who fought Wilson for political advantage was led by the Massachusetts aristocrat-scholar-politician Henry Cabot Lodge, long a power in the Republican Party and now, in the 66th Congress, both the Senate Majority Leader and the chairman of the Foreign Relations Committee. No one had fathomed the reasons for Lodge's dislike of Wilson. Perhaps he resented Wilson's position as Washington's leading scholar. In any case Wilson reciprocated the feeling. The treaty therefore faced many difficulties in its labyrinthine course through the Senate, yet few people in the early summer of 1919 doubted that it would be approved as it stood.

While Wilson was at Versailles there had gathered a group of thirteen Republican Senators who felt no compunction about destroying the treaty in order to keep the United States out of the League. These "irreconcilables" or "bitter-enders"—many of whom were progressives—expressed isolationist fears that Article x would commit the United States to fight in European wars. They pictured the Covenant as the law of the land, and they saw foreign races and peoples actually telling Americans what to do. The irreconcilables were strong beyond their number: they held the balance of power in the Senate, which the Republicans controlled by only two votes. Repeatedly, the irreconcilables forced Lodge to make important concessions to them. Lodge appointed six of them to the Foreign Relations Committee, thus enabling them to constitute a majority of the Republicans who sat on it. Yet it was through this Committee that the treaty had to pass before reaching the Senate floor!

The rest of the Senate—that is, nearly three-fourths of the Republicans and all of the Democrats—supported American participation in the League, but they differed over the conditions. They differed over Article x. About a third of the pro-League Republicans were "strict" reservationists. This meant that they wanted to qualify the terms under which obligations were imposed upon member states. The remainder of the Republicans were "mild" reservationists; they favored some gesture to prove that America was not absolutely beholden to the League. Nearly all Democrats accepted the Covenant as it stood, supporting Wilson down the line. But the Senate Democrats suffered from poor leadership. The man who had been designated to lead Wilson's fight, the shrewd and venerable Thomas Martin of Virginia, had died just before the treaty came up for debate. Gilbert Hitchcock of Nebraska, who took Martin's place, was easily outmaneuvered by Lodge and the irreconcilables and—equally important—lacked the prestige or strength to stand up to Wilson.

In the months of July and August relations between Wilson and the Senate Republican leadership deteriorated further. Lodge's tactics unnerved him. After reading the entire treaty—264 pages of fine text—to an empty Senate, Lodge kept it bottled up in the Foreign Relations Committee for two months, during which the committee heard an army of hostile witnesses whose testimony was widely publicized. Wilson was given a chance to gauge his opposition in an unusual three-hour question and answer session with the whole committee on August 19. The Republicans, as was obvious from their questions, came to the White House on that fateful day to expose, not to explore. By the end of August, Wilson had made up his mind: he was engaged in a fight to the finish, and he had to take drastic measures to defend the Covenant and the hopes of mankind which it embodied.

Wilson brought the issue directly to the people in a heroic contest of strength with his enemies. The importance of the issue, he thought, demanded no less. And, to judge from the punishing tour he set for himself, he must have been prepared to give his life if necessary. He was sixty-three, his health was delicate, and he had, for the past two and a half years, labored continually under brutal strain. Now he was undertaking a 9,500-mile tour through the West; in twenty-two days he intended to give thirty-eight major speeches as well as any number of minor ones. The extraordinary thing is that he held up as long as he did.

In one speech after another he called upon the people to sustain the great project which had been created in their name. The League Covenant, he emphasized, if it was to guarantee peace in a world of free and democratic nations, must have the support of the United States, the freest, most democratic, and strongest of the nations. He took his Senate opponents to task for trying to draw the teeth from the Covenant by imposing reservations on Article x. Any reservation, he held, was equivalent to rejection. Better to reject the treaty outright then to emasculate the League. America would not have such an opportunity again to serve mankind—and herself. He repeatedly called attention to the fact that he came from a family of "Covenanters" and that he, like his ancestors, would fight to the end for a cause that was right.

Wilson seemed to be having success. He was generating excitement throughout the country and particularly in and around the communities he visited. But then what was developing into one of the momentous political debates of modern times suddenly ended. On September 25, after delivering a long speech in Pueblo, Colorado, he collapsed of exhaustion and was taken at once back to Washington. A week later he suffered a stroke which completely incapacitated him for over a month and crippled him for the rest of his life.

This meant that he was cut off from Democratic leaders in the Senate and from responsible and friendly politicians generally. For the remainder of his term of office he depended almost entirely on his wife and physician, who determined what visitors and what written matter he would see. Illness and isolation deepened the intractibility and rigidity that had always been part of his character, but that nonetheless had often served him well: in precisely such situations as he now found himself, he had possessed also the subtle capacity to compromise at the right moment. That capacity was gone and with it effective leadership.

The initiative in the conflict over the treaty now passed to Henry Cabot Lodge. The Foreign Relations Committee released the treaty on September 10 along with a majority report that bristled with epithets against the League—undoubtedly the work of the irreconcilables—and included forty-nine proposed changes: forty-five amendments and four reservations. Lodge reduced these to fourteen reservations which represented the official Republican position. Though annoying and unnecessary, these reservations did not seriously impair America's obligation to the League. The most important of them, dealing of course with Article x, stated that the United States would aid other nations against aggression only with the approval of Congress. The reservation was completely gratuitous, for Congress would have to give its approval in any case. Lodge's obvious strategy was to force Wilson to defeat the treaty himself. Lodge knew that Wilson would not allow the treaty to pass with these reservations, and Lodge had the votes to assure that it would not pass without them.

A heavy share of the blame for defeat of the treaty must therefore fall on Wilson. His strategy was to hold out for the mildest possible reservations. Defeat of the Lodge reservations, he thought, would result in a compromise favorable to those which the Democrats were offering. Wilson himself had secretly drafted reservations for the Democrats which differed only slightly from Lodge's. On November 18, the day before the vote on the treaty, Wilson wrote a letter to the Senate Democrats which insured defeat of the League. The Lodge resolution (which embodied the fourteen reservations) "does not" he said, "provide for ratification, but, rather for nullification of the Treaty. I sincerely hope that the friends and supporters of the Treaty will vote against the Lodge resolution of ratification." The folly of his strategy becomes clear in the next line: "I understand that the door will then be open for a genuine resolution of ratification."

The Lodge resolution, which came up first for vote, was defeated 55–39. Thirty-five Republicans and four Democrats voted for it; forty-two Democrats and the thirteen irreconcilables voted against it. The second vote was for the treaty without reservations. Wilson thought that enough mild reservationist Republicans would join the Democrats to pass it. But it lost decisively, 53–38; only Democrats voted for it; all the Republicans and four Democrats voted against it. And so the treaty was dead—but not yet buried.

The country was stunned by what had taken place in the Senate. How could the League have been defeated when all but thirteen Senators favored America's participation in it? A flood of indignant letters and telegrams poured into the Senate; leading national organizations protested to Lodge; Republican statesmen, notably William Howard Taft, Elihu Root and Herbert Hoover, thought the defeat a travesty. Lodge weakened under the pressure and entered into negotiations with the Democrats to reconsider his reservations. It was also decided that the treaty would again come up for a vote.

But once again Wilson's obduracy, the irreconcilables' resourcefulness, and Lodge's opportunism conspired to defeat the treaty. By early 1920 Wilson was even less eager to compromise than before. In fact he suggested to the Democratic party that no more should be done about the treaty in the 66th Congress and that the issue should be taken to the people in a "solemn referendum" to be held during the presidential election. This would have meant waiting more than a year before the Senate again would consider the treaty—a prospect that delighted the irreconcilables who were confident that time was on their side. Meanwhile the irreconcilables threatened to bolt the Republican party and so depose Lodge from Senate leadership unless Lodge broke off negotiations with the Democrats. Lodge submitted at once.

On March 19, 1920, the treaty again came to a vote. It seemed as though nothing had changed. The setting was the same. Again Wilson admonished the Democrats against voting for the Lodge resolution (which now contained fifteen reservations, an absurd one having been added on independence for Ireland). "Either," Wilson asserted, "we should enter the League fearlessly, accepting the responsibility and not fearing the role of leadership which we now enjoy, contributing our efforts towards establishing a just and permanent peace, or we should retire as gracefully as possible from the great concert of powers, by which the world was saved."

This time Democratic solidarity cracked. In the vote on the Lodge resolution only twenty-three Democrats joined the twelve irreconcilables to oppose it; twenty-one Democrats were among the forty-nine who favored it. Had seven more Democrats switched, the treaty would have carried. There were to be no more votes. The treaty was dead—and buried.

It would be futile here to apportion blame for the defeat. Certainly Wilson proved to be a bad strategist and politician. It would have been best had the United States joined the League without any reservations. But as this was not possible, joining with the Lodge reservations would have been better than not joining at all. Wilson's political acumen did not measure up to his great vision and hope. He foresaw that the world would not have peace unless guaranteed by the most powerful democracy. America's failure to accept the obligation which was hers of necessity had catastrophic consequences for mankind. Defeat of the League was followed by two decades of American isolationism during which time the world moved relentlessly toward the holocaust of the Second World War.

After the second vote, public interest in the treaty waned. Wilson's physical condition was a ghastly symbol of what was also happening to his ideals. The people had had enough of progressivism, of wars to end all wars, of covenants of peace. They were weary of struggling for selfless ends and were disillusioned by their once exalted hopes. In the presidential election of 1920 the Democratic party, whose candidates—James M. Cox and Franklin D. Roosevelt—made an issue of the League, received one of the worst drubbings in American political history. The Republicans had selected in Warren G. Harding and Calvin Coolidge precisely the men whom the country wanted and deserved. They had promised a return to earlier and more relaxed days, before government had come under the domination of reformers and internationalists. The heavily Republican 67th Congress ended the war by joint resolution on July 21, 1921, and separate peace treaties were signed with the Central Powers. Harding and his successors hardly mentioned the League. It was as though it did not exist.

In the three years before his death on February 3, 1924, Wilson occasionally broke his silence to remind the errant nation of its neglected responsibilities. But his was a voice of the distant past —or future.

The following selection of Wilson's speeches, letters and state papers deals almost entirely with his political career and philosophy. Very little—in effect none at all—deals with his personal life. The documents are arranged chronologically to correspond to the important events in his political life.

The first part opens with his earliest essay, goes through his pre-political years, and concludes with his resignation as president of Princeton.

The second part takes in the period of his extraordinary rise, from his New Jersey gubernatorial candidacy in 1910 through his presidential candidacy in 1912.

The third compasses the New Freedom at home and the New Diplomacy abroad—roughly from 1913 through 1915.

The fourth emphasizes his struggles between August, 1914, and February, 1917, to work out a neutrality policy with Britain and Germany and also includes the Second New Freedom of 1916.

The fifth presents Wilson's war aims and negotiations eventuating in the armistice and the Versailles Conference.

The sixth is devoted entirely to the Treaty of Versailles, the emphasis being on Wilson's work in conceiving, drafting, and defending the League of Nations Covenant.

The seventh and last contains the important aspects of his struggle with the Senate Republicans over the League, and his tragic defeat at their hands.

One

PREPARATION
1856–1910

1. By the Genius of a Single Man

Article on Bismarck, November, 1877

Wilson was twenty-one and a sophomore at Princeton when he wrote his first article, published by the Nassau Literary Magazine *of November, 1877. In this sympathetic analysis of Bismarck, he sounds the theme of his pre-political years: the necessity of strong leadership informed by a deep sense of duty.*

FEW CENTURIES seem to have been more fruitful in crises, in revolutions and counter-revolutions, in the establishment, convulsion, and overthrow of empires and kingdoms than our own. From the period upon the teeming pages of whose history falls the glitter of the first and great Napoleon's sword to that which witnessed the sudden downfall of the third Napoleon, innovation and revolution have been the rule rather than the exception in Europe. With Thiers passed away the last of those illustrious men who figured amid the memorable events which crowded upon one another in rapid succession after the great revolution and its attending convulsions. With the appearance of Bismarck upon the political stage began the rule of a new line of statesmen. Stern Time had superseded Thiers. Upon his will had hung the destinies of France. He had seen his country at the zenith of her glory; he lived to see her in deepest degradation at the feet of Bismarck. He lingered only long enough to see his country once more recover some of her wonted energy and then reluctantly made way for a younger generation of statesmen.

The death of Thiers has naturally led us to think of those whom he has left behind him in the field of European politics. And upon the character and life of Bismarck, now the foremost figure of Europe, we would dwell for a little. We may, from the vantage ground of disinterested observation, be able, in the light of the eventful sixty-two years of his life, to estimate his merits without the hatred of the Austrian, the fear-begotten bitterness of the Frenchman, or the prejudice of the Englishman, to warp our judgment. . . .

Events called into action the man from whose will so many events have sprung. In 1862, when every rumor indicated a close alliance between Russia, Prussia, and France, and every circumstance seemed to be calling upon Prussia for immediate and energetic action, William had need to call into his counsels a vigorous mind, and it did not long remain doubtful to whom the position of chief adviser belonged by right of statesmanlike genius. Bismarck's character and commanding talents rendered him a necessity to the king. In his new position, which proved to be the most responsible in Europe, he acted with a boldness and energy combined with foresight and prudence which have made him the most prominent figure in modern history. To sketch his career since 1862 would be to recapitulate the history of Europe for the last fifteen years and such a sketch cannot be attempted here. It will be our aim simply to delineate with all possible care his mental and moral character.

We can form no just conception of Bismarck's capacities as a statesman by comparing him with any of those great English statesmen to whom we have been wont to accord a large place in our notice and admiration, or with any of those honored men and able statesmen who brought our republic in safety and honor through the storms of her early existence. Neither those talents so necessary to the English statesman as a leader of Parliament nor those peculiar gifts always to be found in the guide of popular opinion and guard of popular institutions are necessary to the Prussian statesman. All the energies of the English or American statesman must be spent in governing great popular assemblies, in manipulating parties, in directing and controlling popular opinion. The Prussian statesman, on the other hand, must exert all his powers in rendering himself supreme in the royal closet; his power does not depend upon popular assemblies whose favor he must win and whose support he must command, but rests entirely with his royal master; he is comparatively independent of party relations and ties. Besides great intellect, the English statesman must have eloquence and tact; in the Prussian statesman eloquence and tact are nothing unless accompanied by marked administrative and diplomatic talents and a controlling influence over the royal mind. The triumphs of the English statesman are gained upon the floor of Parliament; those of the Prussian statesman are won in the cabinet of his king. The powers of the English statesman are apt to be dwarfed in being so constantly exercised for the acquirement of nothing more than skill in dialectic fence; intrigue is apt to demean the powers and sully the character of the Prussian statesman. For all the officers of the Prussian ministry are directly responsible to the king alone, and the prime minister, exercising no direct supervision over them, must control his subordinates through the king, their common master. And, while many a triumph over external difficulties and opponents, many a masterstroke of policy, and many a victory in war have all combined to attest the pre-eminence of his genius, Bismarck's character is not altogether free from the stain which intrigue invariably brings. In his dealings with the diplomatic world or even with his royal master, he has not always proved himself above deceit. But still he may justly be regarded as a grand type of his class of statesmen—men of independent conviction, full of self-trust, and themselves the spirit of their country's institutions. In Bismarck are united the moral force of Cromwell and the political shrewdness of Richelieu; the comprehensive intellect of Burke, without his learning, and the diplomatic ability of Talleyrand, without his coldness. In haughtiness, a rival of Chatham; in devotion to his country's interests, a peer of Hampden; in boldness of speech, and action, an equal of Brougham; Bismarck's qualities are in most unique combination. . . .

Bismarck's vivid conceptive powers are naturally combined with an impulsiveness which, if not checked by judgment and restrained by circumstances, might betray him into rashness. But, being under the constant necessity of carefully thinking out every line of action and laboriously planning every mode of execution, in order that his measures may be acceptable to his royal master, every tendency to rashness has been counterbalanced and neutralized by the necessity for deliberation. And, though the great chancellor often chafes fiercely under the restraints thus imposed upon him, he, nevertheless, owes to this very restraint much of his success. William always yielded in more important matters to the genius of his great subject, but frequently only after long and severe struggles, which have greatly worn upon the chancellor at the same time that they have purged his schemes of every rash element. The king possesses more force of moral character and stubbornness of will than clearness of intellectual insight, and his favor, often so hard to win, is therefore essential even to the all-powerful Bismarck. Only an unconquerable energy and an indomitable will have prevented the premier from retiring from a position necessarily so harassing. Obstacles seem only to whet his activity and increase his power.

With unmeasured energy and surprising power of concentration are combined the firmness, the quickness of resolve, and the ability for prompt action so necessary to leaders. But Bismarck's firmness, while pointed with intrepidity, is disfigured by harshness. Nothing could be harsher than his means of removing from his path some antagonist or rival and he has often proved unscrupulous in the use of these means. But our condemnation of Bismarck's occasional bad faith should be surrounded by many qualifications and explanations. We can never justify the willful disregard of justice or the willful breaking of faith. But in a man who is conscious of great powers, whose mind is teeming and overflowing with great political plans and dreaming of grand national triumphs, and who, withal, is hampered on every side by almost every circumstance of his surroundings we can at least understand an occasional breach of honor, and, in the presence of so many grand and peerless qualities and so many noble purposes, can perhaps forgive a want of integrity which so seldom exhibits itself. And even when uprightness is wanting in his purposes or in his choice of means, its place is filled by uncommon wisdom in action.

Burke has somewhere spoken of what, in his usually happy manner, he has styled "retrospective wisdom and historic patriotism"; of these the wisdom and patriotism of Bismarck are the direct opposites. His is the wisdom that penetrates and provides for the future; his is the patriotism that impels him to exhibit his love for his country in constant endeavors to secure for her permanent power and prosperity.

The history of modern times furnishes few examples of such minds as that of this now famous German. We can find on record few instances in which a comparatively small and virtually dependent kingdom has been raised in eight years to the proud place of a first-class power by the genius of a single man. Few indeed are the modern statesmen who have possessed even a small part of Bismarck's creative power backed and pointed by his insight and energy. The man who has of late modified and directed the whole course of European events; the man who was able to destroy the power of Austria, humble France, unify Germany, endow Prussia with immense and unwonted strength, and command the uniform support of Russia; the man who was bold enough to take all temporal power from the German Roman Catholic Church in the face of so many thousands of German Roman Catholics; the man who, by mere genius and force of character, has attained the proudest position in all Europe, will not soon be forgotten. Prussia will not soon find another Bismarck.

2. The Degradation of Our Political Parties

"Cabinet Government in the United States," August, 1879

Written when Wilson was a senior at Princeton, this essay embodies the ideas later incorporated in his most important book, Congressional Government. *The failure of leadership in the United States, he had become convinced, could be traced to deep-seated constitutional reasons, not to the virtues or shortcomings of individual men. The article appeared in the August, 1879, issue of* International Review, *edited by the man who was to become his great adversary—Henry Cabot Lodge.*

OUR PATRIOTISM seems of late to have been exchanging its wonted tone of confident hope for one of desponding solicitude. Anxiety about the future of our institutions seems to be daily becoming stronger in the minds of thoughtful Americans. A feeling of uneasiness is undoubtedly prevalent, sometimes taking the shape of a fear that grave, perhaps radical, defects in our mode of government are militating against our liberty and prosperity. A marked and alarming decline in statesmanship, a rule of levity and folly instead of wisdom and sober forethought in legislation, threaten to shake our trust not only in the men by whom our national policy is controlled, but also in the very principles upon which our Government rests. Both State and National legislatures are looked upon with nervous suspicion, and we hail an adjournment of Congress as a temporary immunity from danger. In casting about for the chief cause of the admitted evil, many persons have convinced themselves that it is to be found in the principle of universal suffrage. When Dr. Woolsey, in his admirable work on Political Science, speaks with despondency of the influence of this principle upon our political life, he simply gives clear expression to misgivings which he shares with a growing minority of his countrymen. We must, it is said, purge the constituencies of their ignorant elements, if we would have highminded, able, worthy representatives. We see adventurers, who in times of revolution and confusion were suffered to climb to high and responsible places, still holding positions of trust; we perceive that our institutions, when once thrown out of gear, seem to possess no power of self-readjustment—and we hasten to cast discredit upon that principle the establishment of which has been regarded as America's greatest claim to political honor—the right of every man to a voice in the Government under which he lives. The existence of such sentiments is in itself an instructive fact. But while it is indisputably true that universal suffrage is a constant element of weakness, and exposes us to many dangers which we might otherwise escape, its operation does not suffice alone to explain existing evils. Those who make this the scapegoat of all our national grievances have made too superficial an analysis of the abuses about which they so loudly complain.

What is the real cause of this solicitude and doubt? It is, in our opinion, to be found in the absorption of all power by a legislature which is practically irresponsible for its acts. But even this would not necessarily be harmful, were it not for the addition of a despotic principle which it is my present purpose to consider.

At its highest development, *representative* government is that form which best enables a free people to govern themselves. The main object of a representative assembly, therefore, should be the discussion of public business. They should legislate as if in the presence of the whole country, because they come under the closest scrutiny and fullest criticism of all the representatives of the country speaking in open and free debate. Only in such an assembly, only in such an atmosphere of publicity, only by means of such a vast investigating machine, can the different sections of a great country learn each other's feelings and interests. It is not enough that the general course of legislation is known to all. Unless during its progress it is subjected to a thorough, even a tediously prolonged, process of public sifting, to the free comment of friend and foe alike, to the ordeal of battle among those upon whose vote its fate depends, an act of open legislation may have its real intent and scope completely concealed by its friends and undiscovered by its enemies, and it may be as fatally mischievous as the darkest measures of an oligarchy or a despot. Nothing can be more obvious than the fact that the very life of free, popular institutions is dependent upon their breathing the bracing air of thorough, exhaustive, and open discussions, or that select Congressional committees, whose proceedings must from their very nature be secret, are, as means of legislation, dangerous and unwholesome. Parliaments are forces for freedom; for "talk is persuasion, persuasion is force, the one force which can sway free men to deeds such as those which have made England what she is," or our English stock what it is.

Congress is a deliberative body in which there is little real deliberation; a legislature which legislates with no real discussion of its business. Our Government is practically carried on by irresponsible committees. Too few Americans take the trouble to inform themselves as to the methods of Congressional management; and, as a consequence, not many have perceived that almost *absolute* power has fallen into the hands of men whose irresponsibility prevents the regulation of their conduct by the people from whom they derive their authority. The most important, most powerful man in the government of the United States in time of peace is the Speaker of the House of Representatives. Instead of being merely an executive officer, whose principal duties are those immediately connected with the administration of the rules of order, he is a potent party chief, the only chief of any real potency—and must of necessity be so. He must be the strongest and shrewdest member of his party in the lower House; for almost all the real business of that House is transacted by committees whose members are his nominees. Unless the rules of the House be suspended by a special two-thirds vote, every bill introduced must be referred, without debate, to the proper Standing Committee, with whom rests the privilege of embodying it, or any part of it, in their reports, or of rejecting it altogether. The House very seldom takes any direct action upon any measures introduced by individual members; its votes and discussions are almost entirely confined to committee reports and committee dictation. The whole attitude of business depends upon forty-seven Standing Committees. Even the discussions upon their directive reports are merely nominal—liberal forms, at most. Take, as an example of the workings of the system, the functions and privileges of the Committee of Ways and Means. To it is intrusted the financial policy of the country; its chairman is, in reality, our Chancellor of the Exchequer. With the aid of his colleagues he determines the course of legislation upon finance; in English political phrase, he draws up the *budget*. All the momentous questions connected with our finance are debated in the private sessions of this committee, and there only. For, when the budget is submitted to the House for its consideration, only a very limited time is allowed for its discussion; and, besides the member of the committee to whom its introduction is intrusted, no one is permitted to speak save those to whom he through courtesy yields the floor, and who must have made arrangements beforehand with the Speaker to be recognized. Where, then, is there room for thorough discussion—for discussion of any kind? If carried, the provisions of the budget must be put into operation by the Secretary of the Treasury, who may be directly opposed to the principles which it embodies. If lost, no one save Congress itself is responsible for the consequent embarrassment into which the nation is brought—and Congress as a body is not readily punishable.

It must at once be evident to every thinking man that a policy thus regulated cannot be other than vacillating, uncertain, devoid of plan or consistency. This is certainly a phase of representative government peculiar to ourselves. And yet its development was most natural and apparently necessary. It is hardly possible for a body of several hundred men, without official or authoritative leaders, to determine upon any line of action without interminable wrangling and delays injurious to the interests under their care. Left to their own resources, they would be as helpless as any other mass meeting. Without leaders having authority to guide their deliberations and give a definite direction to the movement of legislation; and, moreover, with none of that sense of responsibility which constantly rests upon those whose duty it is to work out to a successful issue the policies which they themselves originate, yet with full power to dictate policies which others must carry into execution—a recognition of the need of some sort of leadership, and of a division of labor, led to the formation of these Standing Committees, to which are intrusted the shaping of the national policy in the several departments of administration, as well as the prerogatives of the initiative in legislation and leadership in debate. When theoretically viewed, this is an ingenious and apparently harmless device, but one which, in practice, subverts that most fundamental of all the principles of a free State—the right of the people to a potential voice in their own government. Great measures of legislation are discussed and determined, not conspicuously in public session of the people's representatives, but in the unapproachable privacy of committee rooms.

But what less imperfect means of representative government can we find without stepping beyond the bounds of a true republicanism? Certainly none other than those which were rejected by the Constitutional Convention. When the Convention of 1787, upon the submission of the report of the Committee of Detail, came to consider the respective duties and privileges of the legislative and executive departments, and the relations which these two branches of the Government should sustain towards each other, many serious questions presented themselves for solution. One of the gravest of these was, whether or not the interests of the public service would be furthered by *allowing some of the higher officers of State to occupy seats in the legislature.* The propriety and practical advantage of such a course were obviously suggested by a similar arrangement under the British Constitution, to which our political fathers often and wisely looked for useful hints. But since the spheres of the several departments were in the end defined with all the clearness, strictness, and care possible to a written instrument, the opinion prevailed among the members of the Convention that it would be unadvisable to establish any such connection between the Executive and Congress. They thought, in their own fervor of patriotism and intensity of respect for written law, that paper barriers would prove sufficient to prevent the encroachments of any one department upon the prerogatives of any other; that these vaguely broad laws—or principles of law—would be capable of securing and maintaining the harmonious and mutually helpful co-operation of the several branches; that the exhibition of these general views of government would be adequate to the stupendous task of preventing the legislature from rising to the predominance of influence, which, nevertheless, constantly lay within its reach. But, in spite of constitutional barriers, the legislature has become the imperial power of the State, as it must of necessity become under every representative system; and experience of the consequences of a complete separation of the legislative and executive branches long since led that able and sagacious commentator upon the Constitution, Chief Justice Story, to remark that, "if it would not have been safe to trust the heads of departments, as representatives, to the choice of the people, as their constituents, it would have been at least some gain to have allowed them seats, like territorial delegates, in the House of Representatives, where they might freely debate without a title to vote." In short, the framers of the Constitution, in endeavoring to act in accordance with the principle of Montesquieu's celebrated and unquestionably just political maxim—that the legislative, executive, and judicial departments of a free State should be *separate*—made their separation so complete as to amount to *isolation.* To the methods of representative government which have sprung from these provisions of the Constitution, by which the Convention thought so carefully to guard and limit the powers of the legislature, we must look for an explanation, in a large measure, of the evils over which we now find ourselves lamenting.

What, then, is Cabinet government? What is the change proposed? Simply to give to the heads of the Executive departments—the members of the Cabinet—seats in Congress, with the privilege of the initiative in legislation and some part of the unbounded privileges now commanded by the Standing Committees. But the advocates of such a change—and they are now not a few—deceive themselves when they maintain that it would not necessarily involve the principle of ministerial responsibility—that is, the resignation of the Cabinet upon the defeat of any important part of their plans. For, if Cabinet officers sit in Congress as official representatives of the Executive, this principle of responsibility must of necessity come sooner or later to be recognized. Experience would soon demonstrate the practical impossibility of their holding their seats, and continuing to represent the Administration, after they had found themselves unable to gain the consent of a majority to their policy. Their functions would be peculiar. They would constitute a link between the legislative and executive branches of the general Government, and, as representatives of the Executive, must hold the right of the initiative in legislation. Otherwise their position would be an anomalous one indeed. There would be little danger and evident propriety in extending to them the first right of introducing measures relative to the administration of the several departments; and they could possess such a right without denying the fullest privileges to other members. But, whether granted this initiative or not, the head of each department would undoubtedly find it necessary to take a decided and open stand for or against every measure bearing upon the affairs of his department, by whomsoever introduced. No high-spirited man would long remain in an office in the business of which he was not permitted to pursue a policy which tallied with his own principles and convictions. If defeated by both Houses, he would naturally resign; and not many years would pass before resignation upon defeat would have become an established precedent—and resignation upon defeat is the essence of responsible government. In arguing, therefore, for the admission of Cabinet officers into the legislature, we are logically brought to favor *responsible Cabinet government* in the United States.

But, to give to the President the right to choose whomsoever he pleases as his constitutional advisers, after having constituted Cabinet officers *ex officio* members of Congress, would be to empower him to appoint a limited number of representatives, and would thus be plainly at variance with republican principles. The highest order of responsible government could, then, be established in the United States only by laying upon the President the necessity of selecting his Cabinet from among the number of representatives already chosen by the people, or by the legislatures of the States.

Such a change in our legislative system would not be so radical as it might at first appear: it would certainly be very far from revolutionary. Under our present system we suffer all the inconveniences, are hampered by all that is defective in the machinery, of responsible government, without securing any of the many benefits which would follow upon its complete establishment. Cabinet officers are now appointed only with the consent of the Senate. Such powers as a Cabinet with responsible leadership must possess are now divided among the forty-seven Standing Committees, whose prerogatives of irresponsible leadership savor of despotism, because exercised for the most part within the secret precincts of a committee room, and not under the eyes of the whole House, and thus of the whole country. These committees, too, as has been said, rule without any of that freedom of public debate which is essential to the liberties of the people. Their measures are too often mere partisan measures, and are hurried through the forms of voting by a party majority whose interest it is that all serious opposition, all debate that might develop obstructive antagonism, should be suppressed. Under the conditions of Cabinet government, however, full and free debates are sure to take place. For what are these conditions? According as their policy stands or falls, the ministers themselves stand or fall; to the party which supports them each discussion involves a trial of strength with their opponents; upon it depends the amount of their success as a party; while to the opposition the triumph of ministerial plans means still further exclusion from office, their overthrow, accession to power. To each member of the assembly every debate offers an opportunity for placing himself, by able argument, in a position to command a place in any future Cabinet that may be formed from the ranks of his own party; each speech goes to the building up (or the tearing down) of his political fortunes. There is, therefore, an absolute certainty that every phase of every subject will be drawn carefully and vigorously, will be dwelt upon with minuteness, will be viewed from every possible standpoint. The legislative, holding full power of final decision, would find itself in immediate contact with the executive and its policy. Nor would there be room for factious government or factious opposition. Plainly, ministers must found their policies, an opposition must found its attacks, upon well-considered principles; for in this open sifting of debate, when every feature of every measure, even to the motives which prompted it, is the subject of outspoken discussion and keen scrutiny, no chicanery, no party craft, no questionable principles can long hide themselves. Party trickery, legislative jobbery, are deprived of the very air they breathe—the air of secrecy, of concealment. The public is still surprised whenever they find that dishonest legislation has been allowed to pass unchallenged. Why surprised? As things are, measures are determined in the interests of corporations, and the suffering people know almost nothing of them until their evil tendencies crop out in actual execution. Under lobby pressure from interested parties, they have been cunningly concocted in the closest sessions of partisan committees, and, by the all-powerful aid of party machinery, have been hurried through the stages of legislation without debate; so that even Press correspondents are often as ignorant of the real nature of such special measures as the outside public. Any searching debate of such questions would at once have brought the public eye upon them, and how could they then have stood? Lifting the lid of concealment must have been the discovery to all concerned of their unsavory character. Light would have killed them.

We are thus again brought into the presence of the cardinal fact of this discussion—that *debate* is the essential function of a popular representative body. In the severe, distinct, and sharp enunciation of underlying principles, the unsparing examination and telling criticism of opposite positions, the careful, painstaking unravelling of all the issues involved, which are incident to the free discussion of questions of public policy we see the best, the only effective, means of educating public opinion. . . .

When we come to speak of the probable influence of responsible Cabinet government upon the development of statesmanship and the renewal of the now perishing growth of statesmanlike qualities, we come upon a vital interest of the whole question. Will it bring with it worthy successors of Hamilton and Webster? Will it replace a leadership of trickery and cunning device by one of ability and moral strength? If it will not, why advocate it? If it will, how gladly and eagerly and imperatively ought we to demand it! The most despotic of Governments under the control of wise statesmen is preferable to the freest ruled by demagogues. Now, there are few more common, and perhaps few more reasonable, beliefs than that at all times, among the millions of population who constitute the body of this great nation, there is here and there to be found a man with all the genius, all the deep and strong patriotism, all the moral vigor, and all the ripeness of knowledge and variety of acquisition which gave power and lasting fame to the greater statesmen of our past history. We bewail and even wonder at the fact that these men do not find their way into public life, to claim power and leadership in the service of their country. We naturally ascribe their absence to the repugnance which superior minds must feel for the intrigues, the glaring publicity, and the air of unscrupulousness and even dishonesty which are the characteristics, or at least the environments, of political life. In our disappointment and vexation that they do not, even at the most distressing sacrifice of their personal convenience and peace, devote themselves to the study and practice of statecraft, we turn for comfort to reread history's lesson—that many countries find their greatest statesmen in times of extraordinary crisis or rapid transition and progress; the intervals of slow growth and uninteresting everyday administration of the government being noted only for the elevation of mediocrity, or at most of shrewd cunning, to high administrative places. We take cold consolation from the hope that times of peril—which sometimes seem close enough at hand—will not find us without strong leaders worthy of the most implicit confidence. Thus we are enabled to arrive at the comfortable and fear-quieting conclusion that it is from no fault of ours, certainly from no defects in our forms of government, that we are ruled by scheming, incompetent, political tradesmen, whose aims and ambitions are merely personal, instead of by broad-minded, masterful statesmen, whose sympathies and purposes are patriotic and national.

To supply the conditions of statesmanship is, we conclude, beyond our power; for the causes of its decline and the means necessary to its development are beyond our ken. Let us take a new departure. Let us, drawing light from every source within the range of our knowledge, make a little independent analysis of the conditions of statesmanship, with a view to ascertaining whether or not it is in reality true that we cannot contribute to its development, or even perchance give it a perennial growth among us. We learn from a critical survey of the past, that, so far as political affairs are concerned, great critical epochs are the man-making epochs of history, that revolutionary influences are man-making influences. And why? If this be the law, it must have some adequate reason underlying it; and we seem to find the reason a very plain and conspicuous one. Crises give birth and a new growth to statesmanship because they are peculiarly periods of action, in which talents find the widest and the freest scope. They are periods not only of action, but also of unusual opportunity for gaining leadership and a controlling and guiding influence. It is opportunity for transcendent influence, therefore, which calls into active public life a nation's greater minds—minds which might otherwise remain absorbed in the smaller affairs of private life. And we thus come upon the principle—a principle which will appear the more incontrovertible the more it is looked into and tested—that governmental forms will call to the work of administration able minds and strong hearts constantly or infrequently, according as they do or do not afford them at all times an opportunity of gaining and retaining a commanding authority and an undisputed leadership in the nation's councils. Now it certainly needs no argument to prove that government by supreme committees, whose members are appointed at the caprice of an irresponsible party chief, by seniority, because of reputation gained in entirely different fields, or because of partisan shrewdness, is not favorable to a full and strong development of statesmanship. Certain it is that statesmanship has been steadily dying out in the United States since that stupendous crisis during which its government felt the first throbs of life. In the government of the United States there is no place found for the leadership of men of real ability. Why, then, complain that we have no leaders? The President can seldom make himself recognized as a leader; he is merely the executor of the sovereign legislative will; his Cabinet officers are little more than chief clerks, or superintendents, in the Executive departments, who advise the President as to matters in most of which he has no power of action independently of the concurrence of the Senate. The most ambitious representative can rise no higher than the chairmanship of the Committee of Ways and Means, or the Speakership of the House. The cardinal feature of Cabinet government, on the other hand, is responsible leadership—the leadership and authority of a small body of men who have won the foremost places in their party by a display of administrative talents, by evidence of high ability upon the floor of Congress in the stormy play of debate. None but the ablest can become leaders and masters in this keen tournament in which arguments are the weapons, and the people the judges. Clearly defined, definitely directed policies arouse bold and concerted opposition; and leaders of oppositions become in time leaders of Cabinets. Such a recognized leadership it is that is necessary to the development of statesmanship under popular, republican institutions; for only such leadership can make politics seem worthy of cultivation to men of high mind and aim.

And if party success in Congress—the ruling body of the nation—depends upon power in debate, skill and prescience in policy, successful defense of or attacks upon ruling ministries, how ill can contending parties spare their men of ability from Congress! To keep men of the strongest mental and moral fiber in Congress would become a party necessity. Party triumph would then be a matter of might in debate, not of supremacy in subterfuge. The two great national parties—and upon the existence of two great parties, with clashings and mutual jealousies and watchings, depends the health of free political institutions—are dying for want of unifying and vitalizing principles. Without leaders, they are also without policies, without aims. With leaders there must be followers, there must be parties. And with leaders whose leadership was earned in an open war of principle against principle, by the triumph of one opinion over all opposing opinions, parties must from the necessities of the case have definite policies. Platforms, then, must mean something. Broken promises will then end in broken power. A Cabinet without a policy that is finding effect in progressive legislation is, in a country of frequent elections, inviting its own defeat. Or is there, on the other hand, a determined, aggressive opposition? Then the ministry have a right to ask them what they would do under similar circumstances, were the reins of government to fall to them. And if the opposition are then silent, they cannot reasonably expect the country to intrust the government to them. . . .

Eight words contain the sum of the present degradation of our political parties: *No leaders, no principles; no principles, no parties.* Congressional leadership is divided infinitesimally; and with divided leadership there can be no great party units. Drill in debate, by giving scope to talents, invites talents; raises up a race of men habituated to the methods of public business, skilled parliamentary chiefs. And, more than this, it creates a much-to-be-desired class who early make attendance upon public affairs the business of their lives, devoting to the service of their country all their better years. Surely the management of a nation's business will, in a well-ordered society, be as properly a matter of life-long training as the conduct of private affairs.

3. The Best Men of the Country

Address to Princeton Undergraduates, April 15, 1905

Even before he became president of Princeton on October 25, 1902, Wilson proposed establishment of a preceptorial system designed to raise the college to intellectual preeminence. The plan proposed that, in conjunction with classwork, tutors would, in the manner of English dons, personally guide students. Faculty and trustees liked the idea, and it was launched in the fall of 1905. Before long Princeton developed into a first-rate college. Below, Wilson summarizes the intentions of the preceptorial system to the Princeton Undergraduate Press Club.

. . . THE TUTORIAL system is a plan to get hold of the personal equation of each man, giving him freedom with some guidance, in the things toward which his taste runs, showing him his weak points, and training him to see the value in the things which he does not naturally like. Under this plan each man will be treated individually, with the purpose of putting zest into his work. The tutor will bring out and strengthen the individual characteristics of each man.

The importance of the whole system lies in the character of the men who are being obtained. In the first place they are being selected along very careful lines, and only those will be taken who feel a certain love for the place, and who are in entire sympathy with its spirit, and understand the scope of the plan which is being developed. They are to be selected primarily upon their standing as gentlemen, as men who are companionable, clubable, whose personal qualities of association give them influence over the minds of younger men. If their qualities as gentlemen and as scholars conflict, the former will win them the place. It has been found that when a man at another institution has been invited here, he is immediately offered inducements to stay where he is. These are the kind of men wanted.

The new system is not for advertisement, but in order that the best men of the country shall be attracted here, and that Princeton shall turn out a body of men possessing such sound learning, such high development in all the essential characteristics of manliness that whenever there is anything really difficult to be done in the nation, Princeton and Princeton men will have to be consulted for advice and counsel.

4. We Can Lead in Social Example

Report to the Board of Trustees, June 10, 1907

For the preceptorial system to succeed something had to be done about the notoriously exclusive eating clubs which served as fraternal aristocracies among the student body. According to Wilson, these eating clubs severed students' intellectual activities from social activities. Wilson's indictment of them is contained in his report to the board of trustees of June 10, 1907 (published in the Princeton Alumni Weekly *of June 12, 1907). As the substitute for eating clubs, Wilson proposed his famous quadrangle plan: the students were to be formed into resident quadrangles, each containing a dining hall and study and social rooms. Publication of Wilson's report and address to the board let loose a torrent of controversy. For now he was threatening the whole aristocratic and class arrangement of the college. Some faculty members, led by Andrew F. West, dean of the faculty, resolutely opposed the quad plan. Almost all the young preceptors supported it. The alumni overwhelmingly resisted it. By August, 1907 the board of trustees had become wary of going ahead with it. The struggle continued through the early months of 1908. At one point Wilson was on the verge of resigning. The quad fight ended in April, 1908, when a committee made up of Wilson's own friends reported against it to the board of trustees. Wilson was defeated by his own forces. The whole affair left on all sides a bitterness that was to be assuaged only with Wilson's departure from Princeton in 1910. Wilson himself was not to mention it again in public.*

WE HAVE witnessed in the last few years the creation of a new Princeton, as the result—the astonishingly prompt result—of our attempt to give the University a vital, spontaneous intellectual life—not a life of pedants and grinds or of youngsters held inexorably to formal tasks, but a life of young men led by many influences to read and think for themselves along great lines of study, emancipated from school methods and stimulated to use their minds outside the class room. We realized that, for all its subtle charm and beguiling air of academic distinction, Princeton, so far as her undergraduates were concerned, had come to be merely a delightful place of residence, where young men, for the most part happily occupied by other things, were made to perform certain academic tasks; that, although we demanded at stated times a certain part of the attention of our pupils for intellectual things, their life and consciousness were for the rest wholly unacademic and detached from the interests which in theory were the all-important interests of the place. For a great majority of them residence here meant a happy life of comradeship and sport interrupted by the grind of perfunctory "lessons" and examinations, to which they attended rather because of the fear of being cut off from the life than because they were seriously engaged in getting the training which would fit their faculties and their spirits for the tasks of the world which they knew they must face after their happy freedom was over.

Undoubtedly, if we would give Princeton the highest distinction and that academic leadership in the country which she may now so easily gain, we must study at every turn the means by which to lift her intellectual life and achievements out of mediocrity not only, but also into such an order of naturalness and energy and distinction as shall make her by reason of her way of success a conspicuous model and example. There is no true intellectual life for the undergraduate in the mere faithful performance of set tasks, no matter how eagerly or with what concentration he devote himself to them, if between tasks his mind be emptied of the interest they have created and his life run entirely free of their influence. There must somehow be brought about an interpenetration of his experience inside the class room and conference and his experience outside academic exercises, where men register their interests by what they do and say and let their minds have play upon. A college without sport and without a great deal of irresponsible boyish disengagement from serious talk and thoughtful effort no one can desire who understands the real economics and needs of the mind.

The more wholesome sport and thoughtless fun the better both the work and the intimate comradeships upon which intellectual endeavor depends for energy and enlargement. But leisure and study ought not to be separated in air-tight compartments. Leisure ought to be enriched and diversified by the interests which study creates. In the midst of play there ought to be a constant consciousness of what the place means and must be made to stand for—a place of thoughtful, manly, disinterested men, disciples of university ideals.

When we introduced the preceptorial system we made the greatest strategic move in that direction that has been made in the whole history of American universities. By it we meant to say that the intellectual life of a college did not consist of attendance upon class exercises or of preparation for recitations, but consisted, rather, of constant contact with study and the intimate association of teacher and pupil outside the class room, where the tradition of lectures and recitations was forgotten, rejected, and a thoroughly natural and human relationship, the relationship of fellow-students, substituted. And that meaning has at once been made evident to the whole country. The contrast with the old order of things is most marked in the case of the intercourse of undergraduates with those preceptors who invite them often to their houses or who live in the same dormitories with them. A natural and easy social relationship, an informal, frequent exchange of calls, the easy, unconstrained talks of ordinary comradeship make study itself seem a thing natural and human, a thing not so much of formal exaction under rules as of the vital contact of minds. It is, by intention and in actual fact, a widening of the atmosphere of study to seem a natural medium of life and serious enjoyment.

But the new process, vital as it is in itself, suited as it is to the object we have had in view, may be checked and even nullified by hostile or unfavorable influences. Our new methods of study require as their soil and indispensable environment a new social coordination—a coordination which will not only make sure of a constant and natural intercourse between teacher and pupil, but also knit the student body itself together in some truly organic way which will ensure vital intellectual and academic contacts, the comradeships of a common life with common ends. Your

Committee is of the opinion that this can best be done by combining the undergraduates in residential groups—groups so made up that the forms and conditions under which each man in residence lives may so far as possible be the forms and conditions which are common to all.

Princeton has not since the earliest years of her development been in any full sense a residential college. She provides her students with lodgings, but with nothing else; and not all of them with that. And even the buildings in which she lodges them have never as yet been drawn together into such geographical relations as might be expected to bring their occupants into natural groups of association. They form no closed units, suggesting intimate associations; there are no common rooms; lodgings are assigned by lot, and close neighbors may never know each other. Our social life for generations together has formed itself around the boarding house and club tables. Men have associated themselves with congenial groups of companions to eat together, and, when no sufficiently comfortable boarding house could be found, have rented or built quarters of their own in which they could command their own comforts and their own bill of fare in pleasing independence.

The outcome in our own day has been the development of the upper-class clubs with their attractive club houses, in each of which there are not only dining rooms and kitchens and servants' quarters, but also well-appointed common rooms, libraries, billiard rooms, smoking rooms, private dining rooms for parties, and sleeping rooms for visitors. The members of the Freshman and Sophomore classes are not admitted to membership in these clubs; but the Sophomores maintain clubs of their own upon a more simple scale in rented houses; and in providing, as we have recently provided, eating places for the Freshmen, instead of organizing a commons for the whole class, as economy and ordinary usage would have suggested, we have felt obliged to provide a large number of separate dining rooms in which they could distribute themselves in groups as inchoate clubs, and to set aside for each group which thus formed itself a separate common room in addition, to which the members of the group could resort after meals to smoke and spend a pleasant half hour of diversion together. And that is our social organization. The dormitories are mere sleeping places and places for study, or for the briefer social calls that break the busy hours of the evening.

The evident peculiarity of this life is that it severs the social from the intellectual interests of the place, and does not, with its scattered clubs and divided classes, make us up into a community even on the social side. The vital units are the club units. They divide all four classes into segments and sharply separate the classes as wholes from one another during the two earlier years of the undergraduate course, when characters are being formed and points of view established. Their organization is entirely outside university action; has no organic connection whatever with anything academic; produces interests which absorb the attention and the energy of the best undergraduates as of all others, and yet nowhere interpenetrates the associations which arise out of study, carries no flavour with it which it might not as well have in any other town or in any other similar environment.

It absorbs the attention and all the planning faculties of the undergraduates because all social ambitions turn upon it. It would be difficult to exaggerate the importance in the life of the undergraduate of the question whether at the end of his Sophomore year he is going to be taken into one of the upper-class clubs. His thought is constantly fixed upon that object throughout the first two years of his university course with a great intensity and uneasiness whenever he thinks either of his social standing, his comradeships, or his general social consideration among his fellows. The clubs do not take in all the members of the Junior and Senior classes. About one-third are left out in the elections; and their lot is little less than deplorable. They feel that they cannot continue to associate on terms of intimacy with friends who have been elected into the clubs, for fear that they will be thought to be seeking to make favor with them and obtain a belated invitation to join; and, even when many of them as individuals are not disappointed at having been passed by, they must seek their comradeships with other classmates who are very much disappointed and who feel their isolation with a good deal of bitterness. It is difficult for them to arrange for comfortable eating places; and the places at which they do board are only too much like caves of Adullam. They go forward to their graduation almost like men who are in the University and yet not of it. Often they are cheerful and steadfast enough; individuals here and there are sometimes quite indifferent to their comparative isolation, being absorbed in their books or in the task of earning the money necessary to pay their college expenses, but as a class their position is most trying, and most discreditable to our university democracy. It often happens that men who fail of election into one of the clubs at the end of the Sophomore year leave the University and go to some other college or abandon altogether the idea of completing their university course.

There is a great deal of admirable solidarity still in our undergraduate life. The "Princeton Spirit" of which we so often speak, and which is so strong and excellent a force in everything that affects either the life or the fortunes of the University, has impelled the leading spirits among the undergraduates to strive with the utmost loyalty to keep the upper-class clubs from becoming factional centers and dividing the undergraduate body into cliques which would prefer the interests of their clubs to the interests of the University as a whole. They have felt that the upper-class clubs differed very radically, and very much for the better, from the fraternities which have cut the undergraduate body of other colleges into segments and factions, because they include only Juniors and Seniors in their membership and leave the Sophomores and Freshmen undivided, to acquire the democratic habit and united feeling of the place. So soon as the practice threatened to grow up of seeking out attractive and especially desirable under-classmen and pledging them in advance to accept elections into particular upper-class clubs, a treaty of the most stringent character was entered into by the clubs which sought to make it an act of personal dishonor on the part of any upper-classman who was a member of a club even to cultivate relations of personal intimacy with under-classmen for fear such ends might be in view. That treaty has again and again been violated, and again and again renewed, in stricter and stricter form, until, in its present shape, as now pending for readoption, it practically seeks to fix an impassable gulf between the upper and lower classes in order that such attempts and suspicions may be altogether avoided.

It even goes further. It attempts to minimize the personal and social intercourse between Sophomores and Freshmen, and so segregates the Sophomores entirely. Because the Sophomores, since they cannot be sought or solicited as prospective candidates for membership in upper-class clubs, which are the natural goal of their social ambition, associate themselves in groups to seek admission—not openly or avowedly, but none the less systematically and effectively. That is the recognized object of the Sophomore clubs. It is equally well known, and indeed matter of course, that the groups of Freshmen who form their separate clubs in the several dining rooms in which the Freshmen now eat are formed with a view to being taken at the end of the year into the different Sophomore organizations or "followings" (the so-called "hat lines" described in the President's report), and so making their way, in turn, into the upper-class clubs, where all roads of social preferment in the University end. The makers of the latest inter-club treaty endeavor, in the terms of the document they have just drawn up, to minimize and in part control that tendency also by regulating in some degree the personal and social intercourse between Freshmen and Sophomores, over whom the clubs, the parties to the treaty, clearly have no jurisdiction whatever.

Two very significant and very undesirable, and even dangerous, things have thus come about: the two lower classes, who need above all things the forming and guiding influence of the upper classes, have been almost completely segregated, and the very influences which seemed to render their segregation necessary from the point of view of the clubman have brought about the very result their segregation was meant to prevent—that is, they have cut them up into groups and cliques whose social ambitions give them separate and rival interests quite distinct from, plainly hostile to, the interests of the University as a whole.

No one seems to expect such treaties to be kept. A majority will always respect and obey them, as laws to which they have voluntarily submitted themselves; but a minority will always break and ignore them—with more or less indulgent condemnation from the majority. For it is universally admitted that they are in restraint of human nature: that there is, of course, nothing intrinsically dishonorable in the desire of an upper-classman to secure some friend in the lower class for his own club, and that the natural rivalry of the upper-class clubs, at any rate for the picked men of the lower classes, will frequently lead individuals to break through the artificial restraints of the treaty, no matter what pledges are exacted of them or of their clubs as organizations. In brief, the social ambitions created by the existing system of club life are too strong for individual honor; and treaties in restraint of natural impulses, even if obeyed, do not prevent the social divisions among the Freshmen and Sophomores which it is their main purpose to prevent. And all the while, treaties notwithstanding, the several groups formed by the Freshmen and Sophomores, if not in effect detached sections of the upper-class clubs, are at any rate their satellites and attend them most observantly.

Along with the steadily increasing concentration of the attention of the undergraduates upon the social question and the centering of all social ambitions upon the upper-class clubs has gone a very noticeable, a very rapid, increase in the luxury of the upper-class club houses. The two oldest clubs now have houses of extraordinary elegance and luxury of appointment and five other clubs are maturing plans for replacing their present comfortable structures with buildings which will rival the others in beauty, spaciousness, and comfort. The University, which gives life to these clubs and constitutes their ostensible *raison d'être,* seems in danger of becoming, if the present tendencies of undergraduate organization are allowed to work out their logical results, only an artistic setting and background for life on Prospect Avenue. That life, as it becomes more and more elaborate, will become more and more absorbing, and university interests will fall more and more into the background. The interest of the lower classes will more and more center upon it and the energies of the upper classes will be more and more engrossed by it. The vital life of the place will be outside the University and in large part independent of it.

These tendencies have not been obvious until the last year or two. Though for a long time apparent enough on close observation, they seemed until lately to be without formidable momentum and quite controllable by the conservative influences of the place. But now the undergraduates themselves clearly perceive them and are uneasily aware that they are rapidly getting beyond their control. Before the establishment of the preceptorial system, with its necessary corollary of the intimate association of teacher and pupil—the coordination of the undergraduate life with the teaching of the University—these things were not so near the heart of our plans and hopes for Princeton's intellectual development and academic revitalization. But now they are of the essence of everything we are striving for, whether on the undergraduate or on the graduate side of the University's work, and we are bound to consider the means by which to effect an immediate reintegration of our academic life.

Your Committee is of the opinion that the only adequate means of accomplishing this is the grouping of the undergraduates in residential quadrangles, each with its common dining hall, its common room for intercourse and diversion, and its resident master and preceptors; where members of all four of the classes shall be associated in a sort of family life, not merely as neighbors in the dormitories but also as comrades at meals and in many daily activities—the upper classes ruling and forming the lower, and all in constant association with members of the Faculty fitted to act in sympathetic co-operation with them in the management of their common life. In brief, your Committee is of the opinion that the only way in which the social life of the undergraduates can be prevented from fatally disordering, and perhaps even strangling, the academic life of the University is by the actual absorption of the social life into the academic.

This is not the scheme of the English colleges. Those colleges have separate autonomy. Each separately undertakes the instruction of the undergraduates resident within it. The plan we propose involves only a convenient residential division of the University as a social body. It does not involve its division, or the alteration of its past academic life, in any other respect whatever. It is a plan to substitute for the present segregation of the classes a reunion of the classes, and for the present division of the University into small social segments, which constantly tend to war with one another and to cut the University into factions, larger segments, or, rather, vital groups, which could not possibly develop like rivalries and cliques and which would be permeated by their very organization and environment by the soberer influences of the place—groups which would constitute the best possible *media* for the transmission of such impulses as we are now counting on to transform Princeton entirely. It is a choice between one sort of social transformation and another; and this is clearly the time when the choice must be made.

The effect of this plan upon the upper-class clubs would be either their abolition or their absorption. The withdrawal of the greater part of the Juniors and Seniors from the life of the proposed residential quads would of course be out of the question. A separate club life for them would rob the whole plan of its vitality, and is not to be thought of. But the history of the upper-class clubs has been most honorable and useful. They have served the University in a period of transition, when no plans were thought of for its coordination, as perhaps no other instrumentalities could have served it. Their abolition ought not to be thought of if their adaptation to the new order of things can be effected. It would be a violent breach of historical continuity and out of tone with the traditions and standards of growth which have hitherto kept Princeton intact as an organic whole. Fortunately, if we should be happy enough to secure their co-operation, it will be quite possible to develop them into smaller residential quads as part of the University itself: and this, in the opinion of your Committee, would be the happiest possible solution of the difficulty, giving to clubs which are now in danger of embarrassing and even profoundly demoralizing the life of the University a rôle of singular distinction and public spirit in its organic development, and affording the country at large a new example of Princeton's capacity to lead the way in matters of organization which are now puzzling the authorities of all our larger universities. We can lead in social example, as we are already leading in teaching example. And our alumni and undergraduates will, as usual, be our partners in the enterprise.

Your Committee, therefore, recommend that the President of the University be authorized to take such steps as may seem wisest for maturing this general plan, and for seeking the co-operation and counsel of the upper-class clubs in its elaboration; and that this Committee be continued to consult with the President from time to time as the matter may take shape and as he may require further counsel and advice, and to mature detailed plans for the future consideration of this Board so soon as such plans can be perfected by common counsel among all concerned.

Address to the Board of Trustees

The remedy proposed by the committee whose report I have read is radical, indeed, but not wholly out of line with the organization it is meant to replace. The associations formed in the quads will be like the associations formed in the clubs; with the elective principle left out, indeed, but with all the opportunities for a natural selection of chums and companions that the larger number in residence will afford; and with an added dignity of association, under resident members of the Faculty, fitted for the association and for the function of leadership and example which will naturally fall to them. The elective principle in the clubs at present amounts to little more than the right to choose groups of men (artificially enough formed, as everybody knows) rather than individuals. And, whether the new plan is like the old or not, it is not the social side that our thought is dwelling on. We are not seeking to form better clubs, but academic communities. We are making a university, not devising a method of social pleasure. The social life of the quads will be all-inclusive, and it will serve as the medium for things intellectual.

The question, How the transition from our present social organization to the new organization is to be effected—with what adjustments, accommodations, measures of transformation—is now our main subject of debate; and we can enter on that debate with a frankness and confidence in each other which I believe no other university in the world could hope for in an undertaking of such delicacy and magnitude. We have a body of alumni for whom the interests of the University as a whole, as they may be made to see those interests at any moment of action, take precedence over every other consideration, and over every rival sentiment. They are ready to be partners with the undergraduates and ourselves in accomplishing anything that may be necessary to give free and wholesome vigor to the life of the University and to secure to her the fame which she covets and must win—the fame of distinct intellectual purpose and a clear knowledge of the means by which she proposes to attain them.

I take leave to say that Princeton is the only university in the country which has found itself, which has formulated a clear ideal and deliberately set about the synthesis of plan necessary to realize it. She has set the country an example in the methods of teaching necessary to give a great university the intimacy of contact and the direct efficiency of instruction hitherto supposed to belong only to the small college, and suited to create, besides, something which the small college has seldom known how to create—a habit and freedom of independent reading which makes a "course" something more than the instruction of a single classroom or a single instructor; and now she must take the next step. She must organize her life in such a way that these contacts between the university and the student shall be stuff of daily habit, and not merely matters of formal appointment; not a thing of the classroom and conference merely, but a thing which may touch every hour, any hour, of the day, and fill seasons of leisure and enjoyment with a consciousness of what it is that vitalizes a university and makes it a force in the life of a great nation. Common counsel shall bring us to this consummation—not without trouble, but without serious conflict of opinion or purpose, as a new exhibition of what love of Princeton can do for her regeneration when her sons set themselves to the task. The labor will be pleasant, and the abiding fame of it will belong to all of us in common. . . .

5. Only for Particular Purposes

Article: "The State and The Federal Government," May, 1908

That Wilson was a very conservative Democrat is obvious from this excerpt of his article which appeared in the May, 1908, issue of The North American Review.

. . . WHAT, READING our Constitution in its true spirit, neither sticking in its letter, nor yet forcing it arbitrarily to mean what we wish it to mean, shall be the answer of our generation to the old question of the distribution of powers between Congress and the States? For us, as for previous generations, it is a deeply critical question. The very stuff of all our political principles, of all our political experience, is involved in it. In this all too indistinctly marked field of right choice our statesmanship shall achieve new triumphs or come to eventual shipwreck.

The old theory of the sovereignty of the States, which used so to engage our passions, has lost its vitality. The war between the States established at least this principle, that the Federal Government is, through its courts, the final judge of its own powers. Since that stern arbitrament it would be idle, in any practical argument, to ask by what law of abstract principle the Federal Government is bound and restrained. Its power is "to regulate commerce between the States," and the attempts now made during every session of Congress to carry the implications of that power beyond the utmost boundaries of reasonable and honest inference show that the only limits likely to be observed by politicians are those set by the good sense and conservative temper of the country.

The proposed Federal legislation with regard to the regulation of child labor affords a striking example. If the power to regulate commerce between the States can be stretched to include the regulation of labor in mills and factories, it can be made to embrace every particular of the industrial organization and action of the country. The only limitation Congress would observe, should the Supreme Court assent to such obviously absurd extravagances of interpretation, would be the limitations of opinion and of circumstance.

It is important, therefore, to look at the facts and to understand the real character of the political and economic materials of our own day with a clear and statesmanlike vision, as the makers of the Constitution understood the conditions they dealt with. If the jealousies of the colonies and of the little States which sprang out of them had not obliged the makers of the Constitution to leave the greater part of legal regulation in the hands of the States it would have been wise, it would even have been necessary, to invent such a division of powers as was actually agreed upon. It is not, at bottom, a question of sovereignty or of any other political abstraction; it is a question of vitality. Uniform regulation of the economic conditions of a vast territory and a various people like the United States would be mischievous, if not impossible. The statesmanship which really attempts it is premature and unwise. . . .

The division of powers between the States and the Federal Government effected by our Federal Constitution was the normal and natural division for this purpose. Under it the States possess all the ordinary legal choices that shape a people's life. Theirs is the whole of the ordinary field of law: the regulation of domestic relations and of the relations between employer and employee, the determinaton of property rights and of the validity and enforcement of contracts, the definition of crimes and their punishments, the definition of the many and subtle rights and obligations which lie outside the fields of property and contract, the establishment of the laws of incorporation and of the rules governing the conduct of every kind of business. The presumption insisted upon by the Courts in every argument with regard to the Federal Government is that it has no power not explicitly granted it by the Federal Constitution or reasonably to be inferred as the natural or necessary accompaniment of the powers there conveyed to it; but the presumption with regard to the powers of the States they have always held to be of exactly the opposite kind. It is that the States of course possess every power that government has ever anywhere exercised, except only those powers which their own constitutions or the Constitution of the United States explicitly or by plain inference withheld. They are the ordinary governments of the country; the Federal Government is its instrument only for particular purposes. . . .

The remedy for ill-considered legislation by the States, the remedy alike for neglect and mistake on their part, lies, not outside the States, but within them. The mistakes which they themselves correct will sink deeper into the consciousness of their people than the mistakes which Congress may rush in to correct for them, thrusting upon them what they have not learned to desire. They will either themselves learn their mistakes, by such intimate and domestic processes as will penetrate very deep and abide with them in convincing force, or else they will prove that what might have been a mistake for other States or regions of the country was no mistake for them, and the country will have been saved its wholesome variety. In no case will their failure to correct their own measures prove that the Federal Government might have forced wisdom upon them. . . .

6. I Cannot Consent

To M. Taylor Pyne, December 25, 1909

The graduate-school controversy involved a less important question than the quad plan, though it was more acrimonious and left deeper scars. Andrew F. West, dean of the graduate school, had drawn up a plan in 1906 for using a recent large bequest to build a graduate school off campus; it was to be built to his specifications and to be under his strict control. Wilson thought that the graduate school should be situated on the campus. By early 1909 Wilson had succeeded in withdrawing West's authority over the graduate school curriculum and appointments and placing it in a committee dominated by Wilson men. But on May 10, 1909, West showed Wilson a letter from one William Procter promising $500,000 for the graduate school provided it was located off campus where West wanted it. The board of trustees, hitherto on Wilson's side, yielded to the pressure: on October 21, 1909, it accepted Procter's gift along with Procter's conditions. Such was the setting for Wilson's letter to a trustee who was opposed to him.

. . . THE GRADUATE establishment on the Golf Links cannot succeed. The Faculty has never believed in a graduate establishment which did not constitute the geographical and spiritual center of the University. A Graduate College which lay in every sense at the heart of things was West's first idea, and the modification of his views and purposes has played no small part in depriving him of the confidence of his academic colleagues. He has now lost their confidence completely, and nothing administered by him in accordance with his present ideas can succeed. Indeed, nothing administered by him can now succeed.

When, at my first interview with Mr. Procter, shortly before the October meeting of the Board, I urged upon him the judgment of the Faculty in this all-important matter, and my own clear judgment, in view of all the circumstances, that a Graduate College removed from close neighborhood to the existing life of the University would be a reversal of our whole policy hitherto and of our whole academic conception and hope, he replied that he was sorry, but that he could not agree with the Faculty and with me, or with the majority of the Trustees' Committee on the Graduate School, and must insist that his gift, if accepted at all, must be used only on the condition that the college provided for by Mrs. Swann's bequest be removed to a distance from the present buildings of the University.

I tried, after the meeting of the Board, in October, to accommodate myself as loyally as possible to its decision, in view of Mr. Procter's wishes, to carry out his ideas rather than those of the leading graduate teachers in the Faculty; but I found it against my conscience to assent to the use of Mrs. Swann's money to build on the Golf Links because of the conviction that the directions of Mrs. Swann's will could not be complied with either in letter or in spirit, (a) because she directs that the buildings shall be placed "upon the grounds" of the University and serious doubt exists as to the legality of placing the building on the Golf Links at all, (b) because she directs that the rooms in the building shall be rented "at the best prices they will command, to Graduate, Senior and Junior students of the University," (c) in order to produce an income which shall be devoted to the maintenance of so large a number of fellowships as possible.

I therefore proposed to Mr. Procter, on Wednesday last, that his gift and purpose be separated from Mrs. Swann's; that we carry out her will exactly by erecting Thomson College in close association with the present buildings of the University, and that as much as necessary of his proffered gift be devoted to the erection and maintenance on the Golf Links of such an establishment as he favors. This suggestion meets with the hearty concurrence of my colleagues here. I explained to him that there are already graduate students enough to fill one of these establishments, and that by the time our building operations could be completed there would, at our present rate of growth (certain to be accelerated under a proper policy), be enough to fill both; that the judgment of the Faculty was strongly against Professor West's ideas in this matter; and that it was likely that such a compromise would make it possible to try both experiments under favorable auspices. He did not approve of dividing the graduate students into two separated groups or of associating graduate life with the undergraduate life of the University. He made it much clearer than before that his views were exactly those of

Professor West and Mr. Butler, and that, if his gift was accepted, he would insist upon the use of Mrs. Swann's bequest in connection with it in accordance with those ideas.

You will see, therefore, what I meant when I said in my note from Jersey City that the acceptance of Mr. Procter's gift had taken the guidance of the University out of my hands entirely. Its acceptance by the Board means its acceptance upon the terms prescribed, terms which govern the use of Mrs. Swann's money as well as the use of Mr. Procter's. It has reversed the policy of the Faculty, and the leading conception of my whole administration, in an educational matter of the most fundamental importance. I am not willing to be drawn further into the toils. I cannot accede to the acceptance of gifts upon terms which take the educational policy of the University out of the hands of the Trustees and Faculty and permit it to be determined by those who give money.

I do not wish even to imply a criticism of Mr. Procter. He is in no way at fault. I admire him very much. He has been very generous to the University and in all his dealings with me has acted with the greatest courtesy and kindness. But his attitude means that we must accept his wishes not only with regard to the manner in which his money shall be spent but also with regard to the way in which Mrs. Swann's money shall be expended, and the purposes to which it shall be devoted. I cannot consent, if the gift is deliberately accepted on such terms, to remain responsible for the direction of affairs of the University or for the development of her educational policy.

This is a very solemn matter, my dear Momo; but the issue is clear. Neither my conscience nor my self-respect will permit me to avoid it. There is only one position I can take. I take it with real grief that it should be necessary; and with unabated affection for yourself. I know that you have been convinced that you were acting for the best interests of the University. But I must now ask the Board to consider it in a new light. I must ask them to give the University, at whatever cost, its freedom of choice in matters which so nearly touch its life and development.

7. The Same Sympathies as the Common People

Address to Alumni, April 16, 1910

With Wilson—now a public figure—threatening to resign and the board of trustees angrily divided, William Procter withdrew his offer of $500,000. Wilson was gratified. He sought to bring the graduate-school issue before the faculty, but the board turned him down. Following is the incomplete report of his sharply worded address to the Pittsburgh alumni. The last sentence in particular provoked comment in Princeton circles.

Mr. Wilson said in part:

How does the nation judge Princeton? The institution is intended for the service of the country, and it is by the requirements of the country that it will be measured. I trust I may be thought among the last to blame the churches, yet I feel it my duty to say that they—at least the Protestant churches—are serving the classes and not the masses of the people. They have more regard for the pew rents than for men's souls. They are depressing the level of Christian endeavor.

It is the same with the universities. We look for the support of the wealthy and neglect our opportunities to serve the people. It is for this reason the State University is held in popular approval while the privately supported institution to which we belong is coming to suffer a corresponding loss of esteem.

While attending a recent Lincoln celebration I asked myself if Lincoln would have been as serviceable to the people of this country had he been a college man, and I was obliged to say to myself that he would not. The process to which the college man is subjected does not render him serviceable to the country as a whole. It is for this reason that I have dedicated every power in me to a democratic regeneration.

The American college must become saturated in the same sympathies as the common people. The colleges of this country must be reconstructed from the top to the bottom. The American people will tolerate nothing that savors of exclusiveness.

Their political parties are going to pieces. They are busy with their moral regeneration and they want leaders who can help them accomplish it. Only those leaders who seem able to promise something of a moral advance are able to secure a following. The people are tired of pretense, and I ask you, as Princeton men, to heed what is going on.

If she loses her self-possession, America will stagger like France through fields of blood before she again finds peace and prosperity under the leadership of men who know her needs.

8. This Alters the Whole Perspective

To T. D. Jones, May 30, 1910

While Wilson and his opponents were deadlocked, a new situation arose which ensured his defeat. The will of Isaac Wyman, recently deceased, gave an estate of over $2,000,000 to Princeton for the purpose of establishing a graduate school on the lines laid down by Andrew F. West. The trustees of course agreed to it. This time Wilson acquiesced, saying nothing about resigning. But he was defeated and his status as president compromised.

. . . ON WEDNESDAY the 25th, I went in to New York and had a conference at Mr. Cadwalader's office with Mr. Cadwalader and Mr. Palmer. Before that, namely on Monday evening, the 23rd, I had had a long conference with Fine, Daniels, Capps, and Abbott (Conklin being away). They had all been clear as to what ought to be done in the circumstances, and therefore I went to the conference with Mr. Cadwalader and Mr. Palmer with a clear head, though not with a very light heart.

I said to them that in my opinion (it was also, of course, the opinion of the men in the Faculty I have mentioned) West should remain in his present office as Dean of the Graduate School, because it was eminently desirable, in view of the extraordinary discretion granted in Mr. Wyman's will, that he should be included in our counsels, and not excluded from them, and since it was manifestly necessary, in the circumstances, to deal with him as if of course he intended to do the right thing.

I also said to them that this great gift of millions made it clear that we did not have to depend upon the attractions, or fear the repulsions, of the Graduate College in building up a graduate school, that is to say, a body of graduate students and teachers. It enables us to secure a great graduate faculty. Their presence will make a large body of graduate students certain. This alters the whole perspective, therefore, of the question of the graduate residential hall. I deemed it necessary in the circumstances, therefore, that I should accept defeat in the matter of the location of the college. I would no longer fight its location on the Golf Links. . . .

9. It Becomes My Duty

To Princeton Board of Trustees, October 20, 1910

On October 19, 1910, while campaigning for governor, Wilson was asked by the majority of the board of trustees to resign. The next day he read the following letter to them.

ON THE fifteenth of September last the Democratic party of New Jersey nominated me for the office of Governor of the State, and I deemed it my duty to accept the nomination. In view of Princeton's immemorial observance of the obligation of public service, I could not have done otherwise.

Having accepted the nomination, it becomes my duty to resign the presidency of the University I have so long loved and sought to serve. I, therefore, hereby offer my resignation of the great office with which you have honored me, and venture to express the hope that the Board will see its way to act upon the resignation at once. It is my earnest prayer that the University may go forward without halt or hindrance in the path of true scholarship and thoughtful service of the nation.

Two

GOVERNOR AND CANDIDATE

1910–1912

1. The Mere Preliminary

To D. B. Jones, June 27, 1910

D. B. Jones was a Princeton trustee, a close friend and supporter of Wilson. In this illuminating letter Wilson confides to Jones the extraordinary plan underfoot to make him Governor of New Jersey, then President of the United States.

I FIND that the political question I put to you in my brief note the other day has become acute; and I think that I ought to make a full statement of it to you.

It is immediately, as you know, the question of my nomination for the governorship of New Jersey, but this is the mere preliminary of a plan to nominate me in 1912 for the presidency. It is necessary, if I should be fair to all parties, that I should decide this week whether I can accept the nomination for the governorship. There are some half dozen other men who desire it, but they have all told the State Committee that they are willing to withdraw and allow me to have it by acclamation if I will accept it. If I will not, they wish at once to rally their forces, and it is only fair to give them the chance. The convention meets in September.

What appears to be the facts (reinforced by additional evidence since I saw you and talked it over in Chicago) are, that the representative politicians of Indiana, Illinois, Ohio, Minnesota, and Iowa prefer me as a presidential candidate to Harmon and have urged the party men in New Jersey to nominate me for the governorship, in order to elect me by a substantial majority and so make it necessary to consider me; that the New Jersey men are confident that I can be elected by a majority so large as to be very impressive and convincing and are willing to give me the nomination unanimously, without the raising of a finger on my part; and that my chances for the Presidential nomination would in such circumstances be better than those of any other man.

Last evening I dined with Colonel Watterson, of the *Louisville Courier Journal*, Colonel Harvey, of *Harper's Weekly* and James Smith, the reputed Democratic boss of New Jersey. Whatever we may think of Colonel Watterson, there can be no doubt of his immense political influence in his section of the country, and indeed throughout the whole South. He came on to make my acquaintance, and before the evening was over said that, if New Jersey would make me Governor, he would agree to take off his coat and work for my nomination in 1912. The opportunity seems most unusual. . . .

I cannot throw off the feeling, perhaps I should say the fear, that I am in some way imposing upon your kindness and that of the other men by even suggesting that I take the liberty at this juncture of withdrawing from Princeton. Perhaps it is the fear that this will look to you like a mere case of personal ambition. To my mind it is a question of which is the larger duty and opportunity. At any rate, I am sure you will all judge leniently and will understand.

2. I Should Deem It My Duty

To Editor of *Trenton True American*, July 15, 1910

Wilson officially announces that he will be candidate for Governor of New Jersey.

THERE HAS recently been so much talk of the possibility of my being nominated by the Democrats of New Jersey for the Governorship of the State, and I have been asked by so many persons, whom I respect, what my attitude would be toward such a nomination, that it would be an affectation and discourtesy on my part to ignore the matter any longer. I need not say that I am in no sense a candidate for the nomination, and that I would not, in any circumstances, do anything to obtain it.

My present duty and responsibilities are such as should satisfy any man desirous of rendering public service. They certainly satisfy me, and I do not wish to be drawn away from them, but my wish does not constitute my duty, and if it should turn out to be true, as so many well-informed persons have assured me they believe it will, that it is the wish and hope of a decided majority of the thoughtful Democrats of the State that I should consent to accept the party's nomination for the great office of Governor, I should deem it my duty, as well as an honor and a privilege, to do so. I cannot venture to assume that this is the case. It remains to be seen whether it is or not. I should not feel personally disappointed if it should turn out otherwise. . . .

3. The Warm Friend of Organized Labor

To Edgar Williamson, August 23, 1910

The New Jersey State Federation of Labor adopted a resolution in August "condemning" Wilson "as a foe of organized labor." Wilson's sentiments toward labor in past speeches and writings justified this attitude. A member of the Federation, Williamson, asked Wilson for his views. Wilson's reply helped persuade labor to change its opinion.

MY DEAR Mr. Williamson—I warmly appreciate your kind letter of August 18th.

The gross misrepresentations of my views with regard to organized labor which some newspapers have contained have given me no concern. They were willful and deliberate misrepresentations, and such things take care of themselves. The papers that stoop to them will in the end be found out and lose credit altogether.

I was distressed that the New Jersey State Federation of Labor should have allowed itself to be imposed upon—not because its members are likely to remain deceived in this matter, but for the opposite reason: because they are sure to discover their mistake and to feel the mortification of having taken unjust and hasty action.

I was not hurt, because I knew that no injustice was intended. I was simply sorry. It is a pity to see things so handled.

I had, of course, intended to let the incident pass in silence—for two reasons. First, because I knew the whole matter would right itself, and, second, because I have not been seeking the nomination for Governor at the hands of my party, and to argue the matter would seem to be arguing for my nomination, but your letter puts a compulsion upon me of an entirely different kind.

You urged the federation to inform itself about my views and wait until it could be sure that it was acting justly, and having failed in that, you turn to me and frankly ask me what I really think. Your friendliness and candor leave me no choice but to reply. I do so with pleasure.

I have always been the warm friend of organized labor.

It is, in my opinion, not only perfectly legitimate, but absolutely necessary that labor should organize if it is to secure justice from organized capital, and everything that it does to improve the condition of workingmen, to obtain legislation that will impose full legal responsibility upon the employer for his treatment of his employes and for their protection against accident, to secure just and adequate wages, and to put reasonable limits upon the working day and upon all the exactions of those who employ labor, ought to have the hearty support of all fair-minded and public-spirited men; for there is a sense in which the condition of labor is the condition of the Nation itself.

I have criticized some of the things organized labor has occasionally done, but I have criticized them as a friend and because I thought them harmful to the laborers themselves and harmful to the country.

I know of no other standard by which to judge these things than the interest of the whole community. The laboring man cannot benefit himself by injuring the industries of the country.

Many thoughtful laboring men are themselves critics, and very outspoken critics, of many things which the unions do, and I stand with them and with all other right-minded Americans in saying what I honestly think. If I am mistaken, it can easily be shown that I am, and I shall always be glad to have it shown.

I am much more afraid that the great corporations, combinations and trusts will do the country deep harm than I am that the labor organizations will harm it, and yet I believe the corporations to be necessary instruments of modern business.

They are good things so long as they act in the common interest, and very bad things when they do not.

Joint stock corporations, by putting into one enterprise the money of many thousands of persons, concentrate in their managers the power of thousands, a very dangerous power, which should be closely watched and regulated.

Sharp criticism should keep them amenable to public opinion. Strict law should restrain them. The principle is the same for all of us.

But our object, in the one case as in the other, should not be hostile. There has been hostility enough all around. What we need now is to take common counsel as to what is for the common benefit, for the good of the country and of the several communities in which we live and earn our bread, and also our happiness.

We need frank, outspoken, friendly opinion.

We need criticism which is not intended to damage, but to create a better understanding all around.

I have tried in everything that I have said on public questions to contribute to this friendly process of criticism, in order to assist in bringing on better days, and a state of opinion in which all men and all interests shall receive their due. To have any fear or favor in the matter is to be untrue to every standard of public duty.

If all editors and writers and public speakers will deal frankly and fairly as you have done, we shall soon hit upon a just and common policy with regard to the many things that perplex us.

4. It Has Come to Me Unsolicited

Address Accepting Nomination for Governor, September 15, 1910

Wilson was nominated without difficulty on the first ballot despite opposition from progressives. On the same day he delivered a rousing address to the convention. It was his first major political effort.

YOU HAVE conferred upon me a very great honor. I accept the nomination you have tendered me with the deepest gratification that you should have thought me worthy to lead the Democrats of New Jersey in this stirring time of opportunity.

Even more than the great honor of your nomination I feel the deep responsibility it imposes upon me. For responsibility is proportioned to opportunity.

As you know, I did not seek this nomnation. It has come to me absolutely unsolicited. With the consequence that I shall enter upon the duties of the office of Governor, if elected, with absolutely no pledge of any kind to prevent me from serving the people of the State with singleness of purpose. Not only have no pledges of any kind been given, but none have been proposed or desired.

In accepting the nomination, therefore, I am pledging myself only to the service of the people and the party which intends to advance their interests. I can not but regard the circumstances as marking the beginning of a new and more ideal era in our politics. Certainly they enhance very greatly the honor you have conferred upon me and enlarge the opportunities in equal degree.

A day of unselfish purpose is always a day of confident hope. I feel confident that the people of the State will accept the promises you have made in your platform as made sincerely and with a definite purpose to render them effective service. That platform is sound, explicit and businesslike. There can be no mistaking what it means. And the voters of the State will know at once that promises so definitely made are made to be kept, not to be evaded.

Your declaration deserves and will win their confidence. But we shall keep their confidence only by performance, by achievement and by proving our capacity to conduct the administration and reform the legislation of the State in the spirit of our declarations not only, but also with the sagacity and firmness of practical men who not only purpose, but do what is sensible and effective.

It is towards this task of performance that my thoughts turn as I think of soliciting the suffrages of my fellow citizens for the great office of Governor of the State. I shall do so with a very profound sense of the difficulty of solving new and complicated problems in the right way. I take the three great questions before us to be reorganization and economy in administration, the equalization of taxation and the control of corporations. There are other very important questions that confront us as they confront all the other States of the Union in this day of readjustment: the question of the proper liabilty of employers, for example, the question of corrupt practices in elections, the question of conservation, but the three I have named dominate all the rest.

It is imperative that we should not only master them, but also act upon them, and act very definitely.

It is first of all necessary that we should act in the right spirit. And the right spirit is not a spirit of hostility. We shall not act either justly or wisely if we attack established interests as public enemies. There has been too much indictment and too little successful prosecution for wrongs done; too much talk and too few practicable suggestions as to what is to be done. It is easy to condemn wrong and to fulminate against wrong-doers in effective rhetorical phrases; but that does not bring either reform or ease of mind. Reform will come only when we have done some careful thinking as to exactly what the things are that are being done in contravention of the public interest and as to the most simple, direct and effective way of getting at the men who do them. In a self-governed country there is one rule for everybody, and that is the common interest. Everything must be squared by that. We can square it only by knowing its exact shape and movement. Government is not a warfare of interests. We shall not gain our ends by heats and bitterness, which make it impossible to think either calmly or fairly. Government is a matter of common council, and everyone must come into the consultation with the purpose to yield to the general view, the view which seems most nearly to correspond with the common interests. If any decline frank conference, keep out, hold off, they must take the consequences and blame only themselves if they are in the end badly served. There must be implacable determination to see the right done, but strong purpose, which does not flinch because some must suffer, is perfectly compatible with fairness and justice and a clear view of the actual facts.

This should be our spirit in the matter of reform, and this our method. And in this spirit we should do very definite things. It is obvious even to the casual observer that the administration of the State has been unnecessarily complicated and elaborated, too many separate commissions and boards set up, business methods neglected, money wasted, and a state of affairs brought about of which a successful business concern would be ashamed. No doubt the increase of State expenditures which marked the last decade has been in part due to a necessary and desirable increase of function on the part of the State. But it is only too evident that no study of economy has been made, that a careful reconsideration and reorganization of the administrative processes of the State would result in a great saving and enhance responsibility on the part of those who are entrusted with the important work of government. Our system of taxation is as ill-digested, as piecemeal and as haphazardous as our system of administration. It cannot be changed suddenly or too radically, but many changes should be inaugurated and the whole system by degrees, reconsidered and altered, so as to fit modern economical conditions more equitably. Above all the methods of assessment should be changed, in order that inequality between the taxes of individuals and the taxes of corporations, for example, should be entirely eliminated. It is not necessary for the maintenance of our modern industrial enterprises that corporations should be indulged or favored in the matter of taxation and it is extremely demoralizing that they should be. Such inequalities should be effectually removed by law and by the action of the tax assessing authorities of the State and of the locality. This is a matter which will require dispassionate study and action based, not upon hostility, but upon the common interest. The question of the control of corporations is a very difficult one, upon which no man can speak with confidence; but some things are plain. It is plain, as far as New Jersey is concerned, that we must have a Public Service Commission with the amplest powers to oversee and regulate the administration of public service corporations throughout the State. We have abundant experience elsewhere to guide us in this matter, from the admirable commission so long in successful operation in Wisconsin, to the latest legislation in sister States. We need have no doubt of our right course of action here.

It is the States, not the federal authorities, that create corporations. The regulation of corporations is the duty of the State much more directly than it is the duty of the government of the United States. It is my strong hope that New Jersey may lead the way in reform; by scrutinizing very carefully the enterprises she consents to incorporate; their make-up, their objects, the basis and method of capitalization, their organization with respect to liability to control by the State, their conformity to State and Federal statutes. This can be done and done effectually. I covet for New Jersey the honor of doing it.

It is so also, gentlemen, with every other question we face. Let us face it in the spirit of service and with the careful, practical sense of men of affairs. We shall not ask the voters of the State to lend us their suffrages merely because we call ourselves Democrats, but because we mean to serve them like honest and public-spirited men, true Democrats because true lovers of the common interest, servants of no special group of men or of interests, students of the interest of the people and of the country.

The future is not for parties "playing politics," but for measures conceived in the largest spirit, pushed by parties whose leaders are statesmen, not demagogues, who love not their offices, but their duty and their opportunity for service. We are witnessing a renaissance of public spirit, a reawakening of sober public opinion, a revival of the power of the people, the beginning of an age of thoughtful reconstruction that makes our thought hark back to the great age in which Democracy was set up in America. With the new age we shall show a new spirit. We shall serve justice and candor and all things that make for the right. Is not our own ancient party the party disciplined and made ready for this great task? Shall we not forget ourselves in making it the instrument of righteousness for the State and for the Nation?

5. All These Classes Put Together

Speech at Phillipsburg, October 21, 1910

In this speech in a small community Wilson reiterated his friendship for labor—but in terms that would not alienate the middle class, which constituted the base of New Jersey progressivism.

. . . WHEN YOU form a class or caste and get into the habit of thinking in and for it alone, you are helping to make actual popular government an impossibility. Without popular opinion there cannot be popular government. How can there be a popular opinion representing the beliefs and desires at large when the people are divided into classes and organizations narrowing their thinking down to within their own circles.

The trouble is that we do not think of the people in that way.

Do capitalists constitute the people? Certainly not. When you speak of the people are you thinking of levels? Are you thinking of those who are poor, are you thinking of those who are well-to-do, are you thinking of those who are quite well off, are you thinking of those who are very rich? The interesting thing is that the people consist of all these classes put together; it does not consist of any one, it does not consist of any two of them, or any combination except the combination that constitutes the whole.

I have all my life been the consistent friend of workingmen and workingmen's organizations. But when a few of the workingmen's organizations have done things that I thought were not in the general interest, that is to say, were hurting the general interests of the country and reacting on their own interests, I, of course, have criticized what they did. I am not ashamed. I am not afraid to criticize anybody, and I would consider myself a very unfaithful friend if I did not dare make the criticisms that I think are just. . . .

6. The Threshold of a New Era

To George L. Record, October 24, 1910

During the campaign, Wilson had been trying to establish himself as an authentic progressive, but the progressives, led by their redoubtable leader, George L. Record, remained skeptical. On October 17, Record asked Wilson to state his views on nineteen vital questions. Wilson's answers, widely publicized in the press, more than satisfied Record and the other New Jersey progressives that Wilson was their man.

1. "That the public utilities commission should have full power to fix just and reasonable rates to be charged by all public service corporations. Do you favor this?"

Answer to Question One—Yes.

2. "That the physical property of each public utility corporation which is devoted to a public use should be valued by the State. Do you favor this?"

Answer to Question Two—Yes.

3. "That such physical valuation should be taken as the assessment upon which such corporation shall pay local taxes. Do you favor this?"

Answer to Question Three—Yes.

4. "That such valuation should be used as a basis for fixing rates to be charged by these corporations and that such rates should be limited as to allow them to earn not exceeding six per cent upon this valuation. Do you favor this?"

Answer to Question Four—No. I think that such valuation should form a very important part of the basis upon which rates should be fixed, but not the whole basis. All the financial, physical and economic circumstances of the business should be taken into consideration. The percentage of profit should be determined by the commission after full inquiry, and not by statute.

5. "That the present primary law should be extended to the selection of candidates for party nominations for Governor, Congressman and delegates to national conventions. Do you favor this?"

Answer to Question Five—Yes, though I should wish a better primary law than the present.

6. "That United States Senators should be elected by popular vote. Do you favor this?"

Answer to Question Six—Yes.

7. "To apply this principle, I favor a law compelling all candidates for nomination to the legislature to file a pledge to vote for that candidate of their party for United States Senator who shall receive the highest number of votes under the present primary law. Do you favor this?"

Answer to Question Seven—In principle, yes, but I fear that a law "compelling" this would be unconstitutional. Surely, the voters can exact this pledge, and have the matter in their own hands. A better primary law than the present would facilitate this exaction on the part of the voters by obliging the candidate for the State Legislature to state his intention in this matter when accepting his own nomination.

8. "That the names of all candidates at election should be printed on a blanket ballot, and that all ballots shall be distributed to the voter by mail at public expense, or confined to the polling place. Do you favor this?"

Answer to Question Eight—I believe that the ballots should be given out only at the polling places and only by the election officers, and that, while the blanket ballot is the best form yet devised, experience has proved that it is best to put some indication of the source of the nomination after each name. A mere alphabetical list results usually in the election of the top of the alphabet, and there are actually cases on record of would-be candidates who have had their names changed to begin with the first letter of the alphabet in order to increase their chances of election. Amidst a multitude of names on our long ballots the ordinary voter needs some guidance.

9. "That primary and election officers should be appointed by some impartial agency, like a court. Do you favor this?"

Answer to Question Nine—Yes.

10. "There should be a drastic corrupt practices act, forbidding all political expenditures except for the objects named in the act, with drastic penalties for the violation of the act; prohibiting the employment of more than two workers or watchers at the polls on primary day or election day representing any one party or group of candidates; prohibiting the hiring of vehicles for transporting voters; limiting the amount to be expended by candidates; prohibiting political contributions by corporations. Do you favor this?"

Answer to Question Ten—Yes.

11. "That every industry employing workmen shall be compelled to bear the expense of all injuries to employes which happen in the industry without willful negligence of such employe. Do you favor this?"

Answer to Question Eleven—Yes.

12. "That the County Board of Elections law and the Hillery maximum tax law should be repealed. Do you favor this?"

Answer to Question Twelve—Yes.

13. "Does the Democratic platform declare for the choice of candidates for all elective officers by the direct vote system?"

Answer to Question Thirteen—Yes; I so understand it. If it does not, I do.

14. "Do you admit that the boss system exists as I have described it? If so, how do you propose to abolish it?"

Answer to Question Fourteen—Of course, I admit it. Its existence is notorious. I have made it my business for many years to observe and understand that system, and I hate it as thoroughly as I understand it. You are quite right in saying that the system is bipartisan; that it constitutes "the most dangerous condition in the public life of our State and Nation today"; and that it has virtually, for the time being, "destroyed representative government and in its place set up a government of privilege." I would propose to abolish it by the above reforms, by the election to office of men who will refuse to submit to it and bend all their energies to break it up, and by pitiless publicity.

15. "In referring to the Board of Guardians, do you mean such Republican leaders as Baird, Murphy, Kean and Stokes? Wherein do the relations to the special interests of such leaders differ from the relations to the same interests of such Democratic leaders as Smith, Nugent and Davis?"

Answer to Question Fifteen—I refer to the men you name. They differ from the others in this, that they are in control of the government of the State while the others are not and cannot be if the present Democratic ticket is elected.

16. "I join you in condemning the Republican Board of Guardians. I have been fighting them for years and shall continue to fight them. Will you join me in denouncing the Democratic Overlords, as parties to the same political system? If not, why not?"

Answer to Question Sixteen—Certainly; I will join you or any one else in denouncing and fighting any and every one, of either party, who attempts such outrages against the government and public morality.

17. "You say the Democratic party has been reorganized, and the Republican party has not. Can a political party be reorganized without changing either its leaders, or its old leaders changing their point of view and their political character? Will you claim that either of these events has taken place in the Democratic party? If yes, upon what do you base that conclusion?"

Answer to Question Seventeen—I do not remember saying that the Democratic party has been reorganized. I remember saying that it was seeking reorganization, and was therefore at the threshold of a new era. I said this because it is seeking to change its leaders, and will obviously change them if successful at this election. If I am elected, I shall understand that I am chosen leader of my party and the direct representative of the whole people in the conduct of the government. All of this was distinctly understood at the very outset, when my nomination was first proposed, and there has never been the slightest intimation from any quarter to the contrary since. The Republican party is not seeking to change its leaders, and, therefore, is not even seeking reorganization.

18. "Is there any organized movement in the Democratic party in this State which corresponds to the Progressive Republican movement of which you have already spoken?"

Answer to Question Eighteen—I understand the present platform and the present principal nominations of the Democratic party in this State to be such an organized movement. It will be more fully organized if those nominees are elected. This is, as I interpret it, the spirit of the whole remarkable Democratic revival which we are witnessing not only in New Jersey, but in many other States.

Before I pass to the next question, will you not permit me to frame one which you have not asked, but which I am sure lies implied in those I have just answered? You wish to know what my relations would be with the Democrats whose power and influence you fear, should I be elected Governor, particularly in such important matters as appointments and the signing of bills, and I am very glad to tell you. If elected, I shall not, either in the matter of appointments to office or assent to legislation, or in shaping any part of the policy of my administration, submit to the dictation of any person, or persons, special interest or organization. I will always welcome advice and suggestions from any citizen, whether boss, leader, organization man or plain citizen, and I shall constantly seek the advice of influential and disinterested men, representative of their communities and disconnected from political "organizations" entirely; but all suggestions and all advice will be considered on their merits, and no additional weight will be given to any man's advice or suggestion because of his exercising or supposing that he exercises some sort of political influence or control. I should deem myself forever disgraced should I in even the slightest degree co-operate in any such system or any such transactions as you describe in your characterization of the "boss" system. I regard myself as pledged to the regeneration of the Democratic party which I have forecast above.

19. "Will you agree to publicly call upon the Republican and Democratic candidates for the legislature to pledge themselves in writing prior to election in favor of such of the foregoing reforms as you personally favor? If not, why not?"

Answer to Question Nineteen—I will not. Because I think it would be most unbecoming to me to do so. That is the function of the voters in the several counties. Let them test and judge the men, and choose those who are sincere.

Allow me to thank you for this opportunity to express with the greatest possible definiteness my convictions upon the issues of the present campaign and also for your very kind expression of confidence and regard, which I highly appreciate.

7. This Last Unfortunate Stage

Statement Opposing James Smith, Jr., for Senate, December 24, 1910

James Smith, Jr., the Democratic boss who had made Wilson governor, sought to return to the Senate. Very little stood in his way since the legislature was heavily Democratic and largely under his control. But Wilson refused to allow it. Throughout the months of December and January the governor-elect and the Democratic boss struggled for supremacy. As it turned out all the advantages were with Wilson. He easily depicted Smith as a member of the corrupt alliance of political bosses and economic plutocrats. Following is Wilson's public declaration of war upon Smith.

. . . IMMEDIATELY AFTER the election Mr. Smith came to see me, and said that that had been his feelings before election, but that he was feeling stronger, and hoped that the legislature would offer him the seat. I pointed out to him that this action on his part would confirm all the ugliest suspicions of the campaign concerning him, and urged him very strongly not to allow his name to be used at all; but my arguments had no effect upon him.

I subsequently learned that before my nomination and at the very time I was told that he would not desire the seat, he had made an agreement with the leader of the Hudson county organization that the votes of the Hudson county members of the legislature would be cast for him as Senator in case the legislature should be Democratic. The gentlemen who were to be nominated for the assembly from Hudson were not consulted; it was an agreement between leaders. The vote was to be turned over to Mr. Smith by the organization in case of a Democratic victory.

Mr. Smith has at last publicly announced his candidacy, but he has been a candidate from the first. Ever since the election he has been using every means at his disposal to obtain the pledges of Democratic members of the legislature to vote for him as Senator. He has assumed, in dealing with them, that the State organization would be in control of the legislature; that its offices would be distributed as he should suggest; that members would be assigned to committees and the committees made up as he wished them to be. He has offered to assist members in obtaining membership on such committees as they might prefer. In brief, he has assumed that he and other gentlemen not elected to the legislature by the people would have the same control over the action of the houses that is understood to have been exercised by the so-called Board of Guardians of the Republican party in recent years.

I said in my former statement regarding this matter that if Mr. Smith should be sent to the United States Senate he would not go as the representative of the people. I meant that he would go as the representative of particular interests in the Senate with which it is well known he has always been identified. It is significant that his candidacy is supported by the Camden paper known to be owned or controlled by Mr. David Baird. Mr. John W. Griggs, in a letter recently published, has condemned me for taking any part in this matter and has thereby confirmed the impression that he also has clients who are interested in being represented in the Senate by Mr. Smith. So far as the voters of the State are concerned and the State's essential interests, there is no reason why a change should be made from Mr. John Kean to Mr. James Smith, Jr. They are believed to stand for the same influences and to represent the same group of selfish interests. It should be a matter of indifference to both Republicans and Democrats which of the two represents the State at Washington.

I say these things with genuine regret. I made every possible effort, consistent with dignity and self-respect, to induce Mr. Smith to withdraw from his candidacy. It was my sincere desire that he should earn the credit which is due him for the undoubted service of the Democratic State organization in the recent campaign. By withdrawing he would have won the respect and applause and I should have been very glad to join in according him all just praise. I had hoped that it would be possible for me to assume office and enter on the performance of my duties without giving utterance to anything about individuals that would give them pain or draw me away from the attitude of entire respect which I had tried to maintain. But I have been left without a choice in the matter.

The issue is plain. If Mr. Smith is sent back to the United States Senate, the Democratic party and the State itself is once more delivered into the hands of the very influences from which it had struggled to set itself free. Nothing could have been more unfortunate than Mr. Smith's candidacy. It revives the alarm and prejudices which make fair and just legislation so difficult and doubtful. It renews and intensifies the struggle between the people and selfish interests, between popular rights and property rights, between privilege and opportunity, which ought to be accommodated by laws which will be fair to all parties. It is a sad circumstance that the conflict must be fought out through this last unfortunate stage. But of course it must be. Mr. Smith and those whom he represents have made it inevitable.

The people must now speak their minds in unmistakable terms to those whom they have chosen to represent them. It must now be determined whether the present members of the Legislature are representatives of the people or puppets of a bipartisan machine. I believe in organization. I desire to co-operate with Democrats of every affiliation in carrying the party forward by union and harmony of action toward the great service which it can render the country. If it will but be true to its principles. But when organization is used for the elevation and benefit of individuals who do not represent the people, whose interests are opposed to those of the people, I must resist it by every means at my disposal.

Over against all this selfish effort to use a machine, over against all this sinister pressure to put a man into the United States Senate who by common consent will not represent the people, stands the candidacy of Mr. Martine, supported by the votes of a very large majority of the Democrats who chose to express their preference at the primaries. It is my earnest and deliberate judgment that it is the duty of the Democratic members of the Legislature to ratify that expression of preference by electing Mr. Martine a member of the Senate. . . .

8. To Square Business with the General Interest

Inaugural Address for Governor, January 17, 1911

Wilson delivered this address under particularly auspicious conditions. Having defeated the machine which brought him to power, he dominated the state. He thereupon proposed the following general reforms which the legislature promptly enacted into law.

. . . NO WISE man will say, of course, that he sees the whole problem of reform lying plain before him, or knows how to frame the entire body of law that will be necessary to square business with the general interest, and put right and fairness and public spirit in the saddle again in all the transactions of our new society; but some things are plain enough, and upon these we can act.

In the first place, it is plain that our laws with regard to the relations of employer and employe are in many respects wholly antiquated and impossible. They were framed for another age, which nobody now living remembers, which is, indeed, so remote from our life that it would be difficult for many of us to understand it if it were described to us. The employer is now generally a corporation or huge company of some kind; the employe is one of hundreds or of thousands brought together, not by individual masters whom they know and with whom they had personal relations, but by agents of one sort or another. Workingmen are marshalled in great numbers for the performance of a multitude of particular tasks under a common discipline. They generally use dangerous and powerful machinery, over whose repair and renewal they have no control. New rules must be devised with regard to their obligations and their rights, their obligations to their employers and their responsibilities to one another. New rules must be devised for their protection, for their compensation when injured, for their support when disabled.

We call these questions of employers' liability, questions of workingmen's compensation, but those terms do not suggest quite the whole matter. There is something very new and very big and very complex about these new relations of capital and labor. A new economic society has sprung up, and we must effect a new set of adjustments. We must not pit power against weakness. The employer is generally in our day, as I have said, not an individual, but a powerful group of individuals, and yet the workingman is still, under our existing law, an individual when dealing with his employer, in case of accident, for example, or of loss or of illness, as well as in every contractual relationship. We must have a workingman's compensation act which will not put upon him the burden of fighting powerful composite employers to obtain his rights, but which will give him his rights without suit, directly, and without contest, by automatic operation of law, as if of a law of insurance.

This is the first adjustment needed, because it affects the rights, the happiness, the lives and fortunes of the largest number, and because it is the adjustment for which justice cries loudest and with the most direct appeal to our hearts as well as to our consciences.

But there is regulation needed which lies back of that and is much more fundamental. The composite employer himself needs to have his character and powers overhauled, his constitution and rights reconsidered, readjusted to the fundamental and abiding interests of society. If I may speak very plainly, we are much too free with grants of charters to corporations in New Jersey: A corporation exists, not of natural right, but only by license of law, and the law, if we look at the matter in good conscience, is responsible for what it creates. It can never rightly authorize any kind of fraud or imposition. It cannot righteously allow the setting up of a business which has no sound basis, or which follows methods which in any way outrage justice or fair dealing or the principles of honest industry. The law cannot give its license to things of that kind. It thereby authenticates what it ought of right to forbid.

I would urge, therefore, the imperative obligation of public policy and of public honesty we are under to effect such changes in the law of the State as will henceforth effectually prevent the abuse of the privilege of incorporation which has in recent years brought so much discredit upon our State. In order to do this it will be necessary to regulate and restrict the issue of securities, to enforce regulations with regard to bona fide capital, examining very rigorously the basis of capitalization, and to prescribe methods by which the public shall be safeguarded against fraud, deception, extortion, and every abuse of its confidence.

And such scrutiny and regulation ought not to be confined to corporations seeking charters. They ought also to be extended to corporations already operating under the license and authority of the State. For the right to undertake such regulation is susceptible of easy and obvious justification. A modern corporation—that is, a modern joint stock company—is in no proper sense an intimate or private concern. It is not set up on the risk and adventure of a few persons, the persons who originated it, manage it, carry it to failure or success. On the contrary, it is set up at what may be called the common risk. It is a risk and adventure in which the public are invited to share, and the hundreds, perhaps thousands, who subscribe to the stock do in fact share in it, oftentimes without sharing also, in any effectual manner, in the control and development of the business in which their risk is taken. Moreover, these modern enterprises, with their exchequers replenished out of the common store of the savings of the Nation, conduct business transactions whose scope and influence are as wide as whole regions of the Union, often as wide as the Nation itself. They affect sometimes the lives and fortunes of whole communities, dominate prices, determine land values, make and unmake markets, develop or check the growth of city and of countryside. If law is at liberty to adjust the general conditions of society itself, it is at liberty to control these great instrumentalities which nowadays, in so large part, determine the character of society. Wherever we can find what the common interest is in respect of them we shall find a solid enough basis for law, for reform.

The matter is most obvious when we turn to what we have come to designate public service, or public utility, corporations—those which supply us with the means of transportation and with those common necessaries, water, light, heat, and power. Here are corporations exercising peculiar and extraordinary franchises, and bearing such a relation to society in respect of the services they render that it may be said that they are the very medium of its life. They render a public and common service of which it is necessary that practically everybody should avail himself.

We have a Public Utilities Commission in New Jersey, but it has hardly more than powers of inquiry and advice. It could even as it stands be made a powerful instrument of publicity and of opinion, but it may also modestly wait until it is asked before expressing a judgment, and in any case it will have the uncomfortable consciousness that its opinion is gratuitous, and carries no weight of effective authority. This will not do. It is understood by everybody who knows anything of the common interest that it must have complete regulative powers: the power to regulate rates, the power to learn and make public everything that should furnish a basis for the public judgment with regard to the soundness, the efficiency, the economy of the business—the power, in brief, to adjust such service at every point and in every respect, whether of equipment or changes or methods of financing or means of service, to the general interest of the communities affected. This can be done, as experience elsewhere has demonstrated, not only without destroying the profits of such business, but also with the effect of putting it upon a more satisfactory footing for those who conduct it no less than for those who make use of it day by day.

Such regulation, based on thorough and authoritative inquiry, will go far towards disclosing and establishing those debatable values upon which so many questions of taxation turn. There is an uneasy feeling throughout the State, in which, I dare say, we all share, that there are glaring inequalities in our system—or, at any rate, in our practice—of taxation. The most general complaint is that there is great inequality as between individuals and corporations. I do not see how anyone can determine whether there are or not, for we have absolutely no uniform system of assessment. It would seem that in every locality there is some local variety of practice, in the rate, the ratio of assessment value to market value, and that every assessor is a law unto himself. Our whole system of taxation, which is no system at all, needs overhauling from top to bottom. There can be no system, no safety, no regulation in a multitude of boards. An efficient Public Utilities Commission will be a beginning towards a system of taxation as well as towards a system of corporate control. We cannot fairly tax values until we have ascertained and established them.

And the great matter of conservation seems to me like a part of the same subject. The safeguarding of our water supply, the purification of our streams in order to maintain them as sources of life, and their protection against those who would divert them or diminish their volume for private profit, the maintenance of such woodlands as are left us and the reforestation of bare tracts more suited for forest than for field, the sanitation of great urban districts such as cover the northern portions of our State, by thorough systems of drainage and of refuse disposal, the protection of the public health and the facilitation of urban and suburban life—these are all public obligations which fall sooner or later upon you as the lawmakers of the commonwealth, and they are all parts of the one great task of adjustment which has fallen to our generation. Our business is to adjust right to right, interest to interest, and to systematize right and convenience, individual rights and corporate privileges, upon the single basis of the general good, the good of whole communities, the good which no one will look after or suffice to secure if the legislator does not, the common good for whose safeguarding and maintenance government is intended.

This readjustment has not been going on very fast or very favorably in New Jersey. It has been observed that it limped, or was prevented, or neglected, in other States as well. Everywhere there has been confusion of counsel and many a sad miscarriage of plan. There have, consequently, been some very radical criticisms of our methods of political action. There is widespread dissatisfaction with what our legislatures do, and still more serious dissatisfaction with what they do not do. Some persons have said that representative government has proved too indirect and clumsy an instrument, and has broken down as a means of popular control. Others, looking a little deeper, have said that it was not representative government that had broken down, but the effort to get it. They have pointed out that with our present methods of machine nomination and our present methods of elections, which were nothing more than a choice between one set of machine nominees and another, we did not get representative government at all—at least not government representative of the people, but government representative of political managers who served their own interests and the interests of those with whom they found it profitable to establish partnerships.

Obviously this is something that goes to the root of the whole matter. Back of all reform lies the method of getting it. Back of the question what you want lies the question, the fundamental question of all government, how are you going to get it? How are you going to get public servants who will obtain it for you? How are you going to get genuine representatives who will serve your real interests, and not their own or the interests of some special group or body of your fellow citizens whose power is of the few and not of the many? These are the queries which have drawn the attention of the whole country to the subject of the direct primary, the direct choice of representatives by the people, without the intervention of the nominating machine, the nominating organization.

I earnestly commend to your careful consideration in this connection the laws in recent years adopted in the State of Oregon, whose effect has been to bring government back to the people and to protect it from the control of the representatives of selfish and special interests. They seem to me to point the direction which we must also take before we have completed our regeneration of a government which has suffered so seriously and so long as ours has here in New Jersey from private management and organized selfishness. Our primary laws, extended and perfected, will pave the way. They should be extended to every elective office, and to the selection of every party committee or official as well, in order that the people may once for all take charge of their own affairs, their own political organization and association; and the methods of primary selection should be so perfected that the primaries will be put upon the same free footing that the methods of election themselves are meant to rest upon.

We have here the undoubtedly sound chain and sequence of reforms: an actual direct choice by the people of the men who are to organize alike their parties and their government, and those measures which true representatives of the people will certainly favor and adopt—systematic compensation for injured workingmen; the careful regulation in the common interest of all corporations, both in respect of their organization and of their methods of business, and especially of public service corporations; the equalization of taxes; and the conservation of the natural resources of the State and of the health and safety of its people.

Another matter of the most vital consequence goes with all these: namely, systematic ballot reform and thorough and stringent provisions of law against corrupt practices in connection alike with primaries and with elections. We have lagged behind our sister States in these important matters, and should make haste to avail ourselves of their example and their experience. Here, again, Oregon may be our guide.

This is a big programme, but it is a perfectly consistent programme, and a perfectly feasible programme, and one upon whose details it ought to be possible to agree even within the limits of a single legislative session. You may count upon my co-operation at every step of the work.

I have not spoken of the broad question of economy in the administration of the State government, an economy which can probably be effected only through a thorough reorganization upon business principles, the familiar business principles so thoroughly understood and so intelligently practiced by Americans, but so seldom applied to their governments. We make offices for party purposes too often, instead of conducting our public business by the organization best adapted to efficiency and economy. I have not dwelt upon the subject in this address because it is a very complicated one, hardly suited for brief exposition, and because so obvious a requirement of honest government needs hardly more than to be mentioned to be universally endorsed by the public. I shall try to point out to you from time to time the means by which reorganization and economy may be secured with benefit to the public service. . . .

9. It Will Be Remembered as Extraordinary

Remarks at Close of Legislative Session, April 21, 1911

Dominated by Wilson, the 1911 legislature passed a series of progressive laws which placed New Jersey, hitherto controlled by corporations, among the most progressive states in the country. Here Wilson, in the course of his congratulatory remarks, summarizes the work of the legislature.

I THINK it [the legislative session] will be remembered as extraordinary in this, that it witnessed the fulfillment by the Legislature of every campaign pledge.

Much remains to be done in effecting such reorganization of the State government as may result in increasing economy and efficiency, and many reforms remain to be presented and put upon the statute book, but no single Legislature could possibly be expected to accomplish more than this one has accomplished. It has acted not only with unusual diligence and sobriety, but with singular absence of party feeling and party contest. It has had about it the freedom which characterizes men who are acting in the public interest and without regard to private connection and personal interest. In no other way can I account for its extraordinary record.

The Employer's Liability and Workingmen's Compensation Act has given the State a statute more serviceable and more consistent with justice in the field to which it applies than perhaps any in the Union.

The Primary and Election bill has worked a thorough-going reform of the whole electoral process of the State, and has put every process of choice directly in the hands of the people.

The Corrupt Practices Act is singularly thorough-going, and will undoubtedly prove most effective. It will do, perhaps, more than any other piece of legislation on this notable list, to purify elections and secure unbiased action of the people at the polls.

The Public Utilities Act goes the full length of reform in respect of the control of public service corporations. It is a thoroughly business-like act, well conceived and well constructed, and ought to afford a means of settling some of the most perplexing questions connected with the control of corporations.

Add to this list the regulation of cold storage; the substitution of indeterminate for determinate sentences for criminal offenses; the rectification of the abuses in connection with false weights and measures; the administrative reform of the school system; and it must be admitted to constitute one of the most remarkable records of legislation, I venture to think, that has ever distinguished a single legislative session in this country.

10. I Never Want to Forget This

Address on Bryanism, January 8, 1912

Wilson was now a power in the Democratic party and a leading contender for the presidential nomination. He used the occasion of a Jackson Day dinner in Washington, at which Bryan was present, to affirm his militant support of Bryan's principles. It was important that Wilson do so in view of the recent publication of the so-called Joline letter in which Wilson, writing to a friend in 1908, had said that Bryan should be "knocked into a cocked hat." But Bryan, far from being put off, respected Wilson all the more for having converted to the cause of justice.

MR. TOASTMASTER and fellow Democrats, we are met to celebrate an achievement. It is an interesting circumstance that principles have no anniversaries. Only the men who embody principles are celebrated upon occasions like this and only the events to which their concerted action gave rise excite our enthusiasm. You know that the principles of the Democratic party are professed by practically the whole population of the United States. The test of a Democrat is whether he lives up to those principles or not. I have no doubt there are some people in the United States who covertly question the doctrines of Democracy, but nobody challenges them openly. It goes without saying, therefore, that we have not come together merely to state the abstract principles of our party. We have come together to take counsel as to how it is possible, by courageous and concerted action, to translate them into policy and law. The Democratic party has had a long period of disappointment and defeat and I think that we can point out the reason. We do not live in simple times. We live in very conflicting times indeed. No man can be certain that he can say how to weave the threads of Democratic principle throughout all the complicated garment of our civilization, and the reason that the Democratic party has had this period of successive disturbance is that it has been divided into groups just as it was as to the method of fulfilling the principles.

We have differed as to measures; it has taken us sixteen years and more to come to any comprehension of our community of thought in regard to what we ought to do. What I want to say is that one of the most striking things in recent years is that with all the rise and fall of particular ideas, with all the ebb and flow of particular proposals, there has been one interesting fixed point in the history of the Democratic party, and that fixed point has been the character and the devotion and the preachings of William Jennings Bryan.

I, for my part, never want to forget this: That while we have differed with Mr. Bryan upon this occasion and upon that in regard to the specific things to be done, he has gone serenely on pointing out to a more and more convinced people what it was that was the matter. He has had the steadfast vision all along of what it was that was the matter and he has, not any more than Andrew Jackson did, not based his career upon calculation, but has based it upon principle.

Now, what has been the matter? The matter has been that the Government of this country was privately controlled and that the business of this country was privately controlled; that we did not have genuine representative government and that the people of this country did not have the control of their own affairs.

What do we stand for here tonight and what shall we stand for as long as we live? We stand for setting the Government of this country free and the business of this country free. The facts have been disputed by a good many sections of the Democratic party for the last half generation, but they were not clearly recognized.

I make the assertion that the Government was privately controlled. I mean to put it specifically that the Government of this country was managed by politicians who gained the contributions which they used by solicitation from particular groups of business interests, on the understanding, explicit or implied, that the first care of the Government was to be for those particular interests. I am not questioning either the integrity or patriotism of the men concerned. I have no right to. In most instances they were of that old belief, cropping up again and again in America, that the people of this country are not capable of perceiving their own interest and of managing their own affairs; that they have not the contact with large affairs; that they have not the variety of experience which qualifies them to take charge of their own affairs. It is the old Hamiltonian doctrine that those who have the biggest asset in the Government should be the trustees for the rest of us; that the men who conduct the biggest business transactions are the only men who should stand upon an elevation sufficient to see the whole range of our affairs, and that if we will but follow their leadership we may share in their prosperity. That is the Republican doctrine, and I am perfectly willing, as a tribute to their honesty though not to their intelligence, to admit that they really believe it; that they really believe it is unsafe to trust such delicate matters as the complicated business of this country to the general judgment of the country. They believe only a very small coterie of gentlemen are to be trusted with the conduct of large affairs. There was a long period in New Jersey, for example, in which no commissioner of insurance was ever chosen without first consulting or getting the consent of the head of the largest insurance company in the State, and I am willing to admit, at any rate for the sake of argument, that it was supposed he, better than anyone else, knew who was qualified for the job. He did know who was qualified for the job and he had the proper point of view in demonstrating that it was mainly for the benefit of the big interests.

Now, the other thing that has been privately controlled in this country is the business of the country. I do not mean that each man's particular business ought not to be privately controlled, but I mean that the great business transactions of this country are privately controlled by gentlemen whom I can name and whom I will name, if it is desired; men of great dignity of character; men, as I believe, of great purity of purpose, but men who have concentrated, in their own hands, transactions which they are not willing to have the rest of the country interfere with.

Now, the real difficulty in the United States, gentlemen, it seems to me, is not the existence of great individual combinations —that is dangerous enough in all countries—but the real danger is the combination of the combinations, the real danger is that the same groups of men control chains of banks, systems of railways, whole manufacturing enterprises, great mining projects, great enterprises for the developing of the natural water power of this country, and that threaded together in the personnel of a series of boards of directors is a community of interest more formidable than any conceivable combination in the United States.

It has been said that you cannot "unscramble eggs," and I am perfectly willing to admit it, but I can see in all cases before they are scrambled that they are not put in the same basket and entrusted to the same groups of persons.

What we have got to do—and it is a colossal task—a task not to be undertaken with a light head or without judgment—but what we have got to do is to disentangle this colossal community of interest. No matter how we may purpose dealing with a single combination in restraint of trade, you will agree with me in this that I think no combination is big enough for the United States to be afraid of; and when all the combinations are combined and this combination is not disclosed by any process of incorporation or law, but is merely the identity of personnel, then there is something for the law to pull apart, and gently, but firmly and persistently dissect. . . .

A very thoughtful preacher pointed out the other day that one of the first quotations in our Lord's Prayer is, "Give us this day our daily bread," which would seem, perhaps, to indicate that our Lord knew what every statesman must know, that the spiritual life of the Nation cannot exist unless it has physical life; that you cannot be an altruist and patriot on an empty stomach. Nothing shows the utter incapacity of a man to be a Democrat so much as his incapacity to understand what we are after. He does not know that the very seeds of life are in the principles and confidence and lives and virtues of the people of this country, and so when we strike at the trusts, or, rather, I will not say strike at the trusts, because we are not slashing about us—when we move against the trusts, when we undertake the strategy which is going to be necessary to overcome and destroy monopoly, we are rescuing the business of this country, we are not injuring it, and when we separate the interests from each other and disconnect these communities of connection we have in mind a greater community of interest, a vaster community of interest, the community of interest that binds the virtues of all men together, that mankind which is broad and catholic enough to take under the sweep of its comprehension all sorts and conditions of men, and that vision which sees that no society is renewed from the top and every society is renewed from the bottom. Limit opportunity, restrict the field of originative achievement, and you have cut out the heart and root of the prosperity of the country itself.

The only thing that can ever make a free country is to keep a free and hopeful heart under every jacket in it, and then there will be an irrepressible vitality, then there will be an irrepressible ideal which will enable us to be Democrats of the sort that when we die we shall look back and say: "Yes; from time to time we differed with each other as to what ought to be done, but, after all, we followed the same vision, after all we worked slowly, stumbling through dark and doubtful passages onward to a common purpose and a common ideal." Let us apologize to each other that we ever suspected or antagonized one another; let us join hands once more all around the great circle of community of counsel and of interest which will show us at the last to have been indeed the friends of our country and the friends of mankind.

11. It Was My Duty to Stand Guard

Reply to Republican Legislature, April 11, 1912

The 1912 legislature was hostile to Wilson. He believed that the Republicans and the machine Democrats who, together, dominated the legislature, wanted to undo the progressive measures passed in the previous session. Accordingly, he vetoed some forty-nine bills and accompanied his vetoes with stinging rebukes. On April 11, the Republican majority drew up a manifesto accusing Wilson of being ignorant of the bills he vetoed, and of neglecting state affairs. By this time Wilson's presidential campaign had moved into high gear and he spent much time speaking in other states. Below is his reply to the manifesto.

ORDINARILY I would remain entirely silent under partisan attacks of this kind, but feel that it is due to the people of the State that I should speak my very emphatic protest against an uncalled for grossly discourteous attack upon my official career, proceeding as a manifesto from a conference of Republican members of the legislature.

Of my vetoes, I shall say nothing. They speak for themselves and are justified by the bills against which they were uttered. But the statement that I have by frequent absences from the State in any degree neglected my duties as Governor is absolutely false. No important matter of business has been allowed to fall in arrears in my office. Every bill has been read and acted upon within the time prescribed by the constitution. I have been absent from the State only two of the session days of the legislature.

Not ten days, but five days only, under the explicit prescription of the constitution, were available for the consideration of the more than one hundred and fifty bills which were sent to my office just before the temporary adjournment of the legislature on the 29th day of March. I devoted to these bills the full five days allowed me. They received my careful attention. The legislature had, by deliberate arrangement of its Republican leaders, determined to reassemble the following week, so that I was not permitted, under the constitutional provision, to take more time than I did take in the consideration of the bills.

It is a noteworthy circumstance that, although a great many of the important measures sent me at the end of the session were introduced early in the session, they were delayed in their passage until the very end. The bills that came to me while the session lasted were for the most part of an incidental and trivial importance. Almost all the bills of capital consequence were reserved until the last. Among these none were more conspicuous than those which attempted to break down at one point or another the best legislation of the session of 1911, to the maintenance of which both parties were explicitly pledged in the campaign of the autumn of 1911. Bill after bill was introduced to weaken the force of the corrupt practices act and of the Geran Act. This, that and the other door of loose practice was deliberately opened. It was my duty to stand guard against these things, and I have done so. Against the bills to this effect which have been passed over my veto, I wish to utter my earnest protest in the name not only of party obligation—an obligation fairly resting upon both parties—but in the name of the people of the State. The session has been fruitful of nothing so much as of legislation tending to impair rather than to increase the efficiency of the laws of the State.

In my annual message I called attention to the great matters to which I understood both parties to be committed. I did not deem it wise or courteous to avow, as the session advanced, by repeated messages, my fear that these matters were to be neglected, and that the whole force of the session was to be spent upon measures of another sort and of questionable expediency. If the session has been barren and disappointing, as it has been, the people of the State will know where to bestow the blame. It is not yet too late to retrieve the record, if the Republican leaders are themselves aware of the failure. It might reassure the voters of the State to see them turn anew to the task in a new spirit. I am at their service.

12. The Nation Has Awakened

Address Accepting Presidential Nomination, August 7, 1912

At his summer home in Sea Girt, New Jersey, Wilson officially accepted the Democratic party nomination, given to him more than a month before, and delivered the following speech. His thoughts on the subjects he raised were not yet crystallized into the doctrine of the New Freedom. This came later, following his talks with Louis Brandeis on August 28.

. . . WE STAND in the presence of an awakened Nation, impatient of partisan make-believe. The public man who does not realize the fact and feel its stimulation must be singularly unsusceptible to the influences that stir in every quarter about him. The Nation has awakened to a sense of neglected ideals and neglected duties; to a consciousness that the rank and file of her people find life very hard to sustain, that her young men find opportunity embarrassed, and that her older men find business difficult to renew and maintain because of circumstances of privilege and private advantage which have interlaced their subtle threads throughout almost every part of the framework of our present law. She has awakened to the knowledge that she has lost certain cherished liberties and has wasted priceless resources which she had solemnly undertaken to hold in trust for posterity and for all mankind; and to the conviction that she stands confronted with an occasion for constructive statesmanship such as has not arisen since the great days in which her Government was set up.

Plainly, it is a new age. The tonic of such a time is very exhilarating. It requires self-restraint not to attempt too much, and yet it would be cowardly to attempt too little. The path of duty soberly and bravely trod is the way to service and distinction, and many adventurous feet seek to set out upon it.

There never was a time when impatience and suspicion were more keenly aroused by private power selfishly employed; when jealousy of everything concealed or touched with any purpose not linked with general good, or inconsistent with it, more sharply or immediately displayed itself.

Nor was the country ever more susceptible to unselfish appeals or to the high arguments of sincere justice. These are the unmistakable symptoms of an awakening. There is the more need of wise counsel because the people are so ready to heed counsel if it be given honestly and in their interest.

Great Questions of Right and Justice

It is in the broad light of this new day that we stand face to face—with what? Plainly not with questions of party, not with a contest for office, not with a petty struggle for advantage, Democrat against Republican, liberal against conservative, progressive against reactionary. With great questions of right and of justice, rather—questions of national development, of the development of character and of standards of action no less than of a better business system, more free, more equitable, more open to ordinary men, practicable to live under, tolerable to work under, or a better fiscal system whose taxes shall not come out of the pockets of the many to go into the pockets of the few, and within whose intricacies special privilege may not so easily find covert. The forces of the Nation are asserting themselves against every form of special privilege and private control, and are seeking bigger things than they have ever heretofore achieved. They are sweeping away what is unrighteous in order to vindicate once more the essential rights of human life; and, what is very serious for us, they are looking to us for guidance, disinterested guidance, at once honest and fearless.

At such a time, and in the presence of such circumstances, what is the meaning of our platform, and what is our responsibility under it? What are our duty and our purpose? The platform is meant to show that we know what the Nation is thinking about, what it is most concerned about, what it wishes corrected, and what it desires to see attained that is new and constructive and intended for its long future. But for us it is a very practical document. We are not about to ask the people of the United States to adopt our platform; we are about to ask them to intrust us with office and power and the guidance of their affairs. They will wish to know what sort of men we are and of what definite purpose; what translation of action and of policy we intend to give to the general terms of the platform which the convention at Baltimore put forth, should we be elected.

The platform is not a programme. A programme must consist of measures, administrative acts, and acts of legislation. The proof of the pudding is the eating thereof. How do we intend to make it edible and digestible? From this time on we shall be under interrogation. How do we expect to handle each of the great matters that must be taken up by the next Congress and the next administration?

Rule of Justice for Tariff and Trusts

What is there to do? It is hard to sum the great task up, but apparently this is the sum of the matter: There are two great things to do. One is to set up the rule of justice and of right in such matters as the tariff, the regulation of the trusts, and the prevention of monopoly, the adaptation of our banking and currency laws to the various uses to which our people must put them, the treatment of those who do the daily labor in our factories and mines and throughout all our great industrial and commercial undertakings, and the political life of the people of the Philippines, for whom we hold governmental power in trust, for their service, not our own. The other, the additional duty, is the great task of protecting our people and our resources and of keeping open to the whole people the doors of opportunity through which they must, generation by generation, pass if they are to make conquest of their fortunes in health, in freedom, in peace, and in contentment. In the performance of this second great duty we are face to face with questions of conservation and of development, questions of forests and water powers and mines and waterways, of the building of an adequate merchant marine, and the opening of every highway and facility and the setting up of every safeguard needed by a great, industrious, expanding nation.

These are all great matters upon which everybody should be heard. We have got into trouble in recent years chiefly because these large things, which ought to have been handled by taking counsel with as large a number of persons as possible, because they touched every interest and the life of every class and region, have in fact been too often handled in private conference. They have been settled by very small, and often deliberately exclusive, groups of men who undertook to speak for the whole Nation, or rather for themselves in the terms of the whole Nation—very honestly it may be true, but very ignorantly sometimes, and very shortsightedly, too—a poor substitute for genuine common counsel. No group of directors, economic or political, can speak for a people. They have neither the point of view nor the knowledge. Our difficulty is not that wicked and designing men have plotted against us, but that our common affairs have been determined upon too narrow a view, and by too private an initiative. Our task now is to effect a great readjustment and get the forces of the whole people once more into play. We need no revolution; we need no excited change; we need only a new point of view and a new method and spirit of counsel.

Nation Has Been at War Within Itself

We are servants of the people, the whole people. The Nation has been unnecessarily, unreasonably, at war within itself. Interest has clashed with interest when there were common principles of right and of fair dealing which might and should have bound them all together, not as rivals, but as partners. As the servants of all, we are bound to undertake the great duty of accommodation and adjustment.

We cannot undertake it except in a spirit which some find it hard to understand. Some people only smile when you speak of yourself as a servant of the people; it seems to them like affectation or mere demagoguery. They ask what the unthinking crowd knows or comprehends of great complicated matters of government. They shrug their shoulders and lift their eyebrows when you speak as if you really believed in presidential primaries, in the direct election of United States Senators, and in an utter publicity about everything that concerns government, from the sources of campaign funds to the intimate debate of the higher affairs of State.

They do not, or will not, comprehend the solemn thing that is in your thought. You know as well as they do that there are all sorts and conditions of men—the unthinking mixed with the wise, the reckless with the prudent, the unscrupulous with the fair and honest—and you know what they sometimes forget, that every class without exception affords a sample of the mixture, the learned and the fortunate no less than the uneducated and the struggling mass. But you see more than they do. You see that these multitudes of men, mixed, of every kind and quality, constitute somehow an organic and noble whole, a single people, and that they have interests which no man can privately determine without their knowledge and counsel. That is the meaning of representative government itself. Representative government is nothing more or less than an effort to give voice to this great body through spokesmen chosen out of every grade and class. . . .

I am not one of those who think that competition can be established by law against the drift of a world-wide economic tendency; neither am I one of those who believe that business done upon a great scale by a single organization—call it corporation, or what you will—is necessarily dangerous to the liberties, even the economic liberties, of a great people like our own, full of intelligence and of indomitable energy. I am not afraid of anything that is normal. I dare say we shall never return to the old order of individual competition, and that the organization of business upon a great scale of cooperation is, up to a certain point, itself normal and inevitable.

Big Business Not Dangerous Because It Is Big

Power in the hands of great business men does not make me apprehensive, unless it springs out of advantages which they have not created for themselves. Big business is not dangerous because it is big, but because its bigness is an unwholesome inflation created by privileges and exemptions which it ought not to enjoy. While competition cannot be created by statutory enactment, it can in large measure be revived by changing the laws and forbidding the practices that killed it, and by enacting laws that will give it heart and occasion again. We can arrest and prevent monopoly. It has assumed new shapes and adopted new processes in our time, but these are now being disclosed and can be dealt with.

The general terms of the present Federal antitrust law, forbidding "combinations in restraint of trade," have apparently proved ineffectual. Trusts have grown up under its ban very luxuriantly and have pursued the methods by which so many of them have established virtual monopolies without serious let or hindrance. It has roared against them like any sucking dove. I am not assessing the responsibility. I am merely stating the fact. But the means and methods by which trusts have established monopolies have now become known. It will be necessary to supplement the present law with such laws, both civil and criminal, as will effectually punish and prevent those methods, adding such other laws as may be necessary to provide suitable and adequate judicial processes, whether civil or criminal, to disclose them and follow them to final verdict and judgment. They must be specifically and directly met by law as they develop.

Vast Confederacies of Banks and Railways

But the problem and the difficulty are much greater than that. There are not merely great trusts and combinations which are to be controlled and deprived of their power to create monopolies and destroy rivals; there is something bigger still than they are and more subtle, more evasive, more difficult to deal with. There are vast confederacies (as I may perhaps call them for the sake of convenience) of banks, railways, express companies, insurance companies, manufacturing corporations, mining corporations, power and development companies, and all the rest of the circle, bound together by the fact that the ownership of their stock and the members of their boards of directors are controlled and determined by comparatively small and closely interrelated groups of persons who, by their informal confederacy, may control, if they please and when they will, both credit and enterprise. There is nothing illegal about these confederacies, so far as I can perceive. They have come about very naturally, generally without plan or deliberation, rather because there was so much money to be invested, and it was in the hands, at great financial centers, of men acquainted with one another and intimately associated in business, than because any one had conceived and was carrying out a plan of general control; but they are none the less potent a force in our economic and financial system on that account. They are part of our problem. Their very existence gives rise to the suspicion of a "money trust," a concentration of the control of credit which may at any time become infinitely dangerous to free enterprise. If such a concentration and control does not actually exist it is evident that it can easily be set up and used at will. Laws must be devised which will prevent this, if laws can be worked out by fair and free counsel that will accomplish that result without destroying or seriously embarrassing any sound or legitimate business undertaking or necessary and wholesome arrangement.

Let me say again that what we are seeking is not destruction of any kind nor the disruption of any sound or honest thing, but merely the rule of right and of the common advantage. I am happy to say that a new spirit has begun to show itself in the last year or two among influential men of business, and, what is perhaps even more significant, among the lawyers who are their expert advisers; and that this spirit has displayed itself very notably in the last few months in an effort to return, in some degree at any rate, to the practices of genuine competition. Only a very little while ago our men of business were united in resisting every proposal of change and reform as an attack on business, an embarrassment to all large enterprise, an intimation that settled ideas of property were to be set aside and a new and strange order of things created out of hand. While they thought in that way, progress seemed impossible without hot contest and a bitter clash between interests, almost a war of classes. Common counsel seemed all but hopeless, because some of the chief parties in interest would not take part; seemed even to resent discussion as a manifestation of hostility towards themselves. They talked constantly about vested interests and were very hot.

Big Business Men Are Seeing the Light

It is a happy omen that their attitude has changed. They see that what is right can hurt no man; that a new adjustment of interests is inevitable and desirable, is in the interest of everybody; that their own honor, their own intelligence, their own practical comprehension of affairs is involved. They are beginning to adjust their business to the new standards. Their hand is no longer against the Nation; they are part of it; their interests are bound up with its interests. This is not true of all of them; but it is true of enough of them to show what the new age is to be and how the anxieties of statesmen are to be eased if the light that is dawning broadens into day.

If I am right about this, it is going to be easier to act in accordance with the rule of right and justice in dealing with the labor question. The so-called labor question is a question only because we have not yet found the rule of right in adjusting the interests of labor and capital. The welfare, the happiness, the energy and spirit of the men and women who do the daily work in our mines and factories, on our railroads, in our offices and marts of trade, on our farms and on the sea, are of the essence of our national life. There can be nothing wholesome unless their life is wholesome; there can be no contentment unless they are contented. Their physical welfare affects the soundness of the whole Nation. We shall never get very far in the settlement of these vital matters so long as we regard everything done for the workingman, by law or by private agreement, as a concession yielded to keep him from agitation and a disturbance of our peace. Here, again, the sense of universal partnership must come into play if we are to act like statesmen, as those who serve, not a class, but a nation.

First Regard Must Be Care of Working People

The working people of America—if they must be distinguished from the minority that constitutes the rest of it—are, of course, the backbone of the Nation. No law that safeguards their life, that makes their hours of labor rational and tolerable, that gives them freedom to act in their own interest, and that protects them where they cannot protect themselves, can properly be regarded as class legislation or as anything but as a measure taken in the interest of the whole people, whose partnership in right action we are trying to establish and make real and practical. It is in this spirit that we shall act if we are genuine spokesmen of the whole country.

As our programme is disclosed—for no man can forecast it ready-made and before counsel is taken of everyone concerned—this must be its measure and standard, the interest of all concerned. For example, in dealing with the complicated and difficult question of the reform of our banking and currency laws it is plain that we ought to consult very many persons besides the bankers, not because we distrust the bankers, but because they do not necessarily comprehend the business of the country, notwithstanding they are indispensable servants of it and may do a vast deal to make it hard or easy. No mere bankers' plan will meet the requirements, no matter how honestly conceived. It should be a merchants' and farmers' plan as well, elastic in the hands of those who use it as an indispensable part of their daily business. I do not know enough about this subject to be dogmatic about it; I know only enough to be sure what the partnerships in it should be and that the control exercised over any system we may set up should be, as far as possible, a control emanating not from a single special class, but from the general body and authority of the Nation itself. . . .

A presidential campaign may easily degenerate into a mere personal contest and so lose its real dignity and significance. There is no indispensable man. The Government will not collapse and go to pieces if any one of the gentlemen who are seeking to be entrusted with its guidance should be left at home. But men are instruments. We are as important as the cause we represent, and in order to be important must really represent a cause. What is our cause? The people's cause. That is easy to say, but what does it mean? The common as against any particular interest whatever? Yes, but that, too, needs translation into acts and policies. We represent the desire to set up an unentangled government, a government that cannot be used for private purposes, either in the field of business or in the field of politics; a government that will not tolerate the use of the organization of a great party to serve the personal aims and ambitions of any individual, and that will not permit legislation to be employed to further any private interest. It is a great conception, but I am free to serve it, as you also are. I could not have accepted a nomination which left me bound to any man or group of men. No man can be just who is not free; and no man who has to show favors ought to undertake the solemn responsibility of government in any rank or post whatever, least of all in the supreme post of President of the United States.

To be free is not necessarily to be wise. But wisdom comes with counsel, with the frank and free conference of untrammelled men united in the common interest. Should I be entrusted with the great office of President, I would seek counsel wherever it could be had upon free terms. I know the temper of the great convention which nominated me; I know the temper of the country that lay back of that convention and spoke through it. I heed with deep thankfulness the message you bring me from it. I feel that I am surrounded by men whose principles and ambitions are those of true servants of the people. I thank God, and will take courage.

13. To Revive Her Ancient Standards

Campaign Addresses, 1912

Wilson originally hoped to engage in a high-level dialogue with his chief opponent, Theodore Roosevelt, the Progressive candidate. But he discovered that the campaign demanded old-fashioned politicking, and that, moreover, he was a good stump speaker. The campaign slowed down for two weeks following Roosevelt's incapacitation from a gunshot wound inflicted in an assassination attempt on October 14. The candidates resumed their debate only a week before the election. Below are excerpts from several of Wilson's more important or illuminating campaign addresses. They are taken from John Wells Davidson's collection A Crossroads of Freedom *(New Haven: Yale University Press, 1956).*

AT BUFFALO, NEW YORK, SEPTEMBER 2

. . . WHY IS it that the people of this country are in danger of being discontented with the parties that have pretended to serve them? It [is] because in too many instances their promises were not matched by their performances and men began to say to themselves, "What is the use [of] going to the polls and voting? Nothing happens after the election." Is there any man within the hearing of my voice who can challenge the statement that any party that has forfeited the public confidence, has forfeited it by its own nonperformance?

Very well then, when I speak to you today, I want you to regard me as a man who is talking business. I want in the first place to say that I shall be scrupulous to be fair to those with whom I am in opposition. Because there is a great deal to be said for the programs of hopeful men who intend to do things even if they haven't struck upon the right way to do them. And we ought not to divorce ourselves in sympathy with men who want the right thing because we do not think they have found the way to do them.

I want to speak upon this occasion, of course, on the interests of the workingman, of the wage earner, not because I regard the wage earners of this country as a special class, for they are not. After you have made a catalogue of the wage earners of this country, how many of us are left? The wage earners of this country, in the broad sense, constitute the country. And the most fatal thing that we can do in politics is to imagine that we belong to a special class, and that we have an interest which isn't the interest of the whole community. Half of the difficulties, half of the injustices of our politics have been due to the fact that men regarded themselves as having separate interests which they must serve even though other men were done a great disservice by their promoting them.

We are not afraid of those who pursue legitimate pursuits provided they link those pursuits in at every turn with the interest of the community as a whole; and no man can conduct a legitimate business, if he conducts it in the interest of a single class. I want, therefore, to look at the Nation as a whole today. I would like always to look at it as a whole, not divide it up into sections and classes, but I want particularly to discuss with you today the things which interest the wage earner. That is merely looking at the country as a whole from one angle, from one point of view, to which for the time being we will confine ourselves.

I want as a means of illustration, not as a means of contest, to use the platform of the third party as the means of expounding what I have to say today. I want you to read that platform very carefully, and I want to call your attention to the fact that it really consists of two parts. In one part of it, it declares the sympathy of the party with a certain great program of social reform, and promises that all the influence of that party, of the members of that party, will be used for the promotion of that program of social reform. In the other part, it itself lays down a method of procedure, and what I want you to soberly consider is whether the method of procedure is a suitable way of laying the foundations for the realization of that social program—with regard to the social program, the betterment of the condition of men in this occupation and the other, the protection of women, the shielding of children, the bringing about of social justice here, there, and elsewhere. With that program who can differ in his heart, who can divorce himself in sympathy from the great project of advancing the interests of human beings, wherever it is possible to advance them?

But there is a central method, a central purpose, in that platform from which I very seriously dissent. I am a Democrat as distinguished from a Republican because I believe (and I think that it is generally believed) that the leaders of the Republican party—for I always distinguish them from the great body of the Republican voters who have been misled by them—I say not the Republican party, but the leaders of the Republican party have allowed themselves to become so tied up in alliances with special interests that they are not free to serve us all. And that the immediate business, if you are to have any kind of reform at all, is to set your government free, is to break it away from the partnerships and alliances and understandings and [purchases] which have made it impossible for it to look at the country as a whole and made it necessary to serve special interests one at a time. Until that has been done, no program of social reform is possible because a program of social reform depends upon universal sympathy, universal justice, universal cooperation. It depends upon our understanding one another and serving one another.

What is this program? What is the program of the third party with regard to the disentanglement of the government? Mr. Roosevelt has said, and up to a certain point I sympathize with him, that he does not object, for example, to the system of protection except in this circumstance—that it has [not] inured to the benefit of the workingman of this country. It is very interesting to have him admit that because the leaders of the Republican party have been time out of mind putting this bluff up on you men that the protective policy was for your sake, and I would like to know what you ever got out of it that you didn't get out of the better effort of organized labor. I have yet to learn of any instance where you got anything without going and taking it. And the process of our society instead of being a process of peace has sometimes too much resembled a process of war because men felt obliged to go and insist in organized masses upon getting the justice which they couldn't get any other way.

It is interesting, therefore, to have Mr. Roosevelt admit that not enough of the "prize money," as he frankly calls it, has gone into the pay envelope. He admits that not enough of the money has gone into the envelope. I wish it were not prize money, because dividing up prize money and dividing up earnings are two very different things. And it is very much simpler to divide up earnings than to divide up prize money, because the money is prize money for the [reason] that a limited number of men banded themselves together and got it from the Ways and Means Committee of the House and the Finance Committee of the Senate, and we paid the bills.

But Mr. Roosevelt says that his [object] will be to see that a larger proportion gets into the pay envelope. And how does he propose to do it? (For I am here not to make a speech; I am here to argue this thing with you gentlemen.) How does he propose to do it? I don't find any suggestion anywhere in that platform of the way in which he is going to do it, except in one plank. One plank says that the party will favor a minimum wage for women; and then it goes on to say by a minimum wage it means a living wage, enough to live on.

I am going to assume, for the sake of argument, that it proposed more than that, that it proposed to get a minimum wage for everybody, men as well as women; and I want to call your attention to the fact that just as soon as a minimum wage is established by law, the temptation of every employer in the United States will be to bring his wages down as close to that minimum as he dares, because you can't strike against the government of the United States. You can't strike against what is in the law. You can strike against what is in your agreement with your employer, but if underneath that agreement there is the steel and the adamant of Federal law, you can't tamper with that foundation. And who is going to pay these wages? You know that the great difficulty about wages, one of the great difficulties about wages now, is that the control of industry is getting into fewer and fewer hands. And that, therefore, a smaller and smaller number of men are able to determine what wages shall be. In other words, one of the entanglements of our government is that we are dealing not with a community in which men may take their own choice of what they shall do, but in a community whose industry is very largely governed by great combinations of capital in the hands of a comparatively small number of men; that, in other words, we are in the hands, in many industries, of monopoly itself. And the only way in which the workingman can gain more wages is by getting them from the monopoly.

Very well then, what does this platform propose to do? Break up the monopolies? Not at all. It proposes to legalize them. It says in effect: You can't break them up, the only thing you can do is to put them in charge of the Federal Government. It proposes that they shall be adopted and regulated. And that looks to me like a consummation of the partnership between monopoly and government. Because, when once the government regulates monopoly, then monopoly will have to see to it that it regulates the government. This is a [beautiful] circle of change.

We now complain that the men who control these monopolies control the government, and it is in turn proposed that the government should control them. I am perfectly willing to be controlled if it is I, myself, who control me. If this partnership can be continued, then this control can be manipulated and adjusted to its own pleasure. Therefore, I want to call your attention to this fact that these great combined industries have been more inimical to organized labor than any other class of employers in the United States. Is not that so?

These monopolies that the government, it is proposed, should adopt are the men who have made your independent action most difficult. They have made it most difficult that you should take care of yourselves; and let me tell you that the old adage that God takes care of those who take care of themselves is not gone out of date. No Federal legislation can change that thing. The minute you are taken care of by the government you are wards, not independent men. And the minute they are legalized by the government, they are protégés and not monopolies. They are the guardians and you are the wards. Do you want to be taken care of by a combination of the government and the monopolies? [*A voice from the audience:* "No."] Because the workingmen of this country are perfectly aware that they sell their commodity, that is to say labor, in a perfectly open market. There is free trade in labor in the United States. The laboring men of all the world are free to come and offer their labor here and you are similarly free to go and offer your labor in most parts of the world. And the world demand is what establishes for the most part the rate of wages, at the same time that these gentlemen who are paying the wages in a free-trade market are protected by an unfree market against the competition that would make them [bid] higher because [bid] in competition and not [bid] under protection. If I am obliged to refrain from going into a particular industry by reason of the combination that already exists in it, I can't become an employer of labor, and I can't compete with these gentlemen for the employment of labor. And the whole business of the level of wages is artificially and arbitrarily determined.

Now, I say, gentlemen, that a party that proposes that program cannot, if it carries out that program, be forwarding these other industrial purposes of social regeneration, because they have crystallized, they have hardened, they have narrowed the government which is to be the source of this thing. After all this is done, who is to guarantee to us that the government is to be pitiful, that the government is to be righteous, that the government is to be just? Nothing will then control the power of the government except open revolt, and God forbid that we should bring about a state of politics in which open revolt should be substituted for the ballot box.

I believe that the greatest force for peace, the greatest force for righteousness, the greatest force for the elevation of mankind, is organized opinion, is the thinking of men, is the great force which is in the soul of men, and I want men to breathe a free and pure air. And I know that these monopolies are so many cars of juggernaut which are in our very sight being driven over men in such ways as to crush their life out of them. And I don't look forward with pleasure to the time when the juggernauts are licensed. I don't look forward with pleasure to the time when the juggernauts are driven by commissioners of the United States. I am willing to license automobiles, but not juggernauts, because if any man ever dares take a joy ride in one of them, I would like to know what is to become of the rest of us; because the road isn't wide enough for us to get out of the way. We would have to take to the woods and then set the woods afire. I am speaking partly in pleasantry but underneath, gentlemen, there is a very solemn sense in my mind that we are standing at a critical turning point in our [choice].

Now you say, on the other hand, what do the Democrats propose to do? I want to call your attention to the fact that those who wish to support these monopolies by adopting them under the regulation of the government of the United States are the very men why cry out that competition is destructive. They ought to know because it is competition as they conducted it that destroyed our economic freedom. They are certainly experts in destructive competition. And the purpose of the Democratic leaders is this: not to legislate competition into existence again—because statutes can't make men do things—but to regulate competition.

What has created these monopolies? Unregulated competition. It has permitted these men to do anything that they chose to do to squeeze their rivals out and to crush their rivals to the earth. We know the processes by which they have done these things. We can prevent those processes by remedial legislation, and that remedial legislation will so restrict the wrong use of competition that the right use of competition will destroy monopoly. In other words, ours is a program of liberty and theirs is a program of regulation. Ours is a program by which we find we know the wrongs that have been committed and we can stop those wrongs. And we are not going to adopt into the government family the men who forward the wrongs and license them to do the whole business of the country.

I want you men to grasp the point because I want to say to you right now the program that I propose doesn't look quite as much like acting as a Providence for you as the other program looks. But I want to frankly say to you that I am not big enough to play Providence, and my objection to the other program is that I don't believe that there is any other man that is big enough to play Providence. I have never known any body of men, any small body of men, that understood the United States. And the only way the United States is ever going to be taken care of is by having the voice of all the men in it constantly clamorous for the recognition of what is justice as they see life. A little group of men sitting every day in Washington City is not going to have a vision of your lives as a whole. You alone know what your lives are. I say, therefore, take the shackles off of American industry, the shackles of monopoly, and see it grow into manhood, see it grow out of the enshackled childishness into robust manliness, men being able to take care of themselves, and reassert the great power of American citizenship.

These are the ancient principles of government the world over. For when in the history of labor, here in this country or in any other, did the government present its citizens with freedom and with justice? When has there been any fight for liberty that wasn't a fight against this very thing, the accumulation of regulative power in the hands of a few persons? I in my time have read a good deal of history and, if I were to sum up the whole history of liberty, I should say that it consisted at every turn in human life in resisting just such projects as are now proposed to us. If you don't believe it, try it. If you want a great struggle for liberty that will cost you blood, adopt this program, put yourselves at the disposition of a Providence resident in Washington and then see what will come of it.

Ah, gentlemen, we are debating very serious things. And we are debating this: Are we going to put ourselves in a position to enter upon a great program of understanding one another and helping one another? I can't understand you unless you talk to me. I can't understand you by looking at you. I can't understand you by reading books. With apologies to the gentlemen in front of me, I couldn't even understand you by reading the newspapers. I can understand you only by what you know of your own lives and make evident in your own actions. I understand you only in proportion as you "hump" yourselves and take care of yourselves, and make your force evident in the course of politics. And, therefore, I believe in government as a great process of getting together, a great process of debate.

There are gentlemen on this platform with me who have seen a great vision. They have seen this, for example: You know that there are a great many foreigners coming to America and qualifying as American citizens. And if you are widely acquainted among them you will know that this is true: that the grown-up people who come to America take a long time in feeling at home in America. They don't speak the language and there is no place in which they can get together with the general body of American citizens and feel that they are part of them. But their children feel welcome. Where? In the schoolhouse. The schoolhouse is the great melting pot of democracy. And after the children of these men who have joined us in their desire for freedom have grown up and come through the processes of the schools, they have imbibed the full feeling of American life.

Now, somebody has said—somebody repeated to me the other day—the saying of one of these immigrants that when he went to a meeting or to a series of meetings in the evening in a schoolhouse where all the neighborhood joined to discuss the interests of the neighborhood, he for the first time saw America as he had expected to see it. This [was] America as he had imagined it, this frank coming together of all the people in the neighborhood, of all sorts and conditions, to discuss their common interests. And these gentlemen to whom I have referred have devoted their lives to this: to make the schoolhouses of this country the vital centers of opportunity, to open them out of school hours for everybody who desires to discuss anything and for making them, among other things, the clearinghouses where men who are out of jobs can find jobs and where jobs who are out of men can find men. Why shouldn't our whole life center in this place where we learn the fundamentals of our life? Why shouldn't the schoolhouses be the constant year-in-and-year-out places of assembly where things are said which nobody dares ignore? Because, if we haven't had our way in this country, it has been because we haven't been able to get at the ear of those who are conducting our government. And if there is any man in Buffalo, or anywhere else in the United States, who objects to your using the schoolhouses that way, you may be sure that there is something he doesn't want to have discussed.

You know I have been considered as disqualified for politics because I was a school teacher. But there is one thing a school teacher learns that he never forgets, namely, that it is his business to learn all he can and then to communicate it to others. Now, I consider this to be my function. I have tried to find out how to learn things and learn them fast. And I have made up my mind that for the rest of my life I am going to put all I know at the disposal of my fellow citizens. And I know a good many things that I haven't yet mentioned in public which I am ready to mention at the psychological moment. There is no use firing it off when there is nobody to shoot at, but when they are present, then it is sport to say it. And I have undertaken the duty of constituting myself one of the attorneys for the people in any court to which I can get entrance. I don't mean as a lawyer, for while I was a lawyer, I have repented. But I mean in the courts of public opinion wherever I am allowed, as I am indulgently allowed today, to stand on a platform and talk to attentive audiences—for you are most graciously attentive—I want to constitute myself the spokesman so far as I have the proper table of contents for the people whom I wish to serve; for the whole strength of politics is not in the leader but in the followers. By leading I do not mean telling other people what they have go to do. I [mean] finding out what the interests of the community are agreed to be, and then trying my level best to find the methods of solution by common counsel. That is the only feasible program of social uplift that I can imagine, and, therefore, I am bound in conscience to fight everything that crystallizes things so at the center that you can't break in.

It is amazing to me that public-spirited, devoted men in this country have not seen that the program of the third party proclaims purposes and in the same breath provides an organization of government which makes the carrying out of those purposes impossible. I would rather postpone my sympathy for social reform until I had got in a position to make things happen. And I am not in a position to make things happen until I am part of a free organization which can say to every interest in the United States: "You come into this conference room on an equality with every other interest in the United States, and you are going to speak here with open doors. There is to be no whispering behind the hand. There is to be no private communication. What you can't afford to let the country hear had better be left unsaid."

What I fear, therefore, is a government of experts. God forbid that in a democratic country we should resign the task and give the government over to experts. What are we for if we are to be [scientifically] taken care of by a small number of gentlemen who are the only men who understand the job? Because if we don't understand the job, then we are not a free people. We ought to resign our free institutions and go to school to somebody and find out what it is we are about. I want to say I have never heard more penetrating debate of public questions than I have sometimes been privileged to hear in clubs of workingmen; because the man who is down against the daily problem of life doesn't talk about it in rhetoric; he talks about it in facts. And the only thing I am interested in is facts. I don't know anything else that is as solid to stand on. . . .

At Buffalo (Arsenal Address), New York, September 2

. . . Politics differs from philanthropy only in this: that in philanthropy we sometimes do things through pity merely, while in politics we merely do it, if we are righteous men, on the grounds of justice. Sometimes in our pitiful sympathy with our fellow men we must do things that are more than just. We must forgive men. We must help men that have gone wrong. We must help men that have gone criminally wrong. But the law says we are merely going to equalize conditions, see that every man has a fair chance, see that injustice and wrong are not wrought in the name of government. And yet philanthropy and government are linked in this, that they are both meant for the service of humanity. Why, government was set up in America because men of all classes were not served anywhere else in the world! Under every other government in the world, when American government was set up, the government served only some of the classes of the community, and we boasted, we hoped, we were confident that we had set up a government in this country which would serve every class without discrimination—the most humble along with the most powerful. Only so long as we keep American government up to that ideal and standard will it be worthy of the name America.

Therefore, the critical circumstance of the year 1912 is this, that we fear that we have found that our government is not serving all classes, that our government is serving only a [portion], and that the most powerful [portion] of the community, which could take care of itself. I am very much more interested in seeing government take care of the people who are not powerful than I am in seeing it take care of the people who are powerful. And when I see the powerful control the government, then I say, "This is not American government; this is not the government of the people." Our task this year is to place the government back into the hands of all classes of American citizens. That is what we mean by putting it in the hands of the people. . . .

At Minneapolis, Minnesota, September 18

. . . It seems to me that it should be in that spirit of good nature and of frankness we ought to deal with the questions of 1912; and all that I have to suggest to you gentlemen is that there is this explicit choice to be made in 1912. I was saying last night that when you state it it sounds a little bit abstract, but it is the parting of the ways. And two ways may part at a very slight angle that may seem almost to run parallel with one another. But, if you notice, they are diverging, and the goal at the end of one of them is very distant from the goal at the end of the other one. Your direction is what you have got to choose in 1912.

Now, here is the choice: on the one hand, accepted and regulated monopoly; on the other hand, regulated competition which will prevent monopoly. I have studied history, and I dare not take the road that leads to regulated monopoly; because by regulating monopoly you adopt it, you render it permanent, you accept all the things by which it has been established, and by simply adopting it as an inevitable move to make the best of the situation, and with intent to see that it does as little damage as possible in the circumstances. Whereas, in the other direction, instead of leaving yourself tied up with this established domination, you take a road that by slow degrees only diverges from the other, but nevertheless presently radically diverges, in which men can walk with greater and greater freedom; in which they can determine their own lives with the knowledge that while they are little they can't be crushed by the fellow that is big.

Any man who can get beyond the place where he is little and get big, as you know, can either survive separately or get bought up at a profitable figure, but in order even to get bought out he has got to pass the stage where he is little. Because as long as his market is local, he may be crushed, and when his market becomes general, then he may be taken into partnership or bought out.

That has been the process of our development, has it not? Which means that the independent man can't remain independent, and by the nice arrangements—largely accidental, I don't think they are malignant or intentional—but by the nice arrangement of our modern fiscal system, or rather our banking system (I won't say arrangements but systems . . .) it is very difficult indeed for the new adventurer in the economic world to get the necessary credit as against the men who don't want his competition to interfere with their enterprises. Sometimes he needs big credit, and he can't get it, because to get credit makes him big, and there are big fellows who don't want any more big ones.

We have got to see that the little fellows are protected, and that means that we have to meet the criticism of the old, unrestricted competitive system which has been very justly leveled against it. Men who have built up these great monopolistic enterprises, for they virtually are such, have been right in saying that the whole system was of a character to be destructive. They ought to know, because they have done the destroying. They know how the destroying is done, and I admit that it can be done.

And the only way to stop that is not by legalizing the enterprises that have done the destroying, but by seeing that no more destroying is done. And that is what I call regulated competition;

because I know, and every man in his heart knows, that the only way to enrich America is to make it possible for a man that has the brains to get into the game.

And I am not jealous of the size of any business that has grown to that size. I am not jealous of any process of growth, no matter how huge the result, provided the result was obtained by the processes of growth, which are the processes of efficiency, of economy, of intelligence, and of invention.

I am constantly using this illustration, and you gentlemen know that it is a true one: The United States Steel Corporation had to buy Mr. Carnegie out, because Mr. Carnegie organized his business, economized his processes, ordered his plants in such a fashion that he could beat every mother's son of them in manufacturing steel rails. He had the market, because he could legitimately undersell them, and they had to pay him I don't know how many times, three or four times, the value of his property and of his business in order to get rid of him, in order not to be beaten by him in open competition.

Now, do you want that sort of thing to go on? Do you want the efficiency of your business lowered by creating the necessity and the temptation to put those men out who are the most efficient? Isn't America profited by the growth of just such enterprises? And isn't it about time that we put every undertaking in the United States on its mettle; that we said to it: "If you are now conducting a business upon which you have to pay interest on securities that vastly exceed the value of your business and of your properties, then that is your lookout, not ours. You got into that. This country isn't going to pay, isn't going to continue to pay the price of things out of which it gets nothing."?

I am not now inveighing against watered stock. I know all the statistical arguments, and they are many, for capitalizing earning capacity. It is a very attractive and interesting argument, and in many instances it is legitimately used. But there is a line where you cross, and where you are not capitalizing your earning capacity, but capitalizing your control of the market, capitalizing the profits which you got by your control of the market, and did not get by efficiency and economy.

These things are not hidden even from the laymen. These are not even hidden from college men. Their days of innocence have passed, and their days of sophistication have come. And they know what is going on, because we live in a talkative world, full of statistics, full of congressional inquiries, full of trials of all sorts of persons who have attempted to live independently of the statutes of the United States, and so a great many things have come to light under oath, which we must believe upon the credibility of the witnesses, who are in many instances very eminent and respectable witnesses.

Now, I have wandered abroad in this little talk of mine, but I simply wanted to show you the inside of my mind, so that there need be no misunderstanding between us; so that you would not think I was one of those wild fellows running amuck because I knew something was the matter, and did not know exactly what.

This is no Donnybrook fair. I have gotten my shillalah, but I am not hitting every head I see. I have selected the heads, and if they'll only engage in a little hard thinking beneath the endangered craniums, they need not be hit at all. Because the whole thing is as much in their interest as in the interest of the rest of us. If I didn't believe that, I wouldn't touch it; I wouldn't go out.

I was inducted the other day into an association in Sioux City in which I became a good Indian, but that has not bred in me the desire for scalps. I am not out after any man's topknot; I am not aware of entertaining the least feeling that we ought to get even with some one. I am only possessed with the passion to create a condition that will be even for everybody. . . .

At Minneapolis (Parade Grounds), Minnesota, September 18

. . . The strength of America is proportionate to the health, the buoyancy, the elasticity, the hope, the energy of the American people. What would our forests be worth without these intelligent bodies of ambitious men to make use of them? Why should we conserve our natural resources if we could by a sort of magic of industry transmute them into the wealth of the world? Who transmutes them into that wealth, if not the skill and the touch of the great bodies of men who go daily to their toil and who constitute the great body of the American people? What I am interested in is having the government of the United States more concerned about human rights than about property rights. Property is an instrument of humanity. Humanity isn't an instrument of property. And yet when you see some men engaged in some kinds of industries, riding their great industries as if they were driving a car of juggernaut, not looking to see what multitudes prostrate themselves before the car and lose their lives in the crushing effect of their industry, you wonder how long men are going to be permitted to think more of their machinery than they think of their men. Did you never think of it? Men are cheap and machinery is dear, and many a superintendent will be dismissed for overdriving a delicate machine, who wouldn't be dismissed for overdriving an overtaxed man. Because you can discard one man and replace him; there are others ready to come into his place; but you can't without great cost discard your machine and put a new one in its place. You are not looking upon your men as the essential and vital foundation part of your whole business. I say, therefore, that property as compared with humanity, as compared with the vital red blood in the American people, must take second place, not first place; and that we must see to it that there is no overcrowding, that there is no bad sanitation, that there is no unnecessary spread of avoidable diseases, that there is every safeguard against accidents, that women are not driven to impossible tasks and children not permitted to spend their energy before it is fit to be spent, that all the hope of the race must be preserved, and that men must be preserved according to their individual needs and not according to the programs of industry merely. Because, what is the use having industry if we die in producing it? If we die in trying to feed ourselves, why should we feed ourselves? If we die trying to get a foothold in the crowd, why not let the crowd trample us sooner and be done with it? I tell you, gentlemen, that there is beginning to beat in this nation a great pulse of irresistible sympathy which is going to transform the process of government amongst us. (I am sorry, a gentleman seems to have fallen—I am afraid with the heat. What I was about to say has been driven out of my head by another kind of sympathy.)

There is more than the safety of the people to be considered. There are the opportunities of the people; there are the things that we must do for the people in order to facilitate their lives. What I want to call your attention to is that every time we discuss any one of these questions we come up against some economic objection. This is not theoretical with me, because I have handled these matters in the state of New Jersey. I know that men say: "We can't be more pitiful; we can't be more considerate to our men in this shop, because if we were, the men who are less considerate in the next shop—not spending as much money for the safety of their men as we would spend—could underbid us in the market and beat us in the competition."

There is only one thing to do. Therefore, is the government desirous to step in and say that in all shops these safeguards must be observed, these arrangements for the public and the general health? But, gentlemen, these things are not going to be done until you change the point of view of the government. So long as the point of view of the government is the point of view of successful big business merely, it will not yield to the counsel of the rest of us which says that before the interests of big business must come the interests of humanity. In other words, it is perfectly useless to talk about great programs of reform unless you first get a government that is going to institute the reform. Therefore, it is absolutely necessary that I should remind you of the fundamental question of the present campaign.

I want to say here, as I have said on so many other occasions, that there is a great deal in the program of the new third party which attracts all public-spirited and hopeful men, that there is a great program of human uplift included in the platform of that party. A man would be niggardly and untrue to himself who would not say that. But when I ask myself who is going to carry out this program, then the thing wears another aspect. [A *voice: "Shoots it at him."*] You think that I am referring to an individual. I am not. I am referring to the method by which the individual and the others associated with him propose to deal with the central economic difficulty. . . .

At Columbus, Ohio, September 20

I am very much complimented that the busy men of a particularly busy city should take an hour in the middle of the afternoon to come out and give me the pleasure and the privilege of saying a word or two to them. I would very much prefer that you should for the time being forget that I am a candidate for the Presidency because, if I may say so to you very frankly, the consciousness that I am a candidate and am supposed to be soliciting the suffrages of my fellow citizens sometimes embarrasses me. Because I do not wish the thought of an occasion like this, or any other occasion for that matter, to be centered upon myself as an individual. I would a great deal rather if it were possible, if you were not so numerous, hear you talk than talk myself. Because I regard a meeting like this as a sort of conference in which we can become aware of one another's points of view and of one another's opinions about those matters which concern all of us.

One of the most amazing fictions of our politics is that the Democratic party is not interested in the business welfare of the United States. When you reflect that the Democrats of the United States constitute about half of the population, it is very interesting that half of the population should be suspected of the desire to commit commercial hara-kiri. There are Democrats in every walk of life. There is not an important undertaking in this country with which some Democrat is not connected and upon whose success some Democrats' achievements do not depend. Therefore it is amazing to me that any body of citizens should have long entertained the delusion that the Democratic party as such has any desires upon the material prosperity of our country.

What we are privileged to say to one another upon this matter we should say very frankly indeed: Are you satisfied with the business conditions of the United States? Do you feel the same freedom in enterprise that obtained in this country when those of you who are middle-aged were youngsters? Do you feel that your sons have as open a field for the exercise of their gifts in business as they would have had if they had been born a generation ago? Do you feel no stiffening of the structure? Do you feel no concentration of the control of our industrial development in certain quarters? Do you feel no increased difficulty about obtaining the larger kinds of credit in order to start the larger kinds of undertakings? Are there inventors among you? Do you see nothing taking place in the market for inventions? Is this company of businessmen satisfied that they are now as free in business as they used to be, and that America has as untrammeled a future in her material development as she once seemed to have? Are you convinced there is no such thing as monopoly? Are you ignorant of the processes by which monopoly has been created, and are you content to continue to live under conditions which will perpetuate monopoly?

The questions answer themselves. You are not satisfied with the present conditions of business. If you accept them, it is because of a certain kind of despair. You know these things ought not to have happened. You know that the processes ought not to have been permitted by which they were brought about, but you feel that big business has come to stay and you don't see how to break up the present processes of big business and substitute better ones. Therefore with a spirit quite uncharacteristic of America you shrug your shoulders and say: "Well, perhaps the best we can do is to submit and to regulate the thing if we can find men of genius enough to regulate it."

Gentlemen, do you realize why we prefer democracy to monarchy? It is because we can't afford to be anxious as to what kind of sons a man has. If you have a monarchy or an aristocracy, your leaders have to come from the loins of this man. Suppose they don't come. Then you are cheated of the energy of the nation unless you can say, "It doesn't make any difference what kinds of sons they have." There are plenty of sons to take their places from other ranks and the whole structure of liberty has been built up out of the circumstance that the unknown men regardless of the humbleness of their origin or the obscurity of their beginnings have had an absolutely free channel in which to enter with their energy and establish their lordship over those less confident than themselves.

That is the reason that I am a Democrat, and that is the reason that every American man who is thoughtful is at least a democrat with a little "d." And the interesting circumstance about the present campaign is that men are beginning to see the reason there is no use to put it democrat with a little "d" unless you will begin with a big "D." Because the channels open[ed] by those who are not Democrats with a big "D" do not lead to the real processes of democracy with a little "d." They lead to escapement, they lead to the regulation of monopoly, they simply offer to guarantee to us that monopoly will be good to us.

Now, there isn't any living man that can guarantee that unless he will see to it that men all over the country are challenged to come out and beat these fellows at their own business. That is the only law of freedom. Our trammels just now, our political difficulties, arise out of the fact that those who control our government have taken counsel not with the men who are about to make beginnings but with the men who have achieved, who are at the top of industry, who have already earned their mastery and who can see nothing except the desirability of maintaining the conditions under which their mastery has been obtained.

A very subtle and perhaps cynical English writer has made a very interesting remark. He says it is not true altogether to say of a man who has established himself abundantly in business that you can't bribe a man like that. Because, he says, the point is that he has been bribed—not in any gross sense, in any corrupt sense—but he has got his mastery under existing conditions and existing conditions have put him under bond to see to it that they are not changed. He has learned one game and he isn't going to risk another. He has learned how to get to the top by the ladder that is under him now and he doesn't purpose to let anybody change the processes by which men have to climb. He is going to see to it that things are held where he has them and where he wants them to stay. I am not criticizing it. It is perfectly natural and they have to be changed without his consent. I am very sorry. I would apologize to him if I knew him.

But these things will have to be changed without his consent; for the men that I am listening to as well as I can in politics are the men of the next generation, the men knocking at the door of opportunity, thundering at these closed gates and trying to seize us who have built up a great structure of wealth.

But what of us? Where is our hope, where is our opinion, where is our opportunity of achievement? Are you going to shut the gates upon us and keep them shut? Are you going to open just such little wickets as you care to keep the key to and let us slip in and join your organization, or are you going to open the main portals and say, "Come in. The future is yours as much as it is ours, and no man shall contest it with you except by brains and honesty of character." If an artificial obstacle to free opportunity in this country must be battered down, nobody will profit more, nobody will feel the buoyancy and spring more, than the men already in business in the United States.

One of the things that makes the currency question most pressing and significant at this moment is that we are certain now, in my judgment, to remove some of the artificial obstacles to our prosperity in business. The minute you do that there is to be such an increase in the economic activity of America that this stubborn, stiff, antiquated currency system of ours can't stand the strain. You have got to make it elastic. You have got to change it, or else you can't stand your own prosperity. There won't be any means of carrying it. America is now straining at the leash, and I could name some of the gentlemen who hold the leather thong that is attached to the leash. I don't know whether they know who are holding it or not. It doesn't make any difference whether you do or not. The leash is there and America is straining to be free; and God willing, she shall be free. . . .

At New Haven, Connecticut, September 25

. . . The Democratic party does not stand for the limitation of powers of government, either in the field of the state or in the field of the Federal government. There is not a Democrat that I know who is afraid to have the powers of the government exercised to the utmost. But there are a great many of us who are afraid to see them exercised at the discretion of individuals. There are a great many of us who still adhere to that ancient principle that we prefer to be governed by the power of laws, and not by the power of men.

Therefore, we favor as much power as you choose, but power guided by knowledge, power extended in detail, not power given out in the lump to a commission set up as is proposed by the third party and unencumbered by the restrictions of law, to set up a "constructive regulation," as their platform calls it, of the trusts and monopoly. But [we wish] a law which takes its searchlight and casts its illuminating rays down the secret corridors of all the processes by which monopoly has been established and polices those corridors so that highway robbery is no longer committed on them, so that men are no longer waylaid upon them, so that the liberty of individuals to compete is no longer checked by the power of combination stronger than any possible individual can be. We want to see the law administered. We are not afraid of commissions.

It is said, with a good deal of force, I want frankly to admit, that merely to make laws and leave their application to the present courts with their present procedure is not a very likely way to reform, because the present procedure of our courts means that individuals must challenge the power that is being exerted against them, that an individual must wait until he is injured and then go to the court for redress, and that he must have money enough and courage enough to go to the court and ask for redress. For the worst of our present situation, ladies and gentlemen, is that it requires courage to challenge the power of the men now in control of our industries by resorting to any tribunal whatever. Therefore, I am ready to admit that we may have to have special tribunals, special processes, and I am not afraid, for my part, of the creation of special processes and special tribunals; but I am absolutely opposed to leaving it to the choice of those tribunals what the processes of law shall be and the means of remedy.

Therefore, the difference between the Democratic and the Republican parties, or rather between the Democratic party and those various other groups that are masquerading under all sorts of names, is that they are willing to accept the discretionary power of individuals, and we are not willing to accept anything except the certainty of law. That is the only thing that has ever afforded salvation or safety. . . .

At Pittsburgh, Pennsylvania, October 18

. . . I want to see a government which does not condescend, but takes part in the common life. I want to see a government that feels the thrill of the men who are struggling and does not lean down and lend them a helping hand, but walks with them in the common way and says, "Men and brethren, it is a common life; we must live it together; we must do one another justice." Privilege from above? There is no such benevolence. I say it with all reverence, but I believe that the benevolence of God does not consist in pitying us as weak creatures, but in understanding us and putting the whole Providence of God behind the best things that are in us. And so with government, which ought not to be a Providence, but should be merely the expression of the common life. It cannot lend a helping [hand] to mankind; it must speak for mankind.

And, ladies and gentlemen, is not that the American enterprise?

America was created to illuminate the path of progress for the ordinary man. Any country in the world can show you examples of great and powerful and rich men who have prevailed and made their power felt. America is not distinguished for being rich; other countries have been rich and other countries have been disgraced, disgraced in their very heartless use of their wealth and of their power. America will have lost her title deed unless she shows that she is devoted to the interests of the rank and file of humanity.

What I have come tonight, therefore, to urge upon you as an enterprise in which we can all sink our party traditions and unite with the thought of the people, is to propose to you that as Americans we band ourselves together to restore America. And these gentlemen who offer to rescue us have not been associated with America. The men under whom trusts multiplied from forty to a thousand, from forty to ten thousand, have become accustomed to the multiplication of trusts; it is actually come to the pass that they regard monopoly as the law of nature in business. And if that is the law of nature, then America as a free government just goes out of business. Because the statement of the Democratic platform is the statement that sums up history: that private monopoly is absolutely indefensible and intolerable. If it is any monopoly, it must be a public monopoly and not a private monopoly.

You know what the processes of modern society are. They are not individualistic. They are processes of association, and those processes contain in them a danger that governments never saw before. Because men never before had the means or the genius for association that they have now, and the danger at the present moment is that private association will become stronger than public association, and that there will be combinations of men and of money stronger than the government itself. If we take this thing in hand now, it may be that we shall prevail. If we do not take it in hand now, it may be that we shall not prevail. The time is all too long postponed. The danger is so great that it will need all the prudence, all the moderation, all the intelligence, all the good nature of America to revive her ancient standards and re-practice her ancient principles. If we postpone it, our temper may change. And we shall postpone it if we do not put the Democratic party in power. . . .

At New York City, New York, October 31

. . . What the Democratic party proposes to do is to go into power and do the things that the Republican party has been talking about doing for sixteen years. There is a very simple way of doing it—to direct the provisions of your law against every specific process of monopoly which has by crushing competition built up the control of small numbers of men, and then direct the punishment against every individual who disobeys the law. If this is done with clearness and steadiness of purpose, and with absolute fairness and courage, there will be no more monopolies in the United States.

No one desires to discipline business because it is big. All that we need to do is to check those who use big business to crush little business, who use power to prevent anybody coming into competition with their power by a power and an intelligence of his own. For when we talk of restoring the government to the people, we are talking of nothing more than this, of having the action of the government based on the interests of the average man, and the rank and file of the people. It doesn't mean that the people are to go down to Washington and sit in superintendence on the government, but it means that the people won't have to go to Washington in order for the government to know what they are thinking about; because all the channels of counsel will be open, all the channels of sympathy.

And when we have set the government free, what do we mean to do? Do we mean to try to change men's hearts and so direct and modify men's business that they will be kind to one another? That is an impossible enterprise. What we are going to try to do is to see that nothing more than justice is done. Our standard is not pity, but justice. For, my fellow citizens, you are not benefited by the pity of your employer or the pity of your party leader. You are benefited and elevated by having your rights respected.

Government is based upon right, not benevolence. And so when I look abroad and see the great things that are to be done, when I know the things that must be done in order to protect women, in order to protect children, in order to protect the great masses of men who carry the sometimes intolerable burdens of our daily industry, I say to myself: "We are proposing nothing for these people except what is their due as human beings. We are not proposing to go about with condescension; we are not proposing to go about with the helping hands of those who are stronger to lift up the weaker; but we are going about with the strong hand of government to see that nobody imposes on the weak, to see that nobody lowers the levels of American vitality by putting on the working people of this country more than flesh and blood and nerves and heart can bear." And this not because we are trying to do something more than govern, but because government is meant for the conservation of the national life, and, if you depress the levels of vitality, you depress the whole power and hope and achievement of the nation.

The nation does not consist of those who direct industry. The nation consists of those who carry on industry by their daily labor. And when I look about upon a great company like this, I know that they could come to this gathering only in the evening, because from the rising of the sun to the going down of it they must be intent upon those tasks without which they cannot eat or be fed, or take care of those whom they love and are dependent upon them; and the real problems of their day are between sunrise and sunset. They don't come to a hall like this to hear the mere flowers of rhetoric. They come to see if it is possible to find honest men who understand what ought to be done.

There are some things that ought not to be done. That man ought to be ashamed of himself who sets the passion of one class of society aflame against another class. And the task of every honest leader of the people is the task of convincing his fellow citizens that that man who regards himself as in a class apart is an enemy to the progress of mankind; that where there are classes in point of privilege there is not righteousness, there is not justice, there is not fair play; and that to lift the masses, to safeguard those who are weak, to set forward the hopes of those who are merely beginning to come on in the great enterprise of life, is to help those at the top just as much as it is to help those at the bottom. No man's heart is right unless he feels it beat upon the same level with all the other hearts in God's world. . . .

Three

NEW FREEDOM
1913–1915

1. Our Work Is a Work of Restoration

First Inaugural Address, March 4, 1913

Before taking the oath of office Wilson noticed that the people had been moved far back from the speaker's stand. He told the guard, "Let the people come forward"—a phrase often repeated during his first year as President.

MY FELLOW CITIZENS: There has been a change of government. It began two years ago, when the House of Representatives became Democratic by a decisive majority. It has now been completed. The Senate about to assemble will also be Democratic. The offices of President and Vice-President have been put into the hands of Democrats. What does the change mean? That is the question that is uppermost in our minds today. That is the question I am going to try to answer, in order, if I may, to interpret the occasion.

It means much more than the mere success of a party. The success of a party means little except when the Nation is using that party for a large and definite purpose. No one can mistake the purpose for which the Nation now seeks to use the Democratic party. It seeks to use it to interpret a change in its own plans and point of view. Some old things with which we had grown familiar, and which had begun to creep into the very habit of our thought and of our lives, have altered their aspect as we have latterly looked critically upon them, with fresh, awakened eyes; have dropped their disguises and shown themselves alien and sinister. Some new things, as we look frankly upon them, willing to comprehend their real character, have come to assume the aspect of things long believed in and familiar, stuff of our own convictions. We have been refreshed by a new insight into our own life.

We see that in many things that life is very great. It is incomparably great in its material aspects, in its body of wealth, in the diversity and sweep of its energy, in the industries which have been conceived and built up by the genius of individual men and the limitless enterprise of groups of men. It is great, also, very great, in its moral force.

Nowhere else in the world have noble men and women exhibited in more striking forms the beauty and the energy of sympathy and helpfulness and counsel in their efforts to rectify wrong, alleviate suffering, and set the weak in the way of strength and hope. We have built up, moreover, a great system of government, which has stood through a long age as in many respects a model for those who seek to set liberty upon foundations that will endure against fortuitous change, against storm and accident. Our life contains every great thing, and contains it in rich abundance.

But the evil has come with the good, and much fine gold has been corroded. With riches has come inexcusable waste. We have squandered a great part of what we might have used, and have not stopped to conserve the exceeding bounty of nature, without which our genius for enterprise would have been worthless and impotent, scorning to be careful, shamefully prodigal as well as admirably efficient. We have been proud of our industrial achievements, but we have not hitherto stopped thoughtfully enough to count the human cost, the cost of lives snuffed out, of energies overtaxed and broken, the fearful physical and spiritual cost to the men and women and children upon whom the dead weight and burden of it all has fallen pitilessly the years through. The groans and agony of it all had not yet reached our ears, the solemn, moving undertone of our life, coming up out of the mines and factories and out of every home where the struggle had its intimate and familiar seat. With the great Government went many deep secret things which we too long delayed to look into and scrutinize with candid, fearless eyes. The great Government we loved has too often been made use of for private and selfish purposes, and those who used it had forgotten the people.

At last a vision has been vouchsafed us of our life as a whole. We see the bad with the good, the debased and decadent with the sound and vital. With this vision we approach new affairs. Our duty is to cleanse, to reconsider, to restore, to correct the evil without impairing the good, to purify and humanize every process of our common life without weakening or sentimentalizing it. There has been something crude and heartless and unfeeling in our haste to succeed and be great. Our thought has been "Let every man look out for himself, let every generation look out for itself," while we reared giant machinery which made it impossible that any but those who stood at the levels of control should have a chance to look out for themselves. We had not forgotten our morals. We remembered well enough that we had set up a policy which was meant to serve the humblest as well as the most powerful, with an eye single to the standards of justice and fair play, and remembered it with pride. But we were very heedless and in a hurry to be great.

We have come now to the sober second thought. The scales of heedlessness have fallen from our eyes. We have made up our minds to square every process of our national life again with the standards we so proudly set up at the beginning and have always carried at our hearts. Our work is a work of restoration.

We have itemized with some degree of particularity the things that ought to be altered and here are some of the chief items: A tariff which cuts us off from our proper part in the commerce of the world, violates the just principles of taxation, and makes the Government a facile instrument in the hands of private interests; a banking and currency system based upon the necessity of the Government to sell its bonds fifty years ago and perfectly adapted to concentrating cash and restricting credits; an industrial system which, take it on all its sides, financial as well as administrative, holds capital in leading strings, restricts the liberties and limits the opportunities of labor, and exploits without renewing or conserving the natural resources of the country; a body of agricultural activities never yet given the efficiency of great business undertakings or served as it should be through the instrumentality of science taken directly to the farm, or afforded the facilities of credit best suited to its practical needs; watercourses undeveloped, waste places unreclaimed, forests untended, fast disappearing without plan or prospect of renewal, unregarded waste heaps at every mine. We have studied as perhaps no other nation has the most effective means of production, but we have not studied cost or economy as we should either as organizers of industry, as statesmen, or as individuals.

Nor have we studied and perfected the means by which government may be put at the service of humanity, in safeguarding the health of the Nation, the health of its men and its women and its children, as well as their rights in the struggle for existence. This is no sentimental duty. The firm basis of government is justice, not pity. These are matters of justice. There can be no equality of opportunity, the first essential of justice in the body politic, if men and women and children be not shielded in their lives, their very vitality, from the consequences of great industrial and social processes which they can not alter, control, or singly cope with. Society must see to it that it does not itself crush or weaken or damage its own constituent parts. The first duty of law is to keep sound the society it serves. Sanitary laws, pure food laws, and laws determining conditions of labor which individuals are powerless to determine for themselves are intimate parts of the very business of justice and legal efficiency.

These are some of the things we ought to do, and not leave the others undone, the old-fashioned, never-to-be-neglected, fundamental safeguarding of property and of individual right. This is the high enterprise of the new day: to lift everything that concerns our life as a Nation to the light that shines from the hearthfire of every man's conscience and vision of the right. It is inconceivable that we should do this as partisans; it is inconceivable we should do it in ignorance of the facts as they are or in blind haste. We shall restore, not destroy. We shall deal with our economic system as it is and as it may be modified, not as it might be if we had a clean sheet of paper to write upon; and step by step we shall make it what it should be, in the spirit of those who question their own wisdom and seek counsel and knowledge, not shallow self-satisfaction or the excitement of excursions whither they cannot tell. Justice, and only justice, shall always be our motto.

And yet it will be no cool process of mere science. The Nation has been deeply stirred, stirred by a solemn passion, stirred by the knowledge of wrong, of ideals lost, of government too often debauched and made an instrument of evil. The feelings with which we face this new age of right and opportunity sweep across our heartstrings like some air out of God's own presence, where justice and mercy are reconciled and the judge and the brother are one. We know our task to be no mere task of politics but a task which shall search us through and through, whether we be able to understand our time and the need of our people, whether we be indeed their spokesmen and interpreters, whether we have the pure heart to comprehend and the rectified will to choose our high course of action.

This is not a day of triumph; it is a day of dedication. Here muster, not the forces of party, but the forces of humanity. Men's hearts wait upon us; men's lives hang in the balance; men's hopes call upon us to say what we will do. Who shall live up to the great trust? Who dares fail to try? I summon all honest men, all patriotic, all forward-looking men, to my side. God helping me, I will not fail them, if they will but counsel and sustain me!

2. The Lasting Interest of the Peoples

Statement on Latin America, March 11 ,1913

One of Wilson's first items of business was to define a new policy for Latin America. It was necessary to repudiate Dollar Diplomacy and support for such dictators as Huerta of Mexico. Wilson's statement below surprised the diplomats but gratified the American public.

ONE OF the chief objects of my administration will be to cultivate the friendship and deserve the confidence of our sister republics of Central and South America, and to promote in every proper and honorable way the interests which are common to the peoples of the two continents. I earnestly desire the most cordial understanding and cooperation between the peoples and leaders of America and, therefore, deem it my duty to make this brief statement.

Cooperation is possible only when supported at every turn by the orderly processes of just government based upon law, not upon arbitrary or irregular force. We hold, as I am sure all thoughtful leaders of republican government everywhere hold, that just government rests always upon the consent of the governed, and that there can be no freedom without order based upon law and upon the public conscience and approval. We shall look to make these principles the basis of mutual intercourse, respect, and helpfulness between our sister republics and ourselves. We shall lend our influence of every kind to the realization of these principles in fact and practice, knowing that disorder, personal intrigues, and defiance of constitutional rights weaken and discredit government and injure none so much as the people who are unfortunate enough to have their common life and their common affairs so tainted and disturbed. We can have no sympathy with those who seek to seize the power of government to advance their own personal interests or ambition. We are the friends of peace, but we know that there can be no lasting or stable peace in such circumstances. As friends, therefore, we shall prefer those who act in the interest of peace and honor, who protect private rights, and respect the restraints of constitutional provision. Mutual respect seems to us the indispensable foundation of friendship between states, as between individuals.

The United States has nothing to seek in Central and South America except the lasting interests of the peoples of the two continents, the security of governments intended for the people and for no special group or interest, and the development of personal and trade relationships between the two continents which shall redound to the profit and advantage of both and interfere with the rights and liberties of neither.

From these principles may be read so much of the future policy of this Government as it is necessary now to forecast, and in the spirit of these principles I may, I hope, be permitted with as much confidence as earnestness to extend to the Governments of all the Republics of America the hand of genuine disinterested friendship, and to pledge my own honor and the honor of my colleagues to every enterprise of peace and amity that a fortunate future may disclose.

3. This Is the Only Open Door

Statement on Loan to China, March 18, 1913

Wilson had a chance to add meaning to the New Diplomacy when he confronted the impending "Six Power Loan" to China. In 1911 a consortium of banking interests from six countries, including the United States, had been established to lend the Chinese government 125 million dollars to build the Hukuang Railroad. The Taft administration had supported the consortium. But Wilson, in keeping with his new policy of recognizing the independence of nations, and in denying support for Dollar Diplomacy, issued the statement below. The next day the American banking groups withdrew from the consortium.

WE ARE informed that at the request of the last administration a certain group of American bankers undertook to participate in the loan now desired by the Government of China (approximately $125,000,000). Our Government wished American bankers to participate along with the bankers of other nations, because it desired that the good will of the United States toward China should be exhibited in this practical way, that American capital should have access to that great country, and that the United States should be in a position to share with the other powers any political responsibilities that might be associated with the development of the foreign relations of China in connection with her industrial and commercial enterprises. The present administration has been asked by this group of bankers whether it would also request them to participate in the loan. The representatives of the bankers through whom the administration was approached declared that they would continue to seek their share of the loan under the proposed agreements only if expressly requested to do so by the Government. The administration has declined to make such request, because it did not approve the conditions of the loan or the implications of responsibility on its own part which it was plainly told would be involved in the request.

The conditions of the loan seem to us to touch very nearly the administrative independence of China itself, and this administration does not feel that it ought, even by implication, to be a party to those conditions. The responsibility on its part which would be implied in requesting the bankers to undertake the loan might conceivably go the length in some unhappy contingency of forcible interference in the financial, and even the political, affairs of that great oriental State, just now awakening to a consciousness of its power and of its obligations to its people. The conditions include not only the pledging of particular taxes, some of them antiquated and burdensome, to secure the loan, but also the administration of those taxes by foreign agents. The responsibility on the part of our Government implied in the encouragement of a loan thus secured and administered is plain enough and is obnoxious to the principles upon which the government of our people rests.

The Government of the United States is not only willing, but earnestly desirous, of aiding the great Chinese people in every way that is consistent with their untrammeled development and its own immemorial principles. The awakening of the people of China to a consciousness of their responsibilities under free government is the most significant, if not the most momentous, event of our generation. With this movement and aspiration the American people are in profound sympathy. They certainly wish to participate, and participate very generously, in the opening to the Chinese and to the use of the world the almost untouched and perhaps unrivaled resources of China.

The Government of the United States is earnestly desirous of promoting the most extended and intimate trade relationship between this country and the Chinese Republic. The present administration will urge and support the legislative measure necessary to give American merchants, manufacturers, contractors, and engineers the banking and other financial facilities which they now lack and without which they are at a serious disadvantage as compared with their industrial and commercial rivals. This is its duty. This is the main material interest of its citizens in the development of China. Our interests are those of the open door—a door of friendship and mutual advantage. This is the only door we care to enter.

4. Masters of Competitive Supremacy

Address to Congress on the Tariff, April 8, 1913

Since Reconstruction, the tariff had been the most important single issue before the nation. The Democrats on the whole had traditionally favored lower tariffs, and it was expected that some attempt at reform would be made now that they held the presidency and—with the help of a handful of progressive Republicans—dominated Congress. On April 7, Wilson called Congress for a special session to reform the Payne-Aldrich Tariff of 1909. The next day he gave the following address, the first presidential speech to Congress since John Adams's administration.

GENTLEMEN OF the Congress: I am very glad indeed to have this opportunity to address the two Houses directly and to verify for myself the impression that the President of the United States is a person, not a mere department of the Government hailing Congress from some isolated island of jealous power, sending messages, not speaking naturally and with his own voice—that he is a human being trying to co-operate with other human beings in a common service. After this pleasant experience I shall feel quite normal in all our dealings with one another.

I have called the Congress together in extraordinary session because a duty was laid upon the party now in power at the recent elections which it ought to perform promptly, in order that the burden carried by the people under existing law may be lightened as soon as possible, and in order, also, that the business interests of the country may not be kept too long in suspense as to what the fiscal changes are to be to which they will be required to adjust themselves. It is clear to the whole country that the tariff duties must be altered. They must be changed to meet the radical alteration in the conditions of our economic life which the country has witnessed within the last generation. While the whole face and method of our industrial and commercial life were being changed beyond recognition the tariff schedules have remained what they were before the change began, or have moved in the direction they were given when no large circumstance of our industrial development was what it is today. Our task is to square them with the actual facts. The sooner that is done the sooner we shall escape from suffering from the facts and the sooner our men of business will be free to thrive by the law of nature—the nature of free business—instead of by the law of legislation and artificial arrangement.

We have seen tariff legislation wander very far afield in our day—very far indeed from the field in which our prosperity might have had a normal growth and stimulation. No one who looks the facts squarely in the face or knows anything that lies beneath the surface of action can fail to perceive the principles upon which recent tariff legislation has been based. We long ago passed beyond the modest notion of "protecting" the industries of the country and moved boldly forward to the idea that they were entitled to the direct patronage of the Government. For a long time —a time so long that the men now active in public policy hardly remember the conditions that preceded it—we have sought in our tariff schedules to give each group of manufacturers or producers what they themselves thought that they needed in order to maintain a practically exclusive market as against the rest of the world. Consciously or unconsciously, we have built up a set of privileges and exemptions from competition behind which it was easy by any, even the crudest, forms of combination to organize monopoly; until at last nothing is normal, nothing is obliged to stand the tests of efficiency and economy, in our world of big business, but everything thrives by concerted arrangement. Only new principles of action will save us from a final hard crystallization of monopoly and a complete loss of the influences that quicken enterprise and keep independent energy alive.

It is plain what those principles must be. We must abolish everything that bears even the semblance of privilege or of any kind of artificial advantage, and put our business men and producers under the stimulation of a constant necessity to be efficient, economical, and enterprising, masters of competitive supremacy, better workers and merchants than any in the world. Aside from the duties laid upon articles which we do not, and probably can not, produce, therefore, and the duties laid upon luxuries and merely for the sake of the revenues they yield, the object of the tariff duties henceforth laid must be effective competition, the whetting of American wits by contest with the wits of the rest of the world.

It would be unwise to move toward this end headlong, with reckless haste, or with strokes that cut at the very roots of what has grown up amongst us by long process and at our own invitation. It does not alter a thing to upset it and break it and deprive it of a chance to change. It destroys it. We must make changes in our fiscal laws, in our fiscal system, whose object is development, a more free and wholesome development, not revolution or upset or confusion. We must build up trade, especially foreign trade. We need the outlet and the enlarged field of energy more than we ever did before. We must build up industry as well, and must adopt freedom in the place of artificial stimulation only so far as it will build, not pull down. In dealing with the tariff the method by which this may be done will be a matter of judgment exercised item by item. To some not accustomed to the excitements and responsibilities of greater freedom our methods may in some respects and at some points seem heroic but remedies may be heroic and yet be remedies. It is our business to make sure that they are genuine remedies. Our object is clear. If our motive is above just challenge and only an occasional error of judgment is chargeable against us, we shall be fortunate.

We are called upon to render the country a great service in more matters than one. Our responsibility should be met and our methods should be thorough, as thorough as moderate and well considered, based upon the facts as they are, and not worked out as if we were beginners. We are to deal with the facts of our own day, with the facts of no other and to make laws which square with those facts. It is best, indeed it is necessary, to begin with the tariff. I will urge nothing upon you now at the opening of your session which can obscure the first object or divert our energies from that clearly defined duty. At a later time I may take the liberty of calling your attention to reforms which should press close upon the heels of the tariff changes, if not accompany them, of which the chief is the reform of our banking and currency laws; but just now I refrain. For the present, I put these matters on one side and think only of this one thing—of the changes in our fiscal system which may best serve to open once more the free channels of prosperity to a great people whom we would serve to the utmost and throughout both rank and file.

I sincerely thank you for your courtesy.

5. The Control Must Be Public

Address to Congress on Currency and Banking, June 23, 1913

If tariff reform was to be the first step, currency and banking reform was to be the second on the road to a New Freedom. Many of Wilson's advisors, including Bryan, the most radical member of the cabinet, opposed presenting to Congress another important piece of legislation before the first had passed. But Wilson went ahead—and succeeded. The Federal Reserve bill occupied most of his energies between June 23, when he proposed it, and December 23, when he signed it into law.

GENTLEMEN OF the Congress: It is under the compulsion of what seems to me a clear and imperative duty that I have a second time this session sought the privilege of addressing you in person. . . . It is absolutely imperative that we should give the business men of this country a banking and currency system by means of which they can make use of the freedom of enterprise and of individual initiative which we are about to bestow upon them.

We are about to set them free; we must not leave them without the tools of action when they are free. We are about to set them free by removing the trammels of the protective tariff. Ever since the Civil War they have waited for this emancipation and for the free opportunities it will bring with it. It has been reserved for us to give it to them. Some fell in love, indeed, with the slothful security of their dependence upon the Government; some took advantage of the shelter of the nursery to set up a mimic mastery of their own within its walls. Now both the tonic and the discipline of liberty and maturity are to ensue. There will be some readjustments of purpose and point of view. There will follow a period of expansion and new enterprise, freshly conceived. It is for us to determine now whether it shall be rapid and facile and of easy accomplishment. This it can not be unless the resourceful busisness men who are to deal with the new circumstances are to have at hand and ready for use the instrumentalities and conveniences of free enterprise which independent men need when acting on their own initiative.

It is not enough to strike the shackles from business. The duty of statesmanship is not negative merely. It is constructive also. We must show that we understand what business needs and that we know how to supply it. No man, however casual and superficial his observation of the conditions now prevailing in the country, can fail to see that one of the chief things business needs now and will need increasingly as it gains in scope and vigor in the years immediately ahead of us is the proper means by which readily to vitalize its credit, corporate and individual, and its originative brains. What will it profit us to be free if we are not to have the best and most accessible instrumentalities of commerce and enterprise? What will it profit us to be quit of one kind of monopoly if we are to remain in the grip of another and more effective kind? How are we to gain and keep the confidence of the business community unless we show that we know how both to aid and to protect it? What shall we say if we make fresh enterprise necessary and also make it very difficult by leaving all else except the tariff just as we found it? The tyrannies of business, big and little, lie within the field of credit. We know that. Shall we not act upon the knowledge? Do we not know how to act upon it? If a man can not make his assets available at pleasure, his assets of capacity and character and resource, what satisfaction is it to him to see opportunity beckoning to him on every hand when others have the keys of credit in their pockets and treat them as all but their own private possession? It is perfectly clear that it is our duty to supply the new banking and currency system the country needs, and it will need it immediately more than it has ever needed it before.

The only question is, When shall we supply it—now or later, after the demands shall have become reproaches that we were so dull and so slow? Shall we hasten to change the tariff laws and then be laggards about making it possible and easy for the country to take advantage of the change? There can be only one answer to that question. We must act now, at whatever sacrifice to ourselves. It is a duty which the circumstances forbid us to postpone. I should be recreant to my deepest convictions of public obligation did I not press it upon you with solemn and urgent insistence.

The principles upon which we should act are also clear. The country has sought and seen its path in this matter within the last few years—sees it more clearly now than it ever saw it before—much more clearly than when the last legislative proposals on the subject were made. We must have a currency, not rigid as now, but readily, elastically responsive to sound credit, the expanding and contracting credits of everyday transactions, the normal ebb and flow of personal and corporate dealings. Our banking laws must mobilize reserves; must not permit the concentration anywhere in a few hands of the monetary resources of the country or their use for speculative purposes in such volume as to hinder or impede or stand in the way of other more legitimate, more fruitful uses. And the control of the system of banking and of issue which our new laws are to set up must be public, not private, must be vested in the Government itself, so that the banks may be the instruments, not the masters, of business and of individual enterprise and initiative. . . .

6. I Do Approve of the Segregation

To H. A. Bridgman, September 8, 1913

In response to the demands of the Democratic party, Wilson instituted racial segregation in the Federal government. Wilson thus served notice that the New Freedom did not apply to Negroes. Bridgman, a Protestant minister, had complained to Wilson about the new policy.

IN REPLY to your kind letter of September fourth, I would say that I do approve of the segregation that is being attempted in several of the departments. I have not always approved of the way in which the thing was done and have tried to change that in some instances for the better, but I think if you were here on the ground you would see, as I seem to see, that it is distinctly to the advantage of the colored people themselves that they should be organized, so far as possible and convenient, in distinct bureaux where they will center their work. Some of the most thoughtful colored men I have conversed with have themselves approved of this policy. I certainly myself would not have approved of it if I had not thought it to their advantage and likely to remove many of the difficulties which have surrounded the appointment and advancement of colored men and women. . . .

7. The Relationship of a Family

Address on Latin America, October 27, 1913

Wilson learned from the Mexican embroglio that dictatorship and foreign economic imperialism went hand in hand. (He believed that British interests were behind Huerta.) He wanted to make it clear in this address to the Southern Commercial Congress, meeting in Mobile, Alabama, that henceforward American policy would value human rights and popular government over property rights and dictatorial rule.

. . . THE FUTURE, ladies and gentlemen, is going to be very different for this hemisphere from the past. These States lying to the south of us, which have always been our neighbors, will now be drawn closer to us by innumerable ties, and, I hope, chief of all, by the tie of a common understanding of each other. Interest does not tie nations together; it sometimes separates them. But sympathy and understanding does unite them, and I believe that by the new route that is just about to be opened, while we physically cut two continents asunder, we spiritually unite them. It is a spiritual union which we seek. . . .

There is one peculiarity about the history of the Latin American States which I am sure they are keenly aware of. You hear of "concessions" to foreign capitalists in Latin America. You do not hear of concessions to foreign capitalists in the United States. They are not granted concessions. They are invited to make investments. The work is ours, though they are welcome to invest in it. We do not ask them to supply the capital and do the work. It is an invitation, not a privilege; and States that are obliged, because their territory does not lie within the main field of modern enterprise and action, to grant concessions are in this condition, that foreign interests are apt to dominate their domestic affairs, a condition of affairs always dangerous and apt to become intolerable. What these States are going to see, therefore, is an emancipation from the subordination, which has been inevitable, to foreign enterprise and an assertion of the splendid character which, in spite of these difficulties, they have again and again been able to demonstrate. The dignity, the courage, the self-possession, the self-respect of the Latin American States, their achievements in the face of all these adverse circumstances, deserve nothing but the admiration and applause of the world. They have had harder bargains driven with them in the matter of loans than any other peoples in the world. Interest has been exacted of them that was not exacted of anybody else, because the risk was said to be greater; and then securities were taken that destroyed the risk—an admirable arrangement for those who were forcing the terms! I rejoice in nothing so much as in the prospect that they will now be emancipated from these conditions, and we ought to be the first to take part in assisting in that emancipation. I think some of these gentlemen have already had occasion to bear witness that the Department of State in recent months has tried to serve them in that wise. In the future they will draw closer and closer to us because of circumstances of which I wish to speak with moderation and, I hope, without indiscretion.

We must prove ourselves their friends, and champions upon terms of equality and honor. You cannot be friends upon any other terms than upon the terms of equality. You cannot be friends at all except upon the terms of honor. We must show ourselves friends by comprehending their interest whether it squares with our own interest or not. It is a very perilous thing to determine the foreign policy of a nation in the terms of material interest. It not only is unfair to those with whom you are dealing, but it is degrading as regards your own actions.

Comprehension must be the soil in which shall grow all the fruits of friendship, and there is a reason and a compulsion lying behind all this which is dearer than anything else to the thoughtful men of America. I mean the development of constitutional liberty in the world. Human rights, national integrity, and opportunity as against material interests—that, ladies and gentlemen, is the issue which we now have to face. I want to take this occasion to say that the United States will never again seek one additional foot of territory by conquest. She will devote herself to showing that she knows how to make honorable and fruitful use of the territory she has, and she must regard it as one of the duties of friendship to see that from no quarter are material interests made superior to human liberty and national opportunity.

I say this, not with a single thought that anyone will gainsay it, but merely to fix in our consciousness what our real relationship with the rest of America is. It is the relationship of a family of mankind devoted to the development of true constitutional liberty. We know that that is the soil out of which the best enterprise springs. We know that this is a cause which we are making in common with our neighbors, because we have had to make it for ourselves. . . .

8. The Business Conscience and Honor

Address to Congress on Trusts and Monopolies, January 20, 1914

In framing new antitrust legislation, Wilson had two objects in mind: to control more strictly the activities of the trusts in accordance with his campaign promise of 1912, and to exempt labor unions from the antitrust provisions. In his address to Congress on the subject he emphasized the possibility of harmony between government and big business. On January 3 several large Wall Street houses, knowing that legislation was pending, had announced that they were divesting themselves of many directorships. Some of Wilson's friends thought it was "unconditional surrender." His address heralded passage, later in the year, of the Federal Trade Commission Act and the Clayton Antitrust Act.

. . . CONSTRUCTIVE LEGISLATION, when successful, is always the embodiment of convincing experience and of the mature public opinion which finally springs out of that experience. Legislation is a business of interpretation, not of origination; and it is now plain what the opinion is to which we must give effect in this matter. It is not recent or hasty opinion. It springs out of the experience of a whole generation. It has clarified itself by long contest, and those who for a long time battled with it and sought to change it are now frankly and honorably yielding to it and seeking to conform their actions to it. The great business men who organized and financed monopoly and those who administered it in actual everyday transactions have, year after year until now, either denied its existence or justified it as necessary for the effective maintenance and development of the vast business processes of the country in the modern circumstances of trade and manufacture and finance; but all the whole opinion has made head against them. The average business man is convinced that the ways of liberty are also the ways of peace and the ways of success as well; and at last the masters of business on the great scale have begun to yield their preference and purpose, perhaps their judgment also, in honorable surrender.

What we are purposing to do, therefore, is, happily, not to hamper or interfere with business as enlightened business men prefer to do it, or in any sense to put it under the ban. The antagonism between business and Government is over. We are now about to give expression to the best business judgment of America, to what we know to be the business conscience and honor of the land. The Government and business men are ready to meet each other halfway in a common effort to square business methods with both public opinion and the law. The best-informed men of the business world condemn the methods and processes and consequences of monopoly as we condemn them, and the instinctive judgment of the vast majority of business men everywhere goes with them. We shall now be their spokesmen. That is the strength of our position and the sure prophecy of what will ensue when our reasonable work is done.

When serious contest ends, when men unite in opinion and purpose, those who are to change their ways of business joining with those who ask for the change, it is possible to effect it in the way in which prudent and thoughtful and patriotic men would most wish to see it brought about, with as few, as slight, as easy and simple business readjustments as possible in the circumstances, nothing essential disturbed, nothing torn up by the roots, no parts rent asunder which can be left in wholesome combination. Fortunately, no measures of sweeping or novel change are necessary. It will be understood that our object is *not* to unsettle business or anywhere seriously to break its established courses athwart. On the contrary, we desire the laws we are now about to pass to be the bulwarks and safeguards of industry against the forces that now disturb them. What we have to do can be done in a new spirit, in quiet moderation, without revolution of any untoward kind.

We are all agreed that "private monopoly is indefensible and intolerable," and our program is founded upon that conviction. It will be a comprehensive but not a radical or unacceptable program and these are its items, the changes which opinion deliberately sanctions and for which business waits:

It waits with acquiescence, in the first place, for laws which will effectually prohibit and prevent such interlockings of the *personnel* of the directorates of great corporations—banks and railroads, industrial, commercial, and public service bodies—as in effect result in making those who borrow and those who lend practically one and the same, those who sell and those who buy but the same persons trading with one another under different names and in different combinations, and those who affect to compete in fact partners and masters of the whole field of particular kinds of business. Sufficient time should be allowed, of course, in which to effect these changes of organization without inconvenience or confusion.

Such a prohibition will work much more than a mere negative good by correcting the serious evils which have arisen because, for example, the men who have been the directing spirits of the great investment banks have usurped the place which belongs to independent industrial management working in its own behoof. It will bring new men, new energies, a new spirit of initiative, new blood, into the management of our great business enterprises. It will open the field of industrial development and origination to scores of men who have been obliged to serve when their abilities entitled them to direct. It will immensely hearten the young men coming on and will greatly enrich the business activities of the whole country.

In the second place, business men as well as those who direct public affairs now recognize, and recognize with painful clearness, the great harm and injustice which has been done to many, if not all, of the great railroad systems of the country by the way in which they have been financed and their own distinctive interests subordinated to the interests of the men who financed them and of other business enterprises which those men wished to promote. The country is ready, therefore, to accept, and accept with relief as well as approval, a law which will confer upon the Interstate Commerce Commission the power to superintend and regulate the financial operations by which the railroads are henceforth to be supplied with the money they need for their proper development to meet the rapidly growing requirements of the country for increased and improved facilities of transportation. We cannot postpone action in this matter without leaving the railroads exposed to many serious handicaps and hazards; and the prosperity of the railroads and the prosperity of the country are inseparably connected. Upon this question those who are chiefly responsible for the actual management and operation of the railroads have spoken very plainly and very earnestly, with a purpose we ought to be quick to accept. It will be one step, and a very important one, towards the necessary separation of the business of production from the business of transportation.

The business of the country awaits also, has long awaited and has suffered because it could not obtain, further and more explicit legislative definition of the policy and meaning of the existing antitrust law. Nothing hampers business like uncertainty. Nothing daunts or discourages it like the necessity to take chances, to run the risk of falling under the condemnation of the law before it can make sure just what the law is. Surely we are sufficiently familiar with the actual processes and methods of monopoly and of the many hurtful restraints of trade to make definition possible, at any rate up to the limits of what experience has disclosed. These practices, being now abundantly disclosed, can be explicitly and item by item forbidden by statute in such terms as will practically eliminate uncertainty, the law itself and the penalty being made equally plain.

And the business men of the country desire something more than that the menace of legal process in these matters be made explicit and intelligible. They desire the advice, the definite guidance, and information which can be supplied by an administrative body, an interstate trade commission.

The opinion of the country would instantly approve of such a commission. It would not wish to see it empowered to make terms with monopoly or in any sort to assume control of business, as if the Government made itself responsible. It demands such a commission only as an indispensable instrument of information and publicity, as a clearing house for the facts by which both the public mind and the managers of the great business undertakings should be guided, and as an instrumentality for doing justice to business where the processes of the courts or the natural forces of correction outside the courts are inadequate to adjust the remedy to the wrong in a way that will meet all the equities and circumstances of the case.

Producing industries, for example, which have passed the point up to which combination may be consistent with the public interest and the freedom of trade, can not always be dissected into their component units as readily as railroad companies or similar organizations can be. Their dissolution by ordinary legal process may oftentimes involve financial consequences likely to overwhelm the security market and bring upon it breakdown and confusion. There ought to be an administrative commission capable of directing and shaping such corrective processes, not only in aid of the courts but also by independent suggestion, if necessary.

Inasmuch as our object and the spirit of our action in these matters is to meet business half way in its processes of self-correction and disturb its legitimate course as little as possible, we ought to see to it, and the judgment of practical and sagacious men of affairs everywhere would applaud us if we did see to it, that penalties and punishments should fall not upon business itself, to its confusion and interruption, but upon the individuals who use the instrumentalities of business to do things which public policy and sound business practice condemn. Every act of business is done at the command or upon the initiative of some ascertainable person or group of persons. These should be held individually responsible and the punishment should fall upon them, not upon the business organization of which they make illegal use. It should be one of the main objects of our legislation to divest such persons of their corporate cloak and deal with them as with those who do not represent their corporations, but merely by deliberate intention break the law. Business men the country through would, I am sure, applaud us if we were to take effectual steps to see that the officers and directors of great business bodies were prevented from bringing them and the business of the country in general into disrepute and danger.

Other questions remain which will need very thoughtful and practical treatment. Enterprises in these modern days of great individual fortunes are oftentimes interlocked, not by being under the control of the same directors but by the fact that the greater part of their corporate stock is owned by a single person or group of persons who are in some way intimately related in interest. We are agreed, I take it, that holding *companies* should be prohibited, but what of the controlling private ownership of individuals or actually co-operative groups of individuals? Shall the private owners of capital stock be suffered to be themselves in effect holding companies? We do not wish, I suppose, to forbid the purchase of stocks by any person who pleases to buy them in such quantities as he can afford, or in any way arbitrarily to limit the sale of stocks to bona fide purchasers. Shall we require the owners of stock, when their voting power in several companies which ought to be independent of one another would constitute actual control, to make election in which of them they will exercise their right to vote? This question I venture for your consideration.

There is another matter in which imperative considerations of justice and fair play suggest thoughtful remedial action. Not only do many of the combinations effected or sought to be effected in the industrial world work an injustice upon the public in general; they also directly and seriously injure the individuals who are put out of business in one unfair way or another by the many dislodging and exterminating forces of combination. I hope that we shall agree in giving private individuals who claim to have been injured by these processes the right to found their suits for redress upon the facts and judgments proved and entered in suits by the Government where the Government has upon its own initiative sued the combinations complained of and won its suit, and that the statute of limitations shall be suffered to run against such litigants only from the date of the conclusion of the Government's action. It is not fair that the private litigant should be obliged to set up and establish again the facts which the Government has proved. He cannot afford, he has not the power, to make use of such processes of inquiry as the Government has command of. Thus shall individual justice be done while the processes of business are rectified and squared with the general conscience.

I have laid the case before you, no doubt, as it lies in your own mind, as it lies in the thought of the country. What must every candid man say of the suggestions I have laid before you, of the plain obligations of which I have reminded you? That these are new things for which the country is not prepared? No; but that they are old things, now familiar, and must of course be undertaken if we are to square our laws with the thought and desire of the country. Until these things are done, conscientious business men the country over will be unsatisfied. They are in these things our mentors and colleagues. We are now about to write the additional articles of our constitution of peace, the peace that is honor and freedom and prosperity.

9. Such Wrongs and Annoyances

Address to Congress on Tampico and Vera Cruz Incidents, April 20, 1914

American relations with Mexico during Wilson's administration repeatedly mocked his intentions of respecting the sovereignty of Latin American countries. The Tampico and Vera Cruz incidents humiliated the Mexican people and nearly brought on war. In this address to Congress, Wilson explains what happened at Tampico and Vera Cruz. Far from pointing up the despotism of Huerta, as Wilson averred, the intervention united the Mexican people behind the dictator against a common enemy. On April 22, Congress gave Wilson the authority to use force, although American troops had already occupied the city of Vera Cruz. It was not until November 22—seven months later—that they withdrew, thanks to the mediation of Argentina, Brazil and Chile. The ABC Conference, as it was called, succeeded also in forcing Huerta to abdicate (July 15), thus allowing Carranza to take power.

GENTLEMEN OF the Congress: It is my duty to call your attention to a situation which has arisen in our dealings with Gen. Victoriano Huerta at Mexico City which calls for action, and to ask your advice and co-operation in acting upon it.

On April 9 a Paymaster of the U. S. S. *Dolphin* landed at the Iturbide bridge landing at Tampico with a whaleboat and boat's crew to take off certain supplies needed by his ship, and while engaged in loading the boat was arrested by an officer and squad of men of the army of General Huerta. Neither the Paymaster nor any one of the crew was armed. Two of the men were in the boat when the arrest took place, and were obliged to leave it and submit to be taken into custody, notwithstanding that the boat carried, both at her bow and at her stern, the flag of the United States. The officer who made the arrest was proceeding up one of the streets of the town with his prisoners when met by an officer of higher authority, who ordered him to return to the landing and await orders, and within an hour and a half from the time of the arrest, orders were received from the commander of the Huertista forces at Tampico for the release of the Paymaster and his men. The release was followed by apologies from the commander and also by an expression of regret by General Huerta himself. General Huerta urged that martial law obtained at the time at Tampico, that orders had been issued that no one should be allowed to land at the Iturbide bridge, and that our sailors had no right to land there. Our naval commanders at the port had not been notified of any such prohibition, and, even if they had been, the only justifiable course open to the local authorities would have been to request the Paymaster and his crew to withdraw and to lodge a protest with the commanding officer of the fleet. Admiral Mayo regarded the arrest as so serious an affront that he was not satisfied with the apologies offered, but demanded that the flag of the United States be saluted with special ceremony by the military commander of the port.

The incident can not be regarded as a trivial one, especially as two of the men arrested were taken from the boat itself—that is to say, from the territory of the United States; but had it stood by itself, it might have been attributed to the ignorance or arrogance of a single officer.

Unfortunately, it was not an isolated case. A series of incidents have recently occurred which cannot but create the impression that the representatives of General Huerta were willing to go out of their way to show disregard for the dignity and rights of this Government, and felt perfectly safe in doing what they pleased, making free to show in many ways their irritation and contempt.

A few days after the incident at Tampico an orderly from the U. S. S. *Minnesota* was arrested at Vera Cruz while ashore in uniform to obtain the ship's mail, and was for a time thrown into jail. An official dispatch from this Government to its embassy at

Mexico City was withheld by the authorities of the telegraphic service until peremptorily demanded by our *Chargé d'Affaires* in person.

So far as I can learn, such wrongs and annoyances have been suffered to occur only against representatives of the United States. I have heard of no complaints from other governments of similar treatment. Subsequent explanations and formal apologies did not and could not alter the popular impression, which it is possible it had been the object of the Huertista authorities to create, that the Government of the United States was being singled out, and might be singled out with impunity, for slights and affronts in retaliation for its refusal to recognize the pretensions of General Huerta to be regarded as the Constitutional Provisional President of the Republic of Mexico.

The manifest danger of such a situation was that such offenses might grow from bad to worse until something happened of so gross and intolerable a sort as to lead directly and inevitably to armed conflict. It was necessary that the apologies of General Huerta and his representatives should go much further, that they should be such as to attract the attention of the whole population to their significance, and such as to impress upon General Huerta himself the necessity of seeing to it that no further occasion for explanations and professed regrets should arise. I, therefore, felt it my duty to sustain Admiral Mayo in the whole of his demand and to insist that the flag of the United States should be saluted in such a way as to indicate a new spirit and attitude on the part of the Huertistas.

Such a salute General Huerta has refused, and I have come to ask your approval and support in the course I now propose to pursue.

This Government can, I earnestly hope, in no circumstances be forced into war with the people of Mexico. Mexico is torn by civil strife. If we are to accept the tests of its own Constitution, it has no government. General Huerta has set his power up in the City of Mexico, such as it is, without right and by methods for which there can be no justification. Only part of the country is under his control.

If armed conflict should unhappily come as a result of his attitude of personal resentment toward this Government, we should be fighting only General Huerta and those who adhere to him and give him their support, and our object would be only to restore to the people of the distracted republic the opportunity to set up again their own laws and their own government.

But I earnestly hope that war is not now in question. I believe that I speak for the American people when I say that we do not desire to control in any degree the affairs of our sister republic. Our feeling for the people of Mexico is one of deep and genuine friendship, and everything that we have so far done or refrained from doing has proceeded from our desire to help them, not to hinder or embarass them. We would not wish even to exercise the good offices of friendship without their welcome and consent.

The people of Mexico are entitled to settle their own domestic affairs in their own way, and we sincerely desire to respect their right. The present situation need have none of the grave complications of interference if we deal with it promptly, firmly, and wisely.

No doubt I could do what is necessary in the circumstances to force respect for our Government without recourse to the Congress, and yet not exceed my constitutional power as President; but I do not wish to act in a matter possibly of so grave consequence except in close conference and cooperation with both the Senate and House. I therefore come to ask your approval that I should use the armed forces of the United States in such ways and to such an extent as may be necessary to obtain from General Huerta and his adherents the fullest recognition of the rights and dignity of the United States, even amid the distressing conditions now unhappily obtaining in Mexico.

There can in what we do be no thought of aggression or of selfish aggrandizement. We seek to maintain the dignity and authority of the United States only because we wish always to keep our great influence unimpaired for the uses of liberty, both in the United States and wherever else it may be employed for the benefit of mankind.

10. A New Temper in Affairs

To Thomas D. Jones, July 23, 1914

Wilson had nominated Jones to be a member of the Federal Reserve Board. It was an unfortunate choice, since Jones sat on the board of the Harvester trust, then under criminal investigation. Senator Reed of Missouri went so far as to imply that Jones was a criminal and that Wilson committed a wrong in having nominated him. On July 20, Jones asked Wilson to withdraw his name. Following was Wilson's reply to Jones.

YOUR LETTER of the 20th of July brings to me, I think, more kinds of regret than any other letter I have ever received: Regret, first of all, that the country should lose the invaluable services of such a man as I, and all fair-minded men who know you at all, know you to be; regret that I should have brought upon you so unpleasant an experience, in which you were treated with gross and manifest injustice; regret that such circumstances should seem even for a moment to be associated with appointment to high office under the great Government of the United States, representing a generous, fair, and honorable people; regret that the organization of a great banking system should be so embarrassed and obstructed.

You need not think that anything in the present circumstances has embarrassed me in the least. It causes me not the slightest embarrassment. I have no moment of hesitation or flagging enthusiasm in standing by men whom I honor and believe in. It gives me nothing but pleasure and exhilaration to stand by them at any time and to any extent. You may leave my feelings (my feelings for myself) out of the reckoning.

The aspect of the matter which seems to me of the gravest concern and consequence is that the choice of members of the Federal Reserve Board of the new banking system should have been made an occasion of partisan alignment and action. . . . I believe that the judgment and desire of the whole country cry out for a new temper in affairs. The time has come when discrimination against particular classes of men should be absolutely laid aside and discarded as unworthy of the counsels of a great people. The effort for genuine social justice, for peace which is founded in common understanding and for prosperity, the prosperity of co-operation and mutual trust and confidence, should be a united effort, without partisan prejudice or class antagonism. It is only of such and noble elements that the welfare of a great country can be compounded. We have breathed already too long the air of suspicion and distrust. The progress of reform is not retarded by generosity and forebearance. . . .

11. The Nearest Friend

Wilson Plan for Dominican Republic, July 27, 1914

In 1905 President Roosevelt had intervened in the Dominican Republic after a succession of revolutions. In 1907 the United States had taken control of customs collection—the Republic's main source of revenue. Under American coercion the Republic held a free election early in 1914 which led to great political unrest among the different factions. Moreover, the finances of the country were chaotic. Once again the United States intervened. Following is Wilson's policy toward the Dominican Republic. Under the so-called Wilson Plan, stability was achieved temporarily, but a year later American troops were used to enforce its provisions.

THE GOVERNMENT of the United States desires nothing for itself from the Dominican Republic and no concessions or advantages for its citizens which are not accorded citizens of other countries. It desires only to prove its sincere and disinterested friendship for the Republic and its people and to fulfill its responsibilities as the friend to whom in such crises as the present all the world looks to guide Santo Domingo out of its difficulties.

It, therefore, makes the following earnest representations not only to the existing de facto Government of the Dominican Republic, but also to all who are in any way responsible for the present posture of affairs there:

I. It warns everyone concerned that it is absolutely imperative that the present hostilities should cease and that all who are concerned in them should disperse to their several homes, disbanding the existing armed forces and returning to the peaceful occupations upon which the welfare of the people of the Republic depends. This is necessary, and necessary at once. Nothing can be successfully accomplished until this is done.

II. It is also necessary that there should be an immediate reconstitution of political authority in the Republic. To this end the Government of the United States very solemnly advises all concerned with the public affairs of the Republic to adopt the following plan:

(1) Let all those who have any pretensions to be chosen President of the Republic and who can make any sufficient show of exercising a recognized leadership and having an acknowledged following agree upon some responsible and representative man to act as Provisional President of the Republic, it being understood that Mr. Bordas will relinquish his present position and authority. If these candidates can agree in this matter, the Government of the United States will recognize and support the man of their choice as Provisional President. If they cannot agree, the Government of the United States will itself name a Provisional President, sustain him in the assumption of office, and support him in the exercise of his temporary authority. The Provisional President will not be a candidate for President.

(2) At the earliest feasible date after the establishment and recognition of the Provisional Government thus established let elections for a regular President and Congress be held under the authority and direction of the Provisional President, who will, it must of course be understood, exercise during his tenure of office the full powers of President of the Republic; but let it be understood that the Government of the United States will send representatives of its own choosing to observe the election throughout the Republic and that it will expect those observers not only to be accorded a courteous welcome but also to be accorded the freest opportunities to observe the circumstances and processes of the election.

(3) Let it be understood that if the United States Government is satisfied that these elections have been free and fair and carried out under conditions which enable the people of the Republic

to express their real choice, it will recognize the President and Congress thus chosen as the legitimate and constitutional Government of the Republic and will support them in the exercise of their functions and authority in every way it can. If it should not be satisfied that elections of the right kind have been held, let it be understood that another election will be held at which the mistakes observed will be corrected.

III. A regular and constitutional government having thus been set up, the Government of the United States would feel at liberty thereafter to insist that revolutionary movements cease and that all subsequent changes in the Government of the Republic be effected by the peaceful processes provided in the Dominican Constitution. By no other course can the Government of the United States fulfill its treaty obligations with Santo Domingo or its tacitly conceded obligations as the nearest friend of Santo Domingo in her relations with the rest of the world.

12. Neutral in Fact as Well as in Name

Statement on Neutrality, August 18, 1914

The First World War began in the first week of August 1914. In delivering this message to the people, Wilson wanted not only to affirm a policy of strict neutrality but also to keep America in a position to help in the event of peace negotiations.

MY FELLOW countrymen: I suppose that every thoughtful man in America has asked himself, during these last troubled weeks, what influence the European war may exert upon the United States, and I take the liberty of addressing a few words to you in order to point out that it is entirely within our own choice what its effects upon us will be and to urge very earnestly upon you the sort of speech and conduct which will best safeguard the Nation against distress and disaster.

The effect of the war upon the United States will depend upon what American citizens say and do. Every man who really loves America will act and speak in the true spirit of neutrality, which is the spirit of impartiality and fairness and friendliness to all concerned. The spirit of the Nation in this critical matter will be determined largely by what individuals and society and those gathered in public meetings do and say, upon what newspapers and magazines contain, upon what ministers utter in their pulpits, and men proclaim as their opinions on the street.

The people of the United States are drawn from many nations, and chiefly from the nations now at war. It is natural and inevitable that there should be the utmost variety of sympathy and desire among them with regard to the issues and circumstances of the conflict. Some will wish one nation, others another, to succeed in the momentous struggle. It will be easy to excite passion and difficult to allay it. Those responsible for exciting it will assume a heavy responsibility, responsibility for no less a thing than that the people of the United States, whose love of their country and whose loyalty to its Government should unite them as Americans all, bound in honor and affection to think first of her and her interests, may be divided in camps of hostile opinion, hot against each other, involved in the war itself in impulse and opinion if not in action.

Such divisions amongst us would be fatal to our peace of mind and might seriously stand in the way of the proper performance of our duty as the one great nation at peace, the one people holding itself ready to play a part of impartial mediation and speak the counsels of peace and accommodation, not as a partisan, but as a friend.

I venture, therefore, my fellow countrymen, to speak a solemn word of warning to you against that deepest, most subtle, most essential breach of neutrality which may spring out of partisanship, out of passionately taking sides. The United States must be neutral in fact as well as in name during these days that are to try men's souls. We must be impartial in thought as well as in action, must put a curb upon our sentiments as well as upon every transaction that might be construed as a preference of one party to the struggle before another.

My thought is of America. I am speaking, I feel sure, the earnest wish and purpose of every thoughtful American that this great country of ours, which is, of course, the first in our thoughts and in our hearts, should show herself in this time of peculiar trial a Nation fit beyond others to exhibit the fine poise of undisturbed judgment, the dignity of self-control, the efficiency of dispassionate action; a Nation that neither sits in judgment upon others nor is disturbed in her own counsels and which keeps herself fit and free to do what is honest and disinterested and truly serviceable for the peace of the world.

Shall we not resolve to put upon ourselves the restraints which will bring to our people the happiness and the great and lasting influence for peace we covet for them?

13. Promise of the Best Things

To William Gibbs McAdoo, November 7, 1914

In the Congressional election, the Democrats lost heavily in the East while gaining in the West. The election gave the party a more radical cast than it had had. Following is Wilson's summary, in a letter to the Secretary of the Treasury, of the first two years of his New Freedom.

. . . WE HAVE only to look back ten years ago to realize the deep perplexities and dangerous ill humors out of which we have now at last issued, as if from a bewildering fog, a noxious miasma. Ten or twelve years ago the country was torn and excited by an agitation which shook the very foundations of her political life, brought her business ideals into question, condemned her social standards, denied the honesty of her men of affairs, the integrity of her economic processes, the morality and good faith of many of the things which her law sustained.

Those who had power, whether in business or in politics, were almost universally looked upon with suspicion, and little attempt was made to distinguish the just from the unjust. They in their turn seemed to distrust the people and to wish to limit their control. There was ominous antagonism between classes. Capital and labor were in sharp conflict without prospect of accommoda-tion between them. Interests harshly clashed which should have cooperated.

This was not merely the work of irresponsible agitators. There were real wrongs which cried out to be righted and fearless men had called attention to them, demanding that they be dealt with by law. We were living under a tariff which had been purposely contrived to confer favors upon those who were cooperating to keep the party that originated it in power, and in that all too fertile soil all the bad, interlaced growth and jungle of monopoly had sprung up. Credit, the very life of trade, the very air men must breathe if they would meet their opportunities, was too largely in the control of the same small groups who had planted and cultivated monopoly. The control of all big business, and by consequence of all little business, too, was for the most part potentially, if not actually, in their hands.

And the thing stood so until the Democrats came into power last year. The legislation of the past year and a half has in very large measure done away with these things. With their correction, suspicion and ill-will will pass away. For not only have these things been righted, but new things have been put into action which are sure to prove the instruments of a new life in which the mists and distempers which have so embarrassed us will be cleared away; the wrongs and misunderstandings corrected which have brought distrust upon so many honest men unjustly. That is the main ground of my own satisfaction.

The tariff has been recast with a view to supporting the Government rather than supporting the favored beneficiaries of the Government. A system of banking and currency issues has been created which puts credit within the reach of every man who can show a going business, and the supervision and control of the system is in the hands of a responsible agency of the Government itself. A trade tribunal has been created by which those who attempt unjust and oppressive practices in business can be brought to book. Labor has been made something else in the view of the law than a mere mercantile commodity—something human and linked with the privileges of life itself. The soil has everywhere been laid bare out of which monopoly is slowly going to be eradicated. And undoubtedly the means by which credit has been set free is at the heart of all these things—is the keypiece of the whole structure.

This is the more significant because of its opportunities. It is brought to its final accomplishment just as it is most imperatively needed. The war, which has involved the whole of the heart of Europe, has made it necessary that the United States should mobilize its resources in the most effective way possible and make her credit and her usefulness good for the service of the whole world. It has created, too, special difficulties, peculiar situations to be dealt with, like the great embarrassment in selling our immense cotton crop, which all the world needs but against which, for the time being, the markets of the world are in danger of being artificially shut. That situation the bankers of the country are meeting as far as possible in a businesslike fashion and in the spirit of the new time, which is opening before us.

The railroads of the country are almost as much affected, not so much because their business is curtailed as because their credit is called into question by doubt as to their earning capacity. There is no other interest so central to the business welfare of the country as this. No doubt, in the light of the new day, with its new understandings, the problems of the railroads will also be met and dealt with in a spirit of candor and justice.

For the future is clear and bright with promise of the best things. While there was agitation and suspicion and distrust and bitter complaint of wrong, groups and classes were at war with one another, did not see that their interests were common, and suffered only when separated and brought into conflict. Fundamental wrongs once righted, as they may now easily and quickly be, all differences will clear away. . . .

14. The Counsels of Peace and Amity

Second Annual Address to Congress, December 8, 1914

In this message, delivered a day after Congress opened, Wilson sounds a cautious and hesitant note of preparedness for possible war. The bellicose exponents of preparedness, chief among them Theodore Roosevelt, were dissatisfied with Wilson's address.

. . . BEFORE I close may I say a few words upon two topics, much discussed out of doors, upon which it is highly important that our judgments should be clear, definite and steadfast?

One of these is economy in government expenditures. The duty of economy is not debatable. It is manifest and imperative. In the appropriations we pass we are spending the money of the great people whose servants we are—not our own. We are trustees and responsible stewards in the spending. The only thing debatable and upon which we should be careful to make our thought and purpose clear is the kind of economy demanded of us. I assert with the greatest confidence that the people of the United States are not jealous of the amount their Government costs if they are sure that they get what they need and desire for the outlay, that the money is being spent for objects of which they approve, and that it is being applied with good business sense and management.

Governments grow, piecemeal, both in their tasks and in the means by which those tasks are to be performed, and very few Governments are organized, I venture to say, as wise and experienced business men would organize them if they had a clean sheet of paper to write upon. Certainly the Government of the United States is not. I think that it is generally agreed that there should be a systematic reorganization and reassembling of its parts so as to secure greater efficiency and effect considerable savings in expense. But the amount of money saved in that way would, I believe, though no doubt considerable in itself, running, it may be, into the millions, be relatively small—small, I mean, in proportion to the total necessary outlays of the Government. It would be thoroughly worth effecting, as every saving would, great or small. Our duty is not altered by the scale of the saving. But my point is that the people of the United States do not wish to curtail the activities of this Government; they wish, rather, to enlarge them; and with every enlargement, with the mere growth, indeed, of the country itself, there must come, of course, the inevitable increase of expense. The sort of economy we ought to practice may be effected, and ought to be effected, by a careful study and assessment of the tasks to be performed; and the money spent ought to be made to yield the best possible returns in efficiency and achievement. And, like good stewards, we should so account for every dollar of our appropriations as to make it perfectly evident what it was spent for and in what way it was spent.

It is not expenditure but extravagance that we should fear being criticized for; not paying for the legitimate enterprises and undertakings of a great Government whose people command what it should do, but adding what will benefit only a few or pouring money out for what need not have been undertaken at all or might have been postponed or better and more economically conceived and carried out. The Nation is not niggardly; it is very generous. It will chide us only if we forget for whom we pay money out and whose money it is we pay. These are large and general standards, but they are not very difficult of application to particular cases.

The other topic I shall take leave to mention goes deeper into the principles of our national life and policy. It is the subject of national defense.

It can not be discussed without first answering some very searching questions. It is said in some quarters that we are not prepared for war. What is meant by being prepared? Is it meant that we are not ready upon brief notice to put a nation in the field, a nation of men trained to arms? Of course we are not ready to do that; and we shall never be in time of peace so long as we retain our present political principles and institutions. And what is it that it is suggested we should be prepared to do? To defend ourselves against attack? We have always found means to do that, and shall find them whenever it is necessary without calling our people away from their necessary tasks to render compulsory military service in times of peace.

Allow me to speak with great plainness and directness upon this great matter and to avow my convictions with deep earnestness. I have tried to know what America is, what her people think, what they are, what they most cherish and hold dear. I hope that some of their finer passions are in my own heart—some of the great conceptions and desires which gave birth to this Government and which have made the voice of this people a voice of peace and hope and liberty among the peoples of the world, and that, speaking my own thoughts, I shall, at least in part, speak theirs also, however faintly and inadequately, upon this vital matter.

We are at peace with all the world. No one who speaks counsel based on fact or drawn from a just and candid interpretation of realities can say that there is reason to fear that from any quarters our independence or the integrity of our territory is threatened. Dread of the power of any other nation we are incapable of. We are not jealous of rivalry in the fields of commerce or of any other peaceful achievement. We mean to live our own lives as we will; but we mean also to let live. We are, indeed, a true friend to all the nations of the world, because we threaten none, covet the possessions of none, desire the overthrow of none. Our friendship can be accepted and is accepted without reservation, because it is offered in a spirit and for a purpose which no one need ever question or suspect. Therein lies our greatness. We are the champions of peace and of concord. And we should be very jealous of this distinction which we have sought to earn. Just now we should be particularly jealous of it, because it is our dearest present hope that this character and reputation may presently, in God's providence, bring us an opportunity such as has seldom been vouchsafed any nation, the opportunity to counsel and obtain peace in the world and reconciliation and a healing settlement of many a matter that has cooled and interrupted the friendship of nations. This is the time above all others when we should wish and resolve to keep our strength by self-possession, our influence by preserving our ancient principles of action.

From the first we have had a clear and settled policy with regard to military establishments. We never have had, and while we retain our present principles and ideals we never shall have, a large standing army. If asked, Are you ready to defend yourself? we reply, Most assuredly, to the utmost; and yet we shall not turn America into a military camp. We will not ask our young men to spend the best years of their lives making soldiers of themselves. There is another sort of energy in us. It will know how to declare itself and make itself effective should occasion arise. And especially when half the world is on fire we shall be careful to make our moral insurance against the spread of the conflagration very definite and certain and adequate indeed.

Let us remind ourselves, therefore, of the only thing we can do or will do. We must depend in every time of national peril, in the future as in the past, not upon a standing army, nor yet upon a reserve army, but upon a citizenry trained and accustomed to arms. It will be right enough, right American policy, based upon our accustomed principles and practices, to provide a system by which every citizen who will volunteer for the training may be made familiar with the use of modern arms, the rudiments of drill and maneuver, and the maintenance and sanitation of camps. We should encourage such training and make it a means of discipline which our young men will learn to value. It is right that we should provide it not only, but that we should make it as attractive as possible, and so induce our young men to undergo it at such times as they can command a little freedom and can seek the physical development they need, for mere health's sake, if for nothing more. Every means by which such things can be stimulated is legitimate, and such a method smacks of true American ideas. It is right, too, that the National Guard of the States should be developed and strengthened by every means which is not inconsistent with our obligations to our own people or with the established policy of our Government. And this, also, not because the time or occasion specially calls for such measures, but because it should be our constant policy to make these provisions for our national peace and safety.

More than this carries with it a reversal of the whole history and character of our polity. More than this, proposed at this time, permit me to say, would mean merely that we had lost our self-possession, that we had been thrown off our balance by a war with which we have nothing to do, whose causes can not touch us, whose very existence affords us opportunities of friendship and disinterested service which should make us ashamed of any thought of hostility or fearful preparation for trouble. This is assuredly the opportunity for which a people and a government like ours were raised up, the opportunity not only to speak but actually to embody and exemplify the counsels of peace and amity and the lasting concord which is based on justice, and fair and generous dealing. . . .

15. The Right of Political Asylum

Veto of First Immigration Bill, January 28, 1915

From 1885 to 1914 a vast number of people from Eastern and Southern Europe came to America. Between 1904 and 1914 they came at an average of nearly a million a year. Claiming that "cheap labor" kept wages low, labor unions agitated for restricting immigration. In 1914 Congress passed a bill requiring immigrants to take a literacy test as a condition for admittance. Though Wilson successfully vetoed this bill, even as two predecessors had vetoed similar bills, the movement for restriction grew increasingly strong—strong enough to overcome his subsequent vetoes.

TO THE House of Representatives: It is with unaffected regret that I find myself constrained by clear conviction to return this bill (H. R. 6060, "An act to regulate the immigration of aliens to and the residence of aliens in the United States") without my signature. Not only do I feel it to be a very serious matter to exercise the power of veto in any case, because it involves opposing the single judgment of the President to the judgment of a majority of both the Houses of the Congress, a step which no man who realizes his own liability to error can take without great hesitation, but also because this particular bill is in so many important respects admirable, well conceived, and desirable. Its enactment into law would undoubtedly enhance the efficiency and improve the methods of handling the important branch of the public service to which it relates. But candor and a sense of duty with regard to the responsibility so clearly imposed upon me by the Constitution in matters of legislation leave me no choice but to dissent.

In two particulars of vital consequence this bill embodies a radical departure from the traditional and long-established policy of this country, a policy in which our people have conceived the very character of their Government to be expressed, the very mission and spirit of the Nation in respect of its relations to the peoples of the world outside their borders. It seeks to all but close entirely the gates of asylum which have always been open to those who could find nowhere else the right and opportunity of constitutional agitation for what they conceived to be the natural and inalienable rights of men; and it excludes those to whom the opportunities of elementary education have been denied, without regard to their character, their purposes, or their natural capacity.

Restrictions like these, adopted earlier in our history as a Nation, would very materially have altered the course and cooled the humane ardors of our politics. The right of political asylum has brought to this country many a man of noble character and elevated purpose who was marked as an outlaw in his own less fortunate land, and who has yet become an ornament to our citizenship and to our public councils. The children and the compatriots of these illustrious Americans must stand amazed to see the representatives of their Nation now resolved, in the fullness of our national strength and at the maturity of our great institutions, to risk turning such men back from our shores without test of quality or purpose. It is difficult for me to believe that the full effect of this feature of the bill was realized when it was framed and adopted, and it is impossible for me to assent to it in the form in which it is here cast.

The literacy test and the tests and restrictions which accompany it constitute an even more radical change in the policy of the Nation. Hitherto we have generously kept our doors open to all who were not unfitted by reason of disease or incapacity for self-support or such personal records and antecedents as were likely to make them a menace to our peace and order or to the wholesome and essential relationships of life. In this bill it is proposed to turn away from tests of character and of quality and impose tests which exclude and restrict; for the new tests here embodied are not tests of quality or of character or of personal fitness, but tests of opportunity. Those who come seeking opportunity are not to be admitted unless they have already had one of the chief of the opportunities they seek, the opportunity of education. The object of such provisions is restriction, not selection.

If the people of this country have made up their minds to limit the number of immigrants by arbitrary tests and so reverse the policy of all the generations of Americans that have gone before them, it is their right to do so. I am their servant and have no license to stand in their way. But I do not believe that they have. I respectfully submit that no one can quote their mandate to that effect. Has any political party ever avowed a policy of restriction in this fundamental matter, gone to the country on it, and been commissioned to control its legislation? Does this bill rest upon the conscious and universal assent and desire of the American people? I doubt it. It is because I doubt it that I make bold to dissent from it. I am willing to abide by the verdict, but not until it has been rendered. Let the platforms of parties speak out upon this policy and the people pronounce their wish. The matter is too fundamental to be settled otherwise.

I have no pride of opinion in this question. I am not foolish enough to profess to know the wishes and ideals of America better than the body of her chosen representatives know them. I only want instruction direct from those whose fortunes, with ours and all men's, are involved.

16. It Must Be Displayed Naked

To Mrs. Crawford Toy, January 31, 1915

Wilson wrote often to Mrs. Toy, a close friend. Mrs. Toy had complained about his partisan spirit in a recent speech.

. . . OF COURSE you did not like the Indianapolis speech (that palpable lapse of taste, "Woodrow &c." was only a silliness of the moment; was not in the notes; was produced by the psychology of the stump, no doubt, and admits of no excuse); I instinctively knew that you would not: any more than you would like a real fight, or anything that wore the aspect of partisanship. But there is a real fight on. The Republicans are every day employing the most unscrupulous methods of partisanship and false evidence to destroy this administration and bring back the days of private influence and selfish advantage. I would not, if I could, imitate their tactics; but it is no time for mere manners. The barriers of taste may be overstepped in stating the truth as to what is going on: it must be displayed naked. All that I said was true, to my knowledge, though I did not shade it or trace the lines of it artistically or with literary restraint. The struggle that is on, to bring about reaction and regain privilege, is desperate and absolutely without scruple. It cannot be met by gentle speeches or by presidential utterances which smack of no bias of party. A compact and fighting party must be led against them. I think you cannot know to what lengths men like Root and Lodge are going, who I once thought had consciences but now know have none. We must not suffer ourselves to forget or twist the truth as they do, or use their insincere and contemptible methods of fighting; but we must hit them and hit them straight in the face, and not mind if the blood comes. It is a blunt business, and lacks a certain kind of refinement, but so does all war; and this is a war to save the country from some of the worst influences that ever debauched it. Please do not read the speeches in which I use a bludgeon. I do not like to offend your taste; but I cannot fight rottenness with rosewater. Lend me your indulgence. At any rate forgive me, if you can do nothing else.

As for the Shipping bill, it does, as you perceive, permit us to commit blunders, fatal blunders, if we are so stupid or so blind; but it is not a blunder in itself, and, if we use ordinary sense and prudence, it need lead us into no dangers. The only dangers it involves have already been created by the Ship Registry bill and the war risk insurance measure, for which the Republicans hastened to vote, some coming back to Washington to advocate what the shipping interests wanted who had been absent from their seats for weeks. But the shipping interests do not want this bill. They will do nothing themselves without a subsidy, unless, that is, they are given government money out of the taxes to use as they think best for themselves; if they cannot get that, and of course they cannot, they do not mean to let the development take place, because the control of ocean carriage and of ocean rates will pass out of their hands. We are fighting as a matter of fact the most formidable (covert) lobby that has stood against us yet in anything we have attempted; and we shall see the fight to a finish; trying, when we have won, to act like men who know very familiarly the dangers of what they are about to undertake. It pleases me that you should be so generously distressed at the possibility of our doing what will lead to disaster or even danger; but those who speak to you of these risks have a very poor opinion of our practical sense, and are unconsciously misled by what the press represent, for their own purposes, as the main object of the measure when it is not its object at all. One would suppose that this was a bill to authorize the government to buy German ships. There would be just as stiff a fight against it, and from the same quarters, if it merely conferred the power to build ships.

The path is indeed strewn with difficulties at every turn, in this and in many other matters, and God knows I have no serene confidence in my own judgment and discretion: but of one thing I am resolved, to break the control of special interests over this government and this people. Pardon the seriousness of this letter. These are critical things in which much is wrapped up. . . .

Four

NEUTRALITY
1915–1917

1. A Strict Accountability

Note to Germany, February 10, 1915

On February 4 the German Admiralty issued a proclamation stating that the waters around Britain were to be included in the war zone; that enemy ships would be destroyed; and that neutral ships, which Britain was using as subterfuge, would be in danger as well. Wilson wrote the following note to Germany on the basis of Undersecretary of State Lansing's draft.

PLEASE ADDRESS a note immediately to the Imperial German Government to the following effect:

The Government of the United States, having had its attention directed to the proclamation of the German Admiralty issued on the fourth of February, that the waters surrounding Great Britain and Ireland, including the whole of the English Channel, are to be considered as comprised within the seat of war; that all enemy merchant vessels found in those waters after the eighteenth instant will be destroyed, although it may not always be possible to save crews and passengers; and that neutral vessels expose themselves to danger within this zone of war because, in view of the misuse of neutral flags said to have been ordered by the British Government on the thirty-first of January and of the contingencies of maritime warfare, it may not be possible always to exempt neutral vessels from attacks intended to strike enemy ships, feels it to be its duty to call the attention of the Imperial German Government, with sincere respect and the most friendly sentiments but very candidly and earnestly, to the very serious possibilities of the course of action apparently contemplated under that proclamation.

The Government of the United States views those possibilities with such grave concern that it feels it to be its privilege, and indeed its duty in the circumstances, to request the Imperial German Government to consider before action is taken the critical situation in respect of the relations between this country and Germany which might arise were the German naval forces, in carrying out the policy foreshadowed in the Admiralty's proclamation, to destroy any merchant vessel of the United States or cause the death of American citizens.

It is of course not necessary to remind the German Government that the sole right of a belligerent in dealing with neutral vessels on the high seas is limited to visit and search, unless a blockade is proclaimed and effectively maintained, which this Government does not understand to be proposed in this case. To declare or exercise a right to attack and destroy any vessel entering a prescribed area of the high seas without first certainly determining its belligerent nationality and the contraband character of its cargo would be an act so unprecedented in naval warfare that this Government is reluctant to believe that the Imperial Government of Germany in this case contemplates it as possible. The suspicion that enemy ships are using neutral flags improperly can create no just presumption that all ships traversing a prescribed area are subject to the same suspicion. It is to determine exactly such questions that this Government understands the right of visit and search to have been recognized.

This Government has carefully noted the explanatory statement issued by the Imperial German Government at the same time with the proclamation of the German Admiralty, and takes this occasion to remind the Imperial German Government very respectfully that the Government of the United States is open to none of the criticisms for unneutral action to which the German Government believes the governments of certain other neutral nations have laid themselves open; that the Government of the United States has not consented to or acquiesced in any measures which may have been taken by the other belligerent nations in the present war which operate to restrain neutral trade, but has, on the contrary, taken in all such matters a position which warrants it in holding those governments responsible in the proper way for any untoward effects upon American shipping which the accepted principles of international law do not justify; and that it, therefore, regards itself as free in the present instance to take with a clear conscience and upon accepted principles the position indicated in this note.

If the commanders of German vessels of war should act upon the presumption that the flag of the United States was not being used in good faith and should destroy on the high seas an American vessel or the lives of American citizens, it would be difficult for the Government of the United States to view the act in any other light than as an indefensible violation of neutral rights which it would be very hard indeed to reconcile with the friendly relations now so happily subsisting between the two Governments.

If such a deplorable situation should arise, the Imperial German Government can readily appreciate that the Government of the United States would be constrained to hold the Imperial German Government to a strict accountability for such acts of their naval authorities and to take any steps it might be necessary to take to safeguard American lives and property and to secure to American citizens the full enjoyment of their acknowledged rights on the high seas.

The Government of the United States, in view of these considerations, which it urges with the greatest respect and with the sincere purpose of making sure that no misunderstanding may arise and no circumstance occur that might even cloud the intercourse of the two Governments, expresses the confident hope and expectation that the Imperial German Government can and will give assurance that American citizens and their vessels will not be molested by the naval forces of Germany otherwise than by visit and search, though their vessels may be traversing the sea area delimited in the proclamation of the German Admiralty.

It is added for the information of the Imperial Government that representations have been made to His Britannic Majesty's Government in respect to the unwarranted use of the American flag for the protection of British ships.

2. No Individual Life

To Mary A. Hulbert, February 14, 1915

Wilson complains that his "official duties" are denying him his private life.

. . . TOGETHER, ENGLAND and Germany are likely to drive us crazy, because it looks oftentimes as if they were crazy themselves, the unnecessary provocations they invent. To keep cool heads and handle each matter composedly and without excitement as it arises, seeking to see each thing in the large, in the light of what is likely to happen as well as in the light of what is happening now, involves a nervous expenditure such as I never dreamed of, and drives every private matter into the background to wait for a time of exemption from these things which never comes. I go to bed every night absolutely exhausted, trying not to think about anything, and with all my nerves deadened, my own individuality as it were blotted out. . . .

I never knew before that it was possible, when necessary, for a man to lose his own personal existence, seem even to himself to have no individual life apart from his official duties. But it is possible. It has happened. . . .

3. Unlimited Belligerent Rights

Note to Britain, March 30, 1915

It was obvious to Wilson that Britain benefited from his warning to Germany of February 10. In view of Britain's mastery of the seas, Germany had no choice. Recognizing this, the United States, on February 20, requested that Britain relax her blockade of Germany. Britain refused. Following is Wilson's mild protest. Foreign Minister Grey waited four months before sending a final reply.

YOU ARE instructed to deliver the following to His Majesty's Government in reply to your numbers 1795 and 1798 on March 15:

The Government of the United States has given careful consideration to the subjects treated in the British notes of March 13 and March 15, and to the British Order in Council of the latter date.

These communications contain matters of grave importance to neutral nations. They appear to menace their rights of trade and intercourse not only with belligerents but also with one another. They call for frank comment in order that misunderstandings may be avoided. The Government of the United States deems it its duty, therefore, speaking in the sincerest spirit of friendship, to make its own view and position with regard to them unmistakably clear.

The Order in Council of the 15th of March would constitute, were its provisions to be actually carried into effect as they stand, a practical assertion of unlimited belligerent rights over neutral commerce within the whole European area, and an almost unqualified denial of the sovereign rights of the nations now at peace.

This government takes it for granted that there can be no question what those rights are. A nation's sovereignty over its own ships and citizens under its own flag on the high seas in time of peace is, of course, unlimited; and that sovereignty suffers no diminution in time of war, except in so far as the practice and consent of civilized nations has limited it by the recognition of certain now clearly determined rights, which it is conceded may be exercised by nations which are at war.

A belligerent nation has been conceded the right of visit and search, and the right of capture and condemnation, if upon examination a neutral vessel is found to be engaged in unneutral service or to be carrying contraband of war intended for the enemy's government or armed forces. It has been conceded the right to establish and maintain a blockade of an enemy's ports and coasts and to capture and condemn any vessel taken in trying to break the blockade. It is even conceded the right to detain and take to its own ports for judicial examination all vessels which it suspects for substantial reasons to be engaged in unneutral or contraband service and to condemn them if the suspicion is sustained. But such rights, long clearly defined both in doctrine and practice, have hitherto been held to be the only permissible exceptions to the principle of universal equality of sovereignty on the high seas as between belligerents and nations not engaged in war.

It is confidently assumed that His Majesty's Government will not deny that it is a rule sanctioned by general practice that, even though a blockade should exist and the doctrine of contraband as to unblockaded territory be rigidly enforced, innocent shipments may be freely transported to and from the United States through neutral countries to belligerent territory without being subject to the penalties of contraband traffic or breach of blockade, much less to detention, requisition, or confiscation. . . .

The note of His Majesty's Principal Secretary of State for

Foreign Affairs which accompanies the Order in Council, and which bears the same date, notifies the Government of the United States of the establishment of a blockade which is, if defined by the terms of the Order in Council, to include all the coasts and ports of Germany and every port of possible access to enemy territory. But the novel and quite unprecedented feature of that blockade, if we are to assume it to be properly so defined, is that it embraces many neutral ports and coasts, bars access to them, and subjects all neutral ships seeking to approach them to the same suspicion that would attach to them were they bound for the ports of the enemies of Great Britain, and to unusual risks and penalties.

It is manifest that such limitations, risks, and liabilities placed upon the ships of a neutral power on the high seas, beyond the right of visit and search and the right to prevent the shipment of contraband already referred to, are a distinct invasion of the sovereign rights of the nation whose ships, trade, or commerce are interfered with.

The Government of the United States is, of course, not oblivious to the great changes which have occurred in the conditions and means of naval warfare since the rules hitherto governing legal blockade were formulated. It might be ready to admit that the old form of "close" blockade with its cordon of ships in the immediate offing of the blockaded ports is no longer practicable in face of an enemy possessing the means and opportunity to make an effective defense by the use of submarines, mines, and air craft; but it can hardly be maintained that, whatever form of effective blockade may be made use of, it is impossible to conform at least to the spirit and principles of the established rules of war. If the necessities of the case should seem to render it imperative that the cordon of blockading vessels be extended across the approaches to any neighboring neutral port or country, it would seem clear that it would still be easily practicable to comply with the well-recognized and reasonable prohibition of international law against the blockading of neutral ports by according free admission and exit to all lawful traffic with neutral ports through the blockading cordon. This traffic would of course include all outward-bound traffic from the neutral country and all inward-bound traffic to the neutral country except contraband in transit to the enemy. Such procedure need not conflict in any respect with the rights of the belligerent maintaining the blockade since the right would remain with the blockading vessels to visit and search all ships either entering or leaving the neutral territory which they were in fact, but not of right, investing. . . .

4. I Wish I Could See It as You Do

To Secretary of State Bryan, April 28, 1915

On March 28 an American citizen (Leon Thrasher) died when a German submarine sank the British ship Falaba *in the Irish Sea. Wilson intended to send Germany a stern warning. Bryan, fearful of the effect this might have on neutrality, wrote Wilson on April 19, pleading that the German point of view should receive more sympathetic consideration. The Germans were not "unreasonable" in asking why Americans must travel on British ships. Four days later Bryan again wrote to the President, repeating what he had said before. "Is it not better to try to bring peace for the benefit of the whole world than to risk the provoking of war on account of one man?" The exchange between Wilson and Bryan foreshadowed their break in June.*

I HAVE thought a great deal about the contents of the letter you wrote me (the letter written in your own hand) about the Thrasher case. It of course made a deep impression on me.

As I told you yesterday at cabinet, I am not at all confident that we are on the right track in considering such a note as I outlined for Mr. Lansing to work on. I am not sure that my outline really expressed what I would myself say in the note, for, after all, the character of a note is chiefly in the way the thing is said and the points developed. Perhaps it is not necessary to make formal representations in the matter at all.

What I have been thinking about most is your alternative proposition, that we publicly call upon the belligerents to end the war.

I wish I could see it as you do. But in view of what House writes me I cannot. It is known to every government concerned that we believe the war should be ended and that we speak for all neutral nations in that wish. It is known to them that we are seeking to help and that anything they want to say to one another which they are too proud or too prudent to say directly and officially they can say privately through us. They are at present most appreciative and cordial—ready to accept help when they can accept it. We know their minds and we know their difficulties. They are dependent upon their own public opinion (even Germany) and we know what that opinion is. To insist now would be futile and would probably be offensive. We would lose such influence as we have for peace.

I am afraid, Mr. Secretary, that there is much in this that will seem to you disputable; but I can only state my conviction in the matter, and God knows I have searched my mind and conscience both to get the best, the nearest approach to wisdom, there is in them.

5. Neutral Goods to Neutral Ports

To Colonel House, May 5, 1915

Wilson asked House, then in London on a peace mission, to bring the following grievances to the attention of the British Foreign Secretary, Lord Grey.

. . . A VERY serious change is coming over the public sentiment in this country because of the needless delays and many willful interferences in dealing with our neutral cargoes. The country is listening with more and more acquiescence, just because of this intense irritation, to the suggestion that an embargo be placed upon the shipment of arms and war supplies, and if this grows much more before the Congress assembles in December it may be difficult if not impossible for me to prevent action to that end. Please present to Sir Edward Grey very earnestly the wisdom and necessity of giving utmost freedom to our commerce in neutral goods to neutral ports, and the permanent settlement of all questions concerning cargoes seized or detained. . . .

6. Too Proud to Fight

Address on Neutrality, May 10, 1915

Wilson spoke to several thousand Americans who had just been naturalized in Philadelphia. His speech was especially significant as an earnest expression of his neutralist intentions since it came only three days after the sinking of the Lusitania. *Wilson's enemies, especially the preparedness camp, interpreted his address as evidence of his pusillanimity.*

IT WARMS my heart that you should give me such a reception; but it is not of myself that I wish to think tonight, but of those who have just become citizens of the United States.

This is the only country in the world which experiences this constant and repeated rebirth. Other countries depend upon the multiplication of their own native people. This country is constantly drinking strength out of new sources by the voluntary association with it of great bodies of strong men and forward-looking women out of other lands. And so by the gift of the free will of independent people it is being constantly renewed from generation to generation by the same process by which it was originally created. It is as if humanity had determined to see to it that this great Nation, founded for the benefit of humanity, should not lack for the allegiance of the people of the world.

You have just taken an oath of allegiance to the United States. Of allegiance to whom? Of allegiance to no one, unless it be God —certainly not of allegiance to those who temporarily represent this great Government. You have taken an oath of allegiance to a great ideal, to a great body of principles, to a great hope of the human race. You have said, "We are going to America not only to earn a living, not only to seek the things which it was more difficult to obtain where we were born, but to help forward the great enterprises of the human spirit—to let men know that everywhere in the world there are men who will cross strange oceans and go where a speech is spoken which is alien to them if they can but satisfy their quest for what their spirits crave; knowing that whatever the speech there is but one longing and utterance of the human heart, and that is for liberty and justice." And while you bring all countries with you, you come with a purpose of leaving all other countries behind you—bringing what is best of their spirit, but not looking over your shoulders and seeking to perpetuate what you intended to leave behind in them. I certainly would not be one even to suggest that a man cease to love the home of his birth and the nation of his origin—these things are very sacred and ought not to be put out of our hearts—but it is one thing to love the place where you were born and it is another thing to dedicate yourself to the place to which you go. You cannot dedicate yourself to America unless you become in every respect and with every purpose of your will thorough Americans. You cannot become thorough Americans if you think of yourselves in groups. America does not consist of groups. A man who thinks of himself as belonging to a particular national group in America has not yet become an American, and the man who goes among you to trade upon your nationality is no worthy son to live under the Stars and Stripes.

My urgent advice to you would be, not only always to think first of America, but always, also, to think first of humanity. You do not love humanity if you seek to divide humanity into jealous camps. Humanity can be welded together only by love, by sympathy, by justice, not by jealousy and hatred. I am sorry for the man who seeks to make personal capital out of the passions of his fellowmen. He has lost the touch and ideal of America, for America was created to unite mankind by those passions which lift and not by the passions which separate and debase. We came to America, either ourselves or in the persons of our ancestors, to better the ideals of men, to make them see finer things that they had seen before, to get rid of the things that divide and to make sure of the things that unite. It was but an historical accident no doubt that this great country was called the "United States"; yet I am very thankful that it has that word "United" in its title, and the man who seeks to divide man from man, group from group, interest from interest in this great Union is striking at its very heart.

It is a very interesting circumstance to me, in thinking of those of you who have just sworn allegiance to this great Government, that you were drawn across the ocean by some beckoning

THE BETTMANN ARCHIVE

Undergraduate at Princeton, 1875-79

THE BETTMANN ARCHIVE

President of Princeton, 1902–10

PHOTO FROM EUROPEAN

Governor of New Jersey, 1911–13

FROM UNDERWOOD & UNDERWOOD

Campaigning in 1912, Elk Point, South Dakota

President-elect Wilson, President Taft, just before the inauguration, 1913

THE BETTMANN ARCHIVE

FROM UNDERWOOD & UNDERWOOD

Wilson and released American prisoners of war in the court of Buckingham Palace, 1919

The Big Four at Versailles: Orlando, Lloyd George, Clemenceau, Wilson, 1919

FROM UNDERWOOD & UNDERWOOD

THE BETTMANN ARCHIVE

Above. Wilson and his physician, Rear Admiral Cary T. Grayson, 1919

Top right. Henry Cabot Lodge of Massachusetts, Senate Majority Leader and Chairman of the Foreign Relations Committee

Bottom right. Senator William E. Borah of Idaho, one of the leaders of the "irreconcilables"

Below. Wilson two months before his death on February 3, 1924

PHOTO FROM EUROPEAN

FROM UNDERWOOD & UNDERWOOD

FROM UNDERWOOD & UNDERWOOD

William Jennings Bryan, standing in front of his office in Lincoln, Nebraska

PHOTO FROM EUROPEAN

FROM UNDERWOOD & UNDERWOOD

Louis D. Brandeis in 1912

finger of hope, by some belief, by some vision of a new kind of justice, by some expectation of a better kind of life. No doubt you have been disappointed in some of us. Some of us are very disappointing. No doubt you have found that justice in the United States goes only with a pure heart and a right purpose as it does everywhere else in the world. No doubt what you found here did not seemed touched for you, after all, with the complete beauty of the ideal which you had conceived beforehand. But remember this: If we had grown at all poor in the ideal, you brought some of it with you. A man does not go out to seek the thing that is not in him. A man does not hope for the thing that he does not believe in, and if some of us have forgotten what America believed in, you, at any rate, imported in your own hearts a renewal of the belief. That is the reason that I, for one, make you welcome. If I have in any degree forgotten what America was intended for, I will thank God if you will remind me. I was born in America. You dreamed dreams of what America was to be, and I hope you brought the dreams with you. No man that does not see visions will ever realize any high hope or undertake any high enterprise. Just because you brought dreams with you, America is more likely to realize dreams such as you brought. You are enriching us if you came expecting us to be better than we are.

See, my friends, what that means. It means that Americans must have a consciousness different from the consciousness of every other nation in the world. I am not saying this with even the slightest thought of criticism of other nations. You know how it is with a family. A family gets centered on itself if it is not careful and is less interested in the neighbors than it is in its own members. So a nation that is not constantly renewed out of new sources is apt to have the narrowness and prejudice of a family; whereas, America must have this consciousness, that on all sides it touches elbows and touches hearts with all the nations of mankind. The example of America must be a special example. The example of America must be the example not merely of peace because it will not fight, but of peace because peace is the healing and elevating influence of the world and strife is not. There is such a thing as a man being too proud to fight. There is such a thing as a nation being so right that it does not need to convince others by force that it is right.

You have come into this great Nation voluntarily seeking

something that we have to give, and all that we have to give is this: We cannot exempt you from work. No man is exempt from work anywhere in the world. We cannot exempt you from the strife and the heartbreaking burden of the struggle of the day—that is common to mankind everywhere; we cannot exempt you from the loads that you must carry. We can only make them light by the spirit in which they are carried. That is the spirit of hope, it is the spirit of liberty, it is the spirit of justice.

When I was asked, therefore, by the Mayor and the committee that accompanied him to come up from Washington to meet this great company of newly admitted citizens, I could not decline the invitation. I ought not to be away from Washington, and yet I feel that it has renewed my spirit as an American to be here. In Washington men tell you so many things every day that are not so, and I like to come and stand in the presence of a great body of my fellow-citizens, whether they have been my fellow-citizens a long time or a short time, and drink, as it were, out of the common fountains with them and go back feeling what you have so generously given me—the sense of your support and of the living vitality in your hearts of the great ideals which have made America the hope of the world.

7. The Sacred Freedom of the Seas

First *Lusitania* Note, May 13, 1915

On May 1, the German embassy warned Americans in newspaper advertisements against traveling through the war zone in British ships. On the same day the Lusitania, *queen of the Cunard Lines, sailed from New York to London. On May 7, the* Lusitania *was sunk without warning off the Irish coast. There were 124 Americans among the 1,198 passengers who perished. The American public demanded action. But Wilson, in drafting the note below, refused to be moved "by the present emotionalism of the people." His note affirms the doctrine of "strict accountability."*

PLEASE CALL on the Minister of Foreign Affairs and after reading to him this communication leave with him a copy.

In view of recent acts of the German authorities in violation of

American rights on the high seas which culminated in the torpedoing and sinking of the British steamship *Lusitania* on May 7, 1915, by which over 100 American citizens lost their lives, it is clearly wise and desirable that the Government of the United States and the Imperial German Government should come to a clear and full understanding as to the grave situation which has resulted.

The sinking of the British passenger steamer *Falaba* by a German submarine on March 28, through which Leon C. Thrasher, an American citizen, was drowned; the attack on April 28 on the American vessel *Cushing* by a German aeroplane; the torpedoing on May 1 of the American vessel *Gulflight* by a German submarine, as a result of which two or more American citizens met their death; and, finally, the torpedoing and sinking of the steamship *Lusitania*, constitute a series of events which the Government of the United States has observed with growing concern, distress, and amazement.

Recalling the humane and enlightened attitude hitherto assumed by the Imperial German Government in matters of international right, and particularly with regard to the freedom of the seas; having learned to recognize the German views and the German influence in the field of international obligation as always engaged upon the side of justice and humanity; and having understood the instructions of the Imperial German Government to its naval commanders to be upon the same plane of humane action prescribed by the naval codes of other nations, the Government of the United States was loath to believe—it can not now bring itself to believe—that these acts, so absolutely contrary to the rules, the practices, and the spirit of modern warfare, could have the countenance or sanction of that great Government. It feels it to be its duty, therefore, to address the Imperial German Government concerning them with the utmost frankness and in the earnest hope that it is not mistaken in expecting action on the part of the Imperial German Government which will correct the unfortunate impressions which have been created and vindicate once more the position of that Government with regard to the sacred freedom of the seas.

The Government of the United States has been apprised that the Imperial German Government considered themselves to be obliged by the extraordinary circumstances of the present war and the measures adopted by their adversaries in seeking to cut Germany off from all commerce, to adopt methods of retaliation which go much beyond the ordinary methods of warfare at sea, in the proclamation of a war zone from which they have warned neutral ships to keep away. This Government has already taken occasion to inform the Imperial German Government that it cannot admit the adoption of such measures or such a warning of danger to operate as in any degree an abbreviation of the rights of American shipmasters or of American citizens bound on lawful errands as passengers on merchant ships of belligerent nationality; and that it must hold the Imperial German Government to a strict accountability for any infringement of those rights, intentional or incidental. It does not understand the Imperial German Government to question those rights. It assumes, on the contrary, that the Imperial Government accept, as of course, the rule that the lives of noncombatants, whether they be of neutral citizenship or citizens of one of the nations at war, can not lawfully or rightfully be put in jeopardy by the capture or destruction of an unarmed merchantman, and recognize also, as all other nations do, the obligation to take the usual precaution to visit and search to ascertain whether a suspected merchantman is in fact of belligerent nationality or is in fact carrying contraband of war under a neutral flag.

The Government of the United States, therefore, desires to call the attention of the Imperial German Government with the utmost earnestness to the fact that the objection to their present method of attack against the trade of their enemies lies in the practical impossibility of employing submarines in the destruction of commerce without disregarding those rules of fairness, reason, justice, and humanity which all modern opinion regards as imperative. It is practically impossible for the officers of a submarine to visit a merchantman at sea and examine her papers and cargo. It is practically impossible for them to make a prize of her; and, if they can not put a prize crew on board of her, they can not sink her without leaving her crew and all on board of her to the mercy of the sea in her small boats. These facts it is understood the Imperial German Government frankly admit. We are informed that in the instances of which we have spoken time enough for even that poor measure of safety was not given, and in at least two of the cases cited not so much as a warning was received. Manifestly submarines can not be used against merchantmen, as the last few weeks have shown, without an inevitable violation of many sacred principles of justice and humanity.

American citizens act within their indisputable rights in taking their ships and in traveling wherever their legitimate business calls them upon the high seas, and exercise those rights in what should be the well-justified confidence that their lives will not be endangered by acts done in clear violation of universally acknowledged international obligations, and certainly in the confidence that their own Government will sustain them in the exercise of their rights.

There was recently published in the newspapers of the United States, I regret to inform the Imperial German Government, a formal warning, purporting to come from the Imperial German Embassy at Washington, addressed to the people of the United States, and stating, in effect, that any citizen of the United States who exercised his right of free travel upon the seas would do so at his peril if his journey should take him within the zone of waters within which the Imperial German Navy was using submarines against the commerce of Great Britain and France, notwithstanding the respectful but very earnest protest of his Government, the Government of the United States. I do not refer to this for the purpose of calling the attention of the Imperial German Government at this time to the surprising irregularity of a communication from the Imperial German Embassy at Washington addressed to the people of the United States through the newspapers, but only for the purpose of pointing out that no warning that an unlawful and inhumane act will be committed can possibly be accepted as an excuse or palliation for that act or as an abatement of the responsibility for its commission.

Long acquainted as this Government has been with the character of the Imperial German Government and with the high principles of equity by which they have in the past been actuated and guided, the Government of the United States can not believe that the commanders of the vessels which committed these acts of lawlessness did so except under a misapprehension of the orders issued by the Imperial German naval authorities. It takes it for granted that, at least within the practical possibilities of every such case, the commanders even of submarines were expected to do nothing that would involve the lives of noncombatants or the safety of neutral ships, even at the cost of failing of their object of capture or destruction. It confidently expects, therefore, that the Imperial German Government will disavow the acts of which the Government of the United States complains, that they will make reparation so far as reparation is possible for injuries which are without measure, and that they will take immediate steps to prevent the recurrence of anything so obviously subversive of the principles of warfare for which the Imperial German Government have in the past so wisely and so firmly contended.

The Government and people of the United States look to the Imperial German Government for just, prompt, and enlightened action in this vital matter with the greater confidence because the United States and Germany are bound together not only by special ties of friendship but also by the explicit stipulations of the treaty of 1828 between the United States and the Kingdom of Prussia.

Expressions of regret and offers of reparation in case of the destruction of neutral ships sunk by mistake, while they may satisfy international obligations, if no loss of life results, can not justify or excuse a practice, the natural and necessary effect of which is to subject neutral nations and neutral persons to new and immeasurable risks.

The Imperial German Government will not expect the Government of the United States to omit any word or any act necessary to the performance of its sacred duty of maintaining the rights of the United States and its citizens and of safeguarding their free exercise and enjoyment.

8. The Request Is Unnecessary

To Secretary of State Bryan, May 14, 1915

Wilson answers Bryan's objection to the Lusitania *note as it stood.*

. . . AS TO the request to Americans not to take passage on belligerent ships (for I agree with Mr. Lansing that it could be nothing more than a request), my feeling is this: the request is unnecessary, if the object is to save lives because the danger is already fully known and those who do not refrain because of the danger will not, in all probability, refrain because we request them to do so; and this is not the time to make it, not only for the reason Mr. Lansing suggests, but also because, as I urged this morning, it weakens the effect of our saying to Germany that we mean to support our citizens in the exercise of their right to travel both on our ships and on belligerent. . . .

9. To Put These Principles into Practice

Second *Lusitania* Note, June 9, 1915

Replying on May 28 and June 1 to the first Lusitania *note, the German government maintained that though it regretted the loss of American lives, nevertheless the* Lusitania *was armed and carried contraband munitions. The German government further implied that it did not intend to relax its policy of unrestricted submarine warfare. Dissatisfied with these replies, Wilson drew up the following note.*

. . . YOUR EXCELLENCY'S note, in discussing the loss of American lives resulting from the sinking of the steamship *Lusitania*, adverts at some length to certain information which the Imperial German Government has received with regard to the character and outfit of that vessel, and Your Excellency expresses the fear that this information may not have been brought to the attention of the Government of the United States. It is stated in the note that the *Lusitania* was undoubtedly equipped with masked guns, supplied with trained gunners and special ammunition, transporting troops from Canada, carrying a cargo not permitted under the laws of the United States to a vessel also carrying passengers, and serving, in virtual effect, as an auxiliary to the naval forces of Great Britain. Fortunately, these are matters concerning which the Government of the United States is in a position to give the Imperial German Government official information. Of the facts alleged in Your Excellency's note, if true, the Government of the United States would have been bound to take official cognizance in performing its recognized duty as a neutral power and in enforcing its national laws. It was its duty to see to it that the *Lusitania* was not armed for offensive action, that she was not serving as a transport, that she did not carry a cargo prohibited by the statutes of the United States, and that, if in fact she was a naval vessel of Great Britain, she should not receive clearance as a merchantman; and it performed that duty and enforced its statutes with scrupulous vigilance through its regularly constituted officials. It is able, therefore, to assure the Imperial German Government that it has been misinformed. If the Imperial German Government should deem itself to be in possession of convincing evidence that the officials of the Government of the United States did not perform these duties with thoroughness, the Government of the United States sincerely hopes that it will submit that evidence for consideration.

Whatever may be the contentions of the Imperial German Government regarding the carriage of contraband of war on board the *Lusitania* or regarding the explosion of that material by the torpedo, it need only be said that in the view of this Government these contentions are irrelevant to the question of the legality of the methods used by the German naval authorities in sinking the vessel.

But the sinking of passenger ships involves principles of humanity which throw into the background any special circumstances of detail that may be thought to affect the cases, principles which lift it, as the Imperial German Government will no doubt be quick to recognize and acknowledge, out of the class of ordinary subjects of diplomatic discussion or of international controversy. Whatever be the other facts regarding the *Lusitania*, the principal fact is that a great steamer, primarily and chiefly a conveyance for passengers, and carrying more than a thousand souls who had no part or lot in the conduct of the war, was torpedoed and sunk without so much as a challenge or a warning, and that men, women, and children were sent to their death in circumstances unparalleled in modern warfare. The fact that more than one hundred American citizens were among those who perished made it the duty of the Government of the United States to speak of these things and once more, with solemn emphasis, to call the attention of the Imperial German Government to the grave responsibility which the Government of the United States conceives that it has incurred in this tragic occurrence, and to the indisputable principle upon which that responsibility rests. The Government of the United States is contending for something much greater than mere rights of property or privileges of commerce. It is contending for nothing less high and sacred than the rights of humanity, which every government honors itself in respecting and which no government is justified in resigning on behalf of those under its care and authority. Only her actual resistance to capture or refusal to stop when ordered to do so for the purpose of visit could have afforded the commander of the submarine any justification for so much as putting the lives of those on board the ship in jeopardy. This principle the Government of the United States understands the explicit instructions issued on August 3, 1914, by the Imperial German Admiralty to its commanders at sea to have recognized and embodied, as do the naval codes of all other nations, and upon it every traveler and seaman had a right to depend. It is upon this principle of humanity as well as upon the law founded upon this principle that the United States must stand.

The Government of the United States is happy to observe that Your Excellency's note closes with the intimation that the Imperial German Government is willing, now as before, to accept the good offices of the United States in an attempt to come to an understanding with the Government of Great Britain by which the character and conditions of the war upon the sea may be changed. The Government of the United States would consider it a privilege thus to serve its friends and the world. It stands ready at any time to convey to either Government any intimation or suggestion the other may be willing to have it convey and cordially invites the Imperial German Government to make use of its services in this way at its convenience. The whole world is concerned in anything that may bring about even a partial accommodation of interests or in any way mitigate the terrors of the present distressing conflict.

In the meantime, whatever arrangement may happily be made between the parties to the war, and whatever may in the opinion of the Imperial German Government have been the provocation or the circumstantial justification for the past acts of its commanders at sea, the Government of the United States confidently looks to see the justice and humanity of the Government of

Germany vindicated in all cases where Americans have been wronged or their rights as neutrals invaded.

The Government of the United States therefore very earnestly and very solemnly renews the representations of its note transmitted to the Imperial German Government on the 15th of May, and relies in these representations upon the principles of humanity, the universally recognized understandings of international law, and the ancient friendship of the German nation.

The Government of the United States can not admit that the proclamation of a war zone from which neutral ships have been warned to keep away may be made to operate as in any degree an abbreviation of the rights either of American shipmasters or of American citizens bound on lawful errands as passengers on merchant ships of belligerent nationality. It does not understand the Imperial German Government to question those rights. It understands it, also, to accept as established beyond question the principle that the lives of noncombatants can not lawfully or rightfully be put in jeopardy by the capture or destruction of an unresisting merchantman, and to recognize the obligation to take sufficient precaution to ascertain whether a suspected merchantman is in fact of belligerent nationality or is in fact carrying contraband of war under a neutral flag. The Government of the United States therefore deems it reasonable to expect that the Imperial German Government will adopt the measures necessary to put these principles into practice in respect of the safeguarding of American lives and American ships, and asks for assurances that this will be done.

10. Our Objects Are the Same

To Secretary of State Bryan, June 8, 1915

The second Lusitania *note disturbed Bryan. On June 3 he wrote two letters to Wilson repeating his former objections. On June 5 Bryan, very agitated, wrote Wilson again, asserting: "The sober judgment of the people will not sustain any word or act that provokes war. . . ." Bryan also pleaded with Wilson in person, but to no avail. Finally, on June 8, Bryan resigned. He wrote: "Alike desirous of reaching a peaceful solution of the problem arising out of the use of sub-*

marines against merchantmen, we find ourselves differing irreconcilably as to the methods which should be employed.

"It falls to your lot to speak officially for the nation; I consider it to be none the less my duty to endeavor as a private citizen to promote the end which you have in view by means which you do not feel at liberty to use."

Wilson of course knew that Bryan's resignation was inevitable. Obviously relieved when it came, he accepted it at once.

I ACCEPT your resignation only because you insist upon its acceptance; and I accept it with much more than deep regret, with a feeling of personal sorrow. Our two years of close association have been very delightful to me. Our judgments have accorded in practically every matter of official duty and of public policy until now; your support of the work and purposes of the administration has been generous beyond praise; your devotion to the duties of your great office and your eagerness to take advantage of every great opportunity for service it offered have been an example to the rest of us; you have earned our affectionate admiration and friendship. Even now we are not separated in the object we seek but only in the method by which we seek it.

It is for these reasons that my feeling about your retirement from the Secretaryship of State goes so much deeper than regret. I sincerely deplore it. Our objects are the same and we ought to pursue them together. I yield to your desire only because I must and wish to bid you Godspeed in the parting. We shall continue to work for the same causes even when we do not work in the same way.

11. An Unpardonable Offense

Third *Lusitania* Note, July 21, 1915

The German reply of July 8 to the second Lusitania *note reiterated her claim that she had no alternative in view of Britain's uncompromising blockade. As the note below indicates, Wilson was unhappy about the German reply, but nonetheless he was content to allow differences to cool in the belief that Germany had in fact modified her position.*

THE NOTE of the Imperial German Government, dated the 8th of July, 1915, has received the careful consideration of the Government of the United States, and it regrets to be obliged to say that it has found it very unsatisfactory, because it fails to meet the real differences between the two Governments and indicates no way in which the accepted principles of law and humanity may be applied in the grave matter in controversy, but purposes, on the contrary, arrangements for a partial suspension of those principles which virtually set them aside.

The Government of the United States notes with satisfaction that the Imperial German Government recognizes without reservation the validity of the principles insisted on in the several communications which this Government has addressed to the Imperial German Government with regard to its announcement of a war zone and the use of submarines against merchantmen on the high seas—the principle that the high seas are free, that the character and cargo of a merchantman must first be ascertained before she can lawfully be seized or destroyed, and that the lives of noncombatants may in no case be put in jeopardy unless the vessel resists or seeks to escape after being summoned to submit to examination; for a belligerent act of retaliation is *per se* an act beyond the law, and the defense of an act as retaliatory is an admission that it is illegal.

The Government of the United States is, however, keenly disappointed to find that the Imperial German Government regards itself as in large degree exempt from the obligation to observe these principles, even where neutral vessels are concerned, by what it believes the policy and practice of the Government of Great Britain to be in the present war with regard to neutral commerce. The Imperial German Government will readily understand that the Government of the United States can not discuss the policy of the Government of Great Britain with regard to neutral trade except with that Government itself, and that it must regard the conduct of other belligerent governments as irrelevant to any discussion with the Imperial German Government of what this Government regards as grave and unjustifiable violations of the rights of American citizens by German naval commanders.

Illegal and inhuman acts, however justifiable they may be thought to be against an enemy who is believed to have acted in contravention of law and humanity, are manifestly indefensible when they deprive neutrals of their acknowledged rights, particularly when they violate the right to life itself. If a belligerent can not retaliate against an enemy without injuring the lives of neutrals, as well as their property, humanity, as well as justice and a due regard for the dignity of neutral powers, should dictate that the practice be discontinued. If persisted in it would in such circumstances constitute an unpardonable offense against the sovereignty of the neutral nation affected. The Government of the United States is not unmindful of the extraordinary conditions created by this war or of the radical alterations of circumstances and method of attack produced by the use of instrumentalities of naval warfare which the nations of the world can not have had in view when the existing rules of international law were formulated, and it is ready to make every reasonable allowance for these novel and unexpected aspects of war at sea; but it can not consent to abate any essential or fundamental right of its people because of a mere alteration of circumstance. The rights of neutrals in time of war are based upon principle, not upon expediency, and the principles are immutable. It is the duty and obligation of belligerents to find a way to adapt the new circumstances to them.

The events of the past two months have clearly indicated that it is possible and practicable to conduct such submarine operations as have characterized the activity of the Imperial German Navy within the so-called war zone in substantial accord with the accepted practices of regulated warfare. The whole world has looked with interest and increasing satisfaction at the demonstration of that possibility by German naval commanders. It is manifestly possible, therefore, to lift the whole practice of submarine attack above the criticism which it has aroused and remove the chief causes of offense.

In view of the admission of illegality made by the Imperial Government when it pleaded the right of retaliation in defense of its act, and in view of the manifest possibility of conforming to the established rules of naval warfare, the Government of the United States can not believe that the Imperial Government will longer refrain from disavowing the wanton act of its naval commander in the sinking of the *Lusitania* or from offering reparation for the American lives lost, so far as reparation can be made for a needless destruction of human life by an illegal act.

The Government of the United States, while not indifferent to the friendly spirit in which it is made, cannot accept the suggestion of the Imperial German Government that certain vessels be designated and agreed upon which shall be free on the seas now illegally proscribed. The very agreement would, by implication, subject other vessels to illegal attack and would be a curtailment and therefore an abandonment of the principles for which this Government contends and which in times of calmer counsels every nation would concede as of course.

The Government of the United States and the Imperial German Government are contending for the same great object, have long stood together in urging the very principles, upon which the Government of the United States now so solemnly insists. They are both contending for the freedom of the seas. The Government of the United States will continue to contend for that freedom, from whatever quarter violated, without compromise and at any cost. It invites the practical cooperation of the Imperial German Government at this time when cooperation may accomplish most and this great common object be most strikingly and effectively achieved. . . .

12. Take the Bull by the Horns and Restore Order

To Secretary of State Lansing, August 4, 1915

Wilson, who had promised to end the policy of Dollar Diplomacy, found himself affirming it even more strongly than his predecessors. In March, 1915, a revolution in Haiti placed one Vibrun Sam in power at a time when the country was in financial chaos. Sam was overthrown and killed by a mob. On Wilson's order Marines landed on July 29 and occupied the country. The policy under which Haiti became virtually a protectorate of the United States is set forth by Wilson below.

. . . I FEAR we have not the legal authoritory to do what we apparently ought to do; and that if we did do what is necessary it would constitute a case very much like that of Mr. Roosevelt's action in Santo Domingo, and have very much the same issue.

I suppose there is nothing for it but to take the bull by the horns and restore order. A long programme . . . involves legislation and the cooperation of the Senate in treaty-making, and must therefore await the session of our Congress.

In the meantime this is plain to me:

1. We must send to Port au Prince a force sufficient to absolutely control the city not only but also the country immediately about it from which it draws its food. I would be obliged if you would ascertain from the Secretary of the Navy whether he has such a force available that can reach there soon.

2. We must let the present [Haitian] Congress know that we will protect it but that we will not recognize any action on its part which does not put men in charge of affairs whom we can trust to handle and put an end to revolution.

3. We must give all who now have authority there or desire to have it or who think they have it or about to have it to understand that we shall take steps to prevent the payment of debts contracted to finance revolution: in other words, that we consider it our duty to insist on constitutional government there and will, if necessary (that is, if they force us to it as the only way), take charge of elections and see that a real government is erected which we can support. . . .

This will probably involve making the city authorities virtually subordinate to our commanders. They may hand the city government over to us voluntarily.

13. The Constant Renewal of This People

Address to Daughters of American Revolution, October 11, 1915

In the controversy aroused by neutrality, Wilson was concerned that native-born Americans should not become hostile to foreign-born Americans. It was appropriate that Wilson emphasized this point in an address to the DAR.

. . . EVERY INDIVIDUAL, as well as every Nation, wishes to realize the best thing that is in him, the best thing that can be conceived out of the materials of which his spirit in constructed. It has happened in a way that fascinates the imagination that we have not only been augmented by additions from outside, but that we have been greatly stimulated by those additions. Living in the easy prosperity of a free people, knowing that the sun had always been free to shine upon us and prosper our undertakings, we did not realize how hard the task of liberty is and how rare the privilege of liberty is; but men were drawn out of every climate and out of every race because of an irresistible attraction of their spirits to the American ideal. They thought of America as lifting, like that great statue in the harbor of New York, a torch to light the pathway of men to the things that they desire, and men of all sorts and conditions struggled toward that light and came to our shores with an eager desire to realize it, and a hunger for it such as some of us no longer felt, for we were as if satiated and satisfied and were indulging ourselves after a fashion that did not belong to the ascetic devotion of the early devotees of those great principles. Strangers came to remind us of what we had promised ourselves and through ourselves had promised mankind. All men came to us and said, "Where is the bread of life with which you promised to feed us, and have you partaken of it yourselves?" For my part, I believe that the constant renewal of this people out of foreign stocks has been a constant source of reminder to this people of what the inducement was that was offered to men who would come and be of our number. . . .

America has a great cause which is not confined to the American continent. It is the cause of humanity itself. I do not mean in anything that I say even to imply a judgment upon any nation or upon any policy, for my object here this afternoon is not to sit in judgment upon anybody but ourselves and to challenge you to assist all of us who are trying to make America more than ever conscious of her own principles and her own duty. I looked forward to the necessity in every political agitation in the years which are immediately at hand of calling upon every man to declare himself, where he stands. Is it America first or is it not?

We ought to be very careful about some of the impressions that we are forming just now. There is too general an impression, I fear, that very large numbers of our fellow-citizens born in other lands have not entertained with sufficient intensity and affection the America ideal. But the number of such is, I am sure, not large. Those who would seek to represent them are very vocal, but they are not very influential. Some of the best stuff of America has come out of foreign lands, and some of the best stuff in America is in the men who are naturalized citizens of the United States. I would not be afraid upon the test of "America first" to take a census of all the foreign-born citizens of the United States, for I know that the vast majority of them came here because they believed in America; and their belief in America has made them better citizens than some people who were born in America. They can say that they have bought this privilege with a great price. They have left their homes, they have left their kindred, they have broken all the nearest and dearest ties of human life in order to come to a new land, take a new rootage, begin a new life, and so by self-sacrifice express their confidence in a new principle; whereas, it cost us none of these things. We were born into this privilege; we were rocked and cradled in it; we did nothing to create it; and it is, therefore, the greater duty on our part to do a great deal to enhance it and preserve it. I am not deceived as to the balance of opinion among the foreign-born citizens of the United States, but I am in a hurry for an opportunity to have a line-up and let the men who are thinking first of other countries stand on one side and all those that are for America first, last, and all the time on the other side. . . .

14. We Feel Justified

Address Outlining Preparedness, November 4, 1915

This was Wilson's first major policy address on an issue that was to prove one of his most controversial. Americans had never prepared for war in time of peace, and still believed that the European war would not reach them. Wilson took a middle course between the pacifists and the truculent advocates of full-scale preparedness. But not until the Sussex *crisis in the spring of the following year did Wilson see his program through.*

. . . WITHIN A year we have witnessed what we did not believe possible, a great European conflict involving many of the greatest nations of the world. The influences of a great war are everywhere in the air. All Europe is embattled. Force everywhere speaks out with a loud and imperious voice in a titanic struggle of governments, and from one end of our own dear country to the other men are asking one another what our own force is, how far we are prepared to maintain ourselves against any interference with our national action or development.

In no man's mind, I am sure, is there even raised the question of the willful use of force on our part against any nation or any people. No matter what military or naval force the United States might develop, statesmen throughout the whole world might rest assured that we were gathering that force, not for attack in any quarter, not for aggression of any kind, not for the satisfaction of any political or international ambition, but merely to make sure of our own security. We have it in mind to be prepared, not for war, but only for defense; and with the thought constantly in our minds that the principles we hold most dear can be achieved by the slow processes of history only in the kindly and wholesome atmosphere of peace, and not by the use of hostile force. The mission of America in the world is essentially a mission of peace and good will among men. She has become the home and asylum of men of all creeds and races. Within her hospitable borders they have found homes and congenial associations and freedom and a wide and cordial welcome, and they have become part of the bone and sinew and spirit of America itself. America has been made up out of the nations of the world and is the friend of the nations of the world.

But we feel justified in preparing ourselves to vindicate our right to independent and unmolested action by making the force that is in us ready for assertion.

And we know that we can do this in a way that will be itself an illustration of the American spirit. In accordance with our American traditions we want and shall work for only an army adequate to the constant and legitimate uses of times of international peace. But we do want to feel that there is a great body of citizens who have received at least the most rudimentary and necessary forms of military training; that they will be ready to form themselves into a fighting force at the call of the Nation; and that the Nation has the munitions and supplies with which to equip them without delay should it be necessary to call them into action. We wish to supply them with the training they need, and we think we can do so without calling them at any time too long away from their civilian pursuits.

It is with this idea, with this conception, in mind that the plans have been made which it will be my privilege to lay before the Congress at its next session. That plan calls for only such an increase in the regular Army of the United States as experience has proved to be required for the performance of the necessary duties of the Army in the Philippines, in Hawaii, in Puerto Rico, upon the borders of the United States, at the coast fortifications, and at the military posts of the interior. For the rest, it calls for the training within the next three years of a force of 400,000 citizen soldiers to be raised in annual contingents of 133,000, who would be asked to enlist for three years with the colors and three years on furlough, but who during their three years of enlistment with the colors would not be organized as a standing force but would be expected merely to undergo intensive training for a very brief period of each year. Their training would take place in immediate association with the organized units of the regular Army. It would have no touch of the amateur about it, neither would it exact of the volunteers more than they could give in any one year from their civilian pursuits.

And none of this would be done in such a way as in the slightest degree to supersede or subordinate our present serviceable and efficient National Guard. On the contrary, the National Guard itself would be used as part of the instrumentality by which training would be given the citizens who enlisted under the new conditions, and I should hope and expect that the legislation by which all this would be accomplished would put the National Guard itself upon a better and more permanent footing than it has ever been before, giving it not only the recognition which it deserves, but a more definite support from the national government and a more definite connection with the military organization of the Nation.

What we all wish to accomplish is that the forces of the Nation should indeed be part of the Nation and not a separate professional force, and the chief cost of the system would not be in the enlistment or in the training of the men, but in the providing of ample equipment in case it should be necessary to call all forces into the field. . . .

No thoughtful man feels any panic haste in this matter. The country is not threatened from any quarter. She stands in friendly relations with all the world. Her resources are known and her self-respect and her capacity to care for her own citizens and her own rights. There is no fear amongst us. Under the new-world conditions we have become thoughtful of the things which all reasonable men consider necessary for security and self-defense on the part of every nation confronted with the great enterprise of human liberty and independence. That is all.

Is the plan we propose sane and reasonable and suited to the needs of the hour? Does it not conform to the ancient traditions of America? Has any better plan been proposed than this program that we now place before the country? In it there is no pride of opinion. It represents the best professional and expert judgment of the country. But I am not so much interested in programs as I am in safeguarding at every cost the good faith and honor of the country. If men differ with me in this vital matter, I shall ask them to make it clear how far and in what way they are interested in making the permanent interests of the country safe against disturbance.

In the fulfillment of the program I propose I shall ask for the hearty support of the country, of the rank and file of America, of men of all shades of political opinion. For my position in this important matter is different from that of the private individual who is free to speak his own thoughts and to risk his own opinions in this matter. We are here dealing with things that are vital to the life of America itself. In doing this I have tried to purge my heart of all personal and selfish motives. For the time being, I speak as the trustee and guardian of a Nation's rights, charged with the duty of speaking for that Nation in matters involving her sovereignty—a Nation too big and generous to be exacting and yet courageous enough to defend its rights and the liberties of its people wherever assailed or invaded. I would not feel that I was discharging the solemn obligation I owe the country were I not to speak in terms of the deepest solemnity of the urgency and necessity of preparing ourselves to guard and protect the rights and privileges of our people, our sacred heritage of the fathers who struggled to make us an independent nation.

The only thing within our own borders that has given us grave concern in recent months has been that voices have been raised in America professing to be the voices of Americans which were not indeed and in truth American, but which spoke alien sympathies, which came from men who loved other countries better than they loved America, men who were partisans of other causes than that of America and had forgotten that their chief and only allegiance was to the great government under which they live. These voices have not been many, but they have been loud and very clamorous. They have proceeded from a few who were bitter and who were grievously misled. America has not opened its doors in vain to men and women out of other nations. The vast majority of those who have come to take advantage of her hospitality have united their spirits with hers as well as their fortunes. These men who speak alien sympathies are not their spokesmen but are the spokesmen of small groups whom it is high time that the Nation should call to a reckoning. The chief thing necessary in America in order that she should let all of the world know that she is prepared to maintain her own great position is that the real voice of the Nation should sound forth unmistakably and in majestic volume, in the deep unison of a common, unhesitating national feeling. I do not doubt that upon the first occasion, upon the first opportunity, upon the first definite challenge, that voice will speak forth in tones which no man can doubt and with commands which no man dare gainsay or resist. . . .

15. The Clear Rights of American Citizens

To Senator William Stone, February 24, 1916

Many Congressmen opposed Wilson on the question of allowing American passengers to travel upon armed merchant ships. Senator Stone of Missouri, a faithful supporter of the administration, wrote Wilson that members of Congress were "deeply concerned and disturbed" about the President's inflexible policy. This rebellion in Congress jeopardized the whole preparedness program. Wilson's reply below is a lucid summary of his position.

I VERY warmly appreciate your kind and frank letter of today, and feel that it calls for an equally frank reply.

You are right in assuming that I shall do everything in my

power to keep the United States out of war. I think the country will feel no uneasiness about my course in that respect. Through many anxious months I have striven for that object, amidst difficulties more manifold than can have been apparent upon the surface; and so far I have succeeded. The course which the central European powers have announced their intention of following in the future with regard to undersea warfare seems for the moment to threaten insuperable obstacles, but its apparent meaning is so manifestly inconsistent with explicit assurances recently given us by those powers with regard to their treatment of merchant vessels on the high seas that I must believe that explanations will presently ensue which will put a different aspect upon it. We have had no reason to question their good faith or their fidelity to their promises in the past, and I, for one, feel confident that we shall have none in the future.

But in any event our duty is clear. No nation, no group of nations, has the right while war is in progress to alter or disregard the principles which all nations have agreed upon in mitigation of the horrors and sufferings of war; and if the clear rights of American citizens should ever unhappily be abridged or denied by any such action, we should, it seems to me, have in honor no choice as to what our own course should be.

For my own part, I cannot consent to any abridgement of the rights of American citizens in any respect. The honor and self-respect of the Nation is involved. We covet peace, and shall preserve it at any cost but the loss of honor. To forbid our people to exercise their rights for fear we might be called upon to vindicate them would be a deep humiliation indeed. It would be an implicit, all but an explicit, acquiescence in the violation of the rights of mankind everywhere and of whatever nation or allegiance. It would be a deliberate abdication of our hitherto proud position as spokesmen even amidst the turmoil of war for the law and the right. It would make everything this government has attempted and everything that it has achieved during this terrible struggle of nations meaningless and futile.

It is important to reflect that if in this instance we allowed expediency to take the place of principle, the door would inevitably be opened to still further concessions. Once accept a single abatement of right and many other humiliations would certainly follow, and the whole fine fabric of international law might crumble under our hands piece by piece. What we are contending for in this matter is of the very essence of the things that have made America a sovereign nation. She cannot yield them without conceding her own impotency as a nation and making virtual surrender of her independent position among the nations of the world.

I am speaking, my dear Senator, in deep solemnity, without heat, with a clear consciousness of the high responsibilities of my office, and as your sincere and devoted friend. If we should unhappily differ, we shall differ as friends; but where issues so momentous as these are involved we must, just because we are friends, speak our minds without reservation.

16. Effect an Abandonment

Address to Congress on *Sussex* Affair, April 19, 1916

The Germans were determined—within the limits of the Arabic *pledge—to sink armed merchant ships without warning. On March 24, the steamer* Sussex *was sunk in the English Channel. Several Americans on board were injured. Resisting pressure to break with Germany, Wilson sent a very strong note—or rather an ultimatum—to Germany on April 18. Its contents are summed up in his address to Congress.*

A SITUATION has arisen in the foreign relations of the country of which it is my plain duty to inform you very frankly.

It will be recalled that in February, 1915, the Imperial German Government announced its intention to treat the waters surrounding Great Britain and Ireland as embraced within the seat of war and to destroy all merchant ships owned by its enemies that might be found within any part of that portion of the high seas, and that it warned all vessels, of neutral as well as of belligerent ownership, to keep out of the waters it had thus proscribed or else enter them at their peril. The Government of the United States earnestly protested. It took the position that such a policy could not be pursued without the practical certainty of gross and palpable violations of the law of nations, particularly if submarine craft were to be employed as its instruments, inasmuch as the rules prescribed by that law, rules founded upon principles of humanity and established for the protection of the lives of noncombatants at sea, could not in the nature of the case be observed by such vessels. It based its protest on the ground that persons of neutral nationality and vessels of neutral ownership would be exposed to extreme and intolerable risks, and that no right to close any part of the high seas against their use or to expose them to such risks could lawfully be asserted by any belligerent government. The law of nations in these matters, upon which the Government of the United States based its protest, is not of recent origin or founded upon merely arbitrary principles set up by convention. It is based, on the contrary, upon manifest and imperative principles of humanity and has long been established with the approval and by the express assent of all civilized nations.

Notwithstanding the earnest protest of our Government, the Imperial German Government at once proceeded to carry out the policy it had announced. It expressed the hope that the dangers involved, at any rate the dangers to neutral vessels, would be reduced to a minimum by the instructions which it had issued to its submarine commanders, and assured the Government of the United States that it would take every possible precaution both to respect the rights of neutrals and to safeguard the lives of noncombatants.

What has actually happened in the year which has since elapsed has shown that those hopes were not justified, those assurances insusceptible of being fulfilled. In pursuance of the policy of submarine warfare against the commerce of its adversaries, thus announced and entered upon by the Imperial German Government in despite of the solemn protest of this Government, the commanders of German undersea vessels have attacked merchant ships with greater and greater activity, not only upon the high seas surrounding Great Britain and Ireland but wherever they could encounter them, in a way that has grown more and more ruthless, more and more indiscriminate as the months have gone by, less and less observant of restraints of any kind; and have delivered their attacks without compunction against vessels of every nationality and bound upon every sort of errand. Vessels of neutral ownership, even vessels of neutral ownership bound from neutral port to neutral port, have been destroyed along with vessels of belligerent ownership in constantly increasing numbers. Sometimes the merchantman attacked has been warned and summoned to surrender before being fired on or torpedoed; sometimes passengers or crews have been vouchsafed the poor security of being allowed to take to the ship's boats before she was sent to the bottom. But again and again no warning has been given, no escape even to the ship's boats allowed to those on board. What this Government foresaw must happen has happened. Tragedy has followed tragedy on the seas in such fashion, with such attendant circumstances, as to make it grossly evident that warfare of such a sort, if warfare it be, can not be carried on without the most palpable violation of the dictates alike of right and of humanity. Whatever the disposition and intention of the Imperial German Government, it has manifestly proved impossible for it to keep such methods of attack upon the commerce of its enemies within the bounds set by either the reason or the heart of mankind.

In February of the present year the Imperial German Government informed this Government and the other neutral governments of the world that it had reason to believe that the Government of Great Britain had armed all merchant vessels of British ownership and had given them secret orders to attack any submarine of the enemy they might encounter upon the seas, and that the Imperial German Government felt justified in the circumstances in treating all armed merchantmen of belligerent ownership as auxiliary vessels of war, which it would have the right to destroy without warning. The law of nations has long recognized the right of merchantmen to carry arms for protection and to use them to repel attack, although to use them, in such circumstances, at their own risk; but the Imperial German Government claimed the right to set these understandings aside in circumstances which it deemed extraordinary. Even the terms in which it announced its purpose thus still further to relax the restraints it had previously professed its willingness and desire to put upon the operation of its submarines carried the plain implication that at least vessels which were not armed would still be exempt from destruction without warning and that personal safety would be accorded their passengers and crews; but even that limitation, if it was ever practicable to observe it, has in fact constituted no check at all upon the destruction of ships of every sort.

Again and again the Imperial German Government has given this Government its solemn assurances that at least passenger ships with not be thus dealt with, and yet it has again and again permitted its undersea commanders to disregard those assurances with entire impunity. Great liners like the *Lusitania* and the *Arabic* and mere ferryboats like the *Sussex* have been attacked without a moment's warning, sometimes before they had even become aware that they were in the presence of an armed vessel of the enemy, and the lives of noncombatants, passengers and crew have been sacrificed wholesale, in a manner which the Government of the United States cannot but regard as wanton and without the slighest color of justification. No limit of any kind has in fact been set to the indiscriminate pursuit and destruction of merchantmen of all kinds and nationalities within the waters, constantly extending in area, where these operations have been carried on; and the roll of Americans who have lost their lives on ships thus attacked and destroyed has grown month by month until the ominous toll has mounted into the hundreds.

One of the latest and most shocking instances of this method of warfare was that of the destruction of the French cross-channel steamer *Sussex*. It must stand forth, as the sinking of the steamer *Lusitania* did, as so singularly tragical and unjustifiable as to constitute a truly terrible example of the inhumanity of submarine warfare as the commanders of German vessels have for the past twelvemonth been conducting it. If this instance stood alone, some explanation, some disavowal by the German Government, some evidence of criminal mistake or willful disobedience on the part of the commander of the vessel that fired the torpedo might be sought or entertained; but unhappily it does not stand alone. Recent events make the conclusion inevitable that it is only one instance, even though it be one of the most extreme and distressing instances, of the spirit and method of warfare which the Imperial German Government has mistakenly adopted, and which from the first exposed that Government to the reproach of thrusting all neutral rights aside in pursuit of its immediate objects.

The Government of the United States has been very patient. At every stage of this distressing experience of tragedy after tragedy in which its own citizens were involved it has sought to be restrained from any extreme course of action or of protest by a thoughtful consideration of the extraordinary circumstances of this unprecedented war, and actuated in all that it said or did by the sentiments of genuine friendship which the people of the United States have always entertained and continue to entertain towards the German nation. It has of course accepted the successive explanations and assurances of the Imperial German Government as given in entire sincerity and good faith, and has hoped, even against hope, that it would prove to be possible for the German Government so to order and control the acts of its naval commanders as to square its policy with the principles of humanity as embodied in the law of nations. It has been willing to wait until the significance of the facts became absolutely unmistakable and susceptible of but one interpretation.

That point has now unhappily been reached. The facts are susceptible of but one interpretation. The Imperial German Government has been unable to put any limits or restraints upon its warfare against either freight or passenger ships. It has therefore become painfully evident that the position which this Government took at the very outset is inevitable, namely, that the use of submarines for the destruction of an enemy's commerce is of necessity, because of the very character of the vessels employed and the very methods of attack which their employment of course involves, incompatible with the principles of humanity, the long established and incontrovertible rights of neutrals, and the sacred immunities of noncombatants.

I have deemed it my duty, therefore, to say to the Imperial German Government that if it is still its purpose to prosecute relentless and indiscriminate warfare against vessels of commerce by the use of submarines, notwithstanding the now demonstrated impossibility of conducting that warfare in accordance with what the Government of the United States must consider the sacred and indisputable rules of international law and the universally recognized dictates of humanity, the Government of the United States is at last forced to the conclusion that there is but one course it can pursue; and that unless the Imperial German Government should now immediately declare and effect an abandonment of its present methods of warfare against passenger and freight-carrying vessels this Government can have no choice but to sever diplomatic relations with the Government of the German Empire altogether.

This decision I have arrived at with the keenest regret; the possibility of the action contemplated I am sure all thoughtful Americans will look forward to with unaffected reluctance. But we cannot forget that we are in some sort and by the force of circumstances the responsible spokesmen of the rights of humanity, and that we cannot remain silent while those rights seem in process of being swept utterly away in the maelstrom of this terrible war. We owe it to a due regard for our own rights as a nation, to our sense of duty as a representative of the rights of neutrals the world over, and to a just conception of the rights of mankind to take this stand now with the utmost solemnity and firmness.

I have taken it, and taken it in the confidence that it will meet with your approval and support. All sober-minded men must unite in hoping that the Imperial German Government, which has in other circumstances stood as the champion of all that we are now contending for in the interest of humanity, may recognize the justice of our demands and meet them in the spirit in which they are made.

17. This Friend of Justice and of Men

To Senator C. A. Culbertson, May 5, 1916

Louis Brandeis was one of the best known and most respected—or feared—progressives in the country. In the course of his struggles for social justice he had made many enemies. But Wilson was greatly indebted to him since 1912. On January 28, 1916, Wilson nominated Brandeis to the Supreme Court. Conservatives throughout the country—especially conservative lawyers—were outraged and strove with all their might to prevent him from reaching the Bench. Brandeis's confirmation developed into a vital test for the Wilson administration. On May 5, Senator Culbertson, the chairman of the Judiciary Committee which was considering the nomination, asked Wilson why he insisted on Brandeis. Wilson's eloquent response is given below. On June 1, the Senate confirmed the nomination, and the Supreme Court gained a great judge.

I AM very much obliged to you for giving me an opportunity to make clear to the Judiciary Committee my reasons for nominating Mr. Louis D. Brandeis to fill the vacancy in the Supreme Court of the United States created by the death of Mr. Justice Lamar, for I am profoundly interested in the confirmation of the appointment by the Senate.

There is probably no more important duty imposed upon the President in connection with the general administration of the Government than that of naming members of the Supreme Court; and I need hardly tell you that I named Mr. Brandeis as a member of that great tribunal only because I knew him to be singularly qualified by learning, by gifts, and by character for the position.

Many charges have been made against Mr. Brandeis: the report of your subcommittee has already made it plain to you and to the country at large how unfounded those charges were. They threw a great deal more light upon the character and motives of those with whom they originated than upon the qualifications of Mr. Brandeis. I myself looked into them three years ago when I desired to make Mr. Brandeis a member of my Cabinet and found that they proceeded for the most part from those who hated Mr. Brandeis because he had refused to be serviceable to them in the promotion of their own selfish interests, and from those whom they had prejudiced and misled. The propaganda in this matter has been very extraordinary and very distressing to those who love fairness and value the dignity of the great professions.

I perceived from the first that the charges were intrinsically incredible by anyone who had really known Mr. Brandeis. I have known him. I have tested him by seeking his advice upon some of the most difficult and perplexing public questions about which it was necessary for me to form a judgment. I have dealt with him in matters where nice questions of honor and fair play, as well as large questions of justice and the public benefit, were involved. In every matter in which I have made test of his judgment and point of view I have received from him counsel singularly enlightening, singularly clear-sighted and judicial, and, above all, full of moral stimulation. He is a friend of all just men and a lover of the right; and he knows more than how to talk about the right —he knows how to set it forward in the face of its enemies. I knew from direct personal knowledge of the man what I was doing when I named him for the highest and most responsible tribunal of the nation.

Of his extraordinary ability as a lawyer no man who is competent to judge can speak with anything but the highest admiration. You will remember that in the opinion of the late Chief Justice Fuller he was the ablest man who ever appeared before the Supreme Court of the United States. "He is also," the Chief Justice added, "absolutely fearless in the discharge of his duties."

Those who have resorted to him for assistance in settling great industrial disputes can testify to his fairness and love of justice. In the troublesome controversies between the garment workers and manufacturers of New York City, for example, he gave a truly remarkable proof of his judicial temperament and had what must have been the great satisfaction of rendering decisions which both sides were willing to accept as disinterested and even-handed.

Mr. Brandeis has rendered many notable services to the city and state with which his professional life has been identified. He successfully directed the difficult campaign which resulted in obtaining cheaper gas for the City of Boston. It was chiefly under his guidance and through his efforts that legislation was secured in Massachusetts which authorized savings banks to issue insurance policies for small sums at much reduced rates. And some gentlemen who tried very hard to obtain control by the Boston Elevated Railway Company of the subways of the city for a period of ninety-nine years can probably testify as to his ability as the people's advocate when public interests call for an effective champion. He rendered these services without compensation and earned, whether he got it or not, the gratitude of every citizen of the state and city he served. These are but a few of the services of this kind he has freely rendered. It will hearten friends of community and public rights throughout the country to see his quality signally recognized by his elevation to the Supreme Bench. For the whole country is aware of his quality and is interested in this appointment.

I did not in making choice of Mr. Brandeis ask for or depend upon "endorsements." I acted upon public knowledge and personal acquaintance with the man, and preferred to name a lawyer for this great office whose abilities and character were so widely recognized that he needed no endorsement. I did, however, personally consult many men in whose judgment I had great confidence, and am happy to say was supported in my selection by the voluntary recommendation of the Attorney General of the United States, who urged Mr. Brandeis upon my consideration independently of any suggestion from me.

Let me say by way of summing up, my dear Senator, that I nominated Mr. Brandeis for the Supreme Court because it was, and is, my deliberate judgment that, of all the men now at the bar whom it has been my privilege to observe, test, and know, he is exceptionally qualified. I cannot speak too highly of his impartial, impersonal, orderly, and constructive mind, his rare analytical powers, his deep human sympathy, his profound acquaintance with the historical roots of our institutions and insight into their spirit, or of the many evidences he has given of being imbued to the very heart with our American ideals of justice and equality of opportunity; of his knowledge of modern economic conditions and of the way they bear upon the masses of the people, or of his genius in getting persons to unite in common and harmonious action and look with frank and kindly eyes into each other's minds, who had before been heated antagonists. This friend of justice and of men will ornament the high court of which we are all so justly proud. I am glad to have had the opportunity to pay him this tribute of admiration and of confidence; and I beg that your Committee will accept this nomination as coming from me quick with a sense of public obligation and responsibility.

18. Now Happily Abandoned

Note on German Reply to *Sussex* Statement, May 8, 1916

Wilson's ultimatum on the Sussex *affair brought to a head the conflict between the military and civilian leaders in Germany. The latter, led by Chancellor von Bethmann-Hollweg, finally received*

Emperor William's support in their efforts to end unrestricted submarine warfare. For it became clear that unless it was ended the United States would enter the war. In a note of May 4 the German government promised that henceforward its submarines would search vessels before sinking them. It also demanded that the United States compel Britain to obey international law. Wilson took the German note to be a capitulation. In his reply below he denies Germany's conditions.

THE NOTE of the Imperial German Government under date of May 4, 1916, has received careful consideration by the Government of the United States. It is especially noted, as indicating the purpose of the Imperial Government as to the future, that it "is prepared to do its utmost to confine the operations of the war for the rest of its duration to the fighting forces of the belligerents," and that it is determined to impose upon all its commanders at sea the limitations of the recognized rules of international law upon which the Government of the United States has insisted. Throughout the months which have elapsed since the Imperial Government announced, on February 4, 1915, its submarine policy, now happily abandoned, the Government of the United States has been constantly guided and restrained by motives of friendship in its patient efforts to bring to an amicable settlement the critical questions arising from that policy. Accepting the Imperial Government's declaration of its abandonment of the policy which has so seriously menaced the good relations between the two countries, the Government of the United States will rely upon a scrupulous execution henceforth of the now altered policy of the Imperial Government, such as will remove the principal danger to an interruption of the good relations existing between the United States and Germany.

The Government of the United States feels it necessary to state that it takes for granted that the Imperial German Government does not intend to imply that the maintenance of its newly announced policy is in any way contingent upon the course or result of diplomatic negotiations between the Government of the United States and any other belligerent government, notwithstanding the fact that certain passages in the Imperial Government's note of the 4th instant might appear to be susceptible of that construction. In order, however, to avoid any possible misunderstanding, the Government of the United States notifies the Imperial Government that it can not for a moment entertain, much less discuss, a suggestion that respect by German naval authorities for the rights of citizens of the United States upon the high seas should in any way or in the slightest degree be made contingent upon the conduct of any other government affecting the rights of neutrals and noncombatants. Responsibility in such matters is single, not joint; absolute, not relative.

19. This Alternative

To Colonel House, May 16, 1916

Germany had agreed to cease unrestricted submarine warfare. Why should Britain not allow freedom of the seas? Wilson pressed Britain to agree either to peace terms with Germany or to a system of international law in which freedom of the seas would be guaranteed. Such is the burden of this letter to House.

. . . THE AT least temporary removal of the acute German question has concentrated attention here on the altogether indefensible course Great Britain is pursuing with regard to trade to and from neutral ports and her quite intolerable interception of mails on the high seas carried by neutral ships. Recently there has been added the great shock opinion in this country has received from the course of the British Government towards some of the Irish rebels.

We are plainly face to face with this alternative, therefore. The United States must either make a decided move for peace (upon some basis that promises to be permanent) or, if she postpones that, must insist to the limit upon her rights of trade and upon such freedom of the seas as international law already justifies her in insisting on as against Great Britain, with the same plain speaking and firmness that she has used against Germany. And the choice must be made immediately. Which does Great Britain prefer? She cannot escape both. To do nothing is now, for us, impossible.

If we move for peace, it will be along these lines: 1) Such a settlement with regard to their own immediate interests as the belligerents may be able to agree upon. We have nothing material of any kind to ask for ourselves and are quite aware that we are in no sense parties to the quarrel. Our interest is only in peace and its guarantees; 2) a universal alliance to maintain freedom of the seas and to prevent any war begun either a) contrary to treaty covenants or b) without warning and full inquiry—a virtual guarantee of territorial integrity and political independence.

It seems to me to be of imperative and pressing importance that Sir Edward * should understand all this and that the crisis can not be postponed; and it can be done with the most evident spirit of friendliness through you. Will you not prepare a full cable putting the whole thing plainly to him? We must act, and act at once, in the one direction or the other.

20. "For God's Sake Do Not Do It"

Address Opposing Mexican Intervention, June 30, 1916

Had Wilson not made some gesture of reconciliation to Mexico, there probably would have been a war. Mexican soldiers had recently "ambushed" a contingent of Americans, killing twelve and capturing twenty-three. (Actually the Americans had charged the Mexicans, thinking they would meet no resistance.) This event followed several previous clashes between soldiers on both sides, and public opinion in the two countries was inflamed. In the United States the Republicans were calling for decisive action against Mexico. At this juncture Wilson moved to make peace. His address to the New York Press Club on June 31 relieved tensions at once and the way was cleared for eventual reconciliation.

. . . THE EASIEST thing is to strike. The brutal thing is the impulsive thing. No man has to think before taking aggressive action, but before a man really conserves the honor by realizing the ideals of the Nation, he has to think exactly what to do and how he will do it.

Do you think the glory of America would be enhanced by a war of conquest in Mexico? Do you think that any act of violence by a powerful nation like this against a weak and distracted neigh-

* Edward Grey, British Foreign Secretary.

bor would reflect distinction upon the annals of the United States? Do you think it is our duty to carry self-defense to the point of dictation in the affairs of another people? The annals of America are written plain upon every page of American history.

And I want you to know how fully I realize whose servant I am. I do not own the Government of the United States, even for the time being. I have no right in the use of it to express my own passions. I have no right to express my own ambitions for the development of America if those ambitions are not coincident with the ambitions of the Nation itself.

And I have constantly to remind myself that I am not the servant of those who wish to enhance the value of their Mexican investments, but that I am the servant of the rank and file of the people of the United States.

I get a great many letters, my fellow citizens, from important and influential men in this country, but I get many other letters. I get letters from unknown men, from humble women, from people whose names will never be heard and never be recorded and there is but one prayer in all these letters: "Mr. President, do not allow anybody to persuade you that the people of this country want war with anybody."

I got off the train yesterday and as I was bidding goodbye to the engineer, he said in an undertone, "Mr. President, keep us out of Mexico," and if one man has said that to me a thousand have said it to me as I have moved about the country. If I have opportunity to engage them further in conversation they say, "Of course we know that you cannot govern the circumstances of the case altogether, and it may be necessary, but for God's sake do not do it unless it is necessary. . . ."

I am willing, no matter what my personal fortune may be, to play for the verdict of mankind. Personally, it will be a matter of indifference to me what the verdict on the seventh of November is provided I feel any degree of confidence that when a later jury sits, I shall get their judgment in my favor. Not in my favor personally—what difference does that make?—but in my favor as an honest and conscientious spokesman of a great Nation.

There are some gentlemen who are under the delusion that the power of a nation comes from the top; it does not; it comes from the bottom. The power and virtue of the tree does not come from the blossom and the fruits down into the roots, but it comes from the roots in the obscure passages of the earth where the power is derived which displays itself in the blossom and the fruit; and I know that among the silent speechless masses of the American people is slowly coming up the great sap of moral purpose and love of justice and reverence for humanity which constitutes the only virtue and distinction of the American people. . . .

21. The Last Straw

To Colonel House, July 23, 1916

Britain had done nothing to relax her policy of blacklisting goods and seizing the mails. On July 19 the British government published a much more elaborate blacklist. Wilson was shocked. The letter below is angrier than the mild protest which the State Department finally sent on July 26.

. . . I AM, I must admit, about at the end of my patience with Great Britain and the Allies. This blacklist business is the last straw. I have told Spring Rice so, and he sees the reasons very clearly. Both he and Jusserand think it a stupid blunder. I am seriously considering asking Congress to authorize me to prohibit loans and restrict exportations to the Allies. It is becoming clear to me that there lies latent in this policy the wish to prevent our merchants getting a foothold in markets which Great Britain has hitherto controlled and all but dominated. Polk and I are compounding a very sharp note. I may feel obliged to make it as sharp and final as the one to Germany on the submarines. What is your own judgment? Can we any longer endure their intolerable course? . . .

22. In the Interest of Justice

Address to Congress on Eight Hour Day, August 29, 1916

In the spring of 1916 the four railroad unions said they would strike unless their demands for an eight hour day were met. The managers refused. When a board of mediators failed to bring an agreement, Wilson invited the two sides to a White House conference, making it clear to them that a strike would harm the nation's preparedness effort. But the managers and unions failed to come to terms. Wilson then proposed his own settlement: the workers were to be conceded the eight-hour day but denied the overtime pay which they had also demanded, and a federal commission was to be established to investigate labor problems in the industry. The unions accepted these proposals; the managers turned them down. On August 8, Wilson attempted to convince thirty-one railroad executives; again to no avail. Still another attempt was made and this too failed. On August 27, the unions declared a strike for September 4. Yet another appeal to the managers was turned down. Exasperated and angry, Wilson consulted with his party leaders and then presented the following address to Congress. Working with extraordinary speed, Congress passed and the President signed the Adamson Act, which embodied Wilson's original proposals. It settled the strike but became an issue in the 1916 campaign.

I HAVE come to you to seek your assistance in dealing with a very grave situation which has arisen out of the demand of the employees of the railroads engaged in freight train service that they be granted an eight hour working day, safeguarded by payment for an hour and a half of service for every hour of work beyond the eight.

The matter has been agitated for more than a year. The public has been made familiar with the demands of the men and the arguments urged in favor of them, and even more familiar with the objections of the railroads and their counter demand that certain privileges now enjoyed by their men and certain bases of payment worked out through many years of contest be reconsidered, especially in their relation to the adoption of an eight hour day. The matter came some three weeks ago to a final issue and resulted in a complete deadlock between the parties. The means provided by law for the mediation of the controversy failed and the means of arbitration for which the law provides were rejected. The representatives of the railway executives proposed that the demands of the men be submitted in their entirety to arbitration, along with certain questions of readjustment as to pay and conditions of employment which seemed to them to be either closely associated with the demands or to call for reconsideration on their own merits; the men absolutely declined arbitration, especially if any of their established privileges were by that means to be drawn again in question. The law in the matter put no compulsion upon them. The four hundred thousand men from whom the demands proceeded had voted to strike if their demands were refused; the strike was imminent; it has since been set for the fourth of September next. It affects the men who man the freight trains on practically every railway in the country. The freight service throughout the United States must stand still until their places are filled, if, indeed, it should prove possible to fill them at all. Cities will be cut off from their food supplies, the whole commerce of the Nation will be paralyzed, men of every sort and occupation will be thrown out of employment, countless thousands will in all likelihood be brought, it may be, to the very point of starvation, and a tragical national calamity brought on, to be added to the other distresses of the time, because no basis of accommodation or settlement has been found.

Just so soon as it became evident that mediation under the existing law had failed and that arbitration had been rendered impossible by the attitude of the men, I considered it my duty to confer with the representatives of both the railways and the brotherhoods, and myself offer mediation, not as an arbitrator, but merely as spokesman of the Nation, in the interest of justice, indeed, and as a friend of both parties, but not as judge, only as the representative of one hundred millions of men, women, and children who would pay the price, the incalculable price, of loss and suffering should these few men insist upon approaching and concluding the matters in controversy between them merely as employers and employees, rather than as patriotic citizens of the United States looking before and after and accepting the larger responsibility which the public would put upon them.

It seemed to me, in considering the subject-matter of the controversy, that the whole spirit of the time and the preponderant evidence of recent economic experience spoke for the eight hour day. It has been adjudged by the thought and experience of recent years a thing upon which society is justified in insisting as in the interest of health, efficiency, contentment, and a general increase of economic vigor. The whole presumption of modern experience would, it seemed to me, be in its favor, whether there was arbitration or not, and the debatable points to settle were those which arose out of the acceptance of the eight hour day rather than those which affected its establishment. I, therefore, proposed that the eight-hour day be adopted by the railway managements and put into practice for the present as a substitute for the existing ten hour basis of pay and service; that I should appoint, with the permission of the Congress, a small commission to observe the results of the change, carefully studying the figures of the altered operating costs, not only, but also the conditions of labor under which the men worked and the operation of their existing agreements with the railroads, with instructions to report the facts as they found them to the Congress at the earliest possible day, but without recommendation; and that, after the facts had been thus disclosed, and adjustment should in some orderly manner be sought of all the matters now left unadjusted between the railroad managers and the men. . . .

The representatives of the brotherhoods accepted the plan; but the representatives of the railroads declined to accept it. In the face of what I cannot but regard as the practical certainty that they will be ultimately obliged to accept the eight-hour day by the concerted action of organized labor, backed by the favorable judgment of society, the representatives of the railway management have felt justified in declining a peaceful settlement which would engage all the forces of justice, public and private, on their side to take care of the event. They fear the hostile influence of shippers, who would be opposed to an increase of freight rates (for which, however, of course, the public itself would pay); they apparently feel no confidence that the Interstate Commerce Commission could withstand the objections that would be made. They do not care to rely upon the friendly assurances of the Congress or the President. They have thought it best that they should be forced to yield, if they must yield, not by counsel, but by the suffering of the country. While my conferences with them were in progress, and when to all outward appearance those conferences had come to a standstill, the representatives of the brotherhoods suddenly acted and set the strike for the fourth of September.

The railway managers based their decision to reject my counsel in this matter upon their conviction that they must at any cost to themselves or to the country stand firm for the principle of arbitration which the men had rejected. I based my counsel upon the indisputable fact that there was no means of obtaining arbitration. The law supplied none; earnest efforts at mediation had failed to influence the men in the least. To stand firm for the principle of arbitration and yet not get arbitration seemed to me futile, and something more than futile, because it involved incalculable distress to the country and consequences in some respects worse than those of war, and that in the midst of peace.

I yield to no man in firm adherence, alike of conviction and of purpose, to the principle of arbitration in industrial disputes; but matters have come to a sudden crisis in this particular dispute and the country had been caught unprovided with any practicable means of enforcing that conviction in practice (by whose fault we will not now stop to inquire). A situation had to be met whose elements and fixed conditions were indisputable. The practical and patriotic course to pursue, as it seemed to me, was to secure immediate peace by conceding the one thing in the demands of the men which society itself and any arbitrators who represented public sentiment were most likely to approve, and immediately lay the foundations for securing arbitration with regard to everything else involved. The event has confirmed that judgment.

I was seeking to compose the present in order to safeguard the future; for I wished an atmosphere of peace and friendly cooperation in which to take counsel with the representatives of the Nation with regard to the best means for providing—so far as it might prove possible to provide against the recurrence of such unhappy situations in the future—the best and most practicable means of securing calm and fair arbitration of all industrial disputes in the days to come. This is assuredly the best way of vindicating a principle, namely, having failed to make certain of its observance in the present, to make certain of its observance in the future.

But I could only propose. I could not govern the will of others who took an entirely different view of the circumstances of the case, who even refused to admit the circumstances to be what they have turned out to be.

Having failed to bring the parties to this critical controversy to an accommodation, therefore, I turn to you, deeming it clearly our duty as public servants to leave nothing undone that we can do to safeguard the life and interests of the Nation. In the spirit of such a purpose, I earnestly recommend the following legislation:

First, immediate provision for the enlargement and administrative reorganization of the Interstate Commerce Commission along the lines embodied in the bill recently passed by the House of Representatives and now awaiting action by the Senate; in order that the Commission may be enabled to deal with the many great and various duties now devolving upon it with a promptness and thoroughness which are with its present constitution and means of action practically impossible.

Second, the establishment of an eight hour day as the legal basis alike of work and of wages in the employment of all railway employees who are actually engaged in the work of operating trains in interstate transportation.

Third, the authorization of the appointment by the President of a small body of men to observe the actual results in experience of the adoption of the eight hour day in railway transportation alike for the men and for the railroads; its effects in the matter of operating costs, in the application of the existing practices and agreements to the new conditions, and in all other practical aspects, with the provision that the investigators shall report their conclusions to the Congress at the earliest possible date, but without recommendation as to legislative action; in order that the public may learn from an unprejudiced source just what actual developments have ensued.

Fourth, explicit approval by the Congress of the consideration by the Interstate Commerce Commission of an increase of freight rates to meet such additional expenditures by the railroads as may have been rendered necessary by the adoption of the eight hour day and which have not been offset by administrative readjustments and economies, should the facts disclosed justify the increase.

Fifth, an amendment of the existing federal statute which provides for the mediation, conciliation, and arbitration of such controversies as the present by adding to it a provision that in case the methods of accommodation now provided for should fail, a full public investigation of the merits of every such dispute shall be instituted and completed before a strike or lockout may lawfully be attempted.

And, sixth, the lodgement in the hands of the Executive of the power, in case of military necessity, to take control of such portions and such rolling stock of the railways of the country as may be required for military use and to operate them for military purposes, with authority to draft into the military service of the United States such train crews and administrative officials as the circumstances require for their safe and efficient use. . . .

23. The Conditions of a New Age

Address Accepting Nomination, September 2, 1916

Wilson opened his reelection campaign of 1916 with this detailed summary of his progressive accomplishments.

. . . THE REPUBLICAN party was put out of power because of failure, practical failure and moral failure; because it had served special interests and not the country at large; because, under the leadership of its preferred and established guides, of those who still make its choices, it had lost touch with the thoughts and the needs of the Nation and was living in a past age and under a fixed illusion, the illusion of greatness. It had framed tariff laws based upon a fear of foreign trade, a fundamental doubt as to American skill, enterprise, and capacity, and a very tender regard for the profitable privileges of those who had gained control of domestic markets and domestic credits; and yet had enacted antitrust laws which hampered the very things they meant to foster, which were stiff and inelastic, and in part unintelligible. It had permitted the country throughout the long period of its control to stagger from one financial crisis to another under the operation of a national banking law of its own framing which made stringency and panic certain and the control of the larger business operations of the country by the bankers of a few reserve centers inevitable; had made as if it meant to reform the law but had faint-heartedly failed in the attempt, because it could not bring itself to do the one thing necessary to make the reform genuine and effectual, namely, break up the control of small groups of bankers. It had been oblivious, or indifferent, to the fact that the farmers, upon whom the country depends for its food and in the last analysis for its prosperity, were without standing in the matter of commercial credit, without the protection of standards in their market transactions, and without systematic knowledge of the markets themselves; that the laborers of the country, the great army of men who man the industries it was professing to father and promote, carried their labor as a mere commodity to market, were subject to restraint by novel and drastic process in the courts, were without assurance of compensation for industrial accidents, without federal assistance in accommodating labor disputes, and without national aid or advice in finding the places and the industries in which their labor was most needed. The country had no national system of road construction and development. Little intelligent attention was paid to the army, and not enough to the navy. The other republics of America distrusted us, because they found that we thought first of the profits of American investors and only as an afterthought of impartial justice and helpful friendship. Its policy was provincial in all things; its purposes were out of harmony with the temper and purpose of the people and the timely development of the nation's interests.

So thing stood when the Democratic party came into power. How do they stand now? Alike in the domestic field and in the wide field of the commerce of the world, American business and life and industry have been set free to move as they never moved before.

The tariff has been revised, not on the principle of repelling foreign trade, but upon the principle of encouraging it, upon something like a footing of equality with our own in respect of the terms of competition, and a Tariff Board has been created whose function it will be to keep the relations of American with foreign business and industry under constant observation, for the guidance alike of our business men and of our Congress. American energies are now directed towards the markets of the world.

The laws against trusts have been clarified by definition, with a view to making it plain that they were not directed against big business but only against unfair business and the pretense of competition where there was none; and a Trade Commission has been created with powers of guidance and accommodation which have relieved business men of unfounded fears and set them upon the road of hopeful and confident enterprise.

By the Federal Reserve Act the supply of currency at the disposal of active business has been rendered elastic, taking its volume, not from a fixed body of investment securities, but from the liquid assets of daily trade; and these assets are assessed and accepted, not by distant groups of bankers in control of unavailable reserves, but by bankers at the many centers of local exchange who are in touch with local conditions everywhere.

Effective measures have been taken for the re-creation of an American merchant marine and the revival of the American carrying trade indispensable to our emancipation from the control which foreigners have so long exercised over the opportunities, the routes, and the methods of our commerce with other countries.

The Interstate Commerce Commission has been reorganized to enable it to perform its great and important functions more promptly and more efficiently. We have created, extended and improved the service of the parcels post.

So much we have done for business. What other party has understood the task so well or executed it so intelligently and energetically? What other party has attempted it at all? The Republican leaders, apparently, know of no means of assisting business but "protection." How to stimulate it and put it upon a new footing of energy and enterprise they have not suggested.

For the farmers of the country we have virtually created commercial credit, by means of the Federal Reserve Act and the Rural Credits Act. They now have the standing of other business men in the money market. We have successfully regulated speculation in "futures" and established standards in the marketing of grains. By an intelligent Warehouse Act we have assisted to make the standard crops available as never before both for systematic marketing and as a security for loans from the banks. We have greatly added to the work of neighborhood demonstration on the farm itself of improved methods of cultivation, and, through the intelligent extension of the functions of the Department of Agriculture, have made it possible for the farmer to learn systematically where his best markets are and how to get at them.

The workingmen of America have been given a veritable emancipation, by the legal recognition of a man's labor as part of his life, and not a mere marketable commodity; by exempting labor organizations from processes of the courts which treated their members like fractional parts of mobs and not like accessible and responsible individuals; by releasing our seamen from involuntary servitude; by making adequate provision for compensation for industrial accidents; by providing suitable machinery for mediation and conciliation in industrial disputes; and by putting the Federal Department of Labor at the disposal of the workingman when in search of work.

We have effected the emancipation of the children of the country by releasing them from hurtful labor. We have instituted a system of national aid in the building of highroads such as the country has been feeling after for a century. We have sought to equalize taxation by means of an equitable income tax. We have taken the steps that ought to have been taken at the outset to open up the resources of Alaska. We have provided for national defense upon a scale never before seriously proposed upon the responsibility of an entire political party. We have driven the tariff lobby from cover and obliged it to substitute solid argument for private influence.

This extraordinary recital must sound like a platform, a list of sanguine promises; but it is not. It is a record of promises made four years ago and now actually redeemed in constructive legislation.

These things must profoundly disturb the thoughts and confound the plans of those who have made themselves believe that the Democratic party neither understood nor was ready to assist the business of the country in the great enterprises which it is its evident and inevitable destiny to undertake and carry through. The breaking up of the lobby must especially disconcert them; for it was through the lobby that they sought and were sure they had found the heart of things. The game of privilege can be played successfully by no other means.

This record must equally astonish those who feared that the Democratic party had not opened its heart to comprehend the demands of social justice. We have in four years come very near to carrying out the platform of the Progressive party as well as our own; for we also are progressives.

There is one circumstance connected with this program which ought to be very plainly stated. It was resisted at every step by the interests which the Republican party had catered to and fostered at the expense of the country, and these same interests are now earnestly praying for a reaction which will save their privileges—for the restoration of their sworn friends to power before it is too late to recover what they have lost. They fought with particular desperation and infinite resourcefulness the reform of the banking and currency system, knowing that to be the citadel of their control; and most anxiously are they hoping and planning for the amendment of the Federal Reserve Act by the concentration of control in a single bank which the old familiar group of bankers can keep under their eye and direction. But while the "big men" who used to write the tariffs and command the assistance of the Treasury have been hostile—all but a few with vision—the average business man knows that he has been delivered, and that the fear that was once every day in his heart that the men who controlled credit and directed enterprise from the committee rooms of Congress would crush him, is there no more, and will not return—unless the party that consulted only the "big men" should return to power—the party of masterly inactivity and cunning resourcefulness in standing pat to resist change.

The Republican party is just the party that *cannot* meet the new conditions of a new age. It does not know the way and it does not wish new conditions. It tried to break away from the old leaders and could not. They still select its candidates and dictate its policy, still resist change, still hanker after the old conditions, still know no methods of encouraging business but the old methods. When it changes its leaders and its purposes and brings its ideas up to date it will have the right to ask the American people to give it power again; but not until then. A new age, an age of revolutionary change, needs new purposes and new ideas.

In foreign affairs we have been guided by principles clearly conceived and consistently lived up to. Perhaps they have not been fully comprehended because they have hitherto governed international affairs only in theory, not in practice. They are simple, obvious, easily stated, and fundamental to American ideals.

We have been neutral not only because it was the fixed and traditional policy of the United States to stand aloof from the politics of Europe and because we had had no part either of action or of policy in the influences which brought on the present war, but also because it was manifestly our duty to prevent, if it were possible, the indefinite extension of the fires of hate and desolation kindled by that terrible conflict and seek to serve mankind by reserving our strength and our resources for the anxious and difficult days of restoration and healing which must follow, when peace will have to build its house anew.

The rights of our own citizens of course became involved: that was inevitable. Where they did, this was our guiding principle: that property rights can be vindicated by claims for damages when the war is over, and no modern nation can decline to arbitrate such claims; but the fundamental rights of humanity cannot be. The loss of life is irreparable. Neither can direct violations of a nation's sovereignty await vindication in suits for damages. The nation that violates these essential rights must expect to be checked and called to account by direct challenge and resistance. It at once makes the quarrel in part our own. These are plain principles and we have never lost sight of them or departed from them, whatever the stress or the perplexity of circumstance or the provocation to hasty resentment. The record is clear and consistent throughout and stands distinct and definite for anyone to judge who wishes to know the truth about it.

The seas were not broad enough to keep the infection of the conflict out of our own politics. The passions and intrigues of certain active groups and combinations of men amongst us who were born under foreign flags injected the poison of disloyalty into our own most critical affairs, laid violent hands upon many of our industries, and subjected us to the shame of divisions of sentiment and purpose in which America was condemned and forgotten. It is part of the business of this year of reckoning and settlement to speak plainly and act with unmistakable purpose in rebuke of these things, in order that they may be forever hereafter impossible. I am the candidate of a party, but I am above all things else an American citizen. I neither seek the favor nor fear the displeasure of that small alien element amongst us which puts loyalty to any foreign power before loyalty to the United States.

While Europe was at war our own continent, one of our own neighbors, was shaken by revolution. In that matter, too, principle was plain and it was imperative that we should live up to it if we were to deserve the trust of any real partisan of the right as free men see it. We have professed to believe, and we do believe, that the people of small and weak states have the right to expect to be dealt with exactly as the people of big and powerful states would be. We have acted upon that principle in dealing with the people of Mexico.

Our recent pursuit of bandits into Mexican territory was no violation of that principle. We ventured to enter Mexican territory only because there were no military forces in Mexico that could protect our border from hostile attack and our own people from violence, and we have committed there no single act of hostility or interference even with the sovereign authority of the Republic of Mexico herself. It was a plain case of the violation of our own sovereignty which could not wait to be vindicated by damages and for which there was no other remedy. The authorities of Mexico were powerless to prevent it.

Many serious wrongs against the property, many irreparable wrongs against the persons, of Americans have been committed within the territory of Mexico herself during this confused revolution, wrongs which could not be effectually checked so long as there was no constituted power in Mexico which was in a position to check them. We could not act directly in that matter ourselves without denying Mexicans the right to any revolution at all which disturbed us and making the emancipation of her own people await our own interest and convenience.

For it is their emancipation that they are seeking—blindly, it may be, and as yet ineffectually, but with profound and passionate purpose and within their unquestionable right, apply what true American principle you will—any principle that an American would publicly avow. The people of Mexico have not been suffered to own their own country or direct their own institutions. Outsiders, men out of other nations and with interests too often alien to their own, have dictated what their privileges and opportunities should be and who should control their land, their lives, and their resources—some of them Americans, pressing for things they could never have got in their own country. The Mexican people are entitled to attempt their liberty from such influences; and so long as I have anything to do with the action of our great Government I shall do everything in my power to prevent anyone standing in their way. I know that this is hard for some persons to understand; but it is not hard for the plain people of the United States to understand. It is hard doctrine only for those who wish to get something for themselves out of Mexico. There are men, and noble women, too, not a few, of our own people, thank God! whose fortunes are invested in great properties in Mexico who yet see the case with true vision and assess its issues with true American feeling. The rest can be left for the present out of the reckoning until this enslaved people has had its day of struggle towards the light. I have heard no one who was free from such influences propose interference by the United States with the internal affairs of Mexico. Certainly no friend of the Mexican people has proposed it.

The people of the United States are capable of great sympathies and a noble pity in dealing with problems of this kind. As their spokesman and representative, I have tried to act in the spirit they would wish me to show. The people of Mexico are striving for the rights that are fundamental to life and happiness—fifteen million oppressed men, overburdened women, and pitiful children in virtual bondage in their own home of fertile lands and inexhaustible treasure! Some of the leaders of the revolution may often have been mistaken and violent and selfish, but the revolution itself was inevitable and is right. The unspeakable Huerta betrayed the very comrades he served, traitorously overthrew the government of which he was a trusted part, impudently spoke for the very forces that had driven his people to the rebellion with which he had pretended to sympathize. The men who overcame him and drove him out represent at least the fierce passion of reconstruction which lies at the very heart of liberty; and so long as they represent, however imperfectly, such a struggle for deliverance, I am ready to serve their ends when I can. So long as the power of recognition rests with me the Government of the United States will refuse to extend the hand of welcome to any one who obtains power in a sister republic by treachery and violence. No permanency can be given the affairs of any republic by a title based upon intrigue and assassination. I declared that to be the policy of this Administration within three weeks after I assumed the presidency. I here again vow it. I am more interested in the fortunes of oppressed men and pitiful women and children than in any property rights whatever. . . .

24. The Immediate Succession

To Secretary of State Lansing, November 5, 1916

Wilson thought it intolerable that in times of crisis four months should separate a defeated President from his successor. After discussing the matter with Colonel House he wrote the following extraordinary letter.

THERE IS a matter which has occupied my thoughts throughout the campaign and which I want to lay before you before the election, while I can discuss it without any touch of feeling as to the result.

Again and again the question has arisen in my mind, What would it be my duty to do were Mr. Hughes to be elected? Four months would elapse before he could take charge of the affairs of the government, and during those four months I would be without such moral backing from the nation as would be necessary to steady and control our relations with other governments. I would be known to be the rejected, not the accredited, spokesman of the country; and yet the accredited spokesman would be without legal authority to speak for the nation. Such a situation would be fraught with the gravest dangers. The direction of the foreign policy of the government would in effect have been taken out of my hands and yet its new definition would be impossible until March.

I feel that it would be my duty to relieve the country of the perils of such a situation at once. The course I have in mind is dependent upon the consent and cooperation of the Vice President; but, if I could gain his consent to the plan, I would ask your permission to invite Mr. Hughes to become Secretary of State and would then join the Vice President in resigning, and thus open to Mr. Hughes the immediate succession of the presidency.

All my life long I have advocated some such responsible government for the United States as other constitutional systems afford as of course, and as such action on my part would inaugurate, at least by example. Responsible government means government by those whom the people trust, and trust at the time of decision and action. The whole country has long perceived, without knowing how to remedy, the extreme disadvantage of having to live for four months after a[n] election under a party whose guidance has been rejected at the polls. Here is the remedy, at any rate so far as the Executive is concerned. In ordinary times it would perhaps not be necessary to apply it. But it seems to me that in the existing circumstances it would be imperatively necessary. The choice of policy in respect of our foreign relations rests with the Executive. No such critical circumstances in regard to our foreign policy have ever before existed. It would be my duty to step aside so that there would be no doubt in any quarter how that policy was to be directed, towards what objects and by what means. I would have no right to risk the peace of the nation by remaining in office after I had lost my authority.

I hope and believe that your own judgment will run with mine in this critical matter. . . .

P.S. I beg that you will regard this as in the strictest sense confidential until I shall have had an opportunity to discuss it with you in person, should circumstances make it a practical problem of duty.

25. In the Common Interest of Civilization

Draft of Note to Belligerent Powers, November 25, 1916

In September, 1916, the German government decided to seek a peace agreement through Wilson's good offices. Should this fail, unrestricted submarine warfare would resume. Wilson began to act on German peace overtures immediately after the election, which was itself a mandate to keep the peace. By November 25, Wilson completed the draft of a note, the contents of which appear below, to be sent to the belligerent powers. The next day he read it to Colonel House who thought that it would result in friction, perhaps even war, between the United States and the Allies. Wilson then agreed to table the note. On December 12, Germany again expressed the desire to negotiate for peace. Wilson thereupon brought out his draft and revised it in accordance with House's criticisms. The note that was sent to the belligerents on December 18 requested only that they define their war aims.

REASONS WHY I have the right to speak:

The war is disturbing the whole life of the world, making it hard everywhere for governments to serve and safeguard the life of the nations they serve, and all but impossible for the poor to live at all (governments are for the poor if they are for the bulk of mankind).

The war is making the task of neutrals impracticable, the position of neutrals intolerable.

The character to which the war has settled down: a war of exhaustion and attrition, and the result to be expected.

The professions of each side: that they do not desire conquest or the destruction of their antagonists: that they wish to safeguard the rights of small nations and of peoples: that they desire to end war (which cannot be done by conquest or destruction of nationalities).

The danger that the whole future will be prejudiced.

A common object has been professed by the leaders of the governments at war, viz. such a league to enforce peace as will make the future secure.

The United States is willing to lend its whole force of every kind to that end, with equal resolution and enthusiasm.

A little while and it may be too late to realize this object, because of exhaustion and *reaction.*

Triumph and hate cannot accomplish it.

In such circumstances and in the interest not only of all concerned directly in the war itself, of the whole world, rather, I feel that I have the right, with the utmost respect for the rights of all, to call for a parley.

My objects:

To stop the war before it is too late to remedy what it has done;

To reconsider peace on the basis of the rights of the weak along with the rights of the strong, the rights of peoples as well as the rights of governments;

To effect a league of nations based upon a peace which shall be guaranteed against breach by the common force and an intelligent organization of the common interest.

I take the liberty of addressing to you very frankly certain questions which seem to speak out almost of themselves from the circumstances and present progress of the war and of which I feel justified in making myself the spokesman not only because I am privileged to speak as the head of a great nation whose vital interests are being more and more seriously and profoundly affected with each week of the war's continuance but also because my heart and my reason tell me that the time has come to take counsel lest a violence be done civilization itself which cannot be atoned for or repaired.

In every quarter of the world the life of mankind has been altered and disturbed. Everywhere it is hindered and perplexed, rendered harder, more hazardous, more difficult to plan or to live upon any terms. The task of every government, the task of caring for and promoting the interests of its own people, has been hampered and impeded, and the burden falls, as always, upon those least prepared, least able to bear it.

The position of neutral nations, in particular, has been rendered all but intolerable. Their commerce is interrupted, their industries are checked and diverted, the lives of their people are put in constant jeopardy, they are virtually forbidden the accustomed highways of the sea, their energies are drawn off into temporary and novel channels, they suffer at every turn though disengaged and disposed to none but friendly and impartial offices.

And yet the objects which would, if attained, satisfy the one group of belligerents or the other have never been definitely avowed. The world can still only conjecture what definitive results, what actual exchange of guarantees, what political readjustments or changes, what stage or degree of military success even, would bring it to an end. If any other nation now neutral should be drawn in, it would know only that it was drawn in by some force it could not resist, because it had been hurt and saw no remedy but to risk still greater, it might even be irreparable injury, in order to make the weight in the one scale or the other decisive; and even as a participant it would not know how far the scales must tip before the end would come or what was being weighed in the balance!

Authoritative spokesmen of the nations engaged have, indeed, spoken in general terms of the issues involved; but they have nowhere, so far as I know, made any definite statement of the measures which would in their judgment bring those issues to a practical settlement. Whatever may have brought the war on, they believe the very life and political integrity of the nations they represent to be involved. They are fighting, they have declared, to be quit of aggression and of peril to the free and independent development of their peoples' lives and fortunes. They feel that they must push the conflict to a conclusion in order to make themselves secure in the future against its renewal and against the rivalries and ambitions which brought it about. But to what conclusion? These are very general terms. What sort of ending, what sort of settlement, what kind of guarantees will in their conception constitute a satisfactory outcome, promising some prospect of permanency and safety?

Leaders on both sides have declared very earnestly and in terms whose sincerity no one can justly doubt that it was no part of their wish or purpose to crush their antagonists, make conquest of their territories or possessions, deprive them of their equal place and opportunity among the great peoples of the world. They have declared also that they are fighting no less for the rights of small and weak nations and peoples than for those of the great and powerful states immediately involved. They have declared their desire for peace, but for a peace that will last, a peace based, not upon the uncertain balance of powerful alliances offset against one another, but upon guarantees in which the whole civilized world would join, that the rights and privileges of every nation and people should be the common and definite obligation of all governments.

With these objects the people and government of the United States wholeheartedly sympathize. We are ready to join a league of nations that will pledge itself to their accomplishment and definitely unite in an organization not only of purpose but of force as well that will be adequate to assure their realization. They are ready to lend their every resource, whether of men or money or substance, to such a combination, so purposed and organized. If that be the object of the present war, they are ready when the right moment comes to cooperate to bring it about. But how are they to know when that moment comes unless they be apprised by what test the nations now at war will judge the time of settlement and definition to have come? What must constitute victory by the one side or the other, and what must that victory mean?

The conflict moves very sluggishly. Only upon one or two separated fields here and there do armies move with definite success. Along the main lines of battle, so far as we can judge, there can be no rapid change, until ——? Must the contest be decided by slow attrition and ultimate exhaustion, the slow expenditure of millions of human lives until there are no more to offer up on the one side or the other? Triumph so gained might defeat the very ends for which it had been desired. Upon a triumph which overwhelms and humiliates cannot be laid the foundations of peace and equality and good will. A little while and it may be too late to realize the hopes which all men who love peace and justice entertain and which all statesmen must see to be the only hopes worthy to serve as the motive of great and permanent plans for mankind. Exhaustion, reaction, political upheaval, a resentment that can never cool would make such hopes vain and idle. An irreparable damage to civilization cannot promote peace and the secure happiness of the world.

In such circumstances and moved by such considerations, I deem myself to be clearly within my rights as the representative of a great neutral nation whose interests are being daily affected and as the friend of all the nations engaged in the present struggle, and speaking with the utmost respect for the rights of all concerned, in urging, as I do most earnestly urge, that some means be immediately taken, whether by conference or by a separate formulation of demands and conditions, to define the terms upon which a settlement of the issues of the war may be expected. It has become necessary that the nations that are now neutral should have some certain and definite guide for their future policy. It is necessary that they should have some certain means of determining what part they shall henceforth play should the terms defined be impossible of realization and the end of the war be indefinitely postponed.

The simplest means of arriving at this end would be a conference of representatives of the belligerent governments and of the governments not now engaged in the war whose interests may be thought to be most directly involved, and it is such a conference that I take the liberty of urging, whatever its outcome may be. If that be not feasible, it is possible that other means may be found which will in effect accomplish the same result.

My object, my sole object, in pressing this essential issue now is to assist, if I may, in bringing the war to an end before it is too late to remedy what it has done; to bring about an early reconsideration of peace on the basis of the rights alike of the weak and of the strong, the rights of peoples as well as of governments; and to afford an opportunity to form such a league of nations as all now desire, a league united and powerful enough to force and purpose to guarantee the peace of the world against further breach by injustice or aggression—guarantee it by the sheer might of an intelligent and irresistible organization of the major force of mankind in the common interest of civilization.

Let me say, in order that there may be no danger of any misunderstanding, that I am not renewing or seeking to press my offer of mediation made at the outset of the war. I then expressed my desire to be of service to the belligerents by any offices of accommodation looking towards an end of the contest that they might any of them suggest or encourage; and that offer of course stands. But I am not now returning to that. Neither am I proposing peace. I am doing a very simple, a very practical, and a very different thing. I am asking, and assuming that I have the right to ask, for a concrete definition of the guarantees which the belligerents on the one side and the other deem it their duty to demand as a practical satisfaction of the objects they are aiming at in this contest of force, in addition to the very great and substantial guarantee which will, I feel perfectly confident, be supplied by a league of nations formed to unite their force in active cooperation for the preservation of the world's peace when this war is over. To answer these questions need not commit any belligerent to peace at this time; but until they are answered no influential nation of the world not yet involved in the struggle can intelligently determine its future course of action. The United States feels that it can no longer delay to determine its own.

26. Peace Without Victory

Address to Senate on American Peace Aims, January 22, 1917

Wilson's note to the belligerents provoked an angry response from the Allies. On January 12, they replied to Wilson that they would not stop fighting until they destroyed German military power. Two days before, Germany had complained that the Allies sought to prolong while she sought to end the war. Actually, the political masters of Germany had already decided to make an all-out offensive, including resumption of unrestricted submarine warfare on February 1. The passing of notes served therefore only as a prelude to the final act of the war. All this was, of course, unknown to Wilson who proceeded to draw up an inspiring statement of America's peace aims. These he presented to the Senate on January 22.

ON THE eighteenth of December last I addressed an identic note to the governments of the nations now at war requesting them to state, more definitely than they had yet been stated by either group of belligerents, the terms upon which they would deem it possible to make peace. I spoke on behalf of humanity and of the rights of all neutral nations like our own, many of whose most vital interests the war puts in constant jeopardy. The Central Powers united in a reply which stated merely that they were ready to meet their antagonists in conference to discuss terms of peace. The Entente Powers have replied much more definitely and have stated, in general terms, indeed, but with sufficient definiteness to imply details, the arrangements, guarantees, and acts of reparation which they deem to be the indispensable conditions of a satisfactory settlement. We are that much nearer a definite discussion of the peace which shall end the present war. We are that much nearer the discussion of the international concert which must thereafter hold the world at peace. In every discussion of the peace that must end this war it is taken for granted that that peace must be followed by some definite concert of power which will make it virtually impossible that any such catastrophe should ever overwhelm us again. Every lover of mankind, every sane and thoughtful man must take that for granted.

I have sought this opportunity to address you because I thought that I owed it to you, as the counsel associated with me in the final determination of our international obligations, to disclose to you without reserve the thought and purpose that have been taking form in my mind in regard to the duty of our Government in the days to come when it will be necessary to lay afresh and upon a new plan the foundations of peace among the nations.

It is inconceivable that the people of the United States should play no part in that great enterprise. To take part in such a service will be the opportunity for which they have sought to prepare themselves by the very principles and purposes of their policy and the approved practices of their Government ever since the days when they set up a new nation in the high and honorable hope that it might in all that it was and did show mankind the way to liberty. They cannot in honor withhold the service to which they are now about to be challenged. They do not wish to withhold it. But they owe it to themselves and to the other nations of the world to state the conditions under which they will feel free to render it.

That service is nothing less than this, to add their authority and their power to the authority and force of other nations to guarantee peace and justice throughout the world. Such a settlement cannot now be long postponed. It is right that before it comes this Government should frankly formulate the conditions upon which it would feel justified in asking our people to approve its formal and solemn adherence to a League for Peace. I am here to attempt to state those conditions.

The present war must first be ended; but we owe it to candor and to a just regard for the opinion of mankind to say that, so far as our participation in guarantees of future peace is concerned, it makes a great deal of difference in what way and upon what terms it is ended. The treaties and agreements which bring it to an end must embody terms which will create a peace that is worth guaranteeing and preserving, a peace that will win the approval of mankind, not merely a peace that will serve the several interests and immediate aims of the nations engaged. We shall have no voice in determining what those terms shall be, but we shall, I feel sure, have a voice in determining whether they shall be made lasting or not by the guarantees of a universal covenant, and our judgment upon what is fundamental and essential as a condition precedent to permanency should be spoken now, not afterwards when it may be too late.

No covenant of cooperative peace that does not include the peoples of the New World can suffice to keep the future safe against war; and yet there is only one sort of peace that the peoples of America could join in guaranteeing. The elements of that peace must be elements that engage the confidence and satisfy the principles of the American governments, elements consistent with their political faith and with the practical convictions which the peoples of America have once for all embraced and undertaken to defend.

I do not mean to say that any American government would throw any obstacle in the way of any terms of peace the governments now at war might agree upon, or seek to upset them when made, whatever they might be. I only take it for granted that mere terms of peace between the belligerents will not satisfy even the belligerents themselves. Mere agreements may not make peace secure. It will be absolutely necessary that a force be created as a guarantor of the permanency of the settlement so much greater than the force of any nation now engaged or any alliance hitherto formed or projected that no nation, no probable combination of nations, could face or withstand it. If the peace presently to be made is to endure, it must be a peace made secure by the organized major force of mankind.

The terms of the immediate peace agreed upon will determine whether it is a peace for which such a guarantee can be secured. The question upon which the whole future peace and policy of the world depends is this: Is the present war a struggle for a just and secure peace, or only for a new balance of power? If it be only a struggle for a new balance of power, who will guarantee, who can guarantee, the stable equilibrium of the new arrangement? Only a tranquil Europe can be a stable Europe. There must be, not a balance of power, but a community of power; not organized rivalries, but an organized common peace.

Fortunately we have received very explicit assurances on this point. The statesmen of both of the groups of nations now arrayed against one another have said, in terms that could not be misinterpreted, that it was no part of the purpose they had in mind to crush their antagonists. But the implications of these assurances may not be equally clear to all—may not be the same on both sides of the water. I think it will be serviceable if I attempt to set forth what we understand them to be.

They imply, first of all, that it must be a peace without victory. It is not pleasant to say this. I beg that I may be permitted to put my own interpretation upon it and that it may be understood that no other interpretation was in my thought. I am seeking only to face realities and to face them without soft concealments. Victory would mean peace forced upon the loser, a victor's terms imposed upon the vanquished. It would be accepted in humiliation, under duress, at an intolerable sacrifice, and would leave a sting, a resentment, a bitter memory upon which terms of peace would rest, not permanently, but only as upon quicksand. Only a peace between equals can last. Only a peace the very principle of which is equality and a common participation in a common benefit. The right state of mind, the right feeling between nations, is as necessary for a lasting peace as is the just settlement of vexed questions of territory or of racial and national allegiance.

The equality of nations upon which peace must be founded if it is to last must be an equality of rights; the guarantees exchanged must neither recognize nor imply a difference between big nations and small, between those that are powerful and those that are weak. Right must be based upon the common strength, not upon the individual strength, of the nations upon whose concert peace will depend. Equality of territory or of resources there of course cannot be; nor any other sort of equality not gained in the ordinary peaceful and legitimate development of the peoples themselves. But no one asks or expects anything more than an equality of rights. Mankind is looking now for freedom of life, not for equipoises of power.

And there is a deeper thing involved than even equality of rights among organized nations. No peace can last, or ought to last, which does not recognize and accept the principle that governments derive all their just powers from the consent of the governed, and that no right anywhere exists to hand peoples about from sovereignty to sovereignty as if they were property. I take it for granted, for instance, if I may venture upon a single example, that statesmen everywhere are agreed that there should be a united, independent, and autonomous Poland, and that henceforth inviolable security of life, of worship, and of industrial and social development should be guaranteed to all peoples who have lived hitherto under the power of governments devoted to a faith and purpose hostile to their own.

I speak of this, not because of any desire to exalt an abstract political principle which has always been held very dear by those who have sought to build up liberty in America, but for the same reason that I have spoken of the other conditions of peace which seem to me clearly indispensable—because I wish frankly to uncover realities. Any peace which does not recognize and accept this principle will inevitably be upset. It will not rest upon the affections or the convictions of mankind. The ferment of spirit of whole populations will fight subtly and constantly against it, and all the world will sympathize. The world can be at peace only if its life is stable, and there can be no stability where the will is in rebellion, where there is not tranquillity of spirit and a sense of justice, of freedom, and of right.

So far as practicable, moreover, every great people now struggling towards a full development of its resources and of its powers should be assured a direct outlet to the great highways of the sea. Where this cannot be done by the cession of territory, it can no doubt be done by the neutralization of direct rights of way under the general guarantee which will assure the peace itself. With a right comity of arrangement no nation need be shut away from free access to the open paths of the world's commerce.

And the paths of the sea must alike in law and in fact be free. The freedom of the seas is the *sine qua non* of peace, equality, and cooperation. No doubt a somewhat radical reconsideration of many of the rules of international practice hitherto thought to be established may be necessary in order to make the seas indeed free and common in practically all circumstances for the use of mankind, but the motive for such changes is convincing and compelling. There can be no trust or intimacy between the peoples of the world without them. The free, constant, unthreatened intercourse of nations is an essential part of the process of peace and of development. It need not be difficult either to define or to secure the freedom of the seas if the governments of the world sincerely desire to come to an agreement concerning it.

It is a problem closely connected with the limitation of naval armaments and the cooperation of the navies of the world in keeping the seas at once free and safe. And the question of limiting naval armaments opens the wider and perhaps more difficult question of the limitation of armies and of all programs of military preparation. Difficult and delicate as these questions are, they must be faced with the utmost candor and decided in a spirit of real accommodation if peace is to come with healing in its wings, and come to stay. Peace cannot be had without concession and sacrifice. There can be no sense of safety and equality among the nations if great preponderating armaments are henceforth to continue here and there to be built up and maintained. The statesmen of the world must plan for peace and nations must adjust and accommodate their policy to it as they have planned for war and made ready for pitiless contest and rivalry. The question of armaments, whether on land or sea, is the most immediately and intensely practical question connected with the future fortunes of nations and of mankind.

I have spoken upon these great matters without reserve and with the utmost explicitness because it has seemed to me to be necessary if the world's yearning desire for peace was anywhere to find free voice and utterance. Perhaps I am the only person in high authority amongst all the peoples of the world who is at liberty to speak and hold nothing back. I am speaking as an individual, and yet I am speaking also, of course, as the responsible head of a great government, and I feel confident that I have said what the people of the United States would wish me to say. May I not add that I hope and believe that I am in effect speaking for liberals and friends of humanity in every nation and of every program of liberty? I would fain believe that I am speaking for the silent mass of mankind everywhere who have as yet had no place or opportunity to speak their real hearts out concerning the death and ruin they see to have come already upon the persons and the homes they hold most dear.

And in holding out the expectation that the people and Government of the United States will join the other civilized nations of the world in guaranteeing the permanence of peace upon such terms as I have named, I speak with the greater boldness and confidence because it is clear to every man who can think that there is in this promise no breach in either our traditions or our policy as a nation, but a fulfillment, rather, of all that we have professed or striven for.

I am proposing, as it were, that the nations should with one accord adopt the doctrine of President Monroe as the doctrine of the world: that no nation should seek to extend its polity over any other nation or people, but that every people should be left free to determine its own polity, its own way of development, unhindered, unthreatened, unafraid, the little along with the great and powerful.

I am proposing that all nations henceforth avoid entangling alliances which would draw them into competitions of power; catch them in a net of intrigue and selfish rivalry, and disturb their own affairs with influences intruded from without. There is no entangling alliance in a concert of power. When all unite to act in the same sense and with the same purpose all act in the common interest and are free to live their own lives under a common protection.

I am proposing government by the consent of the governed; that freedom of the seas which in international conference after conference representatives of the United States have urged with the eloquence of those who are the convinced disciples of liberty; and that moderation of armaments which makes of armies and navies a power for order merely, not an instrument of aggression or of selfish violence.

These are American principles, American policies. We could stand for no others. And they are also the principles and policies of forward looking men and women everywhere, of every modern nation, of every enlightened community. They are the principles of mankind and must prevail.

27. This Government Has No Alternative

Address to Congress on Breaking Relations with Germany, February 3, 1917

Wilson's noble "peace without victory" address preceded by eight days Germany's declaration that she would resume unrestricted submarine warfare at once. German statesmen knew that war with the United States was now inevitable. Wilson announced the break with Germany in this address to Congress.

THE IMPERIAL German Government on the thirty-first of January announced to this Government and to the governments of other neutral nations that on and after the first day of February, the present month, it would adopt a policy with regard to the use of submarines against all shipping seeking to pass through certain designated areas of the high seas to which it is clearly my duty to call your attention.

Let me remind the Congress that on the eighteenth of April last, in view of the sinking on the twenty-fourth of March of the cross-channel passenger steamer *Sussex* by a German submarine, without summons or warning, and the consequent loss of the lives of several citizens of the United States who were passengers aboard her, this Government addressed a note to the Imperial German Government in which it made the following declaration:

> If it is still the purpose of the Imperial Government to prosecute relentless and indiscriminate warfare against vessels of commerce by the use of submarines without regard to what the Government of the United States must consider the sacred and indisputable rules of international law and the universally recognized dictates of humanity, the Government of the United States is at last forced to the conclusion that there is but one course it can pursue. Unless the Imperial Government should now immediately declare and effect an abandonment of its present methods of submarine warfare against passenger and freight-carrying vessels, the Government of the United States can have no choice but to sever diplomatic relations with the German Empire altogether.

In reply to this declaration the Imperial German Government gave this Government the following assurance:

> The German Government is prepared to do its utmost to confine the operations of war for the rest of its duration to the fighting forces of the belligerents, thereby also insuring the freedom of the seas, a principle upon which the German Government believes, now as before, to be in agreement with the Government of the United States.
>
> The German Government, guided by this idea, notifies the Government of the United States that the German naval forces have received the following orders: In accordance with the general principles of visit and search and destruction of merchant vessels recognized by international law, such vessels, both within and without the area de-

clared as naval war zone, shall not be sunk without warning and without saving human lives, unless these ships attempt to escape or offer resistance.

"But," it added, "neutrals can not expect that Germany, forced to fight for her existence, shall, for the sake of neutral interest, restrict the use of an effective weapon if her enemy is permitted to continue to apply at will methods of warfare violating the rules of international law. Such a demand would be incompatible with the character of neutrality, and the German Government is convinced that the Government of the United States does not think of making such a demand, knowing that the Government of the United States has repeatedly declared that it is determined to restore the principle of the freedom of the seas, from whatever quarter it has been violated."

To this the Government of the United States replied on the eighth of May, accepting, of course, the assurances given, but adding,

> The Government of the United States feels it necessary to state that it takes it for granted that the Imperial German Government does not intend to imply that the maintenance of its newly announced policy is in any way contingent upon the course or result of diplomatic negotiations between the Government of the United States and any other belligerent Government, notwithstanding the fact that certain passages in the Imperial Government's note of the 4th instant might appear to be susceptible of that construction. In order, however, to avoid any possible misunderstanding, the Government of the United States notifies the Imperial Government that it cannot for a moment entertain, much less discuss, a suggestion that respect by German naval authorities for the rights of citizens of the United States upon the high seas should in any way or in the slightest degree be made contingent upon the conduct of any other Government affecting the rights of neutrals and noncombatants. Responsibility in such matters is single, not joint; absolute, not relative.

To this note of the eighth of May the Imperial German Government made no reply.

On the thirty-first of January, the Wednesday of the present week, the German Ambassador handed to the Secretary of State, along with a formal note, a memorandum which contains the following statement:

The Imperial Government, therefore, does not doubt that the Government of the United States will understand the situation thus forced upon Germany by the Entente-Allies' brutal methods of war and by their determination to destroy the Central Powers, and that the Government of the United States will further realize that the now openly disclosed intentions of the Entente-Allies give back to Germany the freedom of action which she reserved in her note addressed to the Government of the United States on May 4, 1916.

Under these circumstances Germany will meet the illegal measures of her enemies by forcibly preventing after February 1, 1917, in a zone around Great Britain, France, Italy, and in the Eastern Mediterranean all navigation, that of neutrals included, from and to England and from and to France, etc., etc. All ships met within the zone will be sunk.

I think that you will agree with me that, in view of this declaration, which suddenly and without prior intimation of any kind deliberately withdraws the solemn assurance given in the Imperial Government's note of the fourth of May, 1916, this Government has no alternative consistent with the dignity and honor of the United States but to take the course which, in its note of the eighteenth of April, 1916, it announced that it would take in the event that the German Government did not declare and effect an abandonment of the methods of submarine warfare which it was then employing and to which it now purposes again to resort.

I have, therefore, directed the Secretary of State to announce to His Excellency the German Ambassador that all diplomatic relations between the United States and the German Empire are severed, and that the American Ambassador at Berlin will immediately be withdrawn; and, in accordance with this decision, to hand to His Excellency his passports.

Notwithstanding this unexpected action of the German Government, this sudden and deeply deplorable renunciation of its assurances, given this Government at one of the most critical moments of tension in the relations of the two governments, I refuse to believe that it is the intention of the German authorities to do in fact what they have warned us they will feel at liberty to do. I cannot bring myself to believe that they will indeed pay no regard to the ancient friendship between their people and our own or to the solemn obligations which have been exchanged between them and destroy American ships and take the lives of American citizens in the willful prosecution of the ruthless naval programme they have announced their intention to adopt. Only actual overt acts on their part can make me believe it even now.

If this inveterate confidence on my part in the sobriety and prudent foresight of their purpose should unhappily prove unfounded; if American ships and American lives should in fact be sacrificed by their naval commanders in heedless contravention of the just and reasonable understandings of international law and the obvious dictates of humanity, I shall take the liberty of coming again before the Congress, to ask that authority be given me to use any means that may be necessary for the protection of our seamen and our people in the prosecution of their peaceful and legitimate errands on the high seas. I can do nothing less. I take it for granted that all neutral governments will take the same course.

We do not desire any hostile conflict with the Imperial German Government. We are the sincere friends of the German people and earnestly desire to remain at peace with the Government which speaks for them. We shall not believe that they are hostile to us unless and until we are obliged to believe it; and we purpose nothing more than the reasonable defense of the undoubted rights of our people. We wish to serve no selfish ends. We seek merely to stand true alike in thought and in action to the immemorial principles of our people which I sought to express in my address to the Senate only two weeks ago—merely to vindicate our right to liberty and justice and an unmolested life. These are the bases of peace, not war. God grant we may not be challenged to defend them by acts of willful injustice on the part of the Government of Germany!

28. A Little Group of Willful Men

Statement on Arming Merchant Ships, March 4, 1917

German threats had the immediate effect of keeping American ships in port. The demands grew to arm or escort merchant ships. Wilson steadfastly refused to act. But then, on February 25, he learned the contents of the Zimmerman Note, a monumental blunder of German statesmanship. The British had intercepted and then sent on to the United States a note from the German Foreign Secretary, Zimmerman, to the German Ambassador in Mexico, stating that in the event of war between the United States and Germany, Mexico, should she join Germany and induce Japan to do likewise, would receive "the lost territory in Texas, New Mexico and Arizona." On February 26 Wilson asked Congress for authority to arm American merchant ships and to use any other means necessary to protect them. While the House offered no resistance, the Senate—or at least, a small group in the Senate—did. These eleven Senators, led by La Follette, objected not so much to arming merchant ships as to the other sweeping powers which Wilson sought. The bill failed in the Senate and the session of Congress ended. Wilson then issued the following bitter statement. But all was not lost. Wilson and his advisers discovered that merchant ships could be armed by executive order under an old law.

THE TERMINATION of the last session of the Sixty-fourth Congress by constitutional limitation disclosed a situation unparalleled in the history of the country, perhaps unparalleled in the history of any modern Government. In the immediate presence of a crisis fraught with more subtle and far-reaching possibilities of national danger than any other the Government has known within the whole history of its international relations, the Congress has been unable to act either to safeguard the country or to vindicate the elementary rights of its citizens. More than 500 of the 531 members of the two houses were ready and anxious to act; the House of Representatives had acted, by an overwhelming majority; but the Senate was unable to act because a little group of eleven Senators had determined that it should not.

The Senate has no rules by which debate can be limited or brought to an end, no rules by which dilatory tactics of any kind can be prevented. A single member can stand in the way of action, if he have but the physical endurance. The result in this case is a complete paralysis alike of the legislative and of the executive branches of the Government.

This inability of the Senate to act has rendered some of the most necessary legislation of the session impossible at a time when the need of it was most pressing and most evident. The bill which would have permitted such combinations of capital and of organization in the export and import trade of the country as the circumstances of international competition have made imperative—a bill which the business judgment of the whole country approved and demanded—has failed. The opposition of one or two Senators has made it impossible to increase the membership of the Interstate Commerce Commission to give it the altered organization necessary for its efficiency. The Conservation bill, which should have released for immediate use the mineral resources which are still locked up in the public lands, now that their release is more imperatively necessary than ever, and the bill which would have made the unused water power of the country immediately available for industry have both failed, though they have been under consideration throughout the sessions of two Congresses and have been twice passed by the House of Representatives. The appropriations for the army have failed, along with the appropriations for the civil establishment of the Government, the appropriations for the Military Academy at West Point and the General Deficiency bill. It has proved impossible to extend the powers of the Shipping Board to meet the special needs of the new situations into which our commerce has been forced or to increase the gold reserve of our national banking system to meet the unusual circumstances of the existing financial situation.

It would not cure the difficulty to call the Sixty-fifth Congress in extraordinary session. The paralysis of the Senate would remain. The purpose and the spirit of action are not lacking now. The Congress is more definitely united in thought and purpose at this moment, I venture to say, than it has been within the memory of any men now in its membership. There is not only the most united patriotic purpose, but the objects members have in view are perfectly clear and definite. But the Senate cannot act unless its leaders can obtain unanimous consent. Its majority is powerless, helpless. In the midst of a crisis of extraordinary peril, when only definite and decided action can make the Nation safe or shield it from war itself by the aggression of others, action is impossible.

Although, as a matter of fact, the Nation and the representatives of the Nation stand back of the Executive with unprecedented unanimity and spirit, the impression made abroad will, of course, be that it is not so and that other Governments may act as they please without fear that this Government can do anything at all. We cannot explain. The explanation is incredible. The Senate of the United States is the only legislative body in the world which cannot act when its majority is ready for action. A little group of willful men, representing no opinion but their own, have rendered the great Government of the United States helpless and contemptible.

The remedy? There is but one remedy. The only remedy is that the rules of the Senate shall be so altered that it can act. The country can be relied upon to draw the moral. I believe that the Senate can be relied on to supply the means of action and save the country from disaster.

Five

WAR
1917–1918

1. We Shall Walk with the Light All About Us

Second Inaugural Address, March 5, 1917

Wilson's second inaugural address was a solemn event. Though he had run in 1916 on the issue of peace, war was now imminent. The only question was when it would come.

THE FOUR years which have elapsed since last I stood in this place have been crowded with counsel and action of the most vital interest and consequence. Perhaps no equal period in our history has been so fruitful of important reforms in our economic and industrial life or so full of significant changes in the spirit and purpose of our political action. We have sought very thoughtfully to set our house in order, correct the grosser errors and abuses of our industrial life, liberate and quicken the processes of our national genius and energy, and lift our politics to a broader view of the people's essential interests. It is a record of singular variety and singular distinction. But I shall not attempt to review it. It speaks for itself and will be of increasing influence as the years go by. This is not the time for retrospect. It is time, rather, to speak our thoughts and purposes concerning the present and the immediate future.

Although we have centered counsel and action with such unusual concentration and success upon the great problems of domestic legislation to which we addressed ourselves four years ago, other matters have more and more forced themselves upon our attention, matters lying outside our own life as a nation and over which we had no control, but which, despite our wish to keep free of them, have drawn us more and more irresistibly into their own current and influence.

It has been impossible to avoid them. They have affected the life of the whole world. They have shaken men everywhere with a passion and an apprehension they never knew before. It has been hard to preserve calm counsel while the thought of our own people swayed this way and that under their influence. We are a composite and cosmopolitan people. We are of the blood of all the nations that are at war. The currents of our thoughts as well as the currents of our trade run quick at all seasons back and forth between us and them. The war inevitably set its mark from the first alike upon our minds, our industries, our commerce, our politics, and our social action. To be indifferent to it or independent of it was out of the question.

And yet all the while we have been conscious that we were not part of it. In that consciousness, despite many divisions, we have drawn closer together. We have been deeply wronged upon the seas, but we have not wished to wrong or injure in return; have retained throughout the consciousness of standing in some sort apart, intent upon an interest that transcended the immediate issues of the war itself. As some of the injuries done us have become intolerable we have still been clear that we wished nothing for ourselves that we were not ready to demand for all mankind—fair dealing, justice, the freedom to live and be at ease against organized wrong.

It is in this spirit and with this thought that we have grown more and more aware, more and more certain that the part we wished to play was the part of those who mean to vindicate and fortify peace. We have been obliged to arm ourselves to make good our claim to a certain minimum of right and of freedom of action. We stand firm in armed neutrality since it seems that in no other way we can demonstrate what it is we insist upon and cannot forego. We may even be drawn on, by circumstances, not by our own purpose or desire, to a more active assertion of our rights as we see them and a more immediate association with the great struggle itself. But nothing will alter our thought or our purpose. They are too clear to be obscured. They are too deeply rooted in the principles of our national life to be altered. We desire neither conquest nor advantage. We wish nothing that can be had only at the cost of another people. We have always professed unselfish purpose and we covet the opportunity to prove that our professions are sincere.

There are many things still to do at home, to clarify our own politics and give new vitality to the industrial processes of our own life, and we shall do them as time and opportunity serve; but we realize that the greatest things that remain to be done must be done with the whole world for a stage and in cooperation with the wide and universal forces of mankind, and we are making our spirits ready for those things. They will follow in the immediate wake of the war itself and will set civilization up again. We are provincials no longer. The tragical events of the thirty months of vital turmoil through which we have just passed have made us citizens of the world. There can be no turning back. Our own fortunes as a nation are involved, whether we would have it so or not.

And yet we are not the less Americans on that account. We shall be the more American if we but remain true to the principles in which we have been bred. They are not the principles of a province or of a single continent. We have known and boasted all along that they were the principles of a liberated mankind. These, therefore, are the things we shall stand for, whether in war or in peace:

That all nations are equally interested in the peace of the world and in the political stability of free peoples, and equally responsible for their maintenance;

That the essential principle of peace is the actual equality of nations in all matters of right or privilege;

That peace cannot securely or justly rest upon an armed balance of power;

That governments derive all their just powers from the consent of the governed and that no other powers should be supported by the common thought, purpose, or power of the family of nations;

That the seas should be equally free and safe for the use of all peoples, under rules set up by common agreement and consent, and that, so far as practicable, they should be accessible to all upon equal terms;

That national armaments should be limited to the necessities of national order and domestic safety;

That the community of interest and of power upon which peace must henceforth depend imposes upon each nation the duty of seeing to it that all influences proceeding from its own citizens meant to encourage or assist revolution in other states should be sternly and effectually suppressed and prevented.

I need not argue these principles to you, my fellow countrymen: they are your own, part and parcel of your own thinking and your own motive in affairs. They spring up native amongst us. Upon this as a platform of purpose and of action we can stand together.

And it is imperative that we should stand together. We are being forged into a new unity amidst the fires that now blaze throughout the world. In their ardent heat we shall, in God's providence, let us hope, be purged of faction and division, purified of the errant humors of party and of private interest, and shall stand forth in the days to come with a new dignity of national pride and spirit. Let each man see to it that the dedication is in his own heart, the high purpose of the Nation in his own mind, ruler of his own will and desire.

I stand here and have taken the high and solemn oath to which you have been audience because the people of the United States have chosen me for this august delegation of power and have by their gracious judgment named me their leader in affairs. I know now what the task means. I realize to the full the responsibility which it involves. I pray God I may be given the wisdom and the prudence to do my duty in the true spirit of this great people. I am their servant and can succeed only as they sustain and guide me by their confidence and their counsel. The thing I shall count upon, the thing without which neither counsel nor action will avail, is the unity of America—an America united in feeling, in purpose, and in its vision of duty, of opportunity, and of service. We are to beware of all men who would turn the tasks and the necessities of the Nation to their own private profit or use them for the building up of private power; beware that no faction or disloyal intrigue break the harmony or embarrass the spirit of our people; beware that our Government be kept pure and incorrupt in all its parts. United alike in the conception of our duty and in the high resolve to perform it in the face of all men, let us dedicate ourselves to the great task to which we must now set our hand. For myself I beg your tolerance, your countenance, and your united aid. The shadows that now lie dark upon our path will soon be dispelled and we shall walk with the light all about us if we be but true to ourselves—to ourselves as we have wished to be known in the counsels of the world and in the thought of all those who love liberty and justice and the right exalted.

2. The World Must Be Made Safe for Democracy

Address to Congress Asking for Declaration of War, April 2, 1917

The important question before Wilson was when *the United States should declare war;* that *it should do so was settled. Several considerations governed his decision: first, the heavy toll taken of American merchant ships and personnel by the German submarines; second, the increasingly close economic relationship between the United States and the Allies; third, the March Russian Revolution which substituted a democratic government for the Czarist autocracy; and fourth, Wilson's desire that the United States participate in any peace arrangements. On March 20 Wilson's cabinet unanimously favored a declaration of war. It had only confirmed his own decision. The next day Wilson asked Congress to meet on April 2 "to receive a communication by the Executive on grave questions of national policy which should be taken immediately under consideration." On April 6 Congress declared war against Germany and on April 7 against Austria–Hungary.*

I HAVE called the Congress into extraordinary session because there are serious, very serious, choices of policy to be made, and made immediately, which it was neither right nor constitutionally permissible that I should assume the responsibility of making.

On the third of February last I officially laid before you the extraordinary announcement of the Imperial German Government that on and after the first day of February it was its purpose to put aside all restraints of law or of humanity and use its submarines to sink every vessel that sought to approach either the ports of Great Britain and Ireland or the western coasts of Europe or any of the ports controlled by the enemies of Germany within the Mediterranean. That had seemed to be the object of the German submarine warfare earlier in the war, but since April of last year the Imperial Government had somewhat restrained the commanders of its undersea craft in conformity with its promise then given to us that passenger boats should not be sunk and that due warning would be given to all other vessels which its submarines might seek to destroy, when no resistance was offered or escape attempted, and care taken that their crews were given at least a fair chance to save their lives in their open boats. The precautions taken were meager and haphazard enough, as was proved in distressing instance after instance in the progress of the cruel and unmanly business, but a certain degree of restraint was observed. The new policy has swept every restriction aside. Vessels of every kind, whatever their flag, their character, their cargo, their destination, their errand, have been ruthlessly sent to the bottom without warning and without thought of help or mercy for those on board, the vessels of friendly neutrals along with those of belligerents. Even hospital ships and ships carrying relief to the sorely bereaved and stricken people of Belgium, though the latter were provided with safe conduct through the proscribed areas by the German Government itself and were distinguished by unmistakable marks of identity, have been sunk with the same reckless lack of compassion or of principle.

I was for a little while unable to believe that such things would in fact be done by any government that had hitherto subscribed to the humane practices of civilized nations. International law had its origin in the attempt to set up some law which would be respected and observed upon the seas, where no nation had right of dominion and where lay the free highways of the world. By painful stage after stage has that law been built up, with meager enough results, indeed, after all was accomplished that could be accomplished, but always with a clear view, at least, of what the heart and conscience of mankind demanded. This minimum of right the German Government has swept aside under the plea of retaliation and necessity and because it had no weapons which it could use at sea except these which it is impossible to employ as it is employing them without throwing to the winds all scruples of humanity or of respect for the understandings that were supposed to underlie the intercourse of the world. I am not now thinking of the loss of property involved, immense and serious as that is, but only of the wanton and wholesale destruction of the lives of noncombatants, men, women, and children, engaged in pursuits which have always, even in the darkest periods of modern history, been deemed innocent and legitimate. Property can be paid for; the lives of peaceful and innocent people cannot be. The present German submarine warfare against commerce is a warfare against mankind.

It is a war against all nations. American ships have been sunk, American lives taken, in ways which it has stirred us very deeply to learn of, but the ships and people of other neutral and friendly nations have been sunk and overwhelmed in the waters in the same way. There has been no discrimination. The challenge is to all mankind. Each nation must decide for itself how it will meet it. The choice we make for ourselves must be made with a moderation of counsel and a temperateness of judgment befitting our character and our motives as a nation. We must put excited feeling away. Our motive will not be revenge or the victorious assertion of the physical might of the nation, but only the vindication of right, of human right, of which we are only a single champion.

When I addressed the Congress on the twenty-sixth of February last I thought that it would suffice to assert our neutral rights with arms, our right to use the seas against unlawful interference, our right to keep our people safe against unlawful violence. But armed neutrality, it now appears, is impracticable. Because submarines are in effect outlaws when used as the German submarines have been used against merchant shipping, it is impossible to defend ships against their attacks as the law of nations has assumed that merchantmen would defend themselves against privateers or cruisers, visible craft giving chase upon the open sea. It is common prudence in such circumstances, grim necessity indeed, to endeavor to destroy them before they have shown their own intention. They must be dealt with upon sight, if dealt with at all. The German Government denies the right of neutrals to use arms at all within the areas of the sea which it has proscribed, even in the defense of rights which no modern publicist has ever before questioned their right to defend. The intimation is conveyed that the armed guards which we have placed on our merchant ships will be treated as beyond the pale of law and subject to be dealt with as pirates would be. Armed neutrality is ineffectual enough at best; in such circumstances and in the fact of such pretensions it is worse than ineffectual: it is likely only to produce what it was meant to prevent; it is practically certain to drawn us into the war without either the rights or the effectiveness of belligerents. There is one choice we cannot make, we are incapable of making: we will not choose the path of submission and suffer the most sacred rights of our Nation and our people to be ignored or violated. The wrongs against which we now array ourselves are no common wrongs; they cut to the very roots of human life.

With a profound sense of the solemn and even tragical character of the step I am taking and of the grave responsibilities which it involves, but in unhesitating obedience to what I deem my constitutional duty, I advise that the Congress declare the recent course of the Imperial German Government to be in fact nothing less than war against the Government and people of the United States; that it formally accept the status of belligerent which has thus been thrust upon it; and that it take immediate steps not only to put the country in a more thorough state of defense but also to exert all its power and employ all its resources to bring the Government of the German Empire to terms and end the war.

What this will involve is clear. It will involve the utmost practicable cooperation in counsel and action with the governments now at war with Germany, and, as incident to that, the extension to those governments of the most liberal financial credits, in order that our resources may so far as possible be added to theirs. It will involve the organization and mobilization of all the material resources of the country to supply the materials of war and serve the incidental needs of the Nation in the most abundant and yet the most economical and efficient way possible. It will involve the immediate full equipment of the navy in all respects but particularly in supplying it with the best means of dealing with the enemy's submarines. It will involve the immediate addition to the armed forces of the United States already provided for by law in case of war at least five hundred thousand men, who should, in my opinion, be chosen upon the principle of universal liability to service, and also the authorization of subsequent additional increments of equal force so soon as they may be needed and can be handled in training. It will involve also, of course, the granting of adequate credits to the Government, sustained, I hope, so far as they can equitably be sustained by the present generation, by well-conceived taxation.

I say sustained so far as may be equitable by taxation because it seems to me that it would be most unwise to base the credits which will now be necessary entirely on money borrowed. It is our duty, I most respectfully urge, to protect our people so far as we may against the very serious hardships and evils which would be likely to arise out of the inflation which would be produced by vast loans.

In carrying out the measures by which these things are to be accomplished we should keep constantly in mind the wisdom of interfering as little as possible in our own preparation and in the equipment of our own military forces with the duty—for it will be a very practical duty—of supplying the nations already at war with Germany with the materials which they can obtain only from us or by our assistance. They are in the field and we should help them in every way to be effective there.

I shall take the liberty of suggesting, through the several executive departments of the Government, for the consideration of your committees, measures for the accomplishment of the several objects I have mentioned. I hope that it will be your pleasure to deal with them as having been framed after very careful thought by the branch of the Government upon which the responsibility of conducting the war and safeguarding the Nation will most directly fall.

While we do these things, these deeply momentous things, let us be very clear, and make very clear to all the world what our motives and our objects are. My own thought has not been driven from its habitual and normal course by the unhappy events of the last two months, and I do not believe that the thought of the Nation has been altered or clouded by them. I have exactly the same things in mind now that I had in mind when I addressed the Senate on the twenty-second of January last; the same that I had in mind when I addressed the Congress on the third of February and on the twenty-sixth of February. Our object now, as then, is to vindicate the principles of peace and justice in the life of the world as against selfish and autocratic power and to set up amongst the really free and self-governed peoples of the world such a concert of purpose and of action as will henceforth insure the observance of those principles. Neutrality is no longer feasible or desirable where the peace of the world is involved and the freedom of its peoples, and the menace to that peace and freedom lies in the existence of autocratic governments backed by organized force which is controlled wholly by their will, not by the will of their people. We have seen the last of neutrality in such circumstances. We are at the beginning of an age in which it will be insisted that the same standards of conduct and of responsibility for wrong done shall be observed among nations and their governments that are observed among the individual citizens of civilized states.

We have no quarrel with the German people. We have no feeling towards them but one of sympathy and friendship. It was not upon their impulse that their government acted in entering the war. It was not with their previous knowledge or approval. It was a war determined upon as wars used to be determined upon in the old, unhappy days when people were nowhere consulted by their rulers and wars were provoked and waged in the interest of dynasties or of little groups of ambitious men who were accustomed to use their fellow men as pawns and tools. Self-governed nations do not fill their neighbor states with spies or set the course of intrigue to bring about some critical posture of affairs which will give them an opportunity to strike and make conquest. Such designs can be successfully worked out only under cover and where no one has the right to ask questions. Cunningly contrived plans of deception or aggression, carried, it may be, from generation to generation, can be worked out and kept from the light only within the privacy of courts or behind the carefully guarded confidences of a narrow and privileged class. They are happily impossible where public opinion commands and insists upon full information concerning all the nation's affairs.

A steadfast concert for peace can never be maintained except by a partnership of democratic nations. No autocratic government could be trusted to keep faith within it or observe its covenants. It must be a league of honor, a partnership of opinion. Intrigue would eat its vitals away; the plottings of inner circles who could plan what they would and render account to no one would be a corruption seated at its very heart. Only free peoples can hold their purpose and their honor steady to a common end and prefer the interests of mankind to any narrow interest of their own.

Does not every American feel that assurance has been added to our hope for the future peace of the world by the wonderful and heartening things that have been happening within the last few weeks in Russia? Russia was known by those who knew it best to have been always in fact democratic at heart, in all the vital habits of her thought, in all the intimate relationships of her people that spoke their natural instinct, their habitual attitude towards life. The autocracy that crowned the summit of her political structure, long as it had stood and terrible as was the reality of its power, was not in fact Russian in origin, character, or purpose; and now it has been shaken off and the great, generous Russian people have been added in all their naïve majesty and might to the forces that are fighting for freedom in the world, for justice, and for peace. Here is a fit partner for a League of Honor.

One of the things that has served to convince us that the Prussian autocracy was not and could never be our friend is that from the very outset of the present war it has filled our unsuspecting communities and even our offices of government with spies and set criminal intrigues everywhere afoot against our national unity of counsel, our peace within and without, our industries and our commerce. Indeed, it is now evident that its spies were here even before the war began; and it is unhappily not a matter of conjecture but a fact proved in our courts of justice that the intrigues which have more than once come perilously near to disturbing the peace and dislocating the industries of the country have been carried on at the instigation, with the support, and even under the personal direction of official agents of the Imperial Government accredited to the Government of the United States. Even in checking these things and trying to extirpate them we have sought to put the most generous interpretation possible upon them because we knew that their source lay not in any hostile feeling or purpose of the German people towards us (who were no doubt as ignorant of them as we ourselves were), but only in the selfish designs of a Government that did what it pleased and told its people nothing. But they have played their part in serving to convince us at last that that Government entertains no real friendship for us and means to act against our peace and security at its convenience. That it means to stir up enemies against us at our very doors the intercepted note to the German Minister at Mexico City is eloquent evidence.

We are accepting this challenge of hostile purpose because we know that in such a Government, following such methods, we can never have a friend; and that in the presence of its organized power, always lying in wait to accomplish we know not what purpose, there can be no assured security for the democratic Governments of the world. We are now about to accept gage of battle with this natural foe to liberty and shall, if necessary, spend the whole force of the Nation to check and nullify its pretensions and its power. We are glad now that we see the facts with no veil of false pretense about them, to fight thus for the ultimate peace of the world and for the liberation of its peoples, the German peoples included: for the rights of nations great and small and the privilege of men everywhere to choose their way of life and of obedience. The world must be made safe for democracy. Its peace must be planted upon the tested foundations of political liberty. We have no selfish ends to serve. We desire no conquest, no dominion. We seek no indemnities for ourselves, no material compensation for the sacrifices we shall freely make. We are but one of the champions of the right of mankind. We shall be satisfied when those rights have been made as secure as the faith and the freedom of nations can make them.

Just because we fight without rancor and without selfish object, seeking nothing for ourselves but what we shall wish to share with all free people, we shall, I feel confident, conduct our operations as belligerents without passion and ourselves observe with proud punctilio the principles of right and of fair play we profess to be fighting for.

I have said nothing of the Governments allied with the Imperial Government of Germany because they have not made war upon us or challenged us to defend our right and our honor. The Austro-Hungarian Government has, indeed, avowed its unqualified indorsement and acceptance of the reckless and lawless submarine warfare adopted now without disguise by the Imperial German Government, and it has therefore not been possible for this Government to receive Count Tarnowski, the Ambassador recently accredited to this Government by the Imperial and Royal Government of Austria-Hungary; but that Government has not actually engaged in warfare against citizens of the United States on the seas, and I take the liberty, for the present at least, of postponing a discussion of our relations with the authorities at Vienna. We enter this war only where we are clearly forced into it because there are no other means of defending our rights.

It will be all the easier for us to conduct ourselves as belligerents in a high spirit of right and fairness because we act without animus, not in enmity towards a people or with the desire to bring any injury or disadvantage upon them, but only in armed opposition to an irresponsible government which has thrown aside all considerations of humanity and of right and is running amuck. We are, let me say again, the sincere friends of the German people, and shall desire nothing so much as the early reestablishment of intimate relations of mutual advantage between us—however hard it may be for them, for the time being, to believe that this is spoken from our hearts. We have borne with their present Government through all these bitter months because of that friendship—exercising a patience and forbearance which would otherwise have been impossible. We shall, happily, still have an opportunity to prove that friendship in our daily attitude and actions towards the millions of men and women of German birth and native sympathy who live amongst us and share our life, and we shall be proud to prove it towards all who are in fact loyal to their neighbors and to the Government in the hour of test. They are, most of them, as true and loyal Americans as if they had never known any other fealty or allegiance. They will be prompt to stand with us in rebuking and restraining the few who may be of a different mind and purpose. If there should be disloyalty, it will be dealt with with a firm hand of stern repression; but, if it lifts its head at all, it will lift it only here and there and without countenance except from a lawless and malignant few.

It is a distressing and oppressive duty, Gentlemen of the Congress, which I have performed in thus addressing you. There are, it may be, many months of fiery trial and sacrifice ahead of us. It is a fearful thing to lead this great peaceful people into war, into the most terrible and disastrous of all wars, civilization itself seeming to be in the balance. But the right is more precious than peace, and we shall fight for the things which we have always carried nearest our hearts—for democracy, for the right of those who submit to authority to have a voice in their own Governments, for the rights and liberties of small nations, for a universal dominion of right by such a concert of free peoples as shall bring peace and safety to all nations and make the world itself at last free. To such a task we can dedicate our lives and our fortunes, everything that we are and everything that we have, with the pride of those who know that the day has come when America is privileged to spend her blood and her might for the principles that gave her birth and happiness and the peace which she has treasured. God helping her, she can do no other.

3. It Is a Matter of Business

Statement on Roosevelt's Offer to Serve, May 18, 1917

As soon as the United States declared war, former President Roosevelt enthusiastically offered to lead his own division into France. Following is Wilson's rejection.

I SHALL not avail myself, at any rate at the present stage of the war, of the authorization conferred by the act to organize volunteer divisions. To do so would seriously interfere with the carrying out of the chief and most immediately important purpose contemplated by this legislation, the prompt creation and early use of an effective army, and would contribute practically nothing to the effective strength of the armies now engaged against Germany.

I understand that the section of this act which authorizes the creation of volunteer divisions in addition to the draft was added with a view to providing an independent command for Mr. Roosevelt and giving the military authorities an opportunity to use his fine vigor and enthusiasm in recruiting the forces now at the western front. It would be very agreeable to me to pay Mr. Roosevelt this compliment and the Allies the compliment of sending to their aid one of our most distinguished public men, an ex-President who has rendered many conspicuous public services and proved his gallantry in many striking ways. Politically, too, it would no doubt have a very fine effect and make a profound impression. But this is not the time or the occasion for compliment or for any action not calculated to contribute to the immediate success of the war. The business now in hand is undramatic, practical, and of scientific definiteness and precision. I shall act with regard to it at every step and in every particular under expert and professional advice, from both sides of the water.

That advice is that the men most needed are men of the ages contemplated in the draft provisions of the present bill, not men of the age and sort contemplated in the section which authorizes the formation of volunteer units, and that for the preliminary training of the men who are to be drafted we shall need all of our experienced officers. Mr. Roosevelt told me, when I had the pleasure of seeing him a few weeks ago, that he would wish to have associated with him some of the most effective officers of the Regular Army. He named many of those whom he would desire to have designated for the service, and they were men who cannot possibly be spared from the too small force of officers at our command for the much more pressing and necessary duty of training Regular troops to be put into the field in France and Belgium as fast as they can be got ready. The first troops sent to France will be taken from the present forces of the Regular Army and will be under the command of trained soldiers only.

The responsibility for the successful conduct of our own part in this great war rests upon me. I could not escape it if I would. I am too much interested in the cause we are fighting for to be interested in anything but success. The issues involved are too immense for me to take into consideration anything whatever except the best, most effective, most immediate means of military action. What these means are I know from the mouths of men who have seen war as it is now conducted, who have no illusions, and to whom the whole grim matter is a matter of business. I shall center my attention upon those means and let everything else wait. I should be deeply to blame should I do otherwise, whatever the argument of policy or of personal gratification or advantage.

4. A Great Deal of Interest and Sympathy

To Amos Pinchot, July 13, 1917

Under the harsh, sweeping provisions of the Espionage Act, passed in mid-June, the Postmaster General was empowered to remove allegedly seditious literature from the mails. Postmaster General Burleson utilized his power to the full. Amos Pinchot, the Pennsylvania progressive, protested to Wilson over the Postmaster's refusal to allow The Masses, *a Socialist magazine, to pass through the mails. Wilson took the matter up with Burleson, as he said he would. But Burleson prevailed.*

THE LETTER of yesterday signed by yourself, Mr. Eastman, and Mr. Reed has just been laid before me and you may be sure has been read with a great deal of interest and sympathy. I am going to take the matter you present about the paper called *The Masses* up with the Postmaster General to see just how the case may best and mostly justly be handled.

You will understand, I am sure, why I would hesitate to make a public statement such as you suggest. It would undoubtedly be taken advantage of by those with whom neither you nor I have been in sympathy at all. . . .

5. The Utmost Freedom of Speech

To Postmaster General Burleson, October 18, 1917

Postmaster General Burleson had recently ordered the Milwaukee Leader *suppressed after a hearing. Though Wilson, in the letter below, finds fault with the action, the suppression remained.*

. . . I AM afraid you will be shocked, but I must say that I do not find this hearing very convincing. Some of the things quoted probably cross the line and I have very little doubt that they were all intended to have sinister results, but I must frankly say that I do not think that most of what is quoted ought to be regarded as unmailable. I have read the hearing with some feeling of misgiving as to the impression that was created upon the representatives of the paper which has been summoned, not because I doubt for a moment the purposes or the intelligence or the careful and conscientious methods of the public officials concerned, but because there is a wide margin of judgment here and I think that doubt ought always to be resolved in favor of the utmost freedom of speech. . . .

6. I Am with You if You Are with Me

Address to American Federation of Labor, November 12, 1917

Wilson always identified the cause of the war with the rights of labor and felt that it was above all in labor's interest to cooperate with the war effort. Such was the burden of this address to the labor convention meeting at Buffalo, New York.

. . . IF WE are true friends of freedom, our own or anybody else's, we will see that the power of this country and the productivity of this country are raised to their absolute maximum, and that absolutely nobody is allowed to stand in the way of it. When I say that nobody is allowed to stand in the way I do not mean that he shall be prevented by the power of the Government, but by the power of the American spirit. Our duty, if we are to do this great thing and show America to be what we believe her to be—the greatest hope and energy of the world—is to stand together night and day until the job is finished.

While we are fighting for freedom we must see, among other things, that labor is free; and that means a number of interesting things. It means not only that we must do what we have declared our purpose to do, see that the conditions of labor are not rendered more onerous by the war, but also that we shall see to it that the instrumentalities by which the conditions of labor are improved are not blocked or checked. That we must do. That has been the matter about which I have taken pleasure in conferring from time to time with your president, Mr. Gompers; and if I may be permitted to do so, I want to express my admiration of his patriotic courage, his large vision, and his statesman-like sense of what has to be done. I like to lay my mind alongside of a mind that knows how to pull in harness. The horses that kick over the traces will have to be put in corral. . . . We are all of the same clay and spirit, and we can get together if we desire to get together. Therefore, my counsel to you is this: Let us show ourselves Americans by showing that we do not want to go off in separate camps or groups by ourselves, but that we want to cooperate with all other classes and all other groups in the common enterprise which is to release the spirits of the world from bondage. I would be willing to set that up as the final test of an American. That is the meaning of democracy. I have been very much distressed, my fellow citizens, by some of the things that have happened recently. The mob spirit is displaying itself here and there in this country. I have sympathy with what some men are saying, but I have no sympathy with the men who take their punishment into their own hands; and I want to say to every man who does join such a mob that I do not recognize him as worthy of the free institutions of the United States. There are some organizations in this country whose object is anarchy and the destruction of law, but I would not meet their efforts by making myself partner in destroying the law. I despise and hate their purposes as much as any man, but I respect the ancient processes of justice; and I would be too proud not to see them done justice, however wrong they are.

So I want to utter my earnest protest against any manifestation of the spirit of lawlessness anywhere or in any cause. Why, gentlemen, look what it means. We claim to be the greatest democratic people in the world, and democracy means first of all that we can govern ourselves. If our men have not self-control, then they are not capable of that great thing which we call democratic government. A man who takes the law into his own hands is not the right man to cooperate in any formation or development of law and institutions, and some of the processes by which the struggle between capital and labor is carried on are processes that come very near to taking the law into your own hands. I do not mean for a moment to compare them with what I have just been speaking of, but I want you to see that they are mere gradations in this manifestation of the unwillingness to cooperate, and that the fundamental lesson of the whole situation is that we must not only take common counsel, but that we must yield to and obey common counsel. Not all of the instrumentalities for this are at hand. I am hopeful that in the very near future new instrumentalities may be organized by which we can see to it that various things that are now going on ought not to go on. There are various processes of the dilution of labor and the unnecessary substitution of labor and the bidding in distant markets and unfairly upsetting the whole competition of labor which ought not to go on. I mean now on the part of employers, and we must interject some instrumentality of cooperation by which the fair thing will be done all around. I am hopeful that some such instrumentalities may be devised, but whether they are or not, we must use those that we have and upon every occasion where it is necessary have such an instrumentality originated upon that occasion.

So, my fellow citizens, the reason I came away from Washington is that I sometimes get lonely down there. So many people come to Washington who know things that are not so, and so few people who know anything about what the people of the United States are thinking about. I have to come away and get reminded of the rest of the country. I have to come away and talk to men who are up against the real thing, and say to them, "I am with you if you are with me." And the only test of being with me is not to think about me personally at all, but merely to think of me as the expression for the time being of the power and dignity and hope of the United States.

7. The Program of the World's Peace

Address to Congress on Fourteen Points, January 8, 1918

Soon after taking power in November, the Bolsheviks published secret treaties between the Czar, France and England, and charged that the war was imperialistic on both sides. It became imperative for the Allies and the United States to state the democratic nature of their war aims. On January 5 British Prime Minister Lloyd George announced that Britain fought for democracy and human rights. Wilson followed with his great Fourteen Points address.

ONCE MORE, as repeatedly before, the spokesmen of the Central Empires have indicated their desire to discuss the objects of the war and the possible bases of a general peace. Parleys have been in progress at Brest-Litovsk between representatives of the Central Powers to which the attention of all the belligerents has been invited for the purpose of ascertaining whether it may be possible to extend these parleys into a general conference with regard to terms of peace and settlement. The Russian representatives presented not only a perfectly definite statement of the principles upon which they would be willing to conclude peace but also an equally definite program of the concrete application of those principles. The representatives of the Central Powers, on their part, presented an outline of settlement which, if much less definite, seemed susceptible of liberal interpretation until their specific program of practical terms was added. That program proposed no concessions at all either to the sovereignty of Russia or to the preferences of the populations with whose fortunes it dealt, but meant, in a word, that the Central Empires were to keep every foot of territory their armed forces had occupied—every province, every city, every point of vantage—as a permanent addition to their territories and their power. It is a reasonable conjecture that the general principles of settlement which they at first suggested originated with the more liberal statesmen of Germany and Austria, the men who have begun to feel the force of their own peoples' thought and purpose, while the concrete terms of actual settlement came from the military leaders who have no thought but to keep what they have got. The negotiations have been broken off. The Russian representatives were sincere and in earnest. They cannot entertain such proposals of conquest and domination.

The whole incident is full of significance. It is also full of perplexity. With whom are the Russian representatives dealing? For whom are the representatives of the Central Empires speaking? Are they speaking for the majorities of their respective parliaments or for the minority parties, that military and imperialistic minority which has so far dominated their whole policy and controlled the affairs of Turkey and of the Balkan states which have felt obliged to become their associates in this war? The Russian representatives have insisted, very justly, very wisely, and in the true spirit of modern democracy, that the conferences they have been holding with the Teutonic and Turkish statesmen should be held within open, not closed, doors, and all the world has been audience, as was desired. To whom have we been listening, then? To those who speak the spirit and intention of the Resolutions of the German Reichstag of the ninth of July last, the spirit and intention of the liberal leaders and parties of Germany, or to those who resist and defy that spirit and intention and insist upon conquest and subjugation? Or are we listening, in fact, to both, unreconciled and in open and hopeless contradiction? These are very serious and pregnant questions. Upon the answer to them depends the peace of the world.

But, whatever the results of the parleys at Brest-Litovsk, whatever the confusions of counsel and of purpose in the utterances of the spokesmen of the Central Empires, they have again attempted to acquaint the world with their objects in the war and have again challenged their adversaries to say what their objects are and what sort of settlement they would deem just and satisfactory. There is no good reason why that challenge should not be responded to, and responded to with the utmost candor. We did not wait for it. Not once, but again and again, we have laid our whole thought and purpose before the world, not in general terms only, but each time with sufficient definition to make it clear what sort of definitive terms of settlement must necessarily spring out of them. Within the last week Mr. Lloyd George has spoken with admirable candor and in admirable spirit for the people and Government of Great Britain. There is no confusion of counsel among the adversaries of the Central Powers, no uncertainty of principle, no vagueness of detail. The only secrecy of counsel, the only lack of fearless frankness, the only failure to make definite statement of the objects of the war, lies with Germany and her Allies. The issues of life and death hang upon these definitions. No statesman who has the least conception of his responsibility ought for a moment to permit himself to continue this tragical and appalling outpouring of blood and treasure unless he is sure beyond a peradventure that the objects of the vital sacrifice are part and parcel of the very life of Society and that the people for whom he speaks think them right and imperative as he does.

There is, moreover, a voice calling for these definitions of principle and of purpose which is, it seems to me, more thrilling and more compelling than any of the many moving voices with which the troubled air of the world is filled. It is the voice of the Russian people. They are prostrate and all but helpless, it would seem, before the grim power of Germany, which has hitherto known no relenting and no pity. Their power, apparently, is shattered. And yet their soul is not subservient. They will not yield either in principle or in action. Their conception of what is right, of what it is humane and honorable for them to accept, has been stated with a frankness, a largeness of view, a generosity of spirit, and a universal human sympathy which must challenge the admiration of every friend of mankind; and they have refused to compound their ideals or desert others that they themselves may be safe. They call to us to say what it is that we desire, in what, if in anything, our purpose and our spirit differ from theirs; and I believe that the people of the United States would wish me to respond, with utter simplicity and frankness. Whether their present leaders believe it or not, it is our heartfelt desire and hope that some way may be opened whereby we may be privileged to assist the people of Russia to attain their utmost hope of liberty and ordered peace.

It will be our wish and purpose that the processes of peace, when they are begun, shall be absolutely open and that they shall involve and permit henceforth no secret understandings of any kind. The day of conquest and aggrandizement is gone by; so is also the day of secret covenants entered into in the interest of particular governments and likely at some unlooked-for moment to upset the peace of the world. It is this happy fact, now clear to the view of every public man whose thoughts do not still linger in an age that is dead and gone, which makes it possible for every nation whose purposes are consistent with justice and the peace of the world to avow now or at any other time the objects it has in view.

We entered this war because violations of right had occurred which touched us to the quick and made the life of our own people impossible unless they were corrected and the world secured once for all against their recurrence. What we demand in this war, therefore, is nothing peculiar to ourselves. It is that the world be made fit and safe to live in; and particularly that it be made safe for every peace-loving nation which, like our own, wishes to live its own life, determine its own institutions, be assured of justice and fair dealing by the other people of the world as against force and selfish aggression. All the peoples of the world are in effect partners in this interest, and for our own part we see very clearly that unless justice be done to others it will not be done to us. The program of the world's peace, therefore, is our program; and that program, the only possible program, as we see it, is this:

I. Open covenants of peace, openly arrived at, after which there shall be no private international understandings of any kind but diplomacy shall proceed always frankly and in the public view.

II. Absolute freedom of navigation upon the seas, outside territorial waters, alike in peace and in war, except as the seas may be closed in whole or in part by international action for the enforcement of international covenants.

III. The removal, so far as possible, of all economic barriers and the establishment of an equality of trade conditions among all the nations consenting to the peace and associating themselves for its maintenance.

IV. Adequate guarantees given and taken that national armaments will be reduced to the lowest point consistent with domestic safety.

V. A free, open-minded, and absolutely impartial adjustment of all colonial claims, based upon a strict observance of the principle that in determining all such questions of sovereignty the interests of the populations concerned must have equal weight with the equitable claims of the government whose title is to be determined.

VI. The evacuation of all Russian territory and such a settlement of all questions affecting Russia as will secure the best and freest cooperation of the other nations of the world in obtaining for her an unhampered and unembarrassed opportunity for the independent determination of her own political development and national policy and assure her of a sincere welcome into the society of free nations under institutions of her own choosing; and, more than a welcome, assistance also of every kind that she may need and may herself desire. The treatment accorded Russia by her sister nations in the months to come will be the acid test of their good will, of their comprehension of her needs as distinguished from their own interests, and of their intelligent and unselfish sympathy.

VII. Belgium, the whole world will agree, must be evacuated and restored, without any attempt to limit the sovereignty which she enjoys in common with all other free nations. No other single act will serve as this will serve to restore confidence among the nations in the laws which they have themselves set and determined for the government of their relations with one another. Without this healing act the whole structure and validity of international law is forever impaired.

VIII. All French territory should be freed and the invaded portions restored, and the wrong done to France by Prussia in 1871 in the matter of Alsace-Lorraine, which has unsettled the peace of the world for nearly fifty years, should be righted, in order that peace may once more be made secure in the interest of all.

IX. A readjustment of the frontiers of Italy should be effected along clearly recognizable lines of nationality.

X. The peoples of Austria-Hungary, whose place among the nations we wish to see safeguarded and assured, should be accorded the freest opportunity of autonomous development.

XI. Rumania, Serbia, and Montenegro should be evacuated; occupied territories restored; Serbia accorded free and secure access to the sea; and the relations of the several Balkan states to one another determined by friendly counsel along historically established lines of allegiance and nationality; and international guarantees of the political and economic independence and territorial integrity of the several Balkan states should be entered into.

XII. The Turkish portions of the present Ottoman Empire should be assured a secure soveignty, but the other nationalities which are now under Turkish rule should be assured an undoubted security of life and an absolutely unmolested opportunity of autonomous development, and the Dardanelles should be permanently opened as a free passage to the ships and commerce of all nations under international guarantees.

XIII. An independent Polish state should be erected which should include the territories inhabited by indisputably Polish populations, which should be assured a free and secure access to the sea, and whose political and economic independence and territorial integrity should be guaranteed by international covenant.

XIV. A general association of nations must be formed under specific covenants for the purpose of affording mutual guarantees of political independence and territorial integrity to great and small states alike.

In regard to these essential rectifications of wrong and assertions of right we feel ourselves to be intimate partners of all the governments and peoples associated together against the imperialists. We cannot be separated in interest or divided in purpose. We stand together until the end.

For such arrangements and covenants we are willing to fight and to continue to fight until they are achieved; but only because we wish the right to prevail and desire a just and stable peace such as can be secured only by removing the chief provocations to war, which this program does remove. We have no jealousy of German greatness, and there is nothing in this program that impairs it. We grudge her no achievement or distinction of learning or of pacific enterprise such as have made her record very bright and very enviable. We do not wish to injure her or to block in any way her legitimate influence or power. We do not wish to fight her either with arms or with hostile arrangements of trade if she is willing to associate herself with us and the other peace-loving nations of the world in covenants of justice and law and fair dealing. We wish her only to accept a place of equality among the peoples of the world—the new world in which we now live—instead of a place of mastery.

Neither do we presume to suggest to her any alteration or modification of her institutions. But it is necessary, we must frankly say, and necessary as a preliminary to any intelligent dealings with her on our part, that we should know whom her spokesmen speak for when they speak to us, whether for the Reichstag majority or for the military party and the men whose creed is imperial domination.

We have spoken now, surely, in terms too concrete to admit of any further doubt or question. An evident principle runs through the whole program I have outlined. It is the principle of justice to all peoples and nationalities, and their right to live on equal terms of liberty and safety with one another, whether they be strong or weak. Unless this principle be made its foundation no part of the structure of international justice can stand. The people of the United States could act upon no other principle; and to the vindication of this principle they are ready to devote their lives, their honor, and everything that they possess. The moral climax of this the culminating and final war for human liberty has come, and they are ready to put their own strength, their own highest purpose, their own integrity and devotion to the test.

8. Why Begin at the Impossible?

To Colonel House, March 22, 1918

House was Wilson's coadjutor in the creation of a league of nations. Both naturally sought to bring influential Republicans into the scheme. In discussing a prospective league, Wilson called attention to precisely the issue that was later to come between him and the Senate Republicans.

YES, INDEED, I think your lunch with Taft, Lowell, and Root is most wise and should be most helpful, if they have any sense among them—which I sometimes seriously doubt.

My own conviction, as you know, is that the administrative *constitution* of the league must *grow* and not be made; that we must *begin* with solemn covenants, covering mutual guarantees of political independence and territorial integrity (if the final territorial agreements of the peace conference are fair and satisfactory and *ought* to be perpetuated), but that the method of carrying those mutual pledges out should be left to develop of itself, case by case. Any attempt to begin by putting executive authority in the hands of any particular group of powers would be to sow a harvest of jealousy and distrust which would spring up at once and choke the whole thing. To take one thing, and only one, but quite sufficient in itself: The United States Senate would never ratify any treaty which put the force of the United States at the disposal of any such group or body. Why begin at the impossible end when there is a possible end and it is feasible to plant a system which will slowly but surely ripen into fruition? . . .

9. The Thing Is Preposterous

Address at Baltimore, April 6, 1918

Wilson, on the occasion of the third liberty loan campaign, launched in Baltimore, again denied any possibility that peace could be made so long as Germany remained autocratic.

. . . I CALL you to witness, my fellow countrymen, that at no stage of this terrible business have I judged the purposes of Germany intemperately. I should be ashamed in the presence of affairs so grave, so fraught with the destinies of mankind throughout all the world, to speak with truculence, to use the weak language of hatred or vindictive purpose. We must judge as we would be judged. I have sought to learn the objects Germany has in this war from the mouths of her own spokesmen, and to deal as frankly with them as I wished them to deal with me. I have laid bare our own ideals, our own purposes, without reserve or doubtful phrase, and have asked them to say as plainly what it is that they seek.

We have ourselves proposed no injustice, no aggression. We are ready, whenever the final reckoning is made, to be just to the German people, deal fairly with the German power, as with all others. There can be no difference between peoples in the final judgment, if it is indeed to be a righteous judgment. To propose anything but justice, even-handed and dispassionate justice, to Germany at any time, whatever the outcome of the war, would be to renounce and dishonor our own cause. For we ask nothing that we are not willing to accord.

It has been with this thought that I have sought to learn from those who spoke for Germany whether it was justice or dominion and the execution of their own will upon the other nations of the world that the German leaders were seeking. They have answered, answered in unmistakable terms. They have avowed that it was not justice but dominion and the unhindered execution of their own will.

The avowal has not come from Germany's statesmen. It has come from her military leaders, who are her real rulers. Her statesmen have said that they wished peace, and were ready to discuss its terms whenever their opponents were willing to sit down at the conference table with them. Her present Chancellor has said—in indefinite and uncertain terms, indeed, and in phrases that often seem to deny their own meaning, but with as much plainness as he thought prudent—that he believed that peace should be based upon the principles which we had declared would be our own in the final settlement. At Brest-Litovsk her civilian delegates spoke in similar terms; professed their desire to conclude a fair peace and accord to the peoples with whose fortunes they were dealing the right to choose their own allegiances. But action accompanied and followed the profession. Their military masters, the men who act for Germany and exhibit her purpose in execution, proclaimed a very different conclusion. We cannot mistake what they have done—in Russia, in Finland, in the Ukraine, in Rumania. The real test of their justice and fair play has come. From this we may judge the rest. They are enjoying in Russia a cheap triumph in which no brave or gallant nation can long take pride. A great people, helpless by their own act, lies for the time at their mercy. Their fair professions are forgotten. They nowhere set up justice, but everywhere impose their power and exploit everything for their own use and aggrandizement; and the peoples of conquered provinces are invited to be free under their dominion!

Are we not justified in believing that they would do the same things at their western front if they were not there face to face with armies whom even their countless divisions cannot overcome? If, when they have felt their check to be final, they should propose favorable and equitable terms with regard to Belgium and France and Italy, could they blame us if we concluded that they did so only to assure themselves of a free hand in Russia and the East?

Their purpose is undoubtedly to make all the Slavic peoples, all the free and ambitious nations of the Baltic peninsula, all the lands that Turkey has dominated and misruled, subject to their will and ambition and build upon that dominion an empire of force upon which they fancy that they can then erect an empire of gain and commercial supremacy—an empire as hostile to the Americas as to the Europe which it will overawe—an empire which will ultimately master Persia, India, and the peoples of the Far East. In such a program our ideals, the ideals of justice and humanity and liberty, the principle of the free self-determination of nations upon which all the modern world insists, can play no part. They are rejected for the ideals of power, for the principle that the strong must rule the weak, that trade must follow the flag, whether those to whom it is taken welcome it or not, that the peoples of the world are to be made subject to the patronage and overlordship of those whose have the power to enforce it.

That program once carried out, America and all who care or dare to stand with her must arm and prepare themselves to contest the mastery of the world, a mastery in which the rights of common men, the rights of women and of all who are weak, must for the time being be trodden under foot and disregarded, and the old, age-long struggle for freedom and right begin again at its beginning. Everything that America has lived for and loved and grown great to vindicate and bring to a glorious realization will have fallen in utter ruin and the gates of mercy once more pitilessly shut upon mankind!

The thing is preposterous and impossible; and yet is not that what the whole course and action of the German armies has meant wherever they have moved? I do not wish, even in this moment of utter disillusionment, to judge harshly or unrighteously. I judge only what the German arms have accomplished with unpitying thoroughness throughout every fair region they have touched.

What, then, are we to do? For myself, I am ready, ready still, ready even now, to discuss a fair and just and honest peace at any time that it is sincerely purposed—a peace in which the strong and the weak shall fare alike. But the answer, when I proposed such a peace, came from the German commanders in Russia, and I cannot mistake the meaning of the answer.

I accept the challenge. I know that you accept it. All the world shall know that you accept it. It shall appear in the utter sacrifice and self-forgetfulness with which we shall give all that we love and all that we have to redeem the world and make it fit for free men like ourselves to live in. This now is the meaning of all that we do. Let everything that we say, my fellow countrymen, everything that we henceforth plan and accomplish, ring true to this response till the majesty and might of our concerted power shall fill the thought and utterly defeat the force of those who flout and misprize what we honor and hold dear. Germany has once more said that force, and force alone, shall decide whether Justice and Peace shall reign in the affairs of men, whether Right as America conceives it or Dominion as she conceives it shall determine the destinies of mankind. There is, therefore, but one response possible from us: Force, Force to the utmost, Force without stint or limit, the righteous and triumphant Force which shall make Right the law of the world, and cast every selfish dominion down in the dust.

10. The Government Will Have to Take Over

Conversation with Dr. Stockton Axson, June 30, 1918

Dr. Axson, the brother of Wilson's first wife and a very close friend, later reprised the following conversation in an interview with Ray Stannard Baker, Wilson's biographer.

THE PRESIDENT and Mrs. Wilson remained home all day, and Dr. Axson, the President's brother-in-law and dear friend, came in for luncheon. It was probably on this occasion that he and the President had a long and intimate conversation which Dr. Axson afterward reported to the author. The President was in one of his "most lovable talking moods."

"Stock," he said, "if you had the naming of the next President, whom would you name?"

"Do you mean present company excepted?"

"Oh, yes, of course."

"Well," said Dr. Axson, "I have such a personal affection for Mac [McAdoo], as well as such faith in his sagacity, that he would be my choice."

"I love Mac as much as you do," the President said, "but I doubt if he is the person for the next President. In my judgment, a great many things are going to be very difficult, and the next President must be not only a man of action, but he must also have great powers of reflection. Now nobody can do things better than Mac, but if Mac ever reflects, I have never caught him in the act! The next President will have to be able to think in terms of the whole world. He must be internationally minded. Now as a matter of fact, the only really internationally minded people are the labor people. They are in touch with world movements.

"The world is going to change radically, and I am satisfied that governments will have to do many things which are now left to individuals and corporations. I am satisfied for instance that the government will have to take over all the great natural resources. What does that mean? That means it will have to take over all the water power; all the coal mines; all the oil fields, etc. They will have to be government-owned.

"If I should say that outside, people would call me a socialist, but I am not a socialist. And it is because I am not a socialist that I believe these things. I think the only way we can prevent communism [Dr. Axson was not sure he used just this word, but he is sure that 'communism' was what he meant] is by some action as that. Now that is going to involve vast problems, and the next President must be a man who will be able not only to *do* things, but, after having taken counsel and made a full survey, he must be able to retire *alone,* behind his own closed door, and think through the processes, step by step. . . ."

11. These Are the Ends

Address on Four Points, July 4, 1918

In these four points, supplementing the fourteen already set forth, Wilson reaffirms America's war aims and implicitly lays the groundwork for the League of Nations.

GENTLEMEN OF the diplomatic corps and my fellow citizens: I am happy to draw apart with you to this quiet place of old counsel in order to speak a little of the meaning of this day of our Nation's independence. The place seems very still and remote. It is as serene and untouched by the hurry of the world as it was in those great days long ago when General Washington was here and held leisurely conference with the men who were to be associated with him in the creation of a nation. From these gentle slopes they looked out upon the world and saw it whole, saw it with the light of the future upon it, saw it with modern eyes that turned away from a past which men of liberated spirits could no longer endure. It is for that reason that we cannot feel, even here, in the immediate presence of this sacred tomb, that this is a place of death. It was a place of achievement. A great promise that was meant for all mankind was here given plan and reality. The associations by which we are here surrounded are the inspiriting associations of that noble death which is only a glorious consummation. From this green hillside we also ought to be able to see with comprehending eyes the world that lies about us and should conceive anew the purposes that must set men free.

It is significant—significant of their own character and purpose and of the influences they were setting afoot—that Washington and his associates, like the barons at Runnymede, spoke and acted, not for a class, but for a people. It has been left for us to see to it that it shall be understood that they spoke and acted, not for a single people only, but for all mankind. They were thinking, not of themselves and of the material interests which centered in the little groups of landholders and merchants and men of affairs with whom they were accustomed to act, in Virginia and the colonies to the north and south of her, but of a people which wished to be done with classes and special interests and the authority of men whom they had not themselves chosen to rule over them. They entertained no private purpose, desired no peculiar privilege. They were consciously planning that men of every class should be free and America a place to which men out of every nation might resort who wished to share with them the rights and privileges of free men. And we take our cue from them—do we not? We intend what they intended. We here in America believe our participation in this present war to be only the fruitage of what they planted. Our case differs from theirs only in this, that it is our inestimable privilege to concert with men out of every nation what shall make not only the liberties of America secure but the liberties of every other people as well. We are happy in the thought that we are permitted to do what they would have done had they been in our place. There must now be settled once for all what was settled for America in the great age upon whose inspiration we draw today. This is surely a fitting place from which calmly to look out upon our task, that we may fortify our spirits for its accomplishment. And this is the appropriate place from which to avow, alike to the friends who look on and to the friends with whom we have the happiness to be associated in action, the faith and purpose with which we act.

This, then, is our conception of the great struggle in which we are engaged. The plot is written plain upon every scene and every act of the supreme tragedy. On the one hand stand the peoples of the world—not only the peoples actually engaged, but many others also who suffer under mastery but cannot act; peoples of many races and in every part of the world—the people of stricken Russia still, among the rest, though they are for the moment unorganized and helpless. Opposed to them, masters of many armies, stand an isolated, friendless group of governments who speak no common purpose but only selfish ambitions of their own by which none can profit but themselves, and whose peoples are fuel in their hands; governments which fear their people and yet are for the time their sovereign lords, making every choice for them and disposing of their lives and fortunes as they will, as well as of the lives and fortunes of every people who fall under their power—governments clothed with the strange trappings and the primitive authority of an age that is altogether alien and hostile to our own. The Past and the Present are in deadly grapple and the peoples of the world are being done to death between them.

There can be but one issue. The settlement must be final. There can be no compromise. No halfway decision would be tolerable. No halfway decision is conceivable. These are the ends for which the associated peoples of the world are fighting and which must be conceded them before there can be peace:

I. The destruction of every arbitrary power anywhere that can separately, secretly, and of its single choice disturb the peace of the world; or, if it cannot be presently destroyed, at the least its reduction to virtual impotence.

II. The settlement of every question, whether of territory, of sovereignty, of economic arrangement, or of political relationship, upon the basis of the free acceptance of that settlement by the people immediately concerned, and not upon the basis of the material interest or advantage of any other nation or people which may desire a different settlement for the sake of its own exterior influence or mastery.

III. The consent of all nations to be governed in their conduct towards each other by the same principles of honor and of respect for the common law of civilized society that govern the individual citizens of all modern states in their relations with one another; to the end that all promises and covenants may be sacredly observed, no private plots or conspiracies hatched, no selfish injuries wrought with impunity, and a mutual trust established upon the handsome foundation of a mutual respect for right.

IV. The establishment of an organization of peace which shall make it certain that the combined power of free nations will check every invasion of right and serve to make peace and justice the more secure by affording a definite tribunal of opinion to which all must submit and by which every international readjustment that cannot be amicably agreed upon by the peoples directly concerned shall be sanctioned.

These great objects can be put into a single sentence. What we seek is the reign of law, based upon the consent of the governed and sustained by the organized opinion of mankind.

These great ends cannot be achieved by debating and seeking to reconcile and accommodate what statesmen may wish, with their projects for balances of power and of national opportunity. They can be realized only by the determination of what the thinking peoples of the world desire, with their longing hope for justice and for social freedom and opportunity.

I can fancy that the air of this place carries the accents of such principles with a peculiar kindness. Here were started forces which the great nation against which they were primarily directed at first regarded as a revolt against its rightful authority but which it has long since seen to have been a step in the liberation of its own people as well as of the people of the United States; and I stand here now to speak—speak proudly and with confident hope—of the spread of this revolt, this liberation, to the great stage of the world itself! The blinded rulers of Prussia have roused forces they knew little of—forces which, once roused, can never be crushed to earth again; for they have at their heart an inspiration and a purpose which are deathless and of the very stuff of triumph!

12. To Regain Control of Their Own Affairs

Aide-Mémoire on Intervention in Russia, July 17, 1918

Throughout the spring of 1918, Wilson resisted Allied pressure to intervene in Russia, who had left the war and was fighting counter-revolutionary armies. But he changed his mind when the Czechoslovak

Legion rebelled in May and seized the Siberian railroad. The American government thought the Czechs wanted to fight Germany, and Wilson, whose chief motive was to prevent a possible German attack on Siberia, decided to send American soldiers to help them. He never intended to side with the counter-revolutionary forces. Following is Wilson's directive outlining the reasons for American intervention.

. . . IT IS the clear and fixed judgment of the Government of the United States, arrived at after repeated and very searching reconsiderations of the whole situation in Russia, that military intervention there would add to the present sad confusion in Russia rather than cure it, injure her rather than help her, and that it would be of no advantage in the prosecution of our main design, to win the war against Germany. It can not, therefore, take part in such intervention or sanction it in principle. Military intervention would, in its judgment, even supposing it to be efficacious in its immediate avowed object of delivering an attack upon Germany from the east, be merely a method of making use of Russia, not a method of serving her. Her people could not profit by it, if they profited by it at all, in time to save them from their present distresses, and their substance would be used to maintain foreign armies, not to reconstitute their own. Military action is admissible in Russia, as the Government of the United States sees the circumstances, only to help the Czecho-Slovaks consolidate their forces and get into successful cooperation with their Slavic kinsmen and to steady any efforts at self-government or self-defense in which the Russians themselves may be willing to accept assistance. Whether from Vladivostok or from Murmansk and Archangel, the only legitimate object for which American or Allied troops can be employed, it submits, is to guard military stores which may subsequently be needed by Russian forces and to render such aid as may be acceptable to the Russians in the organization of their own self-defense. For helping the Czecho-Slovaks there is immediate necessity and sufficient justification. Recent developments have made it evident that that is in the interest of what the Russian people themselves desire, and the Government of the United States is glad to contribute the small force at its disposal for that purpose. It yields, also, to the judgment of the Supreme Command in the matter of establishing a small force at Murmansk, to guard the military stores at Kola, and to make it safe for Russian forces to come together in organized bodies in the north. But it owes to frank counsel to say that it can go no further than these modest and experimental plans. It is not in a position, and has no expectation of being in a position, to take part in organized intervention in adequate force from either Vladivostok or Murmansk and Archangel. It feels that it ought to add, also, that it will feel at liberty to use the few troops it can spare only for the purposes here stated and shall feel obliged to withdraw those forces, in order to add them to the forces at the western front, if the plans in whose execution it is now intended that they should cooperate should develop into others inconsistent with the policy to which the Government of the United States feels constrained to restrict itself.

At the same time the Government of the United States wishes to say with the utmost cordiality and good will that none of the conclusions here stated is meant to wear the least color of criticism of what the other governments associated against Germany may think it wise to undertake. It wishes in no way to embarrass their choices of policy. All that is intended here is a perfectly frank and definite statement of the policy which the United States feels obliged to adopt for herself and in the use of her own military forces. The Government of the United States does not wish it to be understood that in so restricting its own activities it is seeking, even by implication, to set limits to the action or to define the policies of its associates.

It hopes to carry out the plans for safeguarding the rear of the Czecho-Slovaks operating from Vladivostok in a way that will place it and keep it in close cooperation with a small military force like its own from Japan, and if necessary from the other Allies, and that will assure it of the cordial accord of all the Allied powers; and it proposes to ask all associated in this course of action to unite in assuring the people of Russia in the most public and solemn manner that none of the governments uniting in action either in Siberia or in northern Russia contemplates any interference of any kind with the political sovereignty of Russia, any intervention in her internal affairs, or any impairment of her territorial integrity either now or hereafter, but that each of the associated powers has the single object of affording such aid as shall be acceptable, and only such aid as shall be acceptable, to the Russian people in their endeavor to regain control of their own affairs, their own territory, and their own destiny.

It is the hope and purpose of the Government of the United States to take advantage of the earliest opportunity to send to Siberia a commission of merchants, agricultural experts, labor advisers, Red Cross representatives, and agents of the Young Men's Christian Association accustomed to organizing the best methods of spreading useful information and rendering educational help of a modest sort, in order in some systematic manner to relieve the immediate economic necessities of the people there in every way for which opportunity may open. The execution of this plan will follow and will not be permitted to embarrass the military assistance rendered in the rear of the westward-moving forces of the Czecho-Slovaks.

13. A National Home

To Rabbi Stephen J. Wise, August 31, 1918

Wilson publicly endorsed the Balfour Declaration, by which Britain officially sanctioned the aims of Zionism—the establishment of a Jewish national home in Palestine. Rabbi Wise, a leading American Zionist, was a prominent Democrat and a personal friend of Wilson.

MY DEAR Rabbi Wise: I have watched with deep and sincere interest the reconstructive work which the Weitzman Commission has done in Palestine at the instance of the British Government, and I welcome an opportunity to express the satisfaction I have felt in the progress of the Zionist movement in the United States and in the Allied countries since the declaration by Mr. Balfour, on behalf of the British Government, of Great Britain's approval of the establishment in Palestine of a national home for the Jewish people, and his promise that the British Government would use its best endeavors to facilitate the achievement of that object, with the understanding that nothing would be done to prejudice the civil and religious rights of non-Jewish people in Palestine or the rights and political status enjoyed by Jews in other countries.

I think that all Americans will be deeply moved by the report that even in this time of stress the Weitzman Commission has been able to lay the foundation of the Hebrew University at Jerusalem, with the promise that that bears of spiritual rebirth.

14. The Final Triumph

Address on Five Points, September 27, 1918

The tide of battle had turned decisively in favor of the Allies and the United States. It would be only a matter of time before the Germans must surrender or be crushed. Bulgaria had already sued for peace. Under these conditions Wilson supplemented the original Fourteen Points with yet another five, making twenty-three altogether. The occasion was an address at the Metropolitan Opera House in New York City in behalf of the fourth liberty loan.

. . . AT EVERY turn of the war we gain a fresh consciousness of what we mean to accomplish by it. When our hope and expectation are most excited we think more definitely than before of the issues that hang upon it and of the purposes which must be realized by means of it. For it has positive and well-defined purposes which we did not determine and which we cannot alter. No statesman or assembly created them; no statesman or assembly can alter them. They have arisen out of the very nature and circumstances of the war. The most that statesmen or assemblies can do is to carry them out or be false to them. They were perhaps not clear at the outset; but they are clear now. The war has lasted more than four years and the whole world has been drawn into it. The common will of mankind has been substituted for the particular purposes of individual states. Individual statesmen may have started the conflict, but neither they nor their opponents can stop it as they please. It has become a peoples' war, and peoples of all sorts and races, of every degree of power and variety of fortune, are involved in its sweeping processes of change and settlement. We came into it when its character had become fully defined and it was plain that no nation could stand apart or be indifferent to its outcome. Its challenge drove to the heart of everything we cared for and lived for. The voice of the war had become clear and gripped our hearts. Our brothers from many lands, as well as our own murdered dead under the sea, were calling to us, and we responded, fiercely and of course.

The air was clear about us. We saw things in their full, convincing proportions as they were; and we have seen them with steady eyes and unchanging comprehension ever since. We accepted the issues of the war as facts, not as any group of men either here or elsewhere had defined them, and we can accept no outcome which does not squarely meet and settle them. Those issues are these:

Shall the military power of any nation or group of nations be suffered to determine the fortunes of peoples over whom they have no right to rule except the right of force?

Shall strong nations be free to wrong weak nations and make them subject to their purpose and interest?

Shall peoples be ruled and dominated, even in their own internal affairs, by arbitrary and irresponsible force or by their own will and choice?

Shall there be a common standard of right and privilege for all peoples and nations or shall the strong do as they will and the weak suffer without redress?

Shall the assertion of right be haphazard and by casual alliance or shall there be a common concert to oblige the observance of common rights?

No man, no group of men, chose these to be the issues of the struggle. They *are* the issues of it; and they must be settled—by no arrangement or compromise or adjustment of interests, but definitely and once for all and with a full and unequivocal acceptance of the principle that the interest of the weakest is as sacred as the interest of the strongest.

This is what we mean when we speak of a permanent peace, if we speak sincerely, intelligently, and with a real knowledge and comprehension of the matter we deal with.

We are all agreed that there can be no peace obtained by any kind of bargain or compromise with the governments of the Central Empires, because we have dealt with them already and have seen them deal with other governments that were parties to this struggle, at Brest-Litovsk and Bucharest. They have convinced us that they are without honor and do not intend justice. They observe no covenants, accept no principle but force and their own interest. We cannot "come to terms" with them. They have made it impossible. The German people must by this time be fully aware that we cannot accept the word of those who forced this war upon us. We do not think the same thoughts or speak the same language of agreement.

It is of capital importance that we should also be explicitly agreed that no peace shall be obtained by any kind of compromise or abatement of the principles we have avowed as the principles for which we are fighting. There should exist no doubt about that. I am, therefore, going to take the liberty of speaking with the utmost frankness about the practical implications that are involved in it.

If it be in deed and in truth the common object of the Governments associated against Germany and of the nations whom they govern, as I believe it to be, to achieve by the coming settlements a secure and lasting peace, it will be necessary that all who sit down at the peace table shall come ready and willing to pay the price, the only price, that will procure it; and ready and willing, also, to create in some virile fashion the only instrumentality by which it can be made certain that the agreements of the peace will be honored and fulfilled.

That price is impartial justice in every item of the settlement, no matter whose interest is crossed; and not only impartial justice, but also the satisfaction of the several peoples whose fortunes are dealt with. That indispensable instrumentality is a League of Nations formed under covenants that will be efficacious. Without such an instrumentality, by which the peace of the world can be guaranteed, peace will rest in part upon the word of outlaws and only upon that word. For Germany will have to redeem her character, not by what happens at the peace table, but by what follows.

And, as I see it, the constitution of that League of Nations and the clear definition of its objects must be a part, is in a sense the most essential part, of the peace settlement itself. It cannot be formed now. If formed now, it would be merely a new alliance confined to the nations associated against a common enemy. It is not likely that it could be formed after the settlement. It is necessary to guarantee the peace; and the peace cannot be guaranteed as an afterthought. The reason, to speak in plain terms again, why it must be guaranteed is that there will be parties to the peace whose promises have proved untrustworthy, and means must be found in connection with the peace settlement itself to remove that source of insecurity. It would be folly to leave the guarantee to the subsequent voluntary action of the Governments we have seen destroy Russia and deceive Rumania.

But these general terms do not disclose the whole matter. Some details are needed to make them sound less like a thesis and more like a practical program. These, then, are some of the particulars, and I state them with the greater confidence because I can state them authoritatively as representing this Government's interpretation of its own duty with regard to peace:

First, the impartial justice meted out must involve no discrimination between those to whom we wish to be just and those to whom we do not wish to be just. It must be a justice that plays no favorites and knows no standard but the equal rights of the several peoples concerned;

Second, no special or separate interest of any single nation or any group of nations can be made the basis of any part of the settlement which is not consistent with the common interest of all;

Third, there can be no leagues or alliances or special covenants and understandings within the general and common family of the League of Nations;

Fourth, and more specifically, there can be no special, selfish economic combinations within the League and no employment of any form of economic boycott or exclusion except as the power of economic penalty by exclusion from the markets of the world may be vested in the League of Nations itself as a means of discipline and control;

Fifth, all international agreements and treaties of every kind must be made known in their entirety to the rest of the world.

Special alliances and economic rivalries and hostilities have been the prolific source in the modern world of the plans and passions that produce war. It would be an insincere as well as insecure peace that did not exclude them in definite and binding terms.

The confidence with which I venture to speak for our people in these matters does not spring from our traditions merely and the well-known principles of international action which we have always professed and followed. In the same sentence in which I say that the United States will enter into no special arrangements or understandings with particular nations let me say also that the United States is prepared to assume its full share of responsibility for the maintenance of the common covenants and understandings upon which peace must henceforth rest. We still read Washington's immortal warning against "entangling alliances" with full comprehension and an answering purpose. But only special and limited alliances entangle; and we recognize and accept the duty of a new day in which we are permitted to hope for a general alliance which will avoid entanglements and clear the air of the world for common understandings and the maintenance of common rights. . . .

It is the peculiarity of this great war that while statesmen have seemed to cast about for definitions of their purpose and have sometimes seemed to shift their ground and their point of view, the thought of the mass of men, whom statesmen are supposed to instruct and lead, has grown more and more unclouded; more and more certain of what it is that they are fighting for. National purposes have fallen more and more into the background and the common purpose of enlightened mankind has taken their place. The counsels of plain men have become on all hands more simple and straightforward and more unified than the counsels of sophisticated men of affairs, who still retain the impression that they are playing a game of power and playing for high stakes. That is why I have said that this is a peoples' war, not a statesmen's. Statesmen must follow the clarified common thought or be broken.

I take that to be the significance of the fact that assemblies and associations of many kinds made up of plain workaday people have demanded, almost every time they came together, and are still demanding, that the leaders of their Governments declare to them plainly what it is, exactly what it is, that they were seeking in this war, and what they think the items of the final settlement should be. They are not yet satisfied with what they have been told. They still seem to fear that they are getting what they ask for only in statesmen's terms—only in the terms of territorial arrangements and divisions of power, and not in terms of broad-visioned justice and mercy and peace and the satisfaction of those deep-seated longings of oppressed and distracted men and women and enslaved peoples that seem to them the only things worth fighting a war for that engulfs the world. Perhaps statesmen have not always recognized this changed aspect of the whole world of policy and action. Perhaps they have not always spoken in direct reply to the questions asked because they did not know how searching those questions were and what sort of answers they demanded.

But I, for one, am glad to attempt the answer again and again, in the hope that I may make it clearer and clearer that my one thought is to satisfy those who struggle in the ranks and are, perhaps above all others, entitled to a reply whose meaning no one can have any excuse for misunderstanding, if he understands the language in which it is spoken or can get some one to translate it correctly into his own. And I believe that the leaders of the governments with which we are associated will speak, as they have occasion, as plainly as I have tried to speak. I hope that they will feel free to say whether they think that I am in any degree mistaken in my interpretation of the issues involved or in my purpose with regard to the means by which a satisfactory settlement of those issues may be obtained. Unity of purpose and of counsel are as imperatively necessary in this war as was unity of command in the battlefield; and with perfect unity of purpose and counsel will come assurance of complete victory. It can be had in no other way. "Peace drives" can be effectively neutralized and silenced only by showing that every victory of the nations associated against Germany brings the nations nearer the sort of peace which will bring security and reassurance to all peoples and make the recurrence of another such struggle of pitiless force and bloodshed forever impossible, and that nothing else can. Germany is constantly intimating the "terms" she will accept; and always finds that the world does not want terms. It wishes the final triumph of justice and fair dealing.

15. The German People Themselves

Second Note to Germany on Peace, October 14, 1918

With Bulgaria about to leave the war and German armies on the western front near collapse, General Ludendorff advised his government on September 29 to sue for peace on the best terms possible. Three days later Prince Max of Baden, a Liberal, became chancellor and asked the American government for an armistice on the basis of the Fourteen Points; Austria-Hungary immediately followed suit. Wilson's reply of October 8 was mainly an inquiry: was the government of Prince Max, he wanted to know, the same government which conducted the war? On October 12 the German and Austrian governments sent clarifying notes to the United States. Following is Wilson's reply.

IN REPLY to the communication of the German Government, dated the twelfth instant, which you handed me today, I have the honor to request you to transmit the following answer:

"The unqualified acceptance by the present German Government and by a large majority of the German Reichstag of the terms laid down by the President of the United States of America in his address to the Congress of the United States on the eighth of January, 1918, and in his subsequent addresses justifies the President in making a frank and direct statement of his decision with regard to the communications of the German Government of the eighth and twelfth of October, 1918.

"It must be clearly understood that the process of evacuation and the conditions of an armistice are matters which must be left to the judgment and advice of the military advisers of the Government of the United States and the Allied Governments, and the President feels it his duty to say that no arrangement can be accepted by the Government of the United States which does not provide absolutely satisfactory safeguards and guarantees of the maintenance of the present military supremacy of the armies of the United States and of the Allies in the field. He feels cofident that he can safely assume that this will also be the judgment and decision of the Allied Governments.

"The President feels that it is also his duty to add that neither the Government of the United States nor, he is quite sure, the Governments with which the Government of the United States is associated as a belligerent will consent to consider an armistice so long as the armed forces of Germany continue the illegal and inhumane practices which they still persist in. At the very time that the German Government approaches the Government of the United States with proposals of peace its submarines are engaged in sinking passenger ships at sea, and not the ships alone, but the very boats in which their passengers and crews seek to make their way to safety; and in their present enforced withdrawal from Flanders and France the German armies are pursuing a course of wanton destruction which has always been regarded as in direct violation of the rules and practices of civilized warfare. Cities and villages, if not destroyed, are being stripped of all they contain not only, but often of their very inhabitants. The nations associated against Germany cannot be expected to agree to a cessation of arms while acts of inhumanity, spoliation, and desolation are being continued which they justly look upon with horror and with burning hearts.

"It is necessary also in order that there may be no possibility of misunderstanding, that the President should very solemnly call the attention of the Government of Germany to the language and plain intent of one of the terms of peace which the German Government has now accepted. It is contained in the address of the President delivered at Mount Vernon on the fourth of July last. It is as follows: 'The destruction of every arbitrary power anywhere that can separately, secretly, and of its single choice disturb the peace of the world; or, if it cannot be presently destroyed, at least its reduction to virtual impotency.' The power which has hitherto controlled the German Nation is of the sort here described. It is within the choice of the German Nation to alter it. The President's words just quoted naturally constitute a condition precedent to peace, if peace is to come by the action of the German people themselves. The President feels bound to say that the whole process of peace will, in his judgment, depend upon the definiteness and the satisfactory character of the guarantees which can be given in this fundamental matter. It is indispensable that the Governments associated against Germany should know beyond a peradventure with whom they are dealing.

"The President will make a separate reply to the Royal and Imperial Government of Austria-Hungary."

16. The Masters of German Policy

Third Note to Germany on Peace, October 23, 1918

The German note of October 20 took issue with Wilson's second note, affirmed that the government now represented the people, and agreed to evacuate German troops from occupied territory. The British government strongly urged Wilson not to accept these German armistice terms as they provided too few guarantees to Britain. Following is Wilson's reply to the German note—a reply which the German general staff found too harsh, tantamount to unconditional surrender. Ludendorff said it was "unacceptable to us soldiers."

I HAVE the honor to acknowledge the receipt of your note of the twenty-second transmitting a communication under date of the twentieth from the German Government and to advise you that the President has instructed me to reply thereto as follows:

"Having received the solemn and explicit assurance of the German Government that it unreservedly accepts the terms of peace laid down in his address to the Congress of the United States on the eighth of January, 1918, and the principles of settlement enunciated in his subsequent addresses, particularly the address of the twenty-seventh of September, and that it desires to discuss the details of their application, and that this wish and purpose emanate, not from those who have hitherto dictated German policy and conducted the present war on Germany's behalf, but from ministers who speak for the majority of the Reichstag and for an overwhelming majority of the German people; and having received also the explicit promise of the present German Government that the human rules of civilized warfare will be observed both on land and sea by the German armed forces, the President of the United States feels that he cannot decline to take up with the Governments with which the Government of the United States is associated the question of an armistice.

"He deems it his duty to say again, however, that the only armistice he would feel justified in submitting for consideration would be one which should leave the United States and the powers associated with her in a position to enforce any arrangements that may be entered into and to make a renewal of hostilities on the part of Germany impossible. The President has, therefore, transmitted his correspondence with the present German authorities to the Governments with which the Government of the United States is associated as a belligerent, with the suggestion that, if those Governments are disposed to effect peace upon the terms and principles indicated, their military advisers and the military advisers of the United States be asked to submit to the Governments associated against Germany the necessary terms of such an armistice as will fully protect the interests of the peoples involved and insure to the associated Governments the unrestricted power to safeguard and enforce the details of the peace to which the German Government has agreed, provided they deem such an armistice possible from the military point of view. Should such terms of armistice be suggested, their acceptance by Germany will afford the best concrete evidence of her unequivocal acceptance of the terms and principles of peace from which the whole action proceeds.

"The President would deem himself lacking in candor did he not point out in the frankest possible terms the reason why extraordinary safeguards must be demanded. Significant and important as the constitutional changes seem to be which are spoken of by the German Foreign Secretary in his note of the twentieth of October, it does not appear that the principle of a government responsible to the German people has yet been fully worked out or that any guarantees either exist or are in contemplation that the alterations of principle and of practice now partially agreed upon will be permanent. Moreover, it does not appear that the heart of the present difficulty has been reached. It may be that future wars have been brought under the control of the German people, but the present war has not been; and it is with the present war that we are dealing. It is evident that the German people have no means of commanding the acquiescence of the military authorities of the Empire in the popular will; that the power of the King of Prussia to control the policy of the Empire is unimpaired; that the determining initiative still remains with those who have hitherto been the masters of Germany.

"Feeling that the whole peace of the world depends now on plain speaking and straightforward action, the President deems it his duty to say, without any attempt to soften what may seem harsh words, that the nations of the world do not and cannot trust the word of those who have hitherto been the masters of German policy, and to point out once more that in concluding peace and attempting to undo the infinite injuries and injustices of this war the Government of the United States cannot deal with any but veritable representatives of the German people who have been assured of a genuine constitutional standing as the real rulers of Germany. If it must deal with the military masters and the monarchical autocrats of Germany now, or if it is likely to have to deal with them later in regard to the international obligations of the German Empire, it must demand, not peace negotiations, but surrender. Nothing can be gained by leaving this essential thing unsaid."

17. For the Sake of the Nation Itself

Statement in Behalf of Democratic Congress, October 25, 1918

For some time Democratic politicians had been asking Wilson to publicly state his preference for a Democratic Congress in the coming congressional election. Only a Democratic Congress, they had argued, could be counted on to support him in the great work that was to be done. Wilson agreed. But the appeal to the voters which he issued was not only risky in itself—for it opened him to the charge of partisanship in war—it also specifically put his leadership to the test. The chairman of the Republican National Committee called it "an insult . . . to every loyal Republican. . . ." The Republicans won the congressional elections and took over both Houses of Congress.

MY FELLOW Countrymen: The congressional elections are at hand. They occur in the most critical period our country has ever faced or is likely to face in our time. If you have approved of my leadership and wish me to continue to be your unembarrassed spokesman in affairs at home and abroad, I earnestly beg that you will express yourselves unmistakably to that effect by returning a Democratic majority to both the Senate and the House of Representatives. I am your servant and will accept your judgment without cavil, but my power to administer the great trust assigned me by the Constitution would be seriously impaired should your judgment be adverse, and I must frankly tell you so because so many critical issues depend upon your verdict. No scruple of taste must in grim times like these be allowed to stand in the way of speaking the plain truth.

I have no thought of suggesting that any political party is paramount in matters of patriotism. I feel too keenly the sacrifices which have been made in this war by all our citizens, irrespective of party affiliations, to harbor such an idea. I mean only that the difficulties and delicacies of our present task are of a sort that makes it imperatively necessary that the Nation should give its undivided support to the Government under a unified leadership, and that a Republican Congress would divide the leadership.

The leaders of the minority in the present Congress have unquestionably been pro war, but they have been anti-administration. At almost every turn, since we entered the war they have sought to take the choice of policy and the conduct of the war out of my hands and put it under the control of instrumentalities of their own choosing. This is no time either for divided counsel or for divided leadership. Unity of command is as necessary now in civil action as it is upon the field of battle. If the control of the House and Senate should be taken away from the party now in power, an opposing majority could assume control of legislation and oblige all action to be taken amidst contest and obstruction.

The return of a Republican majority to either House of the Congress would, moreover, certainly be interpreted on the other side of the water as a repudiation of my leadership. Spokesmen of the Republican party are urging you to elect a Republican Congress in order to back up and support the President, but even if they should in this way impose upon some credulous voters on this side of the water, they would impose on no one on the other side. It is well understood there as well as here that the Republican leaders desire not so much to support the President as to control him. The peoples of the allied countries with whom we are associated against Germany are quite familiar with the significance of elections. They would find it very difficult to believe that the voters of the United States had chosen to support their President by electing to the Congress a majority controlled by those who are not in fact in sympathy with the attitude and action of the administration.

I need not tell you, my fellow countrymen, that I am asking your support not for my own sake or for the sake of a political party, but for the sake of the Nation itself, in order that its inward unity of purpose may be evident to all the world. In ordinary times I would not feel at liberty to make such an appeal to you. In ordinary times divided counsels can be endured without permanent hurt to the country. But these are not ordinary times. If in these critical days it is your wish to sustain me with undivided minds, I beg that you will say so in a way which it will not be possible to misunderstand either here at home or among our associates on the other side of the sea. I submit my difficulties and my hopes to you.

18. Force the Purpose Boldly

To Colonel House, October 29, 1918

The leaders of the Allied countries, meeting in Paris, objected to or sought to severely modify the Fourteen Points as the basis for a peace settlement. Moreover, according to House, who represented the United States, they wanted to exclude Wilson altogether from the negotiations. Following are Wilson's instructions to House.

. . . CAN BE no real difficulty about peace terms and interpretation of Fourteen Points if the Entente statesmen will be perfectly frank with us and have no selfish aims of their own which would in any case alienate us from them altogether. It is the Fourteen Points that Germany has accepted. England cannot dispense with our friendship in the future and the other Allies cannot without our assistance get their rights as against England. If it is the purpose of the Allied statesmen to nullify my influence force the purpose boldly to the surface and let me speak of it to all the world as I shall. League of Nations underlies freedom of the seas and every other part of peace programme so far as I am concerned. I am ready to repudiate any selfish programme openly, but assume that the Allies cannot honorably turn the present discussion into a peace conference without me.

19. This Great Consummation

Address to Congress Announcing the Armistice, November 11, 1918

At Wilson's insistence, the Entente statesmen accepted the Fourteen Points. But Britain still sought two reservations: the right to define the meaning of freedom of the seas and the right to press Germany to make compensations for damages inflicted on Allied peoples and property. Meanwhile, on November 3, the German revolution broke out, and within a week Kaiser Wilhelm was forced to flee. On November 4 Austria surrendered. Wilson finally accepted Britain's reservations. The commander of the Allied forces, Marshal Foch, was thereupon given permission to work out with his German counterparts the technicalities of the armistice. The negotiations began on November 8 in the forest of Compiègne and concluded at 5:00 A.M. on November 11. Six hours later the fighting ceased. Later that day Wilson delivered the following address.

IN THESE anxious times of rapid and stupendous change it will in some degree lighten my sense of responsibility to perform in person the duty of communicating to you some of the larger circumstances of the situation with which it is necessary to deal.

The German authorities who have, at the invitation of the Supreme War Council, been in communication with Marshal Foch have accepted and signed the terms of armistice which he was authorized and instructed to communicate to them. . . .

The war thus comes to an end; for, having accepted these terms of armistice, it will be impossible for the German command to renew it.

It is not now possible to assess the consequences of this great consummation. We know only that this tragical war, whose consuming flames swept from one nation to another until all the world was on fire, is at an end and that it was the privilege of our own people to enter it at its most critical juncture in such fashion and in such force as to contribute in a way of which we are all deeply proud to the great result. We know, too, that the object of the war is attained; the object upon which all free men had set their hearts; and attained with a sweeping completeness which even now we do not realize. Armed imperialism such as the men conceived who were but yesterday the masters of Germany is at an end, its illicit ambitions engulfed in black disaster. Who will now seek to revive it? The arbitrary power of the military caste of Germany which once could secretly and of its own single choice disturb the peace of the world is discredited and destroyed. And more than that—much more than that—has been accomplished. The great nations which associated themselves to destroy it have now definitely united in the common purpose to set up such a peace as will satisfy the longing of the whole world for disinterested justice, embodied in settlements which are based upon something much better and much more lasting than the selfish competitive interests of powerful states. There is no longer conjecture as to the objects the victors have in mind. They have a mind in the matter, not only, but a heart also. Their avowed and concerted purpose is to satisfy and protect the weak as well as to accord their just rights to the strong.

The humane temper and intention of the victorious Governments has already been manifested in a very practical way. Their representatives in the Supreme War Council at Versailles have by unanimous resolution assured the peoples of the Central Empires that everything that is possible in the circumstances will be done to supply them with food and relieve the distressing want that is in so many places threatening their very lives; and steps are to be taken immediately to organize these efforts at relief in the same systematic manner that they were organized in the case of Belgium. By the use of the idle tonnage of the Central Empires it ought presently to be possible to lift the fear of utter misery from their oppressed populations and set their minds and energies free for the great and hazardous tasks of political reconstruction which now face them on every hand. Hunger does not breed reform; it breeds madness and all the ugly distempers that make an ordered life impossible.

For with the fall of the ancient governments which rested like an incubus upon the peoples of the Central Empires has come political change not merely, but revolution; and revolution which seems as yet to assume no final and ordered form but to run from one fluid change to another, until thoughtful men are forced to ask themselves, With what Governments, and of what sort, are we about to deal in the making of the covenants of peace? With what authority will they meet us, and with what assurance that their authority will abide and sustain securely the international arrangements into which we are about to enter? There is here matter for no small anxiety and misgiving. When peace is made, upon whose promises and engagements besides our own is it to rest?

Let us be perfectly frank with ourselves and admit that these questions cannot be satisfactorily answered now or at once. But the moral is not that there is little hope of an early answer that will suffice. It is only that we must be patient and helpful and mindful above all of the great hope and confidence that lie at the heart of what is taking place. Excesses accomplish nothing. Unhappy Russia has furnished abundant recent proof of that. Disorder immediately defeats itself. If excesses should occur, if disorder should for a time raise its head, a sober second thought will follow and a day of constructive action, if we help and do not hinder.

The present and all that it holds belongs to the nations and the peoples who preserve their self-control and the orderly processes of their governments; the future to those who prove themselves the true friends of mankind. To conquer with arms is to make only a temporary conquest; to conquer the world by earning its esteem is to make permanent conquest. I am confident that the nations that have learned the discipline of freedom and that have settled with self-possession to its ordered practice are now about to make conquest of the world by the sheer power of example and of friendly helpfulness.

The peoples who have but just come out from under the yoke of arbitrary government and who are now coming at last into their freedom will never find the treasures of liberty they are in search of if they look for them by the light of the torch. They will find that every pathway that is stained with the blood of their own brothers leads to the wilderness, not to the seat of their hope. They are now face to face with their initial test. We must hold the light steady until they find themselves. And in the meantime, if it be possible, we must establish a peace that will justly define their place among the nations, remove all fear of their neighbors and of their former masters, and enable them to live in security and contentment when they have set their own affairs in order. I, for one, do not doubt their purpose or their capacity. There are some happy signs that they know and will choose the way of self-control and peaceful accommodation. If they do, we shall put our aid at their disposal in every way that we can. If they do not, we must await with patience and sympathy the awakening and recovery that will assuredly come at last.

Six

TREATY

1918–1919

1. To Secure Peace

First Draft of a League of Nations Covenant, August, 1918

The idea of a league of nations began long before Wilson wrote this draft. In March, 1918, a group of British lawyers drew up a plan for an international organization at the behest of the British government. This was the so-called Phillmore report. Even prior to the Phillmore report, the American League to Enforce Peace, with which Wilson was always in close touch, had drawn up a remarkably similar plan. In June, 1918, Wilson turned his full attention to a covenant for a prospective international organization and asked Colonel House to work on it, using the Phillmore report as the basis for it. On June 16, House sent Wilson a draft consisting of twenty-three articles. The most important provision in the House draft—later to evolve into the famous Article x*—dealt with the guaranty for each nation's "territorial integrity and political independence." To Wilson, a league of nations without such a guaranty was useless. He drew up the following draft soon after receiving House's and finished it in August, 1918. Wilson took it with him to Paris and it became the basis of all subsequent drafts of the League Covenant.*

COVENANT

PREAMBLE

IN ORDER to secure peace, security, and orderly government by the prescription of open and honorable relations between nations, by the firm establishment of the understandings of international law as the actual rule of conduct among governments, and by the maintenance of justice and a scrupulous respect of all treaty obligations in the dealings of all organized peoples with one another, the Powers signatory to this covenant and agreement jointly and severally adopt this constitution of the League of Nations.

ARTICLE I—The action of the Signatory Powers under the terms of this agreement shall be effected throughout the instrumentality of a Body of Delegates which shall consist of the ambassadors and ministers of the Contracting Powers accredited to H. and the Minister for Foreign Affairs of H. The meetings of the Body of Delegates shall be held at the seat of government of H. and the

Minister for Foreign Affairs of H. shall be the Presiding officer of the Body.

Whenever the Delegates deem it necessary or advisable, they may meet temporarily at the seat of government of B. or of S., in which case the Ambassador or Minister to H. of the country in which the meeting is held shall be the Presiding officer *pro tempore.*

ARTICLE II—The Body of Delegates shall regulate their own procedure and shall have power to appoint such committees as they may deem necessary to inquire into and report upon any matters which lie within the field of their action.

They shall organize a Secretariat to act as their ministerial agency, and the expense of the maintenance of the Secretariat shall be borne as they may prescribe.

In all matters covered by this Article the Body of Delegates may decide by a majority vote of the whole Body.

ARTICLE III—The Contracting Powers unite in guaranteeing to each other political independence and territorial integrity; but it is understood between them that such territorial readjustments, if any, as may in the future become necessary by reason of changes in present racial conditions and aspirations or present social and political relationships, pursuant to the principle of self-determination, and also such territorial readjustments as may in the judgment of three-fourths of the Delegates be demanded by the welfare and manifest interest of the peoples concerned, may be effected, if agreeable to those peoples: and that territorial changes may in equity involve material compensation. The Contracting Powers accept without reservation the principle that the peace of the world is superior in importance to every question of political jurisdiction or boundary.

ARTICLE IV—(H. 21) The Contracting Powers recognize the principle that the establishment and maintenance of peace will require the reduction of national armaments to the lowest point consistent with domestic safety and the enforcement by common action of international obligations; and the Delegates are directed to formulate at once plans by which such a reduction may be brought about. The plan so formulated shall be binding when, and only when, unanimously approved by the Governments signatory to this Covenant.

The Contracting Powers further agree that munitions and implements of war shall not be manufactured by private enterprise or for private profit, and that there shall be full and frank publicity as to all national armaments and military or naval programmes.

ARTICLE V—The Contracting Powers agree that all disputes arising between or among them of whatever nature, which shall not be satisfactorily settled by diplomacy, shall be referred for arbitration to three arbitrators, one of the three to be selected by each of the parties to the dispute, when there are but two such parties, and the third by the two thus selected. When there are more than two parties to the dispute, one arbitrator shall be named by each of the several parties and the arbitrators thus named shall add to their number others of their own choice, the number thus added to be limited to the number which will suffice to give a deciding voice to the arbitrators chosen by the contending parties. In case the arbitrators chosen by the contending parties cannot agree upon an additional arbitrator or arbitrators, the additional arbitrator or arbitrators shall be chosen by the Body of Delegates.

On the appeal of a party to the dispute the decision of the arbitrators may be set aside by a vote of three-fourths unanimous, or by a vote of two-thirds of the Delegates in case the decision of the arbitrators was not unanimous, but unless thus set aside shall be finally binding and conclusive.

When any decision of arbitrators shall have been thus set aside the dispute shall again be submitted to arbitrators chosen as heretofore provided, none of whom shall, however, have previously acted as arbitrators in the dispute in question, and the decision of the arbitrators rendered in this second arbitration shall be finally binding and conclusive without right of any appeal.

ARTICLE VI—(H. 14) Any power which the Body of Delegates shall declare to have failed to submit any dispute to arbitration under the terms of Article V of this Covenant or to have refused or failed to carry out any decision of such arbitration shall thereupon lose and be deprived of all rights of commerce and intercourse with any of the Contracting Powers.

ARTICLE VII—If any Power shall declare war or begin hostilities, or take any hostile step short of war, against another Power before submitting the dispute involved to arbitrators as herein provided, or shall declare war or begin hostilities, or take any hostile step short of war, in regard to any dispute which has been decided adversely to it by arbitrators chosen and empowered as herein provided, the Contracting Powers hereby bind themselves not only to cease all commerce and intercourse with that Power but also to unite in blockading and closing the frontiers of that power to commerce or intercourse with any part of the world and to use any force that may be necessary to accomplish that object.

ARTICLE VIII—(H. 5, 7, 8) Any war or threat of war, whether immediately affecting any of the Contracting Powers or not, is hereby declared a matter of concern to the League of Nations and to all Powers signatory hereto, and those Powers hereby reserve the right to take any action that may be deemed wise and effectual to safeguard the peace of nations.

The Delegates shall meet in the interest of peace whenever war is rumored or threatened, and also whenever the Delegate of any Power shall inform the Delegates that a meeting and conference in the interest of peace is advisable.

The Delegates may also meet at such other times and upon such other occasions as they shall from time to time deem best and determine.

ARTICLE IX—(H. 16, 17) In the event of a dispute arising between one of the Contracting Powers and a Power not a party to this Covenant, the Contracting Power involved hereby binds itself to endeavor to obtain the submission of the dispute to judicial decision or to arbitration. If the other Power will not agree to submit the dispute to judicial decision or to arbitration, the Contractng Power shall bring the matter to the attention of the Body of Delegates. The Delegates shall in such case, in the name of the League of Nations, invite the Power not a party to this Covenant to become *ad hoc* a party and to submit its case to judicial decision or to arbitration, and if that Power consents it is hereby agreed that the provisions hereinbefore contained and applicable to the submission of disputes to arbitration shall be in all respects applicable to the dispute both in favor of and against such Power as if it were a party to this Covenant.

In case the Power not a party to this Covenant shall accept the invitation of the Delegates to become *ad hoc* a party, it shall be the duty of the Delegates immediately to institute an inquiry into the circumstances and merits of the dispute involved and to recommend such joint action by the Contracting Powers as may seem best and most effectual in the circumstances disclosed.

ARTICLE X—(H. 18) If hostilities should be begun or any hostile action taken against the Contracting Power by the Power not a party to this Covenant before a decision of the dispute by arbitrators or before investigation, report, and recommendation by the Delegates in regard to the dispute, or contrary to such recommendation, the Contracting Powers shall thereupon cease all commerce and communication with that Power and shall also unite in blockading and closing the frontiers of that Power to all commerce or intercourse with any part of the world, employing jointly any force that may be necessary to accomplish that object. The Contracting Powers shall also unite in coming to the assistance of the Contracting Power against which hostile action has been taken, combining their armed forces in its behalf.

ARTICLE XI—(H. 19) In case of a dispute between states not parties to this Covenant, any Contracting Power may bring the matter to the attention of the Delegates, who shall thereupon tender the good offices of the League of Nations with a view to the peaceable settlement of the dispute.

If one of the states, a party to the dispute, shall offer and agree to submit its interests and cause of action wholly to the control and decision of the League of Nations, that state shall *ad hoc* be deemed a Contracting Power. If no one of the states, parties to the dispute, shall so offer and agree, the Delegates shall of their own motion take such action and make such recommendation to their governments as will prevent hostilities and result in the settlement of the dispute.

ARTICLE XII—(H. 22) Any Power not a party to this Covenant may apply to the Body of Delegates for leave to become a party. If the Delegates shall regard the granting thereof as likely to promote the peace, order, and security of the World, they may act favorably on the application, and their favorable action shall operate to constitute the Power so applying in all respects a full signatory party to this Covenant.

ARTICLE XIII—(H. 23) The Contracting Powers severally agree that the present Covenant is accepted as abrogating all treaty obligations *inter se* which are inconsistent with the terms hereof, and solemnly engage that they will not enter into any engagements inconsistent with the terms hereof.

In case any of the Powers signatory hereto or subsequently admitted to the League of Nations shall, before becoming a party to this Covenant, have undertaken any treaty obligations which are inconsistent with the terms of this Covenant, it shall be the duty of such Power to take immediate steps to procure its release from such obligations.

2. A Way of Pocketing Me

To Colonel House, November 11, 1918

Referring to a recent message from House (No. 107), Wilson charges the Allied statesmen with attempting to neutralize his influence at the impending peace conference.

YOUR 107 upsets every plan we have made. I infer that French and English leaders desire to exclude me from the Conference for fear I might there lead the weaker nations against them. If I were to come to the seat of the Conference and remain outside I would be merely the center of a sort of sublimated lobby. All weak parties would resort to me and there would be exactly the same jealousy that was excited by the Germans addressing themselves exclusively to me. I play the same part in our government that the prime ministers play in theirs. The fact that I am head of the state is of no practical consequence. No point of dignity must prevent our obtaining the results we have set our hearts upon and must have. It is universally expected and generally desired here that I should attend the Conference, but I believe that no one would wish me to sit by and try to steer from the outside. I am thrown into complete confusion by the change of programme. The programme proposed for me by Clemenceau, George, Reading, and the rest seems to me a way of pocketing me. I hope you will be very shy of their advice and give me your own independent judgment after reconsideration.

3. His Presence Is Necessary

Announcement of Pending Trip to Europe, November 18, 1918

This message took the country by surprise. It was the first time that an American President visited Europe. On November 29, Wilson announced who the chief members of his commission would be: Secretary Lansing, Colonel House, General Tasker Bliss and Henry White. No important member of Congress and no important Republican was invited. Wilson and his delegation sailed on December 4.

THE PRESIDENT expects to sail for France immediately after the opening of the regular session of Congress, for the purpose of taking part in the discussion and settlement of the main features of the treaty of peace. It is not likely that it will be possible for him to remain throughout the sessions of the formal Peace Conference, but his presence at the outset is necessary, in order to obviate the manifest disadvantages of discussion by cable in determining the greater outlines of the final treaty, about which he must necessarily be consulted. He will, of course, be accompanied by delegates who will sit as the representatives of the United States throughout the Conference. The names of the delegates will be presently announced.

4. A Great Wind of Moral Force

Address at Paris, December 18, 1918

Five days after arriving in France, Wilson spoke at the University of Paris upon receiving an honorary degree.

. . . I AGREE with the intimation which has been conveyed today that the terrible war through which we have just passed has not been only a war between nations, but that it has been also a war between systems of culture—the one system, the aggressive system, using science without conscience, stripping learning of its moral restraints, and using every faculty of the human mind to do wrong to the whole race; the other system reminiscent of the high traditions of men, reminiscent of all those struggles, some of them obscure but others clearly revealed to the historian, of men of indomitable spirit everywhere struggling toward the right and seeking above all things else to be free. The triumph of freedom in this war means that spirits of that sort now dominate the world. There is a great wind of moral force moving through the world, and every man who opposes himself to that wind will go down in disgrace. The task of those who are gathered here, or will presently be gathered here, to make the settlements of this peace is greatly simplified by the fact that they are masters of no one; they are the servants of mankind, and if we do not heed the mandates of mankind we shall make ourselves the most conspicuous and deserved failures in the history of the world.

My conception of the League of Nations is just this, that it shall operate as the organized moral force of men throughout the world, and that whenever or wherever wrong and aggression are planned or contemplated, this searching light of conscience will be turned upon them and men everywhere will ask, "What are the purposes that you hold in your heart against the fortunes of the world?" Just a little exposure will settle most questions. If the Central Powers had dared to discuss the purposes of this war for a single fortnight, it never would have happened, and if, as should be, they were forced to discuss it for a year, war would have been inconceivable.

So I feel that this war is, as has been said more than once today, intimately related with the university spirit. The university spirit is intolerant of all the things that put the human mind under restraint. It is intolerant of everything that seeks to retard the advancement of ideals, the acceptance of the truth, the purification of life; and every university man can ally himself with the forces of the present time with the feeling that now at last the spirit of truth, the spirit to which universities have devoted themselves, has prevailed and is triumphant. If there is one point of pride that I venture to entertain, it is that it has been my privilege in some measure to interpret the university spirit in the public life of a great nation, and I feel that in honoring me today in this unusual and conspicuous manner you have first of all honored the people whom I represent. The spirit that I try to express I know to be their spirit, and in proportion as I serve them I believe that I advance the cause of freedom.

I, therefore, wish to thank you, sir, from the bottom of my heart for a distinction which has in a singular way crowned my academic career.

5. The Secret Is Out

Address at Boston, February 24, 1919

While Wilson was on the high seas returning to the United States, rumblings of discontent against the League were to be heard coming from the Senate chambers. On February 21, Senator Borah of Idaho, in the course of a scathing speech, called the Covenant "the greatest triumph of English diplomacy in three centuries." Wilson delivered the following speech several hours after his ship docked. He was well aware that the future chairman of the Senate Foreign Relations Committee, Henry Cabot Lodge, came from Boston.

. . . I MET a group of scholars when I was in Paris. Some gentlemen from one of the Greek universities who had come to see me and in whose presence, or rather in the presence of the traditions of learning, I felt very young, indeed. And I told them that I had had one of the delightful revenges that sometimes come to men. All my life I have heard men speak with a sort of condescension of ideals and of idealists, and particularly of those separated, encloistered persons whom they choose to term academic, who were in the habit of uttering ideals in a free atmosphere when they clash with nobody in particular. And as I said I have had this sweet revenge. Speaking with perfect frankness in the name of the people of the United States I have uttered as the objects of this great war ideals, and nothing but ideals, and the war has been won by that inspiration.

Men were fighting with tense muscle and lowered head until they came to realize those things, feeling they were fighting for their lives and their country, and when these accents of what it was all about reached them from America they lifted their heads, they raised their eyes to heaven, then they saw men in khaki coming across the sea in the spirit of crusaders, and they found these were strange men, reckless of danger not only, but reckless because they seemed to see something that made that danger worth while. Men have testified to me in Europe that our men were possessed by something that they could only call religious fervor. They were not like any of the other soldiers. They had vision; they had dream, and they were fighting in dream; and fighting in dream they turned the whole tide of battle, and it never came back. And now do you realize that this confidence we have established throughout the world imposes a burden upon us—if you choose to call it a burden. It is one of those burdens which any nation ought to be proud to carry. Any man who resists the present tides that run in the world will find himself thrown upon a shore so high and barren that it will seem as if he had been separated from his human kind forever.

[The] Europe that I left the other day was full of something that it had never felt fill its heart so full before. It was full of hope. The Europe of the second year of the war—the Europe of the third year of the war—was sinking to a sort of stubborn desperation. They did not see any great thing to be achieved even when the war should be won. They hoped there would be some salvage; they hoped they could clear their territories of invading armies; they hoped they could set up their homes and start their industries afresh. But they thought it would simply be a resumption of the old life that Europe had led—led in fear; led in anxiety; led in constant suspicion and watchfulness. They never dreamed that it would be a Europe of settled peace and justified hope. And now these ideals have wrought this new magic that all the peoples of Europe are buoyed up and confident in the spirit of hope, because they believe that we are at the eve of a new age in the world, when nations will understand one another; when nations will support one another in every just cause; when nations will unite every moral and every physical strength to see that right shall prevail. If America were at this juncture to fail the world, what would come of it?

I do not mean any disrespect to any other great people when I say that America is the hope of the world. And if she does not justify that hope results are unthinkable. Men will be thrown back upon bitterness of disappointment not only but bitterness of despair. All nations will be set up as hostile camps again; men at the Peace Conference will go home with their heads upon their breasts, knowing they have failed—for they were bidden not to come home from there until they did something more than sign the treaty of peace. Suppose we sign the treaty of peace and that it is the most satisfactory treaty of peace that the confusing elements of the modern world will afford and go home and think about our labors, we will know that we have left written upon the historic table at Versailles, upon which Vergennes and Benjamin Franklin wrote their names, nothing but a modern scrap of paper, no nations united to defend it, no great forces combined to make it good, no assurance given to the downtrodden and fearful people of the world that they shall be safe. Any man who thinks that America will take part in giving the world any such rebuff and disappointment as that does not know America. I invite him to test the sentiments of the Nation.

We set this Nation up to make men free and we did not confine our conception and purpose to America, and now we will make men free. If we did not do that all the fame of America would be gone and all her power would be dissipated. She would then have to keep her power for those narrow, selfish, provincial purposes which seem so dear to some minds that have no sweep beyond the nearest horizon. I should welcome no sweeter challenge than that. I have fighting blood in me and it is sometimes a delight to let it have scope, but if it is challenged on this occasion it will be an indulgence. Think of the picture, think of the utter blackness that would fall on the world. America has failed. America made a little essay at generosity and then withdrew. America said, "We are your friends," but it was only for today, not for tomorrow. America said, "Here is our power to vindicate right," and then next day said, "Let right take care of itself and we will take care of ourselves." America said, "We set up light to lead men along the paths of liberty, but we have lowered it—it is intended only to light our own path."

We set up a great ideal of liberty, and then we said, "Liberty is a thing that you must win for yourself." Do not call upon us and think of the world that we would leave. Do you realize how many new nations are going to be set up in the presence of old and powerful nations in Europe and left there, if left by us, without a disinterested friend? Do you believe in the Polish cause as I do? Are you going to set up Poland, immature, inexperienced, as yet unorganized, and leave her with a circle of armies around her? Do you believe in the aspirations of the Czecho-Slovaks and Jugo-Slavs as I do? Do you know how many powers would be quick to pounce upon them if there were not guarantees of the world behind their liberty? Have you thought of the sufferings of Armenia? You poured out your money to help succor Armenians after they suffered. Now set up your strength so that they shall never suffer again.

Arrangements of the present peace cannot stand a generation unless they are guaranteed by the united forces of the civilized world. And if we do not guarantee them can you not see the picture? Your hearts have instructed you where the burden of this war fell. It did not fall upon national treasuries; it did not fall upon the instruments of administration; it did not fall upon the resources of nations. It fell upon the voiceless homes everywhere, where women were toiling in hope that their men would come back. When I think of the homes upon which dull despair would settle if this great hope is disappointed, I should wish for my part never to have had America play any part whatever in this attempt to emancipate the world.

But I talk as if there were any question. I have no more doubt of the verdict of America in this matter than I have doubt of the blood that is in me. And so, my fellow citizens, I have come back to report progress, and I do not believe that progress is going to stop short of the goal. The nations of the world have set their heads now to do a great thing, and they are not going to slacken their purpose. And when I speak of the nations of the world I do not speak of the governments of the world. I speak of peoples who constitute the nations of the world. They are in the saddle, and they are going to see to it that if their present governments do not do their will some other governments shall. The secret is out, and present governments know it. . . .

6. No Man Is Going to Bring Back a Cadaver

Address at New York City, March 4, 1919

The lines of conflict between Wilson and Senate Republicans were being rapidly drawn. On March 2, thirty-nine Republican Senators—more than the third necessary to defeat a treaty—signed a Round Robin proposed by Henry Cabot Lodge. It stated that "the constitution of the League of Nations in the form now proposed to the peace conference should not be accepted" and that a League should be considered only after a treaty of peace was signed. Wilson's address below, delivered at the Metropolitan Opera House on the eve of his departure for Europe, was in direct response to the Round Robin.

. . . I HAVE tried once and again, my fellow citizens, to say to little circles of friends or to larger bodies what seems to be the real hope of the peoples of Europe, and I tell you frankly I have not been able to do so, because when the thought tries to crowd itself into speech the profound emotion of the thing is too much; speech will not carry. I have felt the tragedy of the hope of those suffering peoples.

It is a tragedy because it is a hope which cannot be realized in its perfection; and yet I have felt besides its tragedy its compulsion, its compulsion upon every living man to exercise every influence that he has to the utmost to see that as little as possible of that hope is disappointed, because if men cannot now, after this agony of bloody sweat, come to their self-possession and see how to regulate the affairs of the world we will sink back into a period of struggle in which there will be no hope and therefore no mercy. There can be no mercy where there is no hope, for why should you spare another if you yourself expect to perish? Why should you be pitiful if you can get no pity? Why should you be just if, upon every hand, you are put upon?

There is another thing which I think the critics of this Covenant have not observed. They not only have not observed the temper of the world but they have not even observed the temper of those splendid boys in khaki that they sent across the seas. I have had the proud consciousness of the reflected glory of those boys because the Constitution made me their commander-in-chief, and they have taught me some lessons. When we went into the war we went into it on the basis of declarations which it was my privilege to utter because I believed them to be an interpretation of the purpose and thought of the people of the United States.

And those boys went over there with the feeling that they were sacredly bound to the realization of those ideals; that they were not only going over there to beat Germany; they were not going over there merely with resentment in their hearts against a particular outlaw nation; but that they were crossing those 3,000 miles of sea in order to show to Europe that the United States, when it became necessary, would go anywhere where the rights of mankind were threatened. They would not sit still in the trenches. They would not be restrained by the prudence of experienced continental commanders. They thought they had come over there to do a particular thing, and they were going to do it and do it at once. And just as soon as that rush of spirit as well as the rush of body came in contact with the lines of the enemy they began to break, and they continued to break until the end. They continued to break, my fellow citizens, not merely because of the physical force of those lusty youngsters but because of the irresistible spiritual force of the armes of the United States. It was that that they felt. It was that that awed them. It was that that made them feel if these youngsters ever got a foothold they could never be dislodged, and that therefore every foot of ground that they won was permanently won for the liberty of mankind.

And do you suppose that, having felt that crusading spirit of these youngsters who went over there not to glorify America but to serve their fellow men, I am going to permit myself for one moment to slacken in my effort to be worthy of them and of their cause? What I said at the opening I said with a deeper meaning than perhaps you have caught; I do not mean to come back until it's over over there, and it must not be over until the nations of the world are assured of the permanency of peace.

Gentlemen on this side of the water would be very much profited by getting into communication with some gentlemen on the other side of the water. We sometimes think, my fellow citizens, that the experienced statesmen of European nations are an unusually hardheaded set of men, by which we generally mean, although we do not admit it, they are a bit cynical; they say, "This is a practical world," by which you always mean that it is not an ideal world; that they do not believe things can be settled upon an ideal basis. Well, I never came into intimate contact with them before, but if they used to be that way they are not that way now. They have been subdued, if that was once their temper, by the awful significance of recent events and the awful importance of what is to ensue, and there is not one of them with whom I have come in contact who does not feel he cannot in conscience return to his people from Paris unless he has done his utmost to do something more than attach his name to a treaty of peace. Every man in that conference knows the treaty of peace in itself will be inoperative, as Mr. Taft has said, without this constant support and energy of a great organization such as is supplied by the League of Nations.

And men who, when I first went over there, were skeptical of the possibility of forming a league of nations, admitted that if we could but form it it would be an invaluable instrumentality through which to secure the operation of the various parts of the treaty; and when that treaty comes back gentlemen on this side will find the Covenant not only in it, but so many threads of the treaty tied to the Covenant that you cannot dissect the Covenant from the treaty without destroying the whole vital struture. The structure of peace will not be vital without the League of Nations, and no man is going to bring back a cadaver with him.

I must say that I have been puzzled by some of the criticisms —not by the criticisms themselves—I can understand them perfectly even when there was no foundation for them—but by the fact of the criticism. I cannot imagine how these gentlemen can live and not live in the atmosphere of the world. I cannot imagine how they can live and not be in contact with the events of their times, and I particularly cannot imagine how they can be Americans and set up a doctrine of careful selfishness thought out to the last detail. I have heard no counsel of generosity in their criticism. I have heard no constructive suggestion. I have heard nothing except, "Will it not be dangerous to us to help the world?" It would be fatal to us not to help it.

From being what I will venture to call the most famous and the most powerful nation in the world, we would of a sudden have become the most contemptible. So I did not need to be told, as I have been told, that the people of the United States would support this Covenant. I am an American and I knew they would. What a sweet revenge it is upon the world. They laughed at us once; they thought we did not mean our professions of principle. They thought so until April of 1917. It was hardly credible to them that we would do more than send a few men over and go through the forms of helping, and when they saw multitudes hastening across the sea, and saw what those multitudes were eager to do when they got to the other side, they stood at amaze and said, "The thing is real; this nation is the friend of mankind as it said it was." The enthusiasm, the hope, the trust, the confidence in the future bred by that change of view are indescribable. Take an individual American and you may often find him selfish and confined to his special interests; but take the American in the mass and he is willing to die for an ideal. The sweet revenge therefore is this, that we believed in righteousness and now we are ready to make the supreme sacrifice for it, the supreme sacrifice of throwing in our fortunes with the fortunes of men everywhere. . . .

7. To Assume the Responsibility

Statement on Senate Obstruction, March 4, 1919

Republican Senators, waiting for the next session, when they would have a majority, deliberately obstructed legislation proposed by the President and Democratic leaders. Following is Wilson's statement on the day Congress adjourned.

A GROUP of men in the Senate have deliberately chosen to embarrass the administration of the Government, to imperil the financial interests of the railway systems of the country, and to make arbitrary use of powers intended to be employed in the interests of the people.

It is plainly my present duty to attend the Peace Conference in Paris. It is also my duty to be in close contact with the public business during a session of the Congress. I must make my choice between these two duties, and I confidently hope that the people of the country will think that I am making the right choice. It is not in the interest of the right conduct of public affairs that I should call the Congress in special session while it is impossible for me to be in Washington, because of a more pressing duty elsewhere, to cooperate with the Houses.

I take it for granted that the men who have obstructed and prevented the passage of necessary legislation have taken all of this into consideration and are willing to assume the responsibility of the impaired efficiency of the Government and the embarrassed finances of the country during the time of my enforced absence.

8. To Achieve International Peace and Security

Final Text of the Covenant of the League of Nations, April 28, 1919

In Wilson's three-week absence from Paris (during which time Colonel House sat for him), the other powers, France in particular, worked to separate the League from the treaty as a whole. They were encouraged in this by the senatorial Round Robin of March 2. In securing adoption of the League Covenant, Wilson's chief task was to assuage American fears that the Monroe Doctrine might be compromised by United States involvement in European affairs and French fears that the United States would fail to protect France from further German aggression. In return for French support of the League, Wilson promised a military treaty guaranteeing protection of France. (For the fate of the French Security Treaty, see *Part VII, Document 2.)* *On April 28, a plenary session of the Peace Conference adopted the Covenant and incorporated it in the treaty precisely as Wilson had hoped.*

The High Contracting Parties

In order to promote international cooperation and to achieve international peace and security

by the acceptance of obligations not to resort to war,

by the prescription of open, just and honorable relations between nations, by the firm establishment of the understandings of international law as the actual rule of conduct among Governments, and

by the maintenance of justice and a scrupulous respect for all treaty obligations in the dealings of organized peoples with one another,

Agree to this Covenant of the League of Nations.

ARTICLE 1—The original Members of the League of Nations shall be those of the Signatories which are named in the Annex to this Covenant and also such of those other States named in the Annex as shall accede without reservation to this Covenant. Such accession shall be effected by a Declaration deposited with the Secretariat within two months of the coming into force of the Covenant. Notice thereof shall be sent to all Members of the League.

Any fully self-governing State, Dominion, or Colony not named in the Annex may become a Member of the League if its admission is agreed to by two-thirds of the Assembly, provided that it shall give effective guarantees of its sincere intentions to observe its international obligations, and shall accept such regulations as may be prescribed by the League in regard to its military, naval, and air forces and armaments.

Any Member of the League may, after two years' notice of its intention so to do, withdraw from the League, provided that all its international obligations and all its obligations under this Covenant shall have been fulfilled at the time of its withdrawal.

ARTICLE 2—The action of the League under this Covenant shall be effected through the instrument of an Assembly and of a Council, with a permanent Secretariat.

ARTICLE 3—The Assembly shall consist of Representatives of the Members of the League.

The Assembly shall meet at stated intervals and from time to time as occasions may require at the Seat of the League or at such other place as may be decided upon.

The Assembly may deal at its meetings with any matter within the sphere of action of the League or affecting the peace of the world.

At meetings of the Assembly each Member of the League shall have one vote, and may have not more than three Representatives.

ARTICLE 4—The Council shall consist of Representatives of the Principal Allied and Associated Powers, together with Representatives of four other Members of the League. These four Members of the League shall be selected by the Assembly from time to time in its discretion. Until the appointment of the Representatives of the four Members of the League, first selected by the Assembly, Representatives of Belgium, Brazil, Spain, and Greece shall be members of the Council.

With the approval of the majority of the Assembly, the Council may name additional Members of the League whose Representatives shall always be members of the Council; the Council with like approval may increase the number of Members of the League to be selected by the Assembly for representation on the Council.

The Council shall meet from time to time as occasion may require, and at least once a year, at the Seat of the League, or at such other place as may be decided upon.

The Council may deal at its meetings with any matter within the sphere of action of the League or affecting the peace of the world.

Any Member of the League not represented on the Council shall be invited to send a Representative to sit as a member at any meeting of the Council during the consideration of matters specially affecting the interests of that Member of the League.

At meetings of the Council, each Member of the League represented on the Council shall have one vote, and may have not more than one Representative.

ARTICLE 5—Except where otherwise expressly provided in this Covenant or by the terms of the present Treaty, decisions at any meeting of the Assembly or of the Council shall require the agreement of all the Members of the League represented by the meeting.

All matters of procedure at meetings of the Assembly or of the Council, including the appointment of Committees to investigate particular matters, shall be regulated by the Assembly or by the Council and may be decided by a majority of the Members of the League represented at the meeting.

The first meeting of the Assembly and the first meeting of the Council shall be summoned by the President of the United States of America.

ARTICLE 6—The permanent Secretariat shall be established at the Seat of the League. The Secretariat shall comprise a Secretary General and such secretaries and staff as may be required.

The first Secretary General shall be the person named in the Annex; thereafter the Secretary General shall be appointed by the Council with the approval of the majority of the Assembly.

The secretaries and staff of the Secretariat shall be appointed by the Secretary General with the approval of the Council.

The Secretary General shall act in that capacity at all meetings of the Assembly and of the Council.

The expenses of the Secretariat shall be borne by the Members of the League in accordance with the apportionment of the expenses of the International Bureau of the Universal Postal Union.

ARTICLE 7—The Seat of the League is established at Geneva.

The Council may at any time decide that the Seat of the League shall be established elsewhere.

All positions under or in connection with the League, including the Secretariat, shall be open equally to men and women.

Representatives of the Members of the League and officials of the League when engaged on the business of the League shall enjoy diplomatic privileges and immunities.

The buildings and other property occupied by the League or its officials or by Representatives attending its meetings shall be inviolable.

ARTICLE 8—The Members of the League recognize that the maintenance of peace requires the reduction of national armaments to the lowest point consistent with national safety and the enforcement by common action of international obligations.

The Council, taking account of the geographical situation and circumstances of each State, shall formulate plans for such reduction for the consideration and action of the several Governments.

Such plans shall be subject to reconsideration and revision at least every ten years.

After these plans shall have been adopted by the several Governments, the limits of armaments therein fixed shall not be exceeded without the concurrence of the Council.

The Members of the League agree that the manufacture by private enterprise of munitions and implements of war is open to grave objections. The Council shall advise how the evil effects attendant upon such manufacture can be prevented, due regard being had to the necessities of those Members of the League which are not able to manufacture the munitions and implements of war necessary for their safety.

The Members of the League undertake to interchange full and frank information as to the scale of their armaments, their military, naval and air programs and the condition of such of their industries as are adaptable to war-like purposes.

ARTICLE 9—A permanent Commission shall be constituted to advise the Council on the execution of the provisions of Articles 1 and 8 and on military, naval and air questions generally.

ARTICLE 10—The Members of the League undertake to respect and preserve as against external aggression the territorial integrity and existing political independence of all Members of the League. In case of any such aggression or in case of any threat or danger of such aggression the Council shall advise upon the means by which this obligation shall be fulfilled.

ARTICLE 11—Any war or threat of war, whether immediately affecting any of the Members of the League or not, is hereby declared a matter of concern to the whole League, and the League shall take any action that may be deemed wise and effectual to safeguard the peace of nations. In case any such emergency should arise the Secretary General shall on the request of any Member of the League forthwith summon a meeting of the Council.

It is also declared to be the friendly right of each Member of the League to bring to the attention of the Assembly or of the Council any circumstance whatever affecting international relations which threatens to disturb international peace or the good understanding between nations upon which peace depends.

ARTICLE 12—The Members of the League agree that if there should arise between them any dispute likely to lead to a rupture, they will submit the matter either to arbitration or to inquiry by the Council, and they agree in no case to resort to war until three months after the award by the arbitrators or the report by the Council.

In any case under this Article the award of the arbitrators shall be made within a reasonable time, and the report of the Council shall be made within six months after the submission of the dispute.

ARTICLE 13—The Members of the League agree that whenever any dispute shall arise between them which they recognize to be suitable for submission to arbitration and which cannot be satisfactorily settled by diplomacy, they will submit the whole subject-matter to arbitration.

Disputes as to the interpretation of a treaty, as to any question of international law, as to the existence of any fact which if established would constitute a breach of any international obligation, or as to the extent and nature of the reparation to be made for any such breach, are declared to be among those which are generally suitable for submission to arbitration.

For the consideration of any such dispute the court of arbitration to which the case is referred shall be the court agreed upon by the parties to the dispute or stipulated in any convention existing between them.

The Members of the League agree that they will carry out in full good faith any award that may be rendered, and that they will not resort to war against a Member of the League which complies therewith. In the event of any failure to carry out such an award, the Council shall propose what steps should be taken to give effect thereto.

ARTICLE 14—The Council shall formulate and submit to the Members of the League for adoption plans for the establishment of a Permanent Court of International Justice. The Court shall be competent to hear and determine any dispute of an international character which the parties thereto submit to it. The Court may also give an advisory opinion upon any dispute or question referred to it by the Council or by the Assembly.

ARTICLE 15—If there should arise between Members of the League any dispute likely to lead to a rupture, which is not submitted to arbitration in accordance with Article 13, the Members of the League agree that they will submit the matter to the Council. Any party to the dispute may effect such submission by giving notice of the existence of the dispute to the Secretary General, who will make all necessary arrangements for a full investigation and consideration thereof.

For this purpose the parties to the dispute will communicate to the Secretary General, as promptly as possible, statements of their case with all the relevant facts and papers, and the Council may forthwith direct the publication thereof.

The Council shall endeavor to effect a settlement of the dispute, and if such efforts are successful, a statement shall be made public giving such facts and explanations regarding the dispute and the terms of settlement thereof as the Council may deem appropriate.

If the dispute is not thus settled, the Council either unanimously or by a majority vote shall make and publish a report containing a statement of the facts of the dispute and the recommendations which are deemed just and proper in regard thereto.

Any Member of the League represented on the Council may make public a statement of the facts of the dispute and of its conclusions regarding the same.

If a report by the Council is unanimously agreed to by the Members thereof, other than the Representatives of one or more of the parties to the dispute, the Members of the League agree that they will not go to war with any party to the dispute which complies with the recommendations of the report.

If the Council fails to reach a report which is unanimously agreed to by the Members thereof, other than the Representatives of one or more of the parties to the dispute, the Members of the League reserve to themselves the right to take such action as they shall consider necessary for the maintenance of right and justice.

If the dispute between the parties is claimed by one of them, and is found by the Council to arise out of a matter which by international law is solely within the domestic jurisdiction of that party, the Council shall so report, and shall make no recommendation as to its settlement.

The Council may in any case under this Article refer the dispute to the Assembly. The dispute shall be so referred at the request of either party to the dispute, provided that such request be made within fourteen days after the submission of the dispute to the Council.

In any case referred to the Assembly, all the provisions of this Article and of Article 12 relating to the action and powers of the Council shall apply to the action and powers of the Assembly, provided that a report made by the Assembly, if concurred in by the Representatives of those Members of the League represented on the Council and of a majority of the other Members of the League, exclusive in each case of the Representatives of the parties to the dispute, shall have the same force as a report by the Council concurred in by all the members thereof other than the Representatives of one or more of the parties to the dispute.

ARTICLE 16—Should any Member of the League resort to war in disregard of its covenants under Articles 12, 13 or 15, it shall *ipso facto* be deemed to have committed an act of war against all other Members of the League, which hereby undertake immediately to subject it to the severance of all trade or financial relations, the prohibition of all intercourse between their nationals and the nationals of the covenant-breaking State, and the prevention of all financial, commercial or personal intercourse between the nationals of the covenant-breaking State and the nationals of any other State, whether a Member of the League or not.

It shall be the duty of the Council in such case to recommend to the several Governments concerned what effective military, naval or air force the Members of the League shall severally contribute to the armed forces to be used to protect the covenants of the League.

The Members of the League agree, further, that they will mutually support one another in the financial and economic measures which are taken under this article, in order to minimize the loss and inconvenience resulting from the above measures aimed at one of their number by the covenant-breaking State, and that they will take the necessary steps to afford passage through their territory to the forces of any of the Members of the League which are cooperating to protect the covenants of the League.

Any Member of the League which has violated any covenant of the League may be declared to be no longer a Member of the League by a vote of the Council concurred in by the Representatives of all the other Members of the League represented thereon.

ARTICLE 17—In the event of a dispute between a Member of the League and a State which is not a Member of the League, or between States not Members of the League, the State or States not Members of the League shall be invited to accept the obligations of membership in the League for the purposes of such dispute, upon such conditions as the Council may deem just. If such invitation is accepted, the provisions of Articles 12 to 16 inclusive shall be applied with such modifications as may be deemed necessary by the Council.

Upon such invitation being given the Council shall immediately institute an inquiry into the circumstances of the dispute and recommend such action as may seem best and most effectual in the circumstances.

If a State so invited shall refuse to accept the obligations of membership in the League for the purposes of such dispute, and shall resort to war against a Member of the League, the provisions of Article 16 shall be applicable as against the State taking such action.

If both parties to the dispute when so invited refuse to accept the obligations of membership in the League for the purposes of such dispute, the Council may take such measures and make such recommendations as will result in the settlement of the dispute.

ARTICLE 18—Every treaty or international engagement entered into hereafter by any Member of the League shall be forthwith registered with the Secretariat and shall as soon as possible be published by it. No such treaty or international engagement shall be binding until so registered.

ARTICLE 19—The Assembly may from time to time advise the reconsideration by Members of the League to treaties which have become inapplicable and the consideration of international conditions whose continuance might endanger the peace of the world.

ARTICLE 20—The Members of the League severally agree that this Covenant is accepted as abrogating all obligations or understandings *inter se* which are inconsistent with the terms thereof, and solemnly undertake that they will not hereafter enter into any engagements inconsistent with the terms thereof.

In case any Member of the League shall, before becoming a Member of the League, have undertaken any obligations inconsistent with the terms of this Covenant, it shall be the duty of such Member to take immediate steps to procure its release from such obligations.

ARTICLE 21—Nothing in this Covenant shall be deemed to affect the validity of international engagements, such as treaties of arbitration or regional understandings like the Monroe Doctrine, for securing the maintenance of peace.

ARTICLE 22—To those colonies and territories which as a consequence of the late war have ceased to be under the sovereignty of the States which formerly governed them and which are inhabited by peoples not yet able to stand by themselves under the strenuous conditions of the modern world, there should be applied the principle that the well-being and development of such peoples form a sacred trust of civilization and that securities for the performance of this trust should be embodied in the Covenant.

The best method of giving practical effect to this principle is that the tutelage of such peoples should be entrusted to advanced nations who by reason of their resources, their experience or their geographical position can best undertake this responsibility, and who are willing to accept it, and that this tutelage should be exercised by them as Mandatories on behalf of the League.

The character of the mandate must differ according to the stage of development of the people, the geographical situation of the territory, its economic conditions, and other similar circumstances.

Certain communities formerly belonging to the Turkish Empire have reached a stage of development where their existence as independent nations can be provisionally recognized subject to the rendering of administrative advice and assistance by a Mandatory until such time as they are able to stand alone. The wishes of these communities must be a principal consideration in the selection of the Mandatory.

Other peoples, especially those of Central Africa, are at such a stage that the Mandatory must be responsible for the administration of the territory under conditions which will guarantee freedom of conscience and religion, subject only to the maintenance of public order and morals, the prohibition of abuses such as the slave trade, the arms traffic and the liquor traffic, and the prevention of the establishment of fortifications or military and naval bases and of military training of the natives for other than police purposes and the defense of territory, and will also secure equal opportunities for the trade and commerce of other Members of the League.

There are territories, such as South West Africa and certain of the South Pacific Islands, which, owing to the sparseness of their population, or their small size, or their remoteness from the centers of civilization, or their geographical circumstances, can be best administered under the laws of the Mandatory as integral portions of its territory subject to the safeguards above mentioned in the interests of the indigenous population.

In every case of mandate, the Mandatory shall render to the Council an annual report in reference to the territory committed to its charge.

The degree of authority, control, or administration to be exercised by the Mandatory shall, if not previously agreed upon by the Members of the League, be explicitly defined in each case by the Council.

A permanent Commission shall be constituted to receive and examine the annual reports of the Mandatories and to advise the Council on all matters relating to the observance of the mandates.

ARTICLE 23—Subject to and in accordance with the provisions of international conventions existing or hereafter to be agreed upon, the Members of the League:

a) will endeavor to secure and maintain fair and humane conditions of labor for men, women, and children, both in their own countries and in all countries to which their commercial and industrial relations extend, and for that purpose will establish and maintain the necessary international organizations;

b) will undertake to secure just treatment of the native inhabitants of territories under their control;

c) will entrust the League with the general supervision over the execution of agreements with regard to the traffic in women and children, and the traffic in opium and other dangerous drugs;

d) will entrust the League with the general supervision of the trade in arms and ammunition with the countries in which the control of this traffic is necessary in the common interest;

e) will make provision to secure and maintain freedom of communications and of transit and equitable treatment for the commerce of all Members of the League. In this connection, the special necessities of the regions devastated during the war of 1914–1918 shall be borne in mind;

f) will endeavor to take steps in matters of international concern for the prevention and control of disease.

ARTICLE 24—There shall be placed under the direction of the League all international bureaux already established by general treaties if the parties to such treaties consent. All such international bureaux and all commissions for the regulation of matters of international interest hereafter constituted shall be placed under the direction of the League.

In all matter of international interest which are regulated by general conventions but which are not placed under the control of international bureaux or commissions, the Secretariat of the League shall, subject to the consent of the Council and if desired by the parties, collect and distribute all relevant information and shall render any other assistance which may be necessary or desirable.

The Council may include as part of the expenses of the Secretariat the expenses of any bureau or commission which is placed under the direction of the League.

ARTICLE 25—The Members of the League agree to encourage and promote the establishment and cooperation of duly authorized voluntary national Red Cross organizations having as purposes the improvement of health, the prevention of disease and the mitigation of suffering throughout the world.

ARTICLE 26—Amendments to this Covenant will take effect when ratified by the Members of the League whose Representatives compose the Council and by a majority of the Members of the League whose Representatives compose the Assembly.

No such amendment shall bind any Member of the League which signifies its dissent therefrom, but in that case it shall cease to be a Member of the League.

9. Such Is Our Situation

To Prime Minister Lloyd George, May 5, 1919

Economic reconstruction was of course a primary concern of the delegates at Versailles. John Maynard Keynes, the economist of the British delegation, drew up a plan which would have required the United States to provide cheap credit—in effect, to underwrite German reparations. Wilson rejected Keynes' plan outright on the advice of Thomas Lamont, the Morgan Company banker, and Norman Davis, who represented the Treasury Department. The American delegation presented an economic plan of its own on May 15; its main point was that "credits to Europe should, so far as possible, be extended through the normal channels of private enterprise." Following is Wilson's rejection of the Keynes plan.

I HAVE carefully considered your recent communication enclosing a scheme suggested for the reestablishment of more normal economic and financial conditions in Europe. I am fully alive to the confused conditions that now exist and to the very great importance of trying to clear and improve them, especially in respect to the situation of the new and weaker nations that are to be set up under the Treaty of Peace.

I am sorry to say, however, that Mr. Keynes' plan does not seem feasible from the American point of view. Our Treasury and our financial delegates here in Paris are convinced that the plan as presented lacks many elements of economic and financial soundness. I have asked our Treasury representatives here, Mr. Davis and Mr. Lamont, to explain in detail to your financial advisors the serious objections to the plan which present themselves to us. Personally, I am convinced of the soundness of these objections. I am convinced, moreover, that it would not be possible for me to secure from the Congress of the United States authority to place a Federal guarantee upon bonds of European origin. Whatever aid the Congress may see fit to authorize should, in my judgment, be rendered along independent lines. By that I do not mean in ways that would not involve close and cordial cooperation with European governments, for such harmony and cooperation I consider indispensable. I mean merely that such cooperation should not, so far as America is concerned, take the form of a guarantee upon bonds. Our Treasury also holds the view (and in this again I concur) that to the very limit of what is practicable such credits as it may be wise to grant should be extended through the medium of the usual private channels rather than through the several Governments. Your Treasury, I understand, and certainly ours, believes it wise to retire at the earliest possible moment from "the banking business."

In order, however, that practical progress may be made, I have asked our local advisors here to present to me their views as soon as possible. Meantime, may I not call to your attention the following facts and considerations with regard to Germany's present and prospective financial situation?

a) Germany requires working capital. Without that, she will be unable to start her industrial life again, and therefore unable to make any substantial progress in the way of reparation. . . .

b) The provisions of the reparation clauses of the proposed treaty demand that Germany shall deliver over at once all her working capital, that is, practically the whole of her liquid assets.

c) Simultaneously the suggestion is in effect made that America should in a large measure make good this deficiency, providing in one form or another credit, and thus working capital, to Germany.

Throughout the reparation discussions the American delegation has steadily pointed out to the other delegations that the plans proposed would surely deprive Germany of the means of making any appreciable reparation payments. I myself, as you know, have frequently made the same observation. But whenever any of us was urgent on this point, he was accused of being pro-German. Our delegation finally gave assent to the reparation clauses as drawn, only because the reparation problem was one that chiefly concerned France, Great Britain, Belgium, and the other European countries, and not America.

I venture to point this situation out to you in order that I may make the following point clear. America has, in my judgment, always been ready and will always stand ready to do her full share financially to assist the general situation. But America has grave difficulties of her own. She has been obliged within two years to raise by means of war loans and taxes the sum of forty billion dollars. This has been a very heavy burden, even for our well-to-do commonwealth, especially in view of the fact of the short period during which such sums of money had to be raised; and our Treasury informs me that our investing public have reached, and perhaps passed, the point of complete saturation in respect of investments. Such is our situation.

You have suggested that we all address ourselves to the problem of helping to put Germany on her feet, but how can your experts or ours be expected to work out a *new* plan to furnish working capital to Germany when we deliberately start out by taking away all Germany's *present* capital? How can anyone expect America to turn over to Germany in any considerable measure new working capital to take the place of that which the European nations have determined to take from her? Such questions would appear to answer themselves, but I cannot refrain from stating them, because they so essentially belong to a candid consideration of the whole difficult problem to which we are addressing ourselves, with as sincere a desire as that of their colleagues to reach a serviceable conclusion.

10. We Must Venture Upon Uncharted Seas

Address on International Law, May 9, 1919

In this address to the International Law Society at Paris, Wilson assessed the meaning of the treaty which had two days before been given to Germany for ratification.

. . . I THOUGHT it a privilege to come here tonight, because your studies were devoted to one of the things which will be of most consequence to men in the future, the intelligent development of international law. In one sense, this great, unprecedented war was fought to give validity to international law, to prove that it has a reality which no nation could afford to disregard; that, while it did not have the ordinary sanctions, while there was no international authority as yet to enforce it, it nevertheless had something behind it which was greater than that, the moral rectitude of mankind.

If we can now give to international law the kind of vitality which it can have only if it is a real expression of our moral judgment, we shall have completed in some sense the work which this war was intended to emphasize.

International law has perhaps sometimes been a little too much thought out in the closet. International law has—may I say it without offense?—been handled too exclusively by lawyers. Lawyers like definite lines. They like systematic arrangements. They are uneasy if they depart from what was done yesterday. They dread experiments. They like charted seas and, if they have no charts, hardly venture to undertake the voyage.

Now we must venture upon uncharted seas, to some extent,

in the future. In the new League of Nations we are starting out on uncharted seas, and therefore we must have, I will not say the audacity, but the steadiness of purpose which is necessary in such novel circumstances. And we must not be afraid of new things, at the same time that we must not be intolerant of old things. We must weave out of the old materials the new garments which it is necessary that men should wear.

It is a great privilege if we can do that kind of thinking for mankind—human thinking, thinking that is made up of comprehension of the needs of mankind. And when I think of mankind, I must say I do not always think of well-dressed persons. Most persons are not well dressed. The heart of the world is under very plain jackets, the heart of the world is at very simple firesides, the heart of the world is in very humble circumstances; and, unless you know the pressure of life of the humbler classes, you know nothing of life whatever. Unless you know where the pinch comes you do not know what the pulse has to stand, you do not know what strain the muscles have to bear, you do not know what trial the nerves have to go through to hold on.

To hold on where there is no glee in life is the hard thing. Those of us who can sit sometimes at leisure and read pleasant books and think of the past, the long past, that we have no part in, and project the long future—we are not specimens of mankind. The specimens of mankind have not time to do that, and we must use our leisure when we have it to feel with them and think for them, so that we can translate their desire into a fact, so far as that is possible, and see that that most complicated and elusive of all things which we call justice is accomplished. An easy word to say, and a noble word upon the tongue, but one of the most difficult enterprises of the human spirit!

It is hard to be just to those with whom you are intimate; how much harder it is to conceive the problems of those with whom you are not intimate, and be just to them. To live and let live, to work for people and with people, is at the bottom of the kind of experience which must underlie justice.

The sympathy that has the slightest touch of condescension in it has no touch of helpfulness about it. If you are aware of stooping to help a man, you cannot help him. You must realize that he stands on the same earth with yourself and has a heart like your own, and that you are helping him, standing on that common level and using that common impulse of humanity.

In a sense the old enterprise of national law is played out. I mean that the future of mankind depends more upon the relations of nations to one another, more upon the realization of the common brotherhood of mankind, than upon the separate and selfish development of national systems of law; so that the men who can, if I may express it so, think without language, think the common thoughts of humanity, are the men who will be most serviceable in the immediate future.

God grant that there may be many of them, that many men may see this hope and wish to advance it, and that the plain man everywhere may know that there is no language of society in which he has no brothers or co-laborers, in order to reach the great ends of equity and of high justice.

11. Their Right Advantage as Human Beings

Message to Congress, May 20, 1919

Wilson sent this message to the special session of the 66th Congress. He presented a liberal and in many ways a radical domestic program in regard to labor. The message fell on deaf ears.

THE QUESTION which stands at the front of all others in every country amidst the present great awakening is the question of labor; and perhaps I can speak of it with as great advantage while engrossed in the consideration of interests which affect all countries alike as I could at home and amidst the interests which naturally most affect my thought, because they are the interests of our own people.

By the question of labor I do not mean the question of efficient industrial production, the question of how labor is to be obtained and made effective in the great process of sustaining populations and winning success amidst commercial and industrial rivalries. I mean that much greater and more vital question, how are the men and women who do the daily labor of the world to obtain progressive improvement in the conditions of their labor, to be made happier, and to be served better by the communities and the industries which their labor sustains and advances? How are they to be given their right advantage as citizens and human beings?

We cannot go any further in our present direction. We have already gone too far. We cannot live our right life as a nation or achieve our proper success as an industrial community if capital and labor are to continue to be antagonistic instead of being partners. If they are to continue to distrust one another and contrive how they can get the better of one another. Or, what perhaps amounts to the same thing, calculate by what form and degree of coercion they can manage to extort on the one hand work enough to make enterprise profitable, on the other justice and fair treatment enough to make life tolerable. That bad road has turned out a blind alley. It is no thoroughfare to real prosperity. We must find another, leading in another direction and to a very different destination. It must lead not merely to accommodation but also to a genuine cooperation and partnership based upon a real community of interest and participation in control.

There is now in fact a real community of interest between capital and labor, but it has never been made evident in action. It can be made operative and manifest only in a new organization of industry. The genius of our business men and the sound practical sense of our workers can certainly work such a partnership out when once they realize exactly what it is that they seek and sincerely adopt a common purpose with regard to it.

Labor legislation lies, of course, chiefly with the states; but the new spirit and method of organization which must be effected are not to be brought about by legislation so much as by the common counsel and voluntary cooperation of capitalist, manager, and workman. Legislation can go only a very little way in commanding what shall be done. The organization of industry is a matter of corporate and individual initiative and of practical business arrangement. Those who really desire a new relationship between capital and labor can readily find a way to bring it about; and perhaps Federal legislation can help more than state legislation could.

The object of all reform in this essential matter must be the genuine democratization of industry, based upon a full recognition of the right of those who work, in whatever rank, to participate in some organic way in every decision which directly affects their welfare or the part they are to play in industry. Some positive legislation is practicable. The Congress has already shown the way to one reform which should be worldwide, by establishing the eight-hour day as the standard day in every field of labor over which it can exercise control. It has sought to find the way to prevent child labor, and will, I hope and believe, presently find it. It has served the whole country by leading the way in developing the means of preserving and safeguarding life and health in dangerous industries. It can now help in the difficult task of giving a new form and spirit to industrial organization by coordinating the several agencies of conciliation and adjustment which have been brought into existence by the difficulties and mistaken policies of the present management of industry, and by setting up and developing new Federal agencies of advice and information which may serve as a clearinghouse for the best experiments and the best thought on this great matter, upon which every thinking man must be aware that the future development of society directly depends. Agencies of international counsel and suggestion are presently to be created in connection with the League of Nations in this very field; but it is national action and the enlightened policy of individuals, corporations, and societies within each nation that must bring about the actual reforms. The members of the committees on labor in the two houses will hardly need suggestions from me as to what means they shall seek to make the Federal Government the agent of the whole Nation in pointing out and, if need be, guiding the process of reorganization and reform. . . .

12. Deep Satisfaction and Confident Hope

Statement on Signing of Treaty, June 28, 1919

The treaty had been handed to Germany for ratification on May 7; Allied armies stood poised on the borders. In the following weeks, while Allied statesmen waited in Paris, the German government repeatedly asked for modifications of a treaty which it insisted was at sharp variance with the Fourteen Points. The delay grew intolerable; Britain was even willing to soften the severity of the treaty. But Wilson was adamant. Finally, on June 20, a new German government, the old having resigned, announced its intention of ratifying. The signing was held eight days later in the Hall of Mirrors at Versailles. Following is Wilson's announcement of the event to the American people.

THE TREATY of peace has been signed. If it is ratified and acted upon in full and sincere execution of its terms it will furnish the charter for a new order of affairs in the world. It is a severe treaty in the duties and penalties it imposes upon Germany, but it is severe only because great wrongs done by Germany are to be righted and repaired; it imposes nothing that Germany cannot do; and she can regain her rightful standing in the world by the prompt and honorable fulfillment of its terms.

And it is much more than a treaty of peace with Germany. It liberates great peoples who have never before been able to find the way to liberty. It ends, once for all, an old and intolerable order under which small groups of selfish men could use the peoples of great empires to serve their own ambition for power and dominion. It associates the free governments of the world in a permanent league in which they are pledged to use their united power to maintain peace by maintaining right and justice. It makes international law a reality supported by imperative sanctions. It does away with the right of conquest and rejects the policy of annexation and substitutes a new order under which backward nations—populations which have not yet come to political consciousness and peoples who are ready for independence but not yet quite prepared to dispense with protection and guidance—shall no more be subjected to the domination and exploitation of a stronger nation, but shall be put under the friendly direction and afforded the helpful assistance of governments which undertake to be responsible to the opinion of mankind in the execution of their task by accepting the direction of the League of Nations.

It recognizes the inalienable rights of nationality; the rights of minorities and the sanctity of religious belief and practice. It lays the basis for conventions which shall free the commercial intercourse of the world from unjust and vexatious restrictions and for every sort of international cooperation that will serve to cleanse the life of the world and facilitate its common action in beneficent service of every kind. It furnishes guarantees such as were never given or even contemplated before for the fair treatment of all who labor at the daily tasks of the world.

It is for this reason that I have spoken of it as a great charter for a new order of affairs. There is ground here for deep satisfaction, universal reassurance, and confident hope.

Seven

TRAGEDY
1919–1924

1. We Cannot Turn Back

Address to Senate at Presentation of Treaty, July 10, 1919

Wilson arrived in New York on July 8, carrying the treaty, the contents of which was to have been kept secret until Germany's ratification. But on June 10 Senator Borah had inserted in the Congressional Record an inaccurate version of it, secured clandestinely from Germany. Its contents therefore were known before Wilson's official presentation of it on July 10. Immediately after the President's address the treaty went to the Senate Foreign Relations Committee.

. . . A LEAGUE of free nations had become a practical necessity. Examine the treaty of peace and you will find that everywhere throughout its manifold provisions its framers have felt obliged to turn to the League of Nations as an indispensable instrumentality for the maintenance of the new order it has been their purpose to set up in the world—the world of civilized men.

That there should be a League of Nations to steady the counsels and maintain the peaceful understandings of the world, to make, not treaties alone, but the accepted principles of international law as well, the actual rule of conduct among the governments of the world, had been one of the agreements accepted from the first as the basis of peace with the Central Powers. The statesmen of all the belligerent countries were agreed that such a league must be created to sustain the settlements that were to be effected. But at first I think there was a feeling among some of them that, while it must be attempted, the formation of such a league was perhaps a counsel of perfection which practical men, long experienced in the world of affairs, must agree to very cautiously and with many misgivings. It was only as the difficult work of arranging an all but universal adjustment of the world's affairs advanced from day to day from one stage of conference to another that it became evident to them that what they were seeking would be little more than something written upon paper, to be interpreted and applied by such methods as the chances of politics might make available if they did not provide a means of common counsel which all were obliged to accept, a common authority whose decisions would be recognized as decisions which all must respect.

And so the most practical, the most skeptical among them turned more and more to the League as the authority through which international action was to be secured, the authority without which, as they had come to see it, would be difficult to give assured effect either to this treaty or to any other international understanding upon which they were to depend for the maintenance of peace. The fact that the Covenant of the League was the first substantive part of the treaty to be worked out and agreed upon, while all else was in solution, helped to make the formulation of the rest easier. The Conference was, after all, not to be ephemeral. The concert of nations was to continue, under a definite Covenant which had been agreed upon and which all were convinced was workable. They could go forward with confidence to make arrangements intended to be permanent. The most practical of the conferees were at last the most ready to refer to the League of Nations the superintendence of all interests which did not admit of immediate determination, of all administrative problems which were to require a continuing oversight. What had seemed a counsel of perfection had come to seem a plain counsel of necessity. The League of Nations was the practical statesman's hope of success in many of the most difficult things he was attempting.

And it had validated itself in the thought of every member of the Conference as something much bigger, much greater every way, than a mere instrument for carrying out the provisions of a particular treaty. It was universally recognized that all the peoples of the world demanded of the Conference that it should create such a continuing concert of free nations as would make wars of aggression and spoliation such as this that has just ended forever impossible. A cry had gone out from every home in every stricken land from which sons and brothers and fathers had gone forth to the great sacrifice that such a sacrifice should never again be exacted. It was manifest why it had been exacted. It had been exacted because one nation desired dominion and other nations had known no means of defense except armaments and alliances. War had lain at the heart of every arrangement of the Europe—of every arrangement of the world—that preceded the war. Restive peoples had been told that fleets and armies, which they toiled to sustain, meant peace; and they now knew that they had been lied to: that fleets and armies had been maintained to promote national ambitions and meant war. They knew that no old policy meant anything else but force, force—always force. And they knew that it was intolerable. Every true heart in the world, and every enlightened judgment demanded that, at whatever cost of independent action, every government that took thought for its people or for justice or for ordered freedom should lend itself to a new purpose and utterly destroy the old order of international politics. Statesmen might see difficulties, but the people could see none and could brook no denial. A war in which they had been bled white to beat the terror that lay concealed in every Balance of Power must not end in a mere victory of arms and a new balance. The monster that had resorted to arms must be put in chains that could not be broken. The united power of free nations must put a stop to aggression, and the world must be given peace. If there was not the will or the intelligence to accomplish that now, there must be another and a final war and the world must be swept clean of every power that could renew the terror. The League of Nations was not merely an instrument to adjust and remedy old wrongs under a new treaty of peace; it was the only hope for mankind. Again and again had the demon of war been cast out of the house of the peoples and the house swept clean by a treaty of peace; only to prepare a time when he would enter in again with spirits worse than himself. The house must now be given a tenant who could hold it against all such. Convenient, indeed indispensable, as statesmen found the newly planned League of Nations to be for the execution of present plans of peace and reparation, they saw it in a new aspect before their work was finished. They saw it as the main object of the peace, as the only thing that could complete it or make it worth while. They saw it as the hope of the world, and that hope they did not dare to disappoint. Shall we or any other free people hesitate to accept this great duty? Dare we reject it and break the heart of the world?

And so the result of the Conference of Peace, so far as Germany is concerned, stands complete. The difficulties encountered were very many. Sometimes they seemed insuperable. It was impossible to accommodate the interests of so great a body of nations —interests which directly or indirectly affected almost every nation in the world—without many minor compromises. The treaty, as a result, is not exactly what we would have written. It is probably not what any one of the national delegations would have written. But results were worked out which on the whole bear test. I think that it will be found that the compromises which were accepted as inevitable nowhere cut to the heart of any principle. The work of the Conference squares, as a whole, with the principles agreed upon as the basis of the peace as well as with the practical possibilities of the international situations which had to be faced and dealt with as facts. . . .

America may be said to have just reached her majority as a world power. It was almost exactly twenty-one years ago that the results of the war with Spain put us unexpectedly in possession of rich islands on the other side of the world and brought us into association with other governments in the control of the West Indies. It was regarded as a sinister and ominous thing by the statesmen of more than one European chancellery that we should have extended our power beyond the confines of our continental dominions. They were accustomed to think of new neighbors as a new menace, of rivals as watchful enemies. There were persons amongst us at home who looked with deep disapproval and avowed anxiety on such extensions of our national authority over distant islands and over peoples whom they feared we might exploit, not serve and assist. But we have not exploited them. We have been their friends and have sought to serve them. And our dominion has been a menace to no other nation. We redeemed our honor to the utmost in our dealings with Cuba. She is weak but absolutely free; and it is her trust in us that makes her free. Weak peoples everywhere stand ready to give us any authority among them that will assure them a like friendly oversight and direction. They know that there is no ground for fear in receiving us as their mentors and guides. Our isolation was ended twenty years ago; and now fear of us is ended also, our counsel and association sought after and desired. There can be no question of our ceasing to be a world power. The only question is whether we can refuse the moral leadership that is offered us, whether we shall accept or reject the confidence of the world.

The war and the Conference of Peace now sitting in Paris seem to me to have answered that question. Our participation in the war established our position among the nations and nothing but our own mistaken action can alter it. It was not an accident or a matter of sudden choice that we are no longer isolated and devoted to a policy which has only our own interest and advantage for its object. It was our duty to go in, if we were indeed the champions of liberty and of right. We answered to the call of duty in a way so spirited, so utterly without thought of what we spent of blood or treasure, so effective, so worthy of the admiration of true men everywhere, so wrought out of the stuff of all that was heroic, that the whole world saw at last, in the flesh, in noble action, a great ideal asserted and vindicated, by a Nation they had deemed material and now found to be compact of the spiritual forces that must free men of every nation from every unworthy bondage. It is thus that a new rôle and a new responsibility have come to this great Nation that we honor and which we would all wish to lift to yet higher levels of service and achievement.

The stage is set, the destiny disclosed. It has come about by no plan of our conceiving, but by the hand of God who led us into this way. We cannot turn back. We can only go forward, with lifted eyes and freshened spirit, to follow the vision. It was of this that we dreamed at our birth. America shall in truth show the way. The light streams upon the path ahead, and nowhere else.

2. A New Day Has Dawned

Message to Senate on French Security Pact, July 29, 1919

Wilson had agreed at Versailles to supplement the treaty with a guarantee that the United States would come to the aid of France in case of German aggression. It is curious that Wilson should have submitted the French Security Treaty to the Senate nineteen days after submitting the Versailles Treaty. As it turned out, the Foreign Relations Committee buried the French Security Treaty—an act which the French thought perfidious.

GENTLEMEN OF the Senate: I take pleasure in laying before you a treaty with the Republic of France the object of which is to secure that Republic of the immediate aid of the United States of America in case of any unprovoked movement of aggression against her on the part of Germany. I earnestly hope that this treaty will meet with your cordial approval and will receive an early ratification at your hands, along with the treaty of peace with Germany. Now that you have had an opportunity to examine the great document I presented to you two weeks ago, it seems opportune to lay before you this treaty which is meant to be in effect a part of it.

It was signed on the same day with the treaty of peace and is intended as a temporary supplement to it. It is believed that the treaty of peace with Germany itself provides adequate protection to France against aggression from her recent enemy on the east; but the years immediately ahead of us contain many incalculable possibilities. The Covenant of the League of Nations provides for military action for the protection of its members only upon advice of the Council of the League—advice given, it is to be presumed, only upon deliberation and acted upon by each of the governments of the member States only if its own judgment justifies such action. The object of the special treaty with France which I now submit to you is to provide for immediate military assistance to France by the United States in case of any unprovoked movement of aggression against her by Germany without waiting for the advice of the Council of the League of Nations that such action be taken. It is to be an arrangement, not independent of the League of Nations, but under it.

It is, therefore, expressly provided that this treaty shall be made the subject of consideration at the same time with the treaty of peace with Germany; that this special arrangement shall receive the approval of the Council of the League; and that this special provision for the safety of France shall remain in force only until, upon the application of one of the parties to it, the Council of the League, acting, if necessary, by a majority vote, shall agree that the provisions of the Covenant of the League afford her sufficient protection.

I was moved to sign this treaty by considerations which will, I hope, seem as persuasive and as irresistible to you as they seemed to me. We are bound to France by ties of friendship which we have always regarded, and shall always regard, as peculiarly sacred. She assisted us to win our freedom as a Nation. It is seriously to be doubted whether we could have won it without her gallant and timely aid. We have recently had the privilege of assisting in driving enemies, who were also enemies of the world, from her soil; but that does not pay our debt to her. Nothing can pay such a debt. She now desires that we should promise to lend our great force to keep her safe against the power she has had most reason to fear. Another great nation volunteers the same promise. It is one of the fine reversals of history that that other nation should be the very power from whom France fought to set us free. A new day has dawned. Old antagonisms are forgotten. The common cause of freedom and enlightenment has created new comradeships and a new perception of what it is wise and necessary for great nations to do to free the world of intolerable fear. Two governments who wish to be members of the League of Nations ask leave of the Council of the League to be permitted to go to the assistance of a friend whose situation has been found to be one of peculiar peril, without awaiting the advice of the League to act.

It is by taking such pledges as this that we prove ourselves faithful to the utmost to the high obligations of gratitude and tested friendship. Such an act as this seems to me one of the proofs that we are a people that sees the true heart of duty and prefers honor to its own separate course of peace.

3. A Compelling Moral Obligation

Interview by Members of Foreign Relations Committee, August 19, 1919

Soon after receiving the treaty, Henry Cabot Lodge, the chairman of the Foreign Relations Committee, spent two weeks reading its entire 268 pages to an empty chamber. The committee thereupon began hearings which ran from July 31 through September 12. During this time the breach between Wilson and the Republicans on the committee widened perceptibly. He refused to send the committee secret information on the ground that doing so would break faith with the Allies. On August 14 Lodge asked the President to meet the committee. Wilson consented and they met amidst unprecedented publicity at the White House on the morning of the 19th. Following are excerpts from the interview. The irreconcilables among Wilson's interlocutors are, in the order of their appearance: Borah, Knox, Fall, Harding, Johnson, and Brandegee.

SENATOR BORAH. Mr. President, with reference to article 10—you will observe that I am more interested in the league than any other feature of this discussion—in listening to the reading of your statement I got the impression that your view was that the first obligation of article 10, to wit—

> The members of the league undertake to respect and preserve as against external aggression the territorial integrity and existing political independence of all members of the league—

was simply a moral obligation.

THE PRESIDENT. Yes, sir; inasmuch as there is no sanction in in the treaty.

SENATOR BORAH. But that would be a legal obligation so far as the United States was concerned if it should enter into it; would it not?

THE PRESIDENT. I would not interpret it in that way, Senator, because there is involved the element of judgment as to whether the territorial integrity or existing political independence is invaded or impaired. In other words, it is an attitude of comradeship and protection among the members of the league, which in its very nature is moral and not legal.

SENATOR BORAH. If, however, the actual fact of invasion were beyond dispute, then the legal obligation, it seems to me, would immediately arise. I am simply throwing this out in order to get a full expression of views. The legal obligation would immediately arise if the fact of actual invasion were undisputed?

THE PRESIDENT. The legal obligation to apply the automatic punishments of the covenant, undoubtedly; but not the legal obligation to go to arms and actually to make war. Not the legal obligation. There might be a very strong moral obligation.

SENATOR MC CUMBER. Just so that I may understand definitely what your view is on that subject, Mr. President, do I understand you to mean that while we have two different remedies, and possibly others, we would be the sole judge of the remedy we would apply, but the obligation would still rest upon us to apply some remedy to bring about the result?

THE PRESIDENT. Yes. I can not quite accept the full wording

that you used, sir. We would have complete freedom of choice as to the application of force.

SENATOR MC CUMBER. Would we not have the same freedom of choice as to whether we would apply a commercial boycott? Are they not both under the same language, so that we would be bound by them in the same way?

THE PRESIDENT. Only in regard to certain articles. The breach of certain articles of the covenant does bring on what I have designated as an automatic boycott, and in that we would have no choice.

SENATOR KNOX. Mr. President, allow me to ask this question: Suppose that it is perfectly obvious and accepted that there is an external aggression against some power, and suppose it is perfectly obvious and accepted that it can not be repelled except by force of arms, would we be under any legal obligation to participate?

THE PRESIDENT. No, sir; but we would be under an absolutely compelling moral obligation.

SENATOR KNOX. But no legal obligation?

THE PRESIDENT. Not as I contemplate it.

SENATOR WILLIAMS. Mr. President, each nation, if I understand it, is, of course, left to judge the applicability of the principles stated to the facts in the case, whether there is or is not external aggression?

THE PRESIDENT. Yes.

SENATOR WILLIAMS. And if any country should conclude that there was not external aggression, but that France or some other country had started the trouble indirectly, we would have the same right, if I understand it, that Italy had to declare that her alliance with Germany and Austria was purely defensive, and that she did not see anything defensive in it; so when you come to judgment of the facts, outside of the international law involved, each nation must determine, if I understand, whether or not there has been external aggression?

THE PRESIDENT. I think you are right, sir. Senator [addressing Senator Knox], you were about to ask something?

SENATOR KNOX. I only wanted to tell you that I asked that question because I was a little confused by the language of your message transmitting the proposed Franco-American treaty to the Senate, in which you said, in substance, and, I think, practically in these terms, that this is only binding us to do immediately what we otherwise would have been bound to do under the league of nations?

THE PRESIDENT. Yes.

SENATOR KNOX. Perhaps I am mistaken with respect to its having been in that message. I am sure I am mistaken; it was not in that message; it was in the message that Mr. Tumulty gave out——

THE CHAIRMAN. May 10.

SENATOR KNOX. Yes.

THE PRESIDENT. Yes.

SENATOR KNOX. That it was merely binding us to do immediately, without waiting for any other power, that which we would otherwise have been bound to do under the terms of the league of nations.

THE PRESIDENT. I did not use the word "bound," but "morally bound." Let me say that you are repeating what I said to the other representatives. I said, "Of course, it is understood we would have to be convinced that it was an unprovoked movement of aggression," and they at once acquiesced in that.

SENATOR MC CUMBER. Mr. President, there are a number of Senators who sincerely believe that under the construction of article 10, taken in connection with other clauses and other articles in the treaty, the council can suggest what we should do, and, of course, while they admit the council can only advise and suggest, that it is nevertheless our moral duty to immediately obey the council, without exercising our own judgment as to whether we shall go to war or otherwise. Now, the public, the American people, a great proportion of them, have that same conviction, which is contrary to your view. Do you not think, therefore, that it would be well to have a reservation inserted in our resolution that shall so construe that section as to make it clear, not only to the American people but to the world, that Congress may use its own judgment as to what it will do, and that its failure to follow the judgment of the council will not be considered a breach of the agreement?

THE PRESIDENT. We differ, Senator, only as to the form of action. I think it would be a very serious practical mistake to put it in the resolution of ratification; but I do hope that we are at liberty, contemporaneously with our acceptance of the treaty, to interpret our moral obligation under that article.

SENATOR PITTMAN. Mr. President, I understand that, under the former method, in your opinion, it would have to go back to Germany and the other countries; while under the latter method it would not be required to go back for ratification.

THE PRESIDENT. Yes, sir; that is my judgment.

SENATOR KNOX. Mr. President, is it not true that such matters are ordinarily covered by a mere exchange of notes between powers, stating that they understand in this or that sense, or do not so understand?

THE PRESIDENT. Yes, sir; ordinarily.

SENATOR KNOX. That would be a matter that would require very little time to consummate it, if these constructions have already been placed upon it in their conversations with you.

THE PRESIDENT. But an exchange of notes is quite a different matter from having it embodied in the resolution of ratification.

SENATOR KNOX. If we embody in our resolution of ratification a statement that we understand section 10 or section 16 or section something else in a particular sense, and this Government, through its foreign department, transmits the proposed form of ratification to the chancellors of the other nations that are concerned in this treaty, and if those interpretations are the same as you have agreed upon with them in your conversations, I do not see how we would need anything more than a mere reply to that effect.

THE PRESIDENT. It would need confirmation.

SENATOR KNOX. Yes; it would need confirmation in that sense.

THE PRESIDENT. My judgment is that the embodying of that in the terms of the resolution of ratification would be acquiescence not only in the interpretation but in the very phraseology of the interpretation, because it would form a part of the contract.

SENATOR KNOX. It might with us, because we have so much machinery for dealing with treaties, but in other countries where it is much more simple I should think it would not be.

THE PRESIDENT. It is simple legally, Senator; but, for example, this treaty has been submitted to legislatures to which the Government was not, by law, obliged to submit it, and it is everywhere being treated as a legislative matter—I mean, so far as the ratification is concerned.

SENATOR KNOX. You mean in countries where, under their constitutions, there are provisions that treaties ordinarily are not submitted to the legislative branch of the Government, this treaty is being so submitted?

THE PRESIDENT. So I understand.

SENATOR KNOX. Where there are two branches of the legislative department, an upper and a lower branch, do you know whether it is being submitted to both?

THE PRESIDENT. I think not, sir. I am not certain about that; but my memory is it is not.

SENATOR FALL. Mr. President, the idea has struck me and I have entertained the view, since reading the treaty and the league, that Germany having signed the treaty but not being yet a member of the league, any reservations which we might make here would be met by Germany either joining the league or refusing to join the league. It would not be submitted to her at all now, because she is not a member of the league? You catch the point?

THE PRESIDENT. Yes. I differ with you there, Senator. One of the reasons for putting the league in the treaty was that Germany was not going to be admitted to the league immediately, and we felt that it was very necessary that we should get her acknowledgment—acceptance—of the league as an international authority, partly because we were excluding her, so that she would thereafter have no ground for questioning such authority as the league might exercise under its covenant.

SENATOR FALL. Precisely.

THE PRESIDENT. Therefore, I think it would be necessary for her to acquiesce in a league the powers of which were differently construed.

SENATOR FALL. Precisely; but her acquiescence would be by her accepting the invitation, when extended, either to join the league or not to join the league. In other words, upon ratification by three of the powers, a status of peace is established, and as to those three powers and Germany all the rules and regulations contained in the treaty of peace become operative. As to the other nations which have not ratified, the status of peace exists; that is, war has terminated. Now, that being the case, and Germany being out of the league—not having been invited to join the league—if in ratifying the treaty we ratify it with certain explanations or reservations, even in the ratifying resolution, when the time comes and Germany is invited to become a member of the league, or when she applies, under the admission clause of the league, for membership therein, if she enters she of course accepts our reservations. If she makes a qualified application, then it is for the league itself to consider whether she will be admitted?

THE PRESIDENT. I do not follow your reasoning in the matter, Senator, because this is not merely a question of either membership or nonmembership. The covenant is a part of the treaty, it is a part of the treaty which she has signed, and we are not at liberty to change any part of that treaty without the acquiescence of the other contracting party.

SENATOR FALL. Well, Mr. President, of course it is not my purpose to enter into an argument, but we are here for information. There are provisions for the amendment of the articles. Germany is out of the league. Any amendment proposed by the other members of the league prior to her coming into the league would not be submitted to her, would it, she not being a member?

THE PRESIDENT. I will admit that that point had not occurred to me. No, she would not.

SENATOR FALL. Then so far as we are concerned we could make a recommendation in the nature of an amendment.

SENATOR PITTMAN. She has already agreed by this treaty that she has signed that the members may amend it.

THE PRESIDENT. Yes.

SENATOR FALL. Precisely, and we could come in with an amendment.

SENATOR HITCHCOCK. Did I understand your first reply to Senator Fall to be that Germany under this treaty already had a relationship to the league by reason of its international character, and its participation in a number of questions that Germany was interested in?

THE PRESIDENT. Yes.

SENATOR HITCHCOCK. So that it has a relationship to the league of nations even before the time that it may apply for membership.

THE PRESIDENT. Yes.

SENATOR MC CUMBER. Mr. President, you answered one question that I think possibly may need a little elucidation. If I remember rightly, in reference to reparation your statement was that the commission would have to decide whether the United States should claim her proportion of the reparation.

THE PRESIDENT. That the commission would have to do it? No; we decide whether we claim it or not.

SENATOR MC CUMBER. That is what I want to make clear. I think the question was asked if the commission was to decide that, and I thought your answer said yes. That is the reason I asked the question.

THE PRESIDENT. The claim would have to come from us, of course.

SENATOR MC CUMBER. It would have to be through an act of Congress, would it not?

THE PRESIDENT. I would have to be instructed about that, Senator. I do not know.

SENATOR MC CUMBER. Whatever right the United States would receive under the treaty for reparation or indemnity is one that runs to the United States, and therefore to divest ourselves of that right would require an act of Congress.

THE PRESIDENT. To divest ourselves of it? I suppose so.

SENATOR KNOX. In the question of the Japanese indemnity, that was done by a joint resolution.

SENATOR MC CUMBER. I thought the President said it would have to be decided by the constituted authority.

SENATOR KNOX. I did not understand that he said that.

SENATOR SWANSON. I understand that the reparation is to be decided upon a representation made by the associated powers. It would seem that the President under that agreement with France, Great Britain, and other nations would have to submit it to the Senate for ratification, and the agreement would have to be reported.

SENATOR MC CUMBER. In each case it would have the force of law.

SENATOR SWANSON. If the Senate wanted to ratify it, it would take an act of Congress.

SENATOR WILLIAMS. This question of reparation does not in any way affect our rights to prewar indemnities?

THE PRESIDENT. That is expressly stated.

SENATOR WILLIAMS. That is expressly stated. Now, then, one other question. Germany has signed this treaty with the covenant of the league in it, and she is subject to be dealt with as a non-member under the treaty, and has very much fewer privileges than a member?

THE PRESIDENT. Yes.

SENATOR NEW. Mr. President, may I ask a question here? What effort was made by the delegates there to prevent the proceedings of the reparations committee from being required to be secret?

THE PRESIDENT. I beg your pardon, Senator.

SENATOR NEW. What effort, if any, was made by the American delegates to prevent the proceedings of the reparation commission from being required to be secret, and did the American delegates protest that America be omitted from this commission on account of that thing?

THE PRESIDENT. Nothing was said about it, that I remember.

SENATOR BORAH. Mr. President, coming back for a moment to the subject from which we were diverted a moment ago, and coupling with article 10 article 11, in order that we may have the construction of the committee which framed the league as to both of those articles, as I understand it from your statement, the committee's view was that the obligations under articles 10 and 11, whatever they are, are moral obligations.

THE PRESIDENT. Remind me of the eleventh. I do not remember that by number.

SENATOR BORAH (reading):

> Any war or threat of war, whether immediately affecting any of the members of the league or not, is hereby declared a matter of concern to the whole league, and the league shall take any action that may be deemed wise and effectual to safeguard the peace of nations.

What I am particularly anxious to know is whether or not the construction which was placed upon these two articles by the committee which framed the league was that it was a binding obligation from a legal standpoint, or merely a moral obligation.

THE PRESIDENT. Senator, I tried to answer with regard to article 10.

SENATOR BORAH. Yes; exactly.

THE PRESIDENT. I would apply it equally with regard to article 11, though I ought to hasten to say that we did not formulate these interpretations. I can only speak from my confident impression from the debates that accompanied the formulation of the covenant.

SENATOR BORAH. Yes; I understand; and your construction of article 11 is the same as that of article 10?

THE PRESIDENT. Yes.

SENATOR BORAH. As to the question of legal obligation. That is all I desire to ask at present.

SENATOR HARDING. Right there, Mr. President, if there is nothing more than a moral obligation on the part of any member of the league, what avail articles 10 and 11?

THE PRESIDENT. Why, Senator, it is surprising that that question should be asked. If we undertake an obligation we are bound in the most solemn way to carry it out.

SENATOR HARDING. If you believe there is nothing more to this than a moral obligation, any nation will assume a moral obligation on its own account. Is it a moral obligation? The point I am trying to get at is, suppose something arises affecting the peace of the world, and the council takes steps as provided here to conserve or preserve, and announces its decision, and every nation in the league takes advantage of the construction that you place upon these articles and says, "Well, this is only a moral obligation, and we assume that the nation involved does not deserve our participation or protection," and the whole thing amounts to nothing but an expression of the league council.

THE PRESIDENT. There is a national good conscience in such a matter. I should think that was one of the most serious things that could possibly happen. When I speak of a legal obligation, I mean one that specifically binds you to do a particular thing under certain sanctions. That is a legal obligation. Now a moral obligation is of course superior to a legal obligation, and, if I may say so, has a greater binding force; only there always remains in the moral obligation the right to exercise one's judgment as to whether it is indeed incumbent upon one in those circumstances to do that thing. In every moral obligation there is an element of judgment. In a legal obligation there is no element of judgment.

SENATOR JOHNSON of California. But, Mr. President, when a moral obligation is undoubted it will impel action more readily than a legal obligation.

THE PRESIDENT. If it is undoubted, yes; but that involves the circumstances of the particular case, Senator.

SENATOR JOHNSON of California. Yes; necessarily.

SENATOR HARDING. In answering Senator Knox a moment ago you spoke of a compelling moral obligation. Would you think that any less binding than a specific legal obligation?

THE PRESIDENT. Not less binding, but operative in a different way because of the element of judgment.

SENATOR HARDING. But not less likely to involve us in armed participation?

THE PRESIDENT. In trifling matters, very much less likely.

SENATOR HARDING. To clear my slow mind, let me take a specific case. Suppose the allotted territory which comes under the control of Italy should in some way be assailed from the Balkan States and the council of the league should immediately look upon that as a threat of war involving other nations and should say that the nations of the league should immediately contribute an armed force to stop that war or to bring the attacking nation to terms, would we be a perfidious people, if I may use that term, or would we violate our obligations, if we failed to participate in the defense of Italy?

THE PRESIDENT. We would be our own judges as to whether we were obliged in those circumstances to act in that way or not.

SENATOR HITCHCOCK. In such a case the council would only act unanimously, and our representative on the council of course would have to concur in any advice given.

THE PRESIDENT. Certainly; we would always in such case advise ourselves.

SENATOR WILLIAMS. But if in such case, Mr. President, we concluded that the case provided for and prescribed had arisen and that the extraneous attack existed and that it fell within the terms of the treaty, then we would be untrue if we did not keep our word?

THE PRESIDENT. Certainly.

SENATOR BORAH. In other words, then, that transfers the power to decide whether we should act from the Congress of the United States to one individual who sits on the council.

SENATOR WILLIAMS. No, it does not; it merely provides that when the council acts in accordance with the prescribed terms and we see that it has acted, then Congress will, as a matter of faith keeping, act itself; and, if Congress does not, Congress will do a dishonorable thing.

SENATOR BORAH. Precisely so; so that the matter gets back to the point where one individual has bound Congress.

SENATOR HITCHCOCK. I hope my question to the President will not be interpreted in that way. My question to the President was whether the matter would even come before this country as the advice of the council until the American representative had concurred with the other eight members of the council. After he had concurred it would then be up to Congress to decide.

THE PRESIDENT. You are quite right, Senator. And let me suggest that I find nothing was more clearly in the consciousness of the men who were discussing these very important matters than that most of the nations concerned had popular governments. They were all the time aware of the fact that it would depend upon the approving or disapproving state of opinion of their countries how their representatives in the council would vote in matters of this sort; and it is inconceivable to me that, unless the opinion of the United States, the moral and practical judgment of the people of the United States, approved, the representative of the United States on the council should vote any such advice as would lead us into war.

SENATOR BORAH. Mr. President, does the special alliance treaty with France which has been submitted to us rest upon any other basis as to legal and moral obligation than that of article 10 and article 11 which you have just described?

THE PRESIDENT. No, sir.

SENATOR BORAH. That is also, as you understand it, simply our moral obligations which we enter into with France?

THE PRESIDENT. Yes.

SENATOR WILLIAMS. All international obligations are moral ones.

SENATOR PITTMAN. There is one thing I do not understand about Senator Borah's question. He has stated that he gathers from what you said that it all rests with our representative on the council. Even if our representative on the council advises as a member of the council, and the council is unanimous, is it not then still up to Congress either to accept or reject that advice?

THE PRESIDENT. Oh, yes; but I understood the Senator to mean that it would be dependent on our representative.

SENATOR JOHNSON of California. May I take the example that was just suggested concerning the Balkan States and a possible attack upon the new territories of Italy. Assuming that that is a case of external aggression by the Balkan States concerning the new territory that Italy has acquired by the peace treaty, upon us rests a compelling moral obligation to do our part in preventing that, does there not?

THE PRESIDENT. Yes.

SENATOR JOHNSON of California. And that compelling moral obligation would require us to use such means as would seem appropriate, either economic or force? Is not that correct?

THE PRESIDENT. Deemed appropriate by whom? That is really the point.

SENATOR JOHNSON of California. Of course, deemed appropriate for the purpose of preventing and frustrating the aggression.

THE PRESIDENT. Deemed by us appropriate?

SENATOR JOHNSON of California. I assume of necessity it would have to be deemed by us to bind us as a compelling moral obligation to prevent the aggression in the case named.

THE PRESIDENT. Yes.

SENATOR MC CUMBER. Mr. President, I think, due to my own fault, I do not fully comprehend your distinction between a moral and a legal obligation in a treaty. If we enter into a treaty with France to defend her against aggression from Germany for any length of time, that is a legal obligation, is it not?

THE PRESIDENT. Legal in the sense that a treaty is of binding force; yes.

SENATOR MC CUMBER. Yes; that is what I meant. It is as legal as any treaty could be made legal, and there is also a moral obligation to keep that treaty, is there not?

THE PRESIDENT. Yes, sir. I happened to hear Senator Knox say what I am glad to adopt. It is a legal obligation with a moral sanction.

SENATOR BORAH. That is true generally, is it not?

THE PRESIDENT. Yes, Senator; but I have already defined in what special sense I use the word "legal."

SENATOR MC CUMBER. To my mind those two articles are legal obligations to be carried out by the moral conscience of the American people if the conditions justify it.

THE PRESIDENT. You see we are speaking of two different fields, and therefore the language does not fit. In international law the word "legal" does not mean the same as in national law, and the word hardly applies.

SENATOR BRANDEGEE. I have here the President's statement which he read to us when we met here this morning, and in it he states:

> Nothing, I am led to believe, stands in the way of the ratification of the treaty except certain doubts with regard to the meaning and implication of certain articles of the covenant of the league of nations; and I must frankly say that I am unable to understand why such doubts should be entertained.

Now, I do not believe the President is correctly informed as to the situation if he believes that. There are things in the treaty itself which militate against the ratification, in my opinion, of the treaty without amendment. Did you have in mind, Mr. President, when you read that to us, the Shantung provision of the treaty?

THE PRESIDENT. I certainly had that in mind, Senator, but I did not understand that that stood in the way of ratification. I am, of course, acting only upon such information as I have received.

SENATOR BRANDEGEE. I understand—and that is the reason of taking the liberty of suggesting to you that you may not be well informed in this respect. Of course there is opposition by a great many Senators to the entire covenant of the league of nations, which I have no doubt you know, that is, article 1 of the treaty of Versailles. Then there is opposition to the various parts of the covenants of the league, and not to the whole league, by other Senators. Then there is a great opposition, fundamental and sincere, to the Shantung provision, which is in the body of the treaty itself, and which can only be cured by an amendment. As I understand it, no reservation that we could make in the resolution of ratification would be effective to strike out the Shantung provision. It must be cured, if it is cured, by a straight out-and-out amendment, striking that from the treaty. That, of course, would necessitate the resubmission of the treaty to the signatories who have already signed it.

Now, you state later on that every suggestion of the United States was accepted, that is after you went back, after you had your conference with us last March, and having obtained our views as to the necessity for certain changes in the first draft of the covenant, you state [reading]:

The view of the United States with regard to the questions I have mentioned had, in fact, already been accepted by the commission and there was supposed to be nothing inconsistent with them in the draft of the covenant first adopted.

And omitting a few lines which do not apply to that you say [reading]:

There was absolutely no doubt as to the meaning of any one of the resulting provisions of the covenant in the minds of those who participated in drafting them, and I respectfully submit that there is nothing vague or doubtful in their wording.

Of course that is your opinion, if I may say so.

THE PRESIDENT. Yes, sir.

SENATOR BRANDEGEE. But you are familiar with the statements, I have no doubt, that ex-Senator Root, Justice Hughes, Mr. Taft, and other able lawyers of the country have made with respect to the necessity for reservations if we are to ratify the treaty, are you not?

THE PRESIDENT. Yes, sir.

SENATOR BRANDEGEE. That is, you admit that there are grave doubts among the ablest lawyers of the country as to the necessity for reservations or the alternative between reservations and ratifying the whole treaty, as it is expressed in the vernacular, without the dotting of an "i" or the crossing of a "t."

THE PRESIDENT. I admit that there are those difficulties in a great many minds.

SENATOR BRANDEGEE. Now, of course, it is true, is it not, that if difficulties arise as to the construction of any provision of the treaty after we have passed from the scene, what we thought the provisions of the treaty or of the covenant meant will not be very powerful in the construction that may be placed upon it by those who then have to determine what it means, will it?

THE PRESIDENT. The vote of the United States will be essential.

SENATOR BRANDEGEE. I do not mean that. The fact that you think now that everything in the treaty is plain and that there is no doubt about the meaning of any provisions, and the fact that I think there is grave doubt about many of the provisions, will not seriously affect the opinion of the council or of the arbitrator that finally passes upon the true meaning of the treaty when dispute arises.

THE PRESIDENT. No, Senator; but the plain wording of the treaty will have a great deal to do, and the meaning of the wording is plain.

SENATOR BRANDEGEE. That is simply another way of stating, is it not, that you are clear in your opinion that the provisions of the treaty are plain? But I am suggesting that there will be a dispute between nations as to what the treaty means after we have passed from the scene.

THE PRESIDENT. No, sir; it is a question of being confident of what language means, not confident of an opinion.

SENATOR BRINDEGEE. I mean, we derive our opinions as to the meanings of the treaty from the language of the treaty, do we not?

THE PRESIDENT. Yes.

SENATOR BRANDEGEE. Now they would derive their construction of what the treaty means from the language of it, we not being there?

THE PRESIDENT. Yes.

SENATOR BRANDEGEE. So that what we think about it now will not be determinative in an international court or before an arbitrator twenty years hence in case of a dispute between two nations as to the meaning of the treaty?

THE PRESIDENT. Certainly not, but the language will.

SENATOR BRANDEGEE. Of course they will have the language before them, but the language which determines it is now in dispute between you and certain lawyers of the country and certain Senators as to its meaning. Now what provision is there in the treaty for the determination of a dispute as to the interpretation of a clause of the treaty if such dispute arises?

THE PRESIDENT. The covenant states that there are certain questions which are acknowledged as being especially suitable for submission to arbitraton. One of those is the meaning of the treaty.

SENATOR BRANDEGEE. What does the treaty provide about that?

THE PRESIDENT. You have it there, sir.

SENATOR BRANDEGEE. Yes, sir; I wondered if you remembered it.

THE PRESIDENT. I think I do so, but you have the language.

SENATOR BRANDEGEE. Yes. Article 12 of the league provides [reading]:

The members of the league agree that if there should arise between them any dispute likely to lead to a rupture, they will submit the matter either to arbitration or to inquiry by the council, and they agree in no case to resort to war until three months after the award by the arbitrators or the report by the council.

That is, if there is a dispute, as I construe this, between members of the league as to the meaning of the covenant or any article thereof, it shall be referred to the arbitrators.

THE PRESIDENT. Only if the parties agree.

SENATOR BRANDEGEE. Or to the council?

THE PRESIDENT. Or to the council; yes.

SENATOR BRANDEGEE. That is, the council is to determine the meaning of the covenant?

THE PRESIDENT. No, Senator; I beg your pardon. There are two processes. If the parties agree to submit to arbitration, of course it is submitted to arbitration, and the decision is final. If they think it is a question that they are not willing to submit to arbitration, then they must submit it to the council for an expression of opinion and a recommendation, but that opinion and recommendation do not bind.

SENATOR BRANDEGEE. Is there any possible way authoritatively of determining without war what the treaty means?

THE PRESIDENT. That is true of every treaty, Senator. If you re-express it in the langugae of the Senators to whom you refer and there is a dispute about the meaning of that, the same would apply. You can not use any language, I assume, which could not possibly give rise to some sort of dispute.

SENATOR BRANDEGEE. I assume that if it provided that if there should arise between the members of the league any dispute in relation to the construction of any article of the covenant of the league of nations, such dispute should be referred to an arbitrator, and the members would agree to be bound by its decision; that would be an agreement for an authoritative determination of what the treaty meant.

THE PRESIDENT. Yes.

SENATOR BRANDEGEE. Now, as it is they will submit the matter either to arbitration or to inquiry by the council, and so forth. Now, you say that the opinion of the council to which the dispute has been submitted is only advisory?

THE PRESIDENT. Yes, sir.

SENATOR BRANDEGEE. Then suppose one party to the dispute against whom the council decides declines to abide by it?

THE PRESIDENT. Then there is war, but not within three months of the opinion of the council.

SENATOR BRANDEGEE. Under article 10 the members of the league undertake to respect and preserve as against external aggression the territorial integrity and existing political independence of all members of the league. That is a contract between the signatories. We say: "We undertake to preserve the territorial integrity of the members against external aggression," which means that we contract to do it, does it not?

THE PRESIDENT. We engage to do it.

SENATOR BRANDEGEE. It means an international contract, does it not, a compact, an agreement?

THE PRESIDENT. Yes.

SENATOR BRANDEGEE. Whether that is a moral or legal obligation, it is an obligation?

THE PRESIDENT. Yes.

SENATOR BRANDEGEE. Of course, it is a moral duty to keep a promise, and this is an international promise; so that the distinction between a moral obligation and a legal one seems to me to be not of great importance, because we are obligated in any event.

THE PRESIDENT. Pardon me; I think it is of the great importance, because the element of judgment enters into it as it does not in the other.

SENATOR BRANDEGEE. You mean the judgment as to whether or not it is a moral obligation?

THE PRESIDENT. No. For example, a question is submitted to arbitration and it is agreed that the decision shall be final. The judgment of one of the parties to the controversy may be that the decision is a very bad one, but it has to accept it; the element of judgment is excluded altogether; but, with regard to the method of fulfilling the obligations of a covenant like that under consideration there is freedom of judgment on the part of the individual members of the league. It seems to me that makes a very considerable difference.

SENATOR HARDING. Will the Senator permit me to interrupt right there?

SENATOR BRANDEGEE. I will.

SENATOR HARDING. I dislike to interrupt the Senator.

SENATOR BRANDEGEE. I yield to the Senator.

SENATOR HARDING. The President expressed a while ago surprise that I raised a question as to the value of this compact because of the moral obligation feature. Let me premise by the statement that I look upon a moral obligation as that which the conscience of the contracting party impels. The conscience of any nation in Europe, for example, may be warped by its prejudices, racial, geographical, and otherwise. If that be true and any nation may put aside or exercise its judgment as to the moral obligation in accepting any recommendation of the league, really what do we get out of this international compact in the enforcement of any decree?

THE PRESIDENT. We get the centering upon it generally of the definite opinion of the world, expressed through the authoritative organs of the responsible governments.

SENATOR HARDING. Another question: That is surrendering the suggestion of a moral obligation for this Republic to the prejudices or necessities of the nations of the Old World, is it not?

THE PRESIDENT. I do not understand that we make such a surrender.

SENATOR HARDING. Would you not understand a decree by the council to be a suggestion of this moral obligation?

THE PRESIDENT. Certainly I would, but we would have to concur in that before it had any force of any kind.

SENATOR HARDING. Would it not be quite as moral for this Republic itself to determine its moral obligations?

THE PRESIDENT. Undoubtedly, Senator; but in the meantime the world would not have the knowledge before it that there will be concerted action by all the responsible governments of the world in the protection of the peace of the world. The minute you do away with that assurance to the world you have reached the situation which produced the German war.

SENATOR HARDING. What becomes of our standing among nations if the council fixes a moral obligation upon us and we reject the judgment of the council as to the moral obligation?

THE PRESIDENT. Pardon me if I remind you that we always have to concur in that.

SENATOR HARDING. Precisely; but the council states what constitutes the moral obligation, if we agree; but if we do not agree, then, in the eyes of the world we have rejected its judgment as to a moral obligation.

THE PRESIDENT. Certainly; and I hold that we are at liberty to do that, if our moral judgment honestly differs from the moral judgment of the world.

SENATOR HARDING. Then, let us go back to the original inquiry. What permanent value is there, then, to this compact?

THE PRESIDENT. The greatest permanent value, Senator, is the point that I have raised. We are assuming that the United States will not concur in the general moral judgment of the world. In my opinion, she generally will. If it had been known that this war was coming on, her moral judgment would have concurred with that of the other Governments of the world, with that of the other peoples of the world; and if Germany had known that there was a possibility of that sort of concurrence, she never would have dared to do what she did. Without such notice served on the powers that may wish to repeat the folly that Germany commenced, there is no assurance to the world that there will be peace even for a generation, whereas if they know beforehand that there will be that concert of judgment, there is the most tremendous guaranty.

SENATOR HARDING. But, Mr. President, nobody expressed for us our moral obligation to enter into this war. That was our own expression, was it not?

THE PRESIDENT. Certainly; it was our concurrence in the judgment of the world.

SENATOR HARDING. One of the points I am getting at, if I can make it clear, is the necessity of a written compact for this Republic to fulfill its moral obligations to civilization.

THE PRESIDENT. Senator, this Republic, if I interpret it rightly, does not need a suggestion from any quarter to fulfill its moral obligations.

SENATOR HARDING. I quite agree with that.

THE PRESIDENT. But it steadies the whole world by its promise beforehand that it will stand with other nations of similar judgment to maintain right in the world.

SENATOR FALL. Mr. President, then if the commissioner of the United States on the council were to join with the other members of the council in fixing a moral obligation upon the United States, and the Congress and the President, acting as part of the legislative branch of the Government, were to reject that judgment, would it not have a very disastrous effect upon the league, throw the world into chaos, and undo all that has been done?

THE PRESIDENT. It might; but you are assuming a case——

SENATOR FALL. Certainly; we have to assume cases.

THE PRESIDENT. Where we would have to assume that responsibility, because, being part of the Government, we would in every case really express the judgment of the American people, and if the unhappy time should ever come when that judgment is against the judgment of the rest of the world we would have to express it.

SENATOR FALL. Certainly. Mr. President, I am possibly looking, as Bacon said, at a distance.

SENATOR MCCUMBER. Would our moral conviction of the unrighteousness of the German war have brought us into this war if Germany had not committed any acts against us, without the league of nations, as, of course, we had no league of nations at that time?

THE PRESIDENT. I hope it would eventually, Senator, as things developed.

SENATOR MC CUMBER. Do you think if Germany had committed no act of war or no act of injustice against our citizens that we would have gotten into this war?

THE PRESIDENT. I do think so.

SENATOR MC CUMBER. You think we would have gotten in anyway?

THE PRESIDENT. I do.

SENATOR BRANDEGEE. If I may be allowed to resume, for I kept still all morning——

SENATOR FALL. If the Senator will pardon me a moment, I am going to ask the President to excuse me, as I have an engagement.

THE PRESIDENT. I am sorry, Senator, that you are obliged to leave.

SENATOR FALL. I regret, sir, that I have an engagement with my wife, who is not in very good health.

SENATOR BRANDEGEE. Now, if I may proceed without interruption, which breaks the continuity of my thought and uses a great deal of time, I will be through in a very few minutes. As I understand the President, his construction of article 10 is that if the council considers the question of external aggression upon a member of the league, we, having signed this treaty with article 10 in it, in which we undertake to preserve against external aggression the territorial integrity of all members of the league, can then say, it is a moral question into which the element of judgment enters and we, considering our judgment binding at the time, do not care to agree to the recommendation of the council. If every member of the league is at liberty to take that view of its moral and legal obligations under article 10, and declines to do what the council recommends, and if it is known in advance that that is the construction placed upon article 10 by those who framed it, it does not seem to me—and this is merely my opinion—that the terror to wrongdoers by what is hoped to be the united, concerted action of the members of the league in the concentration of its powers to suppress the wrongdoer will have the effect that the President thinks it will. In other words, I do not think that Germany would have refrained from war if she had known that article 10 was in existence.

Article 10 says:

> In case of any such aggression, or in case of any threat or danger of such aggression, the council shall advise upon the means by which this obligation shall be fulfilled.

There is no doubt that that is an obligation in a contract, and I know of but one way to perform an obligation that you contracted to perform, and that is to perform it. I do not think that it admits of any qualifications after you sign the treaty. I want to call attention also to the fact that the external aggression which we undertake, if we sign this treaty, to repel or guarantee against is not stated in the treaty at all to be an unwarranted aggression. I wish to ask the President, if the league were in existence and Hungary and Roumania were members of it, and Roumania were in the position she now is, having raided the territorial integrity of Hungary and marched through its capital and occupied it, and the council, as its duty would be under the covenant, considered what was best to be done and advised us to send immediately to cooperate with them 100,000 men, whether we would be at liberty to discuss whether we were morally bound by article 10 of the covenant and decline to send the men, and, if we were, could we do it without risking being called an "international slacker" by the other members of the league?

THE PRESIDENT. Senator, since you have made the case a concrete one I am afraid I ought not to answer it, because it involves a judgment as between Roumania and Hungary.

SENATOR BRANDEGEE. I withdraw the names of the two countries, and assume the circumstances.

THE PRESIDENT. Let me say that I take it for granted that in practically every case the United States would respond; but that does not seem to be the question. I quite agree with you that a moral obligation is to be fulfilled, and I am confident that our Nation will fulfill it, but that does not remove from each individual case the element of judgment which we are free to exercise in two stages: We are, first, free to exercise it in the vote of our representative on the council, who will of course act under instructions from the home Government; and, in the second place, we are to exercise it when the President, acting upon the action of the council, makes his recommendation to Congress. Then, Congress is to exercise its judgment as to whether or not the instructions of the Executive to our member of the council were well founded, and whether the case is one of distinct moral obligation.

SENATOR BRANDEGEE. Suppose that each member of the council, as you say, acting under instructions from its home Government, including our representative on the council, should think, for instance, that Roumania was entirely right in some invasion of Hungary, and public sentiment was that way, but that our Government instructed our representative to vote with the foreign members of the council to support Hungary—suppose the public sentiment of the other members and of the people of this country were in favor of Roumania, what sort of a position would we be in to fulfill our guaranty?

THE PRESIDENT. In order to answer that question I must go a little bit afield. In the first place, I understand that article to mean that no nation is at liberty to invade the territorial integrity of another. That does not mean to invade for purposes of warfare, but to impair the territorial integrity of another nation. Its territorial integrity is not destroyed by armed intervention; it is destroyed by the retention of territory, by taking territory away from it; that impairs its territorial integrity. I understand the covenant to mean that that is in no case permissible by the action of a single nation against another; that there is only one permissible method and that is, if territorial arrangements are unsatisfactory, that they should be brought to the attention of the world through the league and that then the league should exercise such rights as it may be able to exercise for a readjustment of boundaries.

I believe that territorial aggression, in the sense of territorial capture, is, by the wording of the act, made illegitimate.

SENATOR BRANDEGEE. The words are not "territorial aggression," but "external aggression."

THE PRESIDENT. But it says the preservation of its territorial integrity against external aggression.

SENATOR BRANDEGEE. Suppose the external aggressor, having gotten within the territory of the aggressee, stays there?

THE PRESIDENT. Then that impairs the territorial integrity.

SENATOR BRANDEGEE. Certainly; and then on a call by the council for us to perform our international contract under article 10, if Congress does not favor performing it, you think we would not be subject to criticism by the other members of the league?

THE PRESIDENT. Oh, we might be subject to criticism; but I think Congress would be at liberty to form its own judgment as to the circumstances.

SENATOR BRANDEGEE. I agree with you entirely, and under our Constitution Congress would have to do so.

THE PRESIDENT. Yes; that is understood by all.

SENATOR BRANDEGEE. Of course; but I am assuming if the council should advise us to do a certain thing, and Congress refused to do it—and if every nation's representative assembly can do the same thing, it seems to me like a rope of sand and not an effective tribunal which would result in promoting peace.

THE PRESIDENT. The reason I do not agree with you, Senator, is that I do not think such a refusal would likely often occur. I believe it would be only upon the gravest grounds—and in case Congress is right, I am indifferent to foreign criticism.

SENATOR BRANDEGEE. Of course, we would always think we were right, I assume. Now, I wish to call your attention to article 15. . . .

4. As Great as the Cause of Mankind

Western Tour, September 4–15, 1919

It was apparent to Wilson following his interview of August 19 that a significant number of Republicans were determined to destroy or cripple the treaty. The long hearings were obviously a delaying tactic. Moreover, an extensive campaign of propaganda against the treaty had gotten under way, thanks to the financial contributions of two of the most reactionary moguls in the country, Henry Clay Frick and Andrew Mellon. And so Wilson, disregarding the advice of his friends, decided to tour the West where his idealism had always received a warm response. The schedule was brutal. Covering 9,500 miles, he delivered some forty speeches, each averaging an hour, in thirty cities; between speechs he participated in parades and spoke to small gatherings. It was inevitable that Wilson should give way under the strain. On September 25 he collapsed after speaking in Pueblo, Colorado. He still wanted to speak at the next stop, Wichita, Kansas, but his strength had completely left him, and he returned to Washington. A week after his collapse he suffered a stroke that incapacitated him for the rest of his life.

At Columbus, Ohio, September 4

. . . SOME GENTLEMEN have feared with regard to the League of Nations that we will be obliged to do things we do not want to do. If the treaty were wrong, that might be so, but if the treaty is right, we will wish to preserve right. I think I know the heart of this great people whom I, for the time being, have the high honor to represent better than some other men that I hear talk. I have been bred, and am proud to have been bred, in the old revolutionary school which set this Government up, when it was set up as the friend of mankind, and I know if they do not that America has never lost that vision or that purpose. But I have not the slightest fear that arms will be necessary if the purpose is there. If I know that my adversary is armed and I am not, I do not press the controversy, and if any nation entertains selfish purposes set against the principles established in this treaty and is told by the rest of the world that it must withdraw its claims, it will not press them.

The heart of this treaty then, my fellow citizens, is not even that it punishes Germany. That is a temporary thing. It is that it rectifies the age-long wrongs which characterized the history of Europe. There were some of us who wished that the scope of the treaty would reach some other age-long wrongs. It was a big job, and I do not say that we wished that it were bigger, but there were other wrongs elsewhere than in Europe and of the same kind which no doubt ought to be righted, and some day will be righted, but which we could not draw into the treaty because we could deal only with the countries whom the war had engulfed and affected. But so far as the scope of our authority went, we rectified the wrongs which have been the fertile source of war in Europe.

Have you ever reflected, my fellow countrymen, on the real source of revolution? Men do not start revolutions in a sudden passion. Do you remember what Thomas Carlyle said about the French Revolution? He was speaking of the so-called Hundred Days Terror which reigned not only in Paris, but throughout France, in the days of the French Revolution, and he reminded his readers that back of that hundred days lay several hundred years of agony and of wrong. The French people had been deeply and consistently wronged by their Government, robbed, their human rights disregarded, and the slow agony of those hundreds of years had after awhile gathered into a hot anger that could not be suppressed. Revolutions do not spring up overnight. Revolutions come from the long suppression of the human spirit. Revolutions come because men know that they have rights and that they are disregarded; and when we think of the future of the world in connection with this treaty we must remember that one of the chief efforts of those who made this treaty was to remove that anger from the heart of great peoples, great peoples who had always been suppressed, who had always been used, and who had always been the tools in the hands of governments, generally alien governments, not their own. The makers of the treaty knew that if these wrongs were not removed, there could be no peace in the world, because, after all, my fellow citizens, war comes from the seed of wrong and not from the seed of right. This treaty is an attempt to right the history of Europe, and, in my humble judgment, it is a measurable success. . . .

We of all peoples in the world, my fellow citizens, ought to be able to understand the questions of this treaty without anybody explaining them to us, for we are made up out of all peoples of the world. I dare say that in this audience there are representatives of practically all the people dealt with in this treaty. You do not have to have me explain national aspirations to you. You have been brought up on them. You have learned of them since you were children, and it is those national aspirations which we sought to release and give an outlet to in this great treaty.

But we did much more than that. This treaty contains among other things a Magna Charta of labor—a thing unheard of until this interesting year of grace. There is a whole section of the treaty devoted to arrangements by which the interests of those who labor with their hands all over the world, whether they be men or women or children, are sought to be safeguarded; and next month there is to meet the first assembly under this section of the League. Let me tell you, it will meet whether the treaty is ratified by that time or not. There is to meet an assembly which represents the interests of laboring men throughout the world. Not their political interests; there is nothing political about it. It is the interests of men concerning the conditions of their labor; concerning the character of labor which women shall engage in, the character of labor which children shall be permitted to engage in; the hours of labor; and, incidentally, of course, the remuneration of labor; that labor shall be remunerated in proportion, of course, to the maintenance of the standard of living, which is proper, for the man who is expected to give his whole brain and intelligence and energy to a particular task. I hear very little said about the Magna Charta of labor which is embodied in this treaty. It forecasts the day, which ought to have come long ago, when statesmen will realize that no nation is fortunate which is not happy and that no nation can be happy whose people are not contented; contented in their lives and fortunate in the circumstances of their lives.

If I were to state what seems to me the central idea of this treaty, it would be this: It is almost a discovery in international conventions that nations do not consist of their governments but consist of their people. That is a rudimentary idea. It seems to us in America to go without saying, but, my fellow citizens, it was never the leading idea in any other international congress that

I ever heard of; that is to say, any international congress made up of the representatives of governments. They were always thinking of national policy, of national advantage, of the rivalries of trade, of the advantages of territorial conquest. There is nothing of that in this treaty. You will notice that even the territories which are taken away from Germany, like her colonies, are not given to anybody. There is not a single act of annexation in this treaty. Territories inhabited by people not yet able to govern themselves, either because of economical or other circumstances, are put under the care of powers, who are to act as trustees—trustees responsible in the forum of the world at the bar of the League of Nations, and the terms upon which they are to exercise their trusteeship are outlined. They are not to use those people by way of draft to fight their wars for them. They are not to permit any form of slavery among them, or of enforced labor. They are to see to it that there are humane conditions of labor with regard not only to the women and children but to the men also. They are to establish no fortifications. They are to regulate the liquor and the opium traffic. They are to see to it, in other words, that the lives of the people whose care they assume—not sovereignty over whom they assume—are kept clean and safe and wholesome. There again the principle of the treaty comes out, that the object of the arrangement is the welfare of the people who live there, and not the advantage of the trustee.

It goes beyond that. It seeks to gather under the common supervision of the League of Nations the various instrumentalities by which the world has been trying to check the evils that were in some places debasing men, like the opium traffic, like the traffic—for it was a traffic—in women and children, like the traffic in other dangerous drugs, like the traffic in arms among uncivilized people who could use arms only for their own detriment. It provides for sanitation, for the work of the Red Cross. Why, those clauses, my fellow citizens, draw the hearts of the world into league, draw the noble impulses of the world together and make a team of them.

I used to be told that this was an age in which mind was monarch, and my comment was that if that was true, the mind was one of those modern monarchs that reigns and does not govern; that, as a matter of fact, we were governed by a great representative assembly made up of the human passions, and that the best we could manage was that the high and fine passions should be in a majority so that they could control the baser passions, so that they could check the things that were wrong. This treaty seeks something like that. In drawing the humane endeavors of the world together it makes a league of the fine passions of the world, of its philanthropic passions, of its passion of pity, of its passion of human sympathy, of its passion of human friendliness and helpfulness, for there is such a passion. It is the passion which has lifted us along the slow road of civilization. It is the passion which has made ordered government possible. It is the passion which has made justice and established it in the world.

That is the treaty. Did you ever hear of it before? Did you ever know before what was in this treaty? Did anybody before ever tell you what the treaty was intended to do? I beg, my fellow citizens, that you and the rest of those Americans with whom we are happy to be associated all over this broad land will read the treaty yourselves, or, if you will not take the time to do that—for it is a technical document—that you will accept the interpretation of those who made it and know what the intentions were in the making of it. I hear a great deal, my fellow citizens, about the selfishness and the selfish ambitions of other governments, and I would not be doing justice to the gifted men with whom I was associated on the other side of the water if I did not testify that the purposes that I have outlined were their purposes. We differed as to the method very often. We had discussions as to the details, but we never had any serious discussion as to the principle. While we all acknowledged that the principles might perhaps in detail have been better realized, we are all back of those principles. There is a concert of mind and of purpose and of policy in the world that was never in existence before. I am not saying that by way of credit to myself or to those colleagues to whom I have alluded, because what happened to us was that we got messages from our people. We were under instructions, whether they were written down or not, and we did not dare come home without fulfilling those instructions. If I could not have brought back the kind of treaty that I did bring back, I never would have come back, because I would have been an unfaithful servant, and you would have had the right to condemn me in any way that you chose to use. So that I testify that this is an American treaty not only, but it is a treaty that expresses the heart of the great peoples who were associated together in the war against Germany.

I said at the opening of this informal address, my fellow citizens, that I had come to make a report to you. I want to add to that a little bit. I have not come to debate the treaty. It speaks for itself, if you will let it. The arguments directed against it are directed against it with a radical misunderstanding of the instrument itself. Therefore, I am not going anywhere to debate the treaty. I am going to expound it, and I am going, as I do here, now, today, to urge you in every vocal method that you can use to assert the spirit of the American people in support of it. Do not let men pull it down. Do not let them misrepresent it. Do not let them lead this Nation away from the high purposes with which this war was inaugurated and fought. As I came through that line of youngsters in khaki a few minutes ago I felt that I could salute them because I had done the job in the way I promised them I would do it, and when this treaty is accepted, men in khaki will not have to cross the seas again. That is the reason I believe in it.

I say "when it is accepted," for it will be accepted. I have never entertained a moment's doubt of that, and the only thing I have been impatient of has been the delay. It is not dangerous delay, except for the temper of the peoples scattered throughout the world who are waiting. Do you realize, my fellow citizens, that the whole world is waiting on America? The only country in the world that is trusted at this moment is the United States, and the peoples of the world are waiting to see whether their trust is justified or not. That has been the ground of my impatience. I knew their trust was justified, but I begrudged the time that certain gentlemen wish to take in telling them so. We shall tell them so in a voice as authentic as any voice in history, and in the years to come men will be glad to remember that they had some part in the great struggle which brought this incomparable consummation of the hopes of mankind.

At St. Louis, Missouri, September 5

This is much too solemn an occasion to care how we look; we ought to care how we think. [A photographer was asking the audience to sit for a picture.] I have come here tonight to ask permission to discuss with you some of the very curious aberrations of thinking that have taken place in this country of late. I have sought—I think I have sought without prejudice—to understand the point of view of the men who have been opposing the treaty and the Covenant of the League of Nations. Many of them are men whose judgment and whose patriotic feeling I have been accustomed to admire and respect, and yet I must admit to you, my fellow countrymen, that it is very hard for me to believe that they have followed their line of thinking to its logical and necessary conclusion, because when you reflect upon their position, it is either that we ought to reject this treaty altogether or that we ought to change it in such a way as will make it necessary to reopen negotiations with Germany and reconsider the settlements of the peace in many essential particulars. We cannot do the latter alone, and other nations will not join us in doing it. The only alternative is to reject the peace and to do what some of our fellow countrymen have been advising us to do, stand alone in the world.

I am going to take the liberty tonight of pointing out to you what this alternative means. I know the course of reasoning which is either uttered or implicit in this advice when it is given us by some of the men who propose this course. They believe that the United States is so strong, so financially strong, so industrially strong, if necessary so physically strong, that it can impose its will upon the world if it is necessary for it to stand out against the world, and they believe that the processes of peace can be processes of domination and antagonism, instead of processes of co-operation and good feeling. I therefore want to point out to you that only those who are ignorant of the world can believe that any nation, even so great a nation as the United States, can stand alone and play a single part in the history of mankind.

Begin with a single circumstance; for I have not come here tonight to indulge in any kind of oratory. I have come here tonight to present to you certain hard facts which I want you to take home with you and think about. I suppose that most of you realize that it is going to be very difficult for the other nations that were engaged in this war to get financially on their feet again. I dare say you read the other day the statement of Mr. Herbert

Hoover's opinion, an opinion which I always greatly respect, that it will be necessary for the United States immediately to advance four or five billion dollars for the rehabilitation of credit and industry on the other side of the water, and I must say to you that I learned nothing in Paris which would lead me to doubt that conclusion. I think the statement of the sum is a reasonable and conservative statement. If the world is going bankrupt, if credit is going to be destroyed, if the industry of the rest of the world is going to be interrupted, our market is confined to the United States. Trade will be impossible, except within our own borders. If we are to save our own markets and rehabilitate our own industries, we must save the financial situation of the world and rehabilitate the markets of the world. Very well, what do these gentlemen propose? That we should do that, for we cannot escape doing it.

Face to face with a situation of this kind, we are not, let us assume, partners in the execution of this treaty. What is one of the central features of the execution of this treaty? It is the application of the reparation clauses. Germany cannot pay for this war unless her industries are revived, and the treaty of peace sets up a great commission known as the Reparation Commission, in which it was intended that there should be a member from the United States as well as from other countries. The business of this commission will be in part to see that the industries of Germany are revived in order that Germany may pay this great debt which she owes to civilization. That Reparation Commission can determine the currents of trade, the conditions of international credit; it can determine how much Germany is going to buy, where it is going to buy, how it is going to pay for it, and if we must, to save ourselves, contribute to the financial rehabilitation of the world, then without being members of this partnership we must put our money in the hands of those who want to get the markets that belong to us. That is what these gentlemen call playing a lone hand. It is indeed playing a lone hand. It is playing a hand that is frozen out! We must contribute the money which other nations are to use in order to rehabilitate their industry and credit, and we must make them our antagonists and rivals and not our partners! I put that proposition to any business man, young or old, in the United States and ask him how he likes it, and whether he considers that a useful way for the United States to stand alone. We have got to carry this burden of reconstitution whether we will or not or be ruined, and the question is, Shall we carry it and be ruined anyhow? For that is what these gentlemen propose, that at every point we shall be embarrassed by the whole financial affairs of the world being in the hands of other nations.

As I was saying at the luncheon that I had the pleasure of eating with the chamber of commerce today, the whole aspect of the matter is an aspect of ignorance. The men who propose these things do not understand the selfish interests of the United States, because here is the rest of the picture: Hot rivalries, burning suspicions, jealousies, arrangements made everywhere if possible to shut us out, because if we will not come in as equals we ought to be shut out. If we are going to keep out of this thing in order to prey upon the rest of the world, then I think we ought to be frozen out of it. That is not the temper of the United States, and it is not like the United States to be ignorant enough to think any such thoughts, because we know that partners profit and enemies lose the game. But that is not all of the picture, my fellow citizens. If every nation is going to be our rival, if every nation is going to dislike and distrust us, and that will be the case, because having trusted us beyond measure the reaction will occur beyond measure (as it stands now they trust us, they look to us, they long that we shall undertake anything for their assistance rather than that any other nation should undertake it)—if we say, "No, we are in this world to live by ourselves, and get what we can out of it by any selfish processes," then the reaction will change the whole heart and attitude of the world towards this great, free, justice-loving people, and after you have changed the attitude of the world, what have you produced? Peace? Why, my fellow citizens, is there any man here or any woman, let me say is there any child here, who does not know that the seed of war in the modern world is industrial and commercial rivalry? The real reason that the war that we have just finished took place was that Germany was afraid her commercial rivals were going to get the better of her, and the reason why some nations went into the war against Germany was that they thought Germany would get the commercial advantage of them. The seed of the jealousy, the seed of the deep-seated hatred was hot, successful commercial and industrial rivalry.

Why, what did the Germans do when they got into Belgium? I have just seen that suffering country. Most of the Belgian factories are standing. You do not witness in Belgium what you witness in France, except upon certain battlefields—factories destroyed, whole towns wiped out. No! the factories are there, the streets are clear, the people are there, but go in the factories. Every piece of machinery that could be taken away has been taken away. If it was too big to take away, experts directed the way in which it should be injured so it could never be used again, and that was because there were textile industries and iron industries in Belgium which the Germans hated Belgium for having, because they were better than the German and outdid them in the markets of the world. This war, in its inception, was a commercial and industrial war. It was not a political war.

Very well, then, if we must stand apart and be the hostile rivals of the rest of the world, then we must do something else. We must be physically ready for anything that comes. We must have a great standing army. We must see to it that every man in America is trained to arms. We must see to it that there are munitions and guns enough for an army that means a mobilized nation; that they are not only laid up in store, but that they are kept up to date; that they are ready to use tomorrow; that we are a nation in arms; because you cannot be unfriendly to everybody without being ready that everybody shall be unfriendly to you. And what does that mean? Reduction of taxes? No. Not only the continuation of the present taxes but the increase of the present taxes; and it means something very much more serious than that. We can stand that, so far as the expense is concerned, if we care to keep up the high cost of living and enjoy the other luxuries that we have recently enjoyed, but, what is much more serious than that, we have got to have the sort of organization which is the only kind of organization that can handle arms of that sort. We may say what we please of the German Government that has been destroyed, my fellow citizens, but it was the only sort of government that could handle an armed nation. You cannot handle an armed nation by vote. You cannot handle an armed nation if it is democratic, because democracies do not go to war that way. You have got to have a concentrated, militaristic organization of government to run a nation of that sort. You have got to think of the President of the United States, not as the chief counsellor of the Nation, elected for a little while, but as the man meant constantly and every day to be the Commander in Chief of the Army and Navy of the United States, ready to order them to any part of the world where the threat of war is a menace to his own people. And you cannot do that under free debate. You cannot do that under public counsel. Plans must be kept secret. Knowledge must be accumulated by a system which we have condemned, because we have called it a spying system. The more polite call it a system of intelligence. You cannot watch other nations with your unassisted eye. You have got to watch them by secret agencies planted everywhere. Let me testify to this, my fellow citizens: I not only did not know it until we got into this war, but I did not believe it when I was told that it was true, that Germany was not the only country that main-ained a secret service. Every country in Europe maintained it, because they had to be ready for Germany's spring upon them, and the only difference between the German secret service and the other secret services was that the German secret service found out more than the others did, and therefore Germany sprang upon the other nations unawares, and they were not ready for it.

And you know what the effect of a military government is upon social questions. You know how impossible it is to effect social reform if everybody must be under orders from the Government. You know how impossible it is, in short, to have a free nation, if it is a military nation and under military order. You may say, "You have been on the other side of the water and got bad dreams." I have got no dreams at all. I am telling you the things, the evidence of which I have seen with awakened eyes and not with sleeping eyes, and I know that this country, if it wishes to stand alone, must stand alone as part of a world in arms. Because, ladies and gentlemen—I do not say it because I am an American and my heart is full of the same pride that fills yours with regard to the power and spirit of this great Nation, but merely because it is a fact which I think everybody would admit, outside of America, as well as inside of America—the organization contemplated by the League of Nations without the United States would merely be an alliance and not a league of nations. It would be an alliance in which the partnership would be between the more powerful European nations and Japan, and the other party to the world arrangement, the antagonist, the disassociated party, the party standing off to be watched by the alliance, would be the United States of America. There can be no league of nations in the true sense without the partnership of this great people.

Now, let us mix the selfish with the unselfish. If you do not want me to be too altruistic, let me be very practical. If we are partners, let me predict we will be the senior partner. The financial leadership will be ours. The industrial primacy will be ours. The commercial advantage will be ours. The other countries of the world are looking to us for leadership and direction. Very well, then, if I am to compete with the critics of this League and of this treaty as a selfish American, I say I want to get in and get in as quick as I can. I want to be inside and know how the thing is run and help to run it. You have the alternative, armed isolation or peaceful partnership. . . .

At Kansas City, Missouri, September 6

. . . There was something else we wanted that is accomplished by this treaty. We wanted to destroy autocratic authority everywhere in the world. We wanted to see to it that there was no place in the world where a small group of men could use their fellow citizens as pawns in a game; that there was no place in the world where a small group of men, without consulting their fellow citizens, could send their fellow citizens to the battlefields and to death in order to accomplish some dynastic ambition, some political plan that had been conceived in private, some object that had been prepared for by universal, world-wide intrigue. That is what we wanted to accomplish. The most startling thing that developed itself at the opening of our participation in this war was, not the military preparation of Germany—we were familiar with that, though we had been dreaming that she would not use it—but her political preparation—to find every community in the civilized world was penetrated by her intrigue. The German people did not know that, but it was known on Wilhelmstrasse, where the central offices of the German Government were, and

Wilhelmstrasse was the master of the German people. And this war, my fellow citizens, has emancipated the German people as well as the rest of the world. We do not want to see anything like that happen again, because we know that democracies will sooner or later have to destroy that form of Government, and if we do not destroy it now the job is still to be done. And by a combination of all the great fighting peoples of the world, to see to it that the aggressive purposes of such governments cannot be realized, you make it no longer worth while for little groups of men to contrive the downfall of civilization in private conference.

I want to say something about that that has a different aspect, and perhaps you will regard it as a slight digression from the discussion which I am asking you to be patient enough to follow. My fellow citizens, it does not make any difference what kind of a minority governs you if it is a minority, and the thing we must see to is that no minority anywhere masters the majority. That is at the heart, my fellow citizens, of the tragical things that are happening in that great country which we long to help and can find no way that is effective to help. I mean the great realm of Russia. The men who are now measurably in control of the affairs of Russia represent nobody but themselves. They have again and again been challenged to call a constitutional convention. They have again and again been challenged to prove that they had some kind of a mandate, even from a single class of their fellow citizens, and they dare not attempt it. They have no mandate from anybody. There are only thirty-four of them, I am told, and there were more than thirty-four men who used to control the destinies of Europe from Wilhelmstrasse. There is a closer monopoly of power in Petrograd and Moscow than there ever was in Berlin, and the thing that is intolerable is, not that the Russian people are having their way, but that another group of men more cruel than the Czar himself is controlling the destinies of that great people.

I want to say here and now that I am against the control of any minority anywhere. Search your own economic history and what have you been uneasy about? Now and again you have said there were small groups of capitalists who were controlling the industry and therefore the development of the United States. Very well, my fellow citizens; if that is so, and sometimes I have feared that it was, we must break up that monopoly. I am not now saying that there is any group of our fellow citizens who are consciously doing anything of the kind. I am saying that these allegations must be proved, but if it is proved that any class, any group, anywhere, is, without the suffrage of their fellow citizens, in control of our affairs, then I am with you to destroy the power of that group. We have got to be frank with ourselves, however: If we do not want minority government in Russia, we must see that we do not have it in the United States. If you do not want little groups of selfish men to plot the future of Europe, we must not allow little groups of selfish men to plot the future of America. Any man that speaks for a class must prove that he also speaks for all his fellow citizens and for mankind, and then we will listen to him. The most difficult thing in a democracy, my fellow citizens, is to get classes, where they unfortunately exist, to understand one another and unite, and you have not got a great democracy until they do understand one another and unite. If we are in for seeing that there are no more Czars and no more Kaisers, then let us do a thorough job and see that nothing of that sort occurs anywhere. . . . I do not want to attempt any flight of fancy, but I can fancy those men of the first generation that so thoughtfully set this great Government up, the generation of Washington and Hamilton and Jefferson and the Adamses—I can fancy their looking on with a sort of enraptured amazement that the American spirit should have made conquest of the world.

I wish you could have seen the faces of some of the people that talked to us over there about the arrival of the American troops. At first they did not know that we were going to be able to send so many, but they got something from the first groups that changed the whole aspect of the war. One of the most influential ladies in Paris, the wife of a member of the cabinet, told us that on the Fourth of July of last year she and others had attended the ceremonies with very sad hearts and merely out of courtesy to the United States, because they did not believe that the aid of the United States was going to be effective, but she said, "After we had been there and seen the faces of those men in khaki, seen the spirit of their swing and attitude and seen the vision that was in their eyes, we came away knowing that victory was in sight." What Europe saw in our boys was not merely men under arms, indomitable men under arms, but men with an ideal in their eyes, men who had come a long way from home to defend other peoples, men who had forgotten the convenience of everything that personally affected them and had turned away from the longing love of the people who were dear to them and gone across the broad sea to rescue the nations of the world from an intolerable oppression.

I tell you, my fellow citizens, the war was won by the American spirit. German orders were picked up on the battlefield directing the commanders not to let the Americans get hold of a particular post, because you never could get them out again. You know what one of our American wits said, that it took only half as long to train an American army as any other, because you had only to train them to go one way. It is true that they never thought of going any other way, and when they were restrained, because they were told it was premature or dangerous, they were impatient, they said, "We didn't come over here to wait, we came over here to fight," and their very audacity, their very indifference to danger, changed the morale of the battlefield. They were not fighting prudently; they were going to get there. And America in this treaty has realized, my fellow countrymen, what those gallant boys we are so proud of fought for. The men who make this impossible or difficult will have a life-long reckoning with the fighting forces of the United States. I have consorted with those boys. I have been proud to call myself their commander in chief. I did not run the business. They did not need anybody to run it. All I had to do was to turn them loose!

And now for a final word, my fellow citizens. If anything that I have said has left the impression on your mind that I have the least doubt of the result, please dismiss the impression. And if you think that I have come out on this errand to fight anybody—any body—please dismiss that from your mind. I have not come to fight or antagonize anybody, or any body of individuals. I have, let me say without the slightest affectation, the greatest respect for the Senate of the United States, but, my fellow citizens, I have come out to fight a cause. That cause is greater than the Senate. It is greater than the Government. It is as great as the cause of mankind, and I intend, in office or out, to fight that battle as long as I live. My ancestors were troublesome Scotchmen, and among them were some of that famous group that were known as the Covenanters. Very well, then, here is the Covenant of the League of Nations. I am a Covenanter! . . .

At Minneapolis, Minnesota, September 9

. . . Very well, then, what are we discussing? What are we debating in the United States? Whether we will take part in guiding and steadying the world or not. And some men hesitate. It is the only country in the world whose leadership and guidance will be accepted. If we do not give it, we may look forward, my fellow citizens, to something like a generation of doubt and of disorder which it will be impossible to pass through without the wreckage of a very considerable part of our slowly constructed civilization. America and her determinations now constitute the balance of moral force in the world, and if we do not use that moral force we will be of all peoples the most derelict. We are in the presence of this great choice, in the presence of this fundamental choice, whether we will stand by the mass of our own people and the mass of mankind. Pick up the great volume of the treaty. It is a great volume. It is as thick as that [illustrating]. You would think it just had three or four articles in it to hear some men talk about it. It is a thick volume, containing the charter of the new order of the world. I took the pains to write down here some of the things that it provides for, and if you will be patient I will read them, because I can make it more brief that way.

It provides for the destruction of autocratic power as an instrument of international control, admitting only self-governing nations to the League of Nations. Had you ever been told that before? No nation is admitted to the League of Nations whose people do not control its Government. That is the reason that we are making Germany wait. She says that henceforth her people are going to control her Government, but we have got to wait and see. If they do control it, she is as welcome to the League as anybody else, because we are not holding nations off. We are holding selfish groups of men off. We are not saying to peoples, "We do not want to be your comrades and serve you along with the rest of our fellow beings," but we are saying, "It depends upon your attitude; if you take charge of your own affairs, then come into the game and welcome." The League of Nations sends autocratic governments to coventry. That is the first point.

It provides for the substitution of publicity, discussion and arbitration for war. That is the supreme thing that it does. I will not go into details now, but every member of the League promises not to go to war until there has been a discussion and a cooling off of nine months, and, as I have frequently said on this tour, if Germany had submitted to discussion for nine days she never would have dared go to war. Though every foreign office in Europe begged her to do so, she would not grant twenty-four hours for a meeting of the representatives of the Governments of the world to ask what it was all about, because she did not dare tell what it was all about. Nine months' cooling off is a very valuable institution in the affairs of mankind. And you have got to have a very good case if you are willing that all your fellow men should know the whole case, for that is provided for, and talk about it for nine months. Nothing is more valuable, if you think your friend is a fool, than to induce him to hire a hall. If you think he is a fool the only way to prove it is to let him address a mass of his fellow citizens and see how they like his ideas. If they like them and you do not, it may be that you are the fools! The proof is presented at any rate.

Instead of using force after this period of discussion, something very much more effective than force is proposed, namely, an absolute boycott of the nation that does not keep its covenant, and when I say an absolute boycott I mean an absolute boycott. There cannot be any kind of intercourse with that nation. It cannot sell or buy goods. It cannot receive or send messages or letters. It cannot have any transactions with the citizens of any member of the League, and when you consider that the League is going to consist of every considerable nation in the world, except Germany, you can see what that boycott will mean. There is not a nation in the world, except this one, that can live without importing goods for nine months, and it does not make any difference to us whether we can or not, because we always fulfill our obligations, and there will never be a boycott for us.

It provides for placing the peace of the world under constant international oversight, in recognition of the principle that the peace of the world is the legitimate and immediate interest of every nation. Why, as it stands at present, my fellow citizens, if there is likely to be trouble between two nations other than the United States it is considered an unfriendly and hostile act for the United States to intervene. This Covenant makes it the right of the United States, and not the right of the United States merely, but the right of the weakest nation in the world, to bring anything that the most powerful nation in the world is doing that is likely to disturb the peace of the world under the scrutiny of mankind. [Voice in audience, "And that is right!"] My friend in the audience says that is right, and it undoubtedly is, because the peace of the world is everybody's business. Yet this is the first document that ever recognized that principle. We now have the attitude of the Irishman, you know, who went into one of those antique institutions known as a saloon. It was rather a large place, and he saw two men fighting over in the corner. He went up to the bartender and he said, "Is this a private fight, or can everybody get in?" Now, in the true Irish spirit, we are abolishing private fights, and we are making it the law of mankind that it is everybody's business and everybody can get in. The consequence is that there will be no attempt at private fights.

It provides for disarmament on the part of the great fighting nations of the world.

It provides in detail for the rehabilitation of oppressed peoples, and that will remove most of the causes of war.

It provides that there shall be no more annexations of territory anywhere, but that those territories whose people are not ready to govern themselves shall be intrusted to the trusteeship of the nations that can take care of them, the trustee nation to be responsible in annual reports to the League of Nations; that is to say, to mankind in general, subject to removal and restricted in respect to anything that might be done to that population which would be to the detriment of the population itself. So that you cannot go into darkest Africa and make slaves of those poor people, as some Governments at times have done.

It abolishes enforced labor. It takes the same care of the women and children of those unschooled races that we try to take of the women and children of ours. Why, my fellow citizens, this is the great humane document of all time.

It provides that every secret treaty shall be invalid. It sweeps the table of all private understandings and enforces the principle that there shall be no private understandings of any kind that anybody is bound to respect. One of the difficulties in framing this treaty was that after we got over there private—secret—treaties were springing up on all sides like a noxious growth. You had to guard your breathing apparatus against the miasma that arose from some of them. But they were treaties, and the war had been fought on the principle of the sacredness of treaties. We could not propose that solemn obligations, however unwisely undertaken, should be disregarded, but we could do the best that was possible in the presence of those understandings and then say, "No more of this; no more secret understandings." And the representatives of every great nation in the world assented without demur—without the slightest difficulty.

I do not think you realize what a change of mind has come over the world. As we used to say in the old days, some men that never got it before have got religion.

It provides for the protection of dependent peoples.

It provides that high standards of labor, such as are observed in the United States, shall be extended to the workingman everywhere in the world.

It provides that all the great humane instrumentalities, like the Red Cross, like the conventions against the opium trade, like the regulation of the liquor traffic with debased and ignorant people, like the prohibition of the selling of arms and ammunition to people who can use them only to their own detriment, shall be under the common direction and control of the League of Nations. Now, did you ever hear of all these things before? That is the treaty, my fellow citizens; and I can only conjecture that some of the men who are fighting the treaty either never read it themselves or are taking it for granted that you will not read it. I say without hesitation that no international agreement has ever before been drawn up along those lines—of the universal consideration of right and the interest of humanity. . . .

At Billings, Montana, September 11

. . . What I have come to say to you today, my friends, is this: We are debating the treaty of peace with Germany and we are making the mistake, I take the liberty of saying, of debating it as if it were an ordinary treaty with some particular country, a treaty which we could ourselves modify without complicating the affairs of the world; whereas, as a matter of fact, this is not merely a treaty with Germany. Matters were drawn into this treaty which affected the peace and happiness of the whole Continent of Europe, and not of the Continent of Europe merely, but of forlorn populations in Africa, of peoples that we hardly know about in Asia, in the Far East and everywhere the influence of German policy had extended and everywhere that influence had to be corrected, had to be checked, had to be altered. What I want to impress upon you today is that it is this treaty or none. It is this treaty because we can have no other.

Consider the circumstances. For the first time in the world some twenty nations sent their most thoughtful and responsible men to consult together at the capital of France to effect a settlement of the affairs of the world, and I want to render my testimony that these gentlemen entered upon their deliberations with great openness of mind. Their discussions were characterized by the utmost candor, and they realize, my fellow citizens, what as a student of history I venture to say no similar body ever acknowledged before, that they were nobody's masters, that they did not have the right to follow the line of any national advantage in determining what the settlements of the peace should be, but that they were the servants of their people and the servants of the people of the world. This settlement, my fellow citizens, is the first international settlement that was intended for the happiness of the average men and women throughout the world. This is indeed and in truth a people's treaty, and it is the first people's treaty, and I venture to express the opinion that it is not wise for Parliaments or Congresses to attempt to alter it. It is a people's treaty, notwithstanding the fact that we call it a treaty with Germany; and while it is a treaty with Germany, and in some senses a very severe treaty, indeed, it is not an unjust treaty, as some have characterized it. My fellow citizens, Germany tried to commit a crime against civilization, and this treaty is justified in making Germany pay for that criminal error up to the ability of her payment. Some of the very gentlemen who are now characterizing this treaty as too harsh are the same men who less than a twelve-month ago were criticizing the administration at Washington in the fear that they would compound with Germany and let her off from the payment of the utmost that she could pay in retribution for what she had done. They were pitiless then; they are pitiful now.

It is very important, my fellow citizens, that we should not forget what this war meant. I am amazed at the indications that we are forgetting what we went through. There are some indications that on the other side of the water they are apt to forget what they went through. I venture to think that there are thousands of mothers and fathers and wives and sisters and sweethearts in this country who are never going to forget. Thousands of our gallant youth lie buried in France, and buried for what? For the redemption of America? America was not directly attacked. For the salvation of America? America was not immediately in danger. No; for the salvation of mankind. It is the noblest errand that troops ever went on. I was saying the other day in the presence of a little handful of men whom I revered, veterans of our Civil War, that it seemed to me that they fought for the greatest thing that there was to fight for in their day, and you know with what reverence we have regarded all the men who fought in the ranks in the Civil War for the Union. I am saying this out of a full heart, though I was born on the other side of the Mason and Dixon line. We revere the men who saved the Union. What are going to be our sentiments with regard to these boys in khaki and the boys who have just been in khaki in this war? Do you not think that when they are old men a halo will seem to be about them, because they were crusaders for the liberty of the world? One of the hardest things for me to do during this war, as for many another man in this country, was merely to try to direct things and not take a gun and go myself. When I feel the pride that I often have felt in having been the commander in chief of these gallant armies and those splendid boys at sea, I think, "Ah, that is fine, but, oh, to have been one of them and to have accomplished this great thing which has been accomplished!"

The fundamental principle of this treaty is a principle never acknowledged before, a principle which had its birth and has had its growth in this country, that the countries of the world belong to the people who live in them, and that they have a right to determine their own destiny and their own form of government and their own policy, and that no body of statesmen, sitting anywhere, no matter whether they represent the overwhelming physical force of the world or not, has the right to assign any great people to a sovereignty under which it does not care to live. This is the great treaty which is being debated. This is the treaty which is being examined with a microscope. This is the treaty which is being pulled about and about which suggestions are made as to changes of phraseology. Why, my friends, are you going to be so nearsighted as to look that way at a great charter of human liberty? The thing is impossible. You cannot have any other treaty, because you can never get together again the elements that agreed to this treaty. You cannot do it by dealing with separate governments. You cannot assemble the forces again that were back of it. You cannot bring the agreement upon which it rests into force again. It was the laborious work of many, many months of the most intimate conference. It has very, very few compromises in it and is, most of it, laid down in straight lines according to American specifications. The choice is either to accept this treaty or play a lone hand. . . .

The central fact of the modern world is universal unrest, and the unrest is not due merely to the excitement of a recent war. The unrest is not due merely to the fact of recent extraordinary circumstances. It is due to a universal conviction that the conditions under which men live and labor are not satisfactory. It is a conviction all over the world that there is no use talking about political democracy unless you have also industrial democracy. You know what this war interrupted in the United States. We were searching our own hearts; we were looking closely at our own methods of doing business. A great many were convinced that the control of the business of this country was in too few hands. Some were convinced that the credit of the country was controlled by small groups of men, and the great Federal Reserve Act and the great Land-Bank Act were passed in order to release the resources of the country on a broader and more generous scale. We had not finished dealing with monopolies. We have not finished dealing with monopolies. With monopolies there can be no industrial democracy. With the control of the few, of whatever kind or class, there can be no democracy of any sort. The world is finding that out in some portions of it in blood and terror.

Look what has happened in Russia, my fellow citizens. I find wherever I go in America that my fellow citizens feel as I do, an infinite pity for that great people, an infinite longing to be of some service to them. Everybody who has mixed with the Russian people tells me that they are among the most lovable people in the world, a very gentle people, a very friendly people, a very simple people, and in their local life a very democratic people, people who easily trust you, and who expect you to be trustworthy as they are. Yet this people is delivered into the hands of an intolerable tyranny. It came out of one tyranny to get into a worse. A little group of some thirty or forty men are the masters of that people at present. Nobody elected them. They chose themselves. They maintain their power by the sword, and they maintain the sword by seizing all the food of the country and letting only those who will fight for them eat, the rest of them to go starved; and because they can command no loyalty we are told by the newspapers that they are about to brand the men under arms for them, so that they will be forever marked as their servants and slaves. That is what pitiful Russia has got in for, and there will be many a bloody year, I am afraid, before she finds herself again.

I speak of Russia. Have you seen no symptoms of the spread of that sort of chaotic spirit into other countries? If you had been across the sea with me you would know that the dread in the mind of every thoughtful man in Europe is that that distemper will spread to their countries, that before there will be settled order there will be tragical disorder. Have you heard nothing of the propaganda of that sort of belief in the United States? That poison is running through the veins of the world, and we have made the methods of communication throughout the world such that all the veins of the world are open and the poison can circulate. The wireless throws it out upon the air. The cable whispers it underneath the sea. Men talk about it in little groups, men talk about it openly in great groups not only in Europe but here also in the United States. There are apostles of Lenin in our own midst. I can not imagine what it means to be an apostle of Lenin. It means to be an apostle of the night, of chaos, of disorder; there can be no creed of disorganization. Our immediate duty, therefore, my fellow countrymen, is to see that no minority, no class, no special interest, no matter how respectable, how rich, how poor, shall get control of the affairs of the United States. . . .

At Spokane, Washington, September 12

. . . The guarantee of this treaty is the part of the Covenant of nations which you have heard most criticized. I mean the now celebrated Article X. Article X is an engagement of the most extraordinary kind in history. It is an engagement by all the fighting nations of the world never to fight upon the plan upon which they always fought before. They, all of them, agree to respect and preserve against external aggression the territorial integrity and existing political independence of the others, and they agree that if there should be any breach of that Covenant, the council of the League shall advise what steps shall be taken to make the promises good. That is the Covenant with which you have been frightened. Frightened, my fellow citizens? Why, it is the only possible or conceivable guarantee against the wars that have ravaged the world, because those wars have habitually begun by territorial aggression, by the seizure of territory that did not belong to the power that was effecting the seizure. How did this great war begin? It began by the invasion of Belgium, and it was admitted by all German statesmen that they never meant to get out of Belgium. By guaranteeing the territorial integrity of a country, you do not mean that you guarantee it against invasion. You guarantee it against the invader staying there and keeping the spoils. The integrity is the title, is the ownership. You agree never to take territory away from the people to whom it belongs, and you agree never to interfere with the political independence of the people living in these territories whose titles are now made clear by a universal international guarantee.

I want to discuss with you very frankly, indeed, just as frankly as I know how, the difficulties that have been suggested, because I say, not in the spirit of criticism, but in a spirit of entire intended fairness, that not one of the qualifications which have been suggested in this discussion is justified by the language of the instrument. Let me take them one by one. In the first article of the Covenant of the League it is provided that any member State may withdraw from the league upon two years' notice, provided at the time of withdrawal it has fulfilled its international obligations and its obligations under the Covenant.

Gentlemen object that it is not said who shall determine whether it has fulfilled its international obligations and its obligations under the covenant or not. Having sat at the table where the instrument was drawn, I know that that was not by accident, because that is a matter upon which no nation can sit in judgment upon another. That is left to the conscience and the independent determination of the nation that is withdrawing, and there is only one jury that it need fear and that is the great embodied jury expressing the opinion of mankind. I want to differentiate myself, therefore, from the men who are afraid of that clause, because I want to record my feeling in the matter that, as an American, I am never afraid that the United States will fail to perform its international obligations; and, being certain that it will never fail in that respect, I have no fear that an occasion will arise when we need be sensitive to the opinion of mankind. That is the only jury set up in the case, and I am ready to go before that jury at any time. These gentlemen want to say what the instrument says, that we can withdraw when we please. The instrument does not say it in those words, but it says it in effect, and the only limitation upon that is that we should not please unless we have done our duty. We never will please, God helping us, to neglect our duty.

The second difficulty—taking them in the order in which they have come in the Covenant itself—is the article I was a moment ago discussing, Article X. Article X, as I told you, says that if the promise to respect and preserve as against external aggression the territorial integrity and existing political independence of the member States is broken, then the council shall advise what is to be done. I do not know any but one meaning for the word "advise." I have been very curious and interested to learn how many other meanings have been put into it. I, in my surprise, have looked in the dictionary to be sure I was not mistaken, and so far as I can find out "advise" means "advise." And more interesting than that, the advice cannot be given without the affirmative vote of the United States. There must be unanimous vote of the council before there is advice, and the United States is a member of the council by the constitution of the League itself, a member now and always a member, so that neither the United States nor any other country can be advised to go to war for the redemption of that promise without the concurrent affirmative vote of the United States. Yet I hear gentlemen say that this is an invasion of our sovereignty. My fellow citizens, if it is anything, it is an exaggeration of our sovereignty, because it puts our sovereignty in a way to put a veto on that advice being given to anybody. Our present sovereignty merely extends to making choice whether we will go to war or not, but this extends our sovereignty to saying whether other nations shall go to war or not. If that does not constitute a very considerable insurance against war, I would like somebody to write a provision which would; because, at every point, my fellow citizens, the position of these gentlemen who criticize this instrument is either that they do not understand the Covenant or that they can suggest something better, and I have not heard one of them suggest anything better. In fact, I have never heard one of them suggest anything. If the world is going to be at peace, it must be this or something better, and I want to say again it is a case of "put up or shut up."

Let me make a slight digression here, if I may, to speak about a matter of some delicacy. I have had a great many men say to me, "I am a Republican, but I am in favor of the League of Nations." Why the "but"? I want to tell you, my fellow citizens, that there is one element in this whole discussion which ought not to be in it. There is, though I say it myself, an element of personal bitterness. One would suppose that this Covenant of the League of Nations was first thought of and first invented and first written by a man named Wilson. I wish it were. If I had done that, I would be willing to have it recorded that I had done that and nothing else. But I did not do it. I, along with thousands of my fellow countrymen, got the idea twenty years ago, chiefly from Republican public men. Take men like ex-Senator Burton, of Ohio. He has been preaching a league of nations for twenty years. I do not want to mention names, because I do not want to record gentlemen against themselves, but go through the list and you will find most of the leading, thinking minds on the Republican side in favor of this very kind of thing, and I want to remind every Republican of the criticism that he and his comrades have usually made of the Democratic party, and the boast that they have generally made of their party. They said that the Democratic party was a party of negations and not a party of constructive policies, and that the Republican party was a party of constructive policy. Very well, then, why that "but"? "I am a Republican, but I am in favor of the greatest constructive thing that has ever been suggested!" If I were a Republican, I would say, "I am a Republican and therefore I am in favor of a League of Nations." My present point is to dissociate the League of Nations from the present speaker. I did not originate it. It is not my handiwork. It has originated out of the consciences and thought of men who wanted justice and loved peace for generations, and my relationship to it is just what my relationship ought to be to every public question, the relationship which a man bears to his fellow citizens when he tries to interpret their thought and their conscience. That is what I conceive to be my part in the League of Nations. I did have a part in some of the phraseology, and every time I did it was to carry out the ideas that these gentlemen are fighting for.

For example, there is one part of the Covenant, the principal part of it, where it speaks of arbitration and discussion, where it provides that any member State failing to keep these particular covenants shall be regarded as thereby *ipso facto* to have committed an act of war against the other members. The way it originally read was, "Shall thereby *ipso facto* be deemed at war with the other members," and I said, "No; I cannot agree to that. That provision would put the United States at war without the consent of the Congress of the United States, and I have no right in this part of the Covenant or any other to assent to a provision which would deprive the Congress of the United States of its free choice whether it makes war or not." There, and at every other point in the Covenant where it was necessary to do so, I insisted upon language which would leave the Congress of the United States free, and yet these gentlemen say that the Congress of the United States is deprived of its liberty. I fought that battle and won it. It is not necessary for them to fight it over again.

You will say, "It is all very well what you say about the vote of the United States being necessary to the advice provided the United States is not one of the parties to the dispute. In that case it cannot vote." That is very true; but in that case it has got the fight on its hands anyhow, because if it is one of the parties to the dispute the war belongs to it. It does not have to go into it, and therefore it cannot be forced by the vote of the United States in the council to go into the war. The only thing the vote can do is to force it out of the war. I want to ask you to think what it means when it is suggested that the United States may be a party. A party to what? A party to seizing somebody else's territory? A party to infringing some other country's political independence? Is any man willing to stand on this platform and say that the United States is likely to do either of those things? I challenge any man to stand up before an American audience and say that that is the danger. "Ah, but somebody else may seek to seize our territory or impair our political independence." Well, who? Who has an arm long enough, who has an audacity great enough to try to take a single inch of American territory or to seek to interfere for one moment with the political independence of the United States? These gentlemen are dreaming of things that cannot happen, and I cannot bring myself to feel uneasy in the presence of things that I know are not so. The great difficulty in this discussion, as in so many others, is in the number of things that men know that are not so.

"But the Monroe Doctrine." I must admit to you, my fellow citizens, I do not know how the Monroe Doctrine could be any more explicitly accepted than it is in the Covenant of the League of Nations. It says that nothing in the Covenant shall be interpreted as impairing the validity of the Monroe Doctrine. What more could you say? I did try while I was in Paris to define the Monroe Doctrine and get it written into the document, but I will confide to you in confidence that when I tried to define it I found that it escaped analysis, that all that you could say was that it was a principle with regard to the interference of foreign powers in the politics of the Western Hemisphere which the United States felt at liberty to apply in any circumstances where it thought it pertinent. That is not a definition. That means that the United States means to play big brother to the Western Hemisphere in any circumstances where it thinks it wise to play big brother. Therefore, inasmuch as you could not or would not define the Monroe Doctrine—at least I would not, because I do not know how much we may want to extend it—what more could you say than that nothing in that instrument shall impair the validity of the Monroe Doctrine? I tell you, my fellow citizens, that is the most extraordinary sentence in that treaty, for this reason: Up to that time there was not a nation in the world that was willing to admit the validity of the Monroe Doctrine. I have made a great many speeches in my life, perhaps too many, but I do not think that I ever put so much of what I hope was the best in me as I put in the speech in the conference on the League of Nations in favor of the Monroe Doctrine, and it was upon that occasion that it was embodied. And we have this extraordinary spectacle, of the world recognizing the validity of the Monroe Doctrine. Yet these gentlemen seem to want something more. What more could you get? Shall we get them to express their belief in the deity of the Monroe Doctrine? They accept it for the first time in the history of the world, and they say that they will do nothing that will interfere with it. I must submit that it is absolutely irrational to ask for anything more.

But there is the question of somebody interfering with the domestic policies of the United States—immigration, naturalization, tariffs; matters of that sort. There, again, I cannot understand or feel the weight of the difficulty because the Covenant says that if any international difficulty is brought under discussion and one of the parties claims and the council finds that it is a matter of domestic jurisdiction, the council shall cease to discuss it and shall make no report about it. The only way you could make the document more clear would be by enumerating the domestic questions you had in mind. Very well. I ask any lawyer here if that would be safe? Might you not be in danger of leaving out something? Might you not be in danger of not mentioning something that would afterwards become important? The danger of making a list is that the mention of the things you do mention constitutes the exclusion of the things you do not mention. Inasmuch as there is no dispute of any authoritative students of international law that these matters that we are most concerned about—immigration, naturalization, tariff, and the rest—are domestic questions, it is inconceivable that the council should ever seek to interfere with or to discuss such questions, unless we had ourselves deliberately made them matters of international agreement, and even the opponents of the League admit they would be suitable and proper subjects for discussion.

Those are the matters upon which they are talking about reservations. . . .

At San Francisco, California, September 17

. . . Again and again, as I have crossed the continent, generous women, women I did not know, have taken me by the hand and said, "God bless you, Mr. President." Some of them, like many of you, had lost sons and husbands and brothers in the war. Why should they bless me? I advised Congress to declare war. I advised Congress to send their sons to their death. As Commander in Chief of the Army, I sent them over the seas, and they were killed. Why should they bless me? Because in the generosity of their hearts they want the sons of other women saved henceforth, and they believe that the methods proposed at any rate create a very hopeful expectation that similar wars will be prevented, and that other armies will not have to go from the United States to die upon distant fields of battle. The moral compulsion upon us, upon us who at the critical stage of the world saved the world and who threw in our fortunes with all the forward-looking peoples of the world—the moral compulsion upon us to stand by and see it through is overwhelming. We cannot now turn back. We made the choice in April, 1917. We cannot with honor reverse it now.

Not only is there the compulsion of honor, but there is the compulsion of interest. I never like to speak of that, because, notwithstanding the reputation that we had throughout the world before we made the great sacrifice of this war, this Nation does love its honor better than it loves its interest. It does yield to moral compulsion more readily than to material compulsion. That is the glory of America. That is the spirit in which she was conceived and born. That is the mission that she has in the world. She always has lived up to it, and, God helping her, she always will live up to it. But if you want, as some of our fellow countrymen insist, to dwell upon the material side of it and our interest in the matter, our commercial interest, draw the picture for yourselves. The other nations of the world are drawing together. We who suggested that they should draw together in this new partnership stand aside. We at once draw their suspicion upon us. We at once draw their intense hostility upon us. We at once renew the thing that had begun to be done before we went into the war. There was a conference in Paris not many months before we went into the war in which the nations then engaged against Germany attempted to draw together in an exclusive economic combination where they should serve one another's interest and exclude those who had not participated in the war from sharing in that interest, and just so certainly as we stay out, every market that can possibly be closed against us will be closed. If you merely look at it from the point of view of the material prosperity of the United States, we are under compulsion to stay in the partnership. I was asking some gentlemen the other day who were engaged in commerce of various sorts, "Can you sell more easily to a man who trusts you or to a man who distrusts you?" There can be but one answer to that question. Can you sell more easily to a man who takes your goods because he cannot do without them or to a man who wants them and believes them the best? The thing demonstrates itself. You make all the lines of trade lines of resistance unless you prove true to the things that you have attempted and undertaken.

Then, there is a deeper compulsion even than those, the compulsion of humanity. If there is one thing that America ought to have learned more promptly than any other country it is that, being made up out of all the ranks of humanity, in serving itself it must serve the human race. I suppose I could not command the words which would exaggerate the present expectations of the world with regard to the United States. Nothing more thrilling, nothing more touching, happened to me on the other side of the water than the daily evidences that, not the weak peoples merely, not the peoples of countries that had been allowed to shift for themselves and had always borne the chief burden of the world's sufferings, but the great peoples as well, the people of France as well as the people of Serbia, the people of all the nations that had looked this terror in the face, were turning to the United States and saying, "We depend upon you to take the lead, to direct us how to go out of this wilderness of doubt and fear and terror." We cannot desert humanity. We are the trustees of humanity, and we must see that we redeem the pledges which are always implicit in so great a trusteeship.

So, feeling these compulsions, the compulsion of honor, the compulsion of interest, and the compulsion of humanity, I wonder what it is that is holding some minds back from acquiescence in this great enterprise of peace. I must admit to you, my fellow citizens, that I have been much puzzled. I cannot conceive a motive adequate to hold men off from this thing, and when I examine the objections which they make to the treaty I can but wonder if they are really thinking, or if, on the other hand, there is some emotion coming from fountains that I do not know of which are obliging them to take this course. . . .

At Salt Lake City, Utah, September 23

. . . The forces of objection being driven out of one position after another are now centering upon the heart of the League itself. I have come here tonight, my fellow countrymen, to discuss that critical matter that you constantly see in the newspapers, which we call "reservations." I want you to have a very clear idea of what is meant by reservations. Reservations are to all intents and purposes equivalent to amendments. I can say, I believe with confidence, that it is the judgment of the people of the United States that neither the treaty nor the Covenant should be amended. Very well, then; look at the character of the reservations. What does a reservation mean? It means a stipulation that this particular Government insists upon interpreting its duty under that Covenant in a special way, insists upon interpreting it in a way in which other Governments, it may be, do not interpret it. This thing, when we ratify it, is a contract. You can not alter so much as the words of a contract without the consent of the other parties. Any reservation will have to be carried to all the other signatories, Germany included, and we shall have to get the consent of Germany, among the rest, to read this Covenant in some special way in which we prefer to read it in the interest of the safety of America. That, to my mind, is one of the most unacceptable things that could happen. To my mind, to reopen the question of the meaning of this clearly written treaty is to reopen negotiations with Germany, and I do not believe that any part of the world is in the temper to do that. In order to put this matter in such a shape as will lend itself to concrete illustration, let me read you what I understand is a proposed form of reservation:

> The United States assumes no obligation under the provisions of Article X to preserve the territorial integrity or political independence

of any other country or to interfere in controversies between other nations, whether members of the League or not, or to employ the military and naval forces of the United States under any article of the treaty for any purpose, unless in any particular case the Congress, which under the Constitution has the sole power to declare war or authorize the employment of the military and naval forces of the United States, shall by act or joint resolution so declare.

That is a rejection of the Covenant. That is an absolute refusal to carry any part of the same responsibility that the other members of the League carry. Does the United States want to be in on that special footing? Does the United States want to say to the nations with whom it stood in this great struggle, "We have seen you through on the battle field, but now we are done. We are not going to stand by you"? Article X is an engagement on the part of all the great fighting nations of the world, because all the great fighting nations are going to be members of the League, that they will respect and preserve as against external aggression the territorial integrity and the existing political independence of the other members of the League. That is cutting at the heart of all wars. Every war of any consequence that you can cite originated in an attempt to seize the territory or interfere with the political independence of some other nation. We went into this war with the sacred promise that we regarded all nations as having the same rights, whether they were weak or strong, and unless we engage to sustain the weak we have guaranteed that the strong will prevail, we have guaranteed that imperialistic enterprise may revive, we have guaranteed that there is no barrier to the ambition of nations that have the power to dominate, we have abdicated the whole position of right and substituted the principle of might. This is the heart of the Covenant, and what are these gentlemen afraid of? Nothing can be done under that article of the treaty without the consent of the United States. I challenge them to draw any other deduction from the provisions of the Covenant itself. In every case where the League takes action the unanimous vote of the council of the League is necessary; the United States is a permanent member of the council of the League, and its affirmative vote is in every case necessary for every affirmative, or for that matter every negative, action.

Let us go into particulars. These gentlemen say, "We do not want the United States drawn into every little European squabble." Of course, we do not, and under the League of Nations it is entirely within our choice whether we will be or not. The normal processes of the action of the League are certainly to be this: When trouble arises in the Balkans, when somebody sets up a fire somewhere in central Europe among those little nations, which are for the time being looking upon one another with a good deal of jealousy and suspicion, because the passions of the world have not cooled—whenever that happens, the council of the League will confer as to the best methods of putting out the fire. If you want to put out a fire in Utah, you do not send to Oklahoma for the fire engine. If you want to put out a fire in the Balkans, if you want to stamp out the smoldering flame in some part of central Europe, you do not send to the United States for troops. The council of the League selects the powers which are most ready, most available, most suitable, and selects them only at their own consent, so that the United States would in no such circumstances conceivably be drawn in unless the flame spread to the world. And would they then be left out, even if they were not members of the League? You have seen the fire spread to the world once, and did not you go in? If you saw it spread again, if you saw human liberty again imperiled, would you wait to be a member of the League to go in?

My fellow citizens, the whole thing goes directly to the conscience of the Nation. If the fight is big enough to draw the United States in, I predict that they will be drawn in anyhow, and if it is not big enough to bring them in inevitably, they can go in or stay out according to their own decision. Why are these gentlemen afraid? There is no force to oblige the United States to do anything except moral force. Is any man, any proud American, afraid that the United States will resist the duress of duty? I am intensely conscious of the great conscience of this Nation. I see the inevitableness, as well as the dignity and the greatness, of such declarations as President Grant has made aligning all the great organized moral forces of the world on the same side. It is inconceivable they should be on different sides.

There is no necessity for the last part of this reservation. Every public man, every statesman, in the world knows, and I say that advisedly, that in order that the United States should go to war it is necessary for the Congress to act. They do not have to be told that, but that is not what this resolution says. This resolution says the United States assumes no obligation under the provisions of Article X to preserve the territorial integrity or political independence of any other country—washes its hands of the whole business; says, "We do not want even to create the presumption that we will do the right thing. We do not want to be committed even to a great principle, but we want to say that every time a case arises the Congress will independently take it up as if there were no Covenant and determine whether there is any moral obligation; and after determining that, determining whether it will act upon that moral obligation or not, it will act." In other words, that is an absolute withdrawal from the obligations of Article X. That is why I say that it would be a rejection of the Covenant and thereby a rejection of the treaty, for the treaty cannot be executed without the Covenant.

I appeal, and I appeal with confidence, my fellow countrymen, to the men whose judgment I am told has approved of reservations of this sort. I appeal to them to look into the matter again. I know some of the gentlemen who are quoted as approving a reservation of that sort; I know them to be high-minded and patriotic Americans, and I know them to be men whose character and judgment I entirely respect, and whose motives I respect as much as I respect the motives of any man, but they have not looked into the matter. Are they willing to ask the rest of the world to go into this Covenant and to let the United States assume none of its obligations? Let us have all the advantages of it and none of the responsibilities? Are they willing that proud America should ask for special exemptions, should show a special timidity, should ask to go into an arrangement depending upon a judgment when its own judgment is a different judgment? I confidently believe, my fellow citizens, that they will do no such thing. This is not an interpretation of the Covenant. I have been trying to interpret it to you. This is a rejection of the Covenant, and if this is adopted, the whole treaty falls to the ground, for, my fellow citizens, we must realize that a great and final choice is before this people. Either we are going to guarantee civilization or we are going to abandon it. I use the word with perhaps the admission that it may carry a slight exaggeration, but nevertheless advisedly, when I say abandon civilization, for what is the present condition of civilization? Everywhere, even in the United States, there is an attitude of antagonism toward the ordered processes of government. We feel the evil influence on this side of the Atlantic, and on the other side of the Atlantic every public man knows that it is knocking at the door of his government. . . .

At Pueblo, Colorado, September 25

. . . My friends, on last Decoration Day I went to a beautiful hillside near Paris, where was located the cemetery of Suresnes, a cemetery given over to the burial of the American dead. Behind me on the slopes was rank upon rank of living American soldiers, and lying before me upon the levels of the plain was rank upon rank of departed American soldiers. Right by the side of the stand where I spoke there was a little group of French women who had adopted those graves, had made themselves mothers of those dear ghosts by putting flowers every day upon those graves, taking them as their own sons, their own beloved, because they had died in the same cause—France was free and the world was free because America had come! I wish some men in public life who are now opposing the settlement for which these men died could visit such a spot as that. I wish that the thought that comes out of those graves could penetrate their consciousness. I wish that they could feel the moral obligation that rests upon us not to go back on those boys, but to see the thing through, to see it through to the end and make good their redemption of the world. For nothing less depends upon this decision, nothing less than the liberation and salvation of the world.

You will say, "Is the League an absolute guarantee against war?" No; I do not know any absolute guarantee against the errors of human judgment or the violence of human passion, but I tell you this: With a cooling space of nine months for human passion, not much of it will keep hot. I had a couple of friends who were in the habit of losing their tempers, and when they lost their tempers they were in the habit of using very unparliamentary language. Some of their friends induced them to make a promise that they never would swear inside the town limits. When the impulse next came upon them, they took a street car to go out of town to swear, and by the time they got out of town they did not want to swear. They came back convinced that they were just what they were, a couple of unspeakable fools, and the habit of getting angry and of swearing suffered great inroads upon it by that experience. Now, illustrating the great by the small, that is true of the passions of nations. It is true of the passions of men however you combine them. Give them space to cool off. I ask you this: If it is not an absolute insurance against war, do you want no insurance at all? Do you want nothing? Do you want not only no probability that war will not recur, but the probability that it will recur? The arrangements of justice do not stand of themselves, my fellow citizens. The arrangements of this treaty are just, but they need the support of the combined power of the great nations of the world. And they will have that support. Now that the mists of this great question have cleared away, I believe that men will see the truth, eye to eye and face to face. There is one thing that the American people always rise to and extend their hand to, and that is the truth of justice and of liberty and of peace. We have accepted that truth and we are going to be led by it, and it is going to lead us, and through us the world, out into pastures of quietness and peace such as the world never dreamed of before.

5. Not Ratification but Nullification

To Senator Hitchcock, November 18, 1919

It was obvious that the treaty could not pass the Senate without reservations, "strong" or "mild." Senate Democratic leaders, following Wilson, hoped for a deadlock which would result in a compromise more favorable to—or rather dictated by—the administraton. On the afternoon of November 19 the vote was held. The Democrats, thanks to the support of twelve irreconcilables, defeated Lodge's resolution (which embodied his thirteen reservations). Next, the irreconcilables joined their Republican brethren to defeat both Democratic proposals: adoption of the treaty with Democratic (the President's) reservations and adoption of it without any reservations. The Treaty of Versailles was dead for the first session of the 66th Congress. Following is Wilson's letter to the Senate Democratic leader warning against any compromise with Lodge.

YOU WERE good enough to bring me word that the Democratic Senators supporting the treaty expected to hold a conference before the final vote on the Lodge resolution of ratification and that they would be glad to receive a word of counsel from me.

I should hesitate to offer it in any detail, but I assume that the Senators only desire my judgment upon the all-important question of the final vote on the resolution containing the many reservations by Senator Lodge. On that I can not hesitate, for, in my opinion, the resolution in that form does not provide for ratification but, rather, for the nullification of the treaty. I sincerely hope that the friends and supporters of the treaty will vote against the Lodge resolution of ratification.

I trust that all true friends of the treaty will refuse to support the Lodge resolution.

6. No Compromise or Concession

Statement on Treaty, December 14, 1919

Wilson wrote this statement and released it to the press through official White House spokesmen.

IT WAS learned from the highest authority at the executive offices today that the hope of the Republican leaders of the Senate that the President would make some move which will relieve the situation with regard to the treaty is entirely without foundation.

He has no compromise or concession of any kind in mind, but intends, so far as he is concerned, that the Republican leaders of the Senate shall continue to bear the undivided responsibility for the fate of the treaty and the present condition of the world in consequence of that fate.

7. Great and Solemn Referendum

To Homer S. Cummings, January 8, 1920

Wilson believed that the only sure way of resolving the treaty conflict was to hold a plebiscite on it in the next general election; this would have meant shelving the treaty for fourteen months.

Wilson proposed this solution in his letter to the Democratic national chairman, who read it to the party faithful at a Jackson Day dinner. As soon as the letter was read, William Jennings Bryan replied by advocating some immediate compromise with Lodge. For his part Lodge was more than willing to take up the gauntlet dropped by Wilson. The irreconcilables were especially happy for they knew the delay would work in their favor.

MY DEAR Mr. Chairman: It is with the keenest regret that I find that I am to be deprived of the pleasure and privilege of joining you and the other loyal Democrats who are to assemble tonight to celebrate Jackson Day and renew their vows of fidelity to the great principles of our party, the principles which must now fulfill the hopes not only of our own people but of the world.

The United States enjoyed the spiritual leadership of the world until the Senate of the United States failed to ratify the treaty by which the belligerent nations sought to effect the settlements for which they had fought throughout the war.

It is inconceivable that at this supreme crisis and final turning point in the international relations of the whole world, when the results of the Great War are by no means determined and are still questionable and dependent upon events which no man can foresee or count upon, the United States should withdraw from the concert of progressive and enlightened nations by which Germany was defeated, and all similar Governments (if the world be so unhappy as to contain any) warned of the consequences of any attempt at a like iniquity, and yet that is the effect of the course which the United States has taken with regard to the Treaty of Versailles.

Germany is beaten, but we are still at war with her, and the old stage is reset for a repetition of the old plot. It is now ready for a resumption of the old offensive and defensive alliances which made settled peace impossible. It is now open again to every sort of intrigue.

The old spies are free to resume their former abominable activities. They are again at liberty to make it impossible for Governments to be sure what mischief is being worked among their own people, what internal disorders are being fomented.

Without the Covenant of the League of Nations there may be as many secret treaties as ever, to destroy the confidence of

Governments in each other, and their validity cannot be questioned.

None of the objects we professed to be fighting for has been secured, or can be made certain of, without this Nation's ratification of the treaty and its entry into the Covenant. This Nation entered the Great War to vindicate its own rights and to protect and preserve free government. It went into the war to see it through to the end, and the end has not yet come. It went into the war to make an end of militarism, to furnish guarantees to weak nations, and to make a just and lasting peace. It entered it with noble enthusiasm. Five of the leading belligerents have accepted the treaty and formal ratifications soon will be exchanged. The question is whether this country will enter and enter wholeheartedly. If it does not do so, the United States and Germany will play a lone hand in the world.

The maintenance of the peace of the world and the effective execution of the treaty depend upon the whole-hearted participation of the United States. I am not stating it as a matter of power. The point is that the United States is the only Nation which has sufficient moral force with the rest of the world to guarantee the substitution of discussion for war. If we keep out of this agreement, if we do not give our guarantees, then another attempt will be made to crush the new nations of Europe.

I do not believe that this is what the people of this country wish or will be satisfied with. Personally, I do not accept the action of the Senate of the United States as the decision of the Nation.

I have asserted from the first that the overwhelming majority of the people of this country desire the ratification of the treaty, and my impression to that effect has recently been confirmed by the unmistakable evidences of public opinion given during my visit to seventeen of the States.

I have endeavored to make it plain that if the Senate wishes to say what the undoubted meaning of the League is I shall have no objection. There can be no reasonable objection to interpretations accompanying the act of ratification itself. But when the treaty is acted upon, I must know whether it means that we have ratified or rejected it.

We cannot rewrite this treaty. We must take it without changes which alter its meaning, or leave it, and then, after the rest of the world has signed it, we must face the unthinkable task of making another and separate treaty with Germany.

But no mere assertions with regard to the wish and opinion of the country are credited. If there is any doubt as to what the people of the country think on this vital matter, the clear and single way out is to submit it for determination at the next election to the voters of the Nation, to give the next election the form of a great and solemn referendum, a referendum as to the part the United States is to play in completing the settlements of the war and in the prevention in the future of such outrages as Germany attempted to perpetrate.

We have no more moral right to refuse now to take part in the execution and administration of these settlements than we had to refuse to take part in the fighting of the last few weeks of the war which brought victory and made it possible to dictate to Germany what the settlements should be. Our fidelity to our associates in the war is in question and the whole future of mankind. It will be heartening to the whole world to know the attitude and purpose of the people of the United States.

I spoke just now of the spiritual leadership of the United States, thinking of international affairs. But there is another spiritual leadership which is open to us and which we can assume.

The world has been made safe for democracy, but democracy has not been finally vindicated. All sorts of crimes are being committed in its name, all sorts of preposterous perversions of its doctrines and practices are being attempted.

This, in my judgment, is to be the great privilege of the democracy of the United States, to show that it can lead the way in the solution of the great social and industrial problems of our time, and lead the way to a happy, settled order of life as well as to political liberty. The program for this achievement we must attempt to formulate, and in carrying it out we shall do more than can be done in any other way to sweep out of existence the tyrannous and arbitrary forms of power which are now masquerading under the name of popular government.

Whenever we look back to Andrew Jackson we should draw fresh inspiration from his character and example. His mind grasped with such a splendid definiteness and firmness the principles of national authority and national action. He was so indomitable in his purpose to give reality to the principles of the Government, that this is a very fortunate time to recall his career and to renew our vows of faithfulness to the principles and the pure practices of democracy.

I rejoice to join you in this renewal of faith and purpose. I hope that the whole evening may be of the happiest results as regards the fortunes of our party and the Nation.

8. Is It True?

To Secretary of State Lansing, February 7, 1920

This letter lent support to Republican charges that the President was a vindictive man. It is curious that Wilson *brought his complaint to Lansing's attention four months after first learning of it.*

IS IT true, as I have been told, that during my illness you have frequently called the heads of the executive departments of the Government into conference? If it is, I feel it my duty to call your attention to considerations which I do not care to dwell upon until I learn from you yourself that this is the fact. Under our constitutional law and practice, as developed hitherto, no one but the President has the right to summon the heads of the executive departments into conference, and no one but the President and the Congress has the right to ask their views or the views of any one of them on any public question.

I take this matter up with you because in the development of every constitutional system, custom and precedent are of the most serious consequence, and I think we will all agree in desiring not to lead in any wrong direction. I have therefore taken the liberty of writing you to ask you this question, and I am sure you will be glad to answer.

I am happy to learn from your recent note to Mrs. Wilson that your strength is returning.

9. A Feeling That Was Growing Upon Me

To Secretary of State Lansing, February 11, 1920

Lansing admitted that he presided over "informal conferences" of the Cabinet. But he denied that he ever went beyond the narrow limits of his office. He then offered to resign. To the President's letter below accepting the resignation, Lansing replied the following day, detailing his grievances very frankly. His main grievance was that since January, 1919, at Paris, Wilson had been bypassing him continually and had evidently lost all confidence in him. Only loyalty had prevented him from resigning sooner. Wilson replaced him with Bainbridge Colby.

I AM very much disappointed by your letter of February 9 in reply to mine asking about the so-called Cabinet meetings. You kindly explain the motives of these meetings, and I find nothing in your letter which justifies your assumption of presidential authority in such a matter. You say you "felt that, in view of the fact that you were denied communication with me, it was wise to confer informally together on interdepartmental matters and matters as to which action could not be postponed until my medical advisers permitted me" to be seen and consulted, but I have to remind you, Mr. Secretary, that no action could be taken without me by the Cabinet, and therefore there could have been no disadvantage in awaiting action with regard to matters concerning which action could not have been taken without me.

This affair, Mr. Secretary, only deepens a feeling that was growing upon me. While we were still in Paris I felt, and have felt increasingly ever since, that you accepted my guidance and direction on questions with regard to which I had to instruct you only with increasing reluctance, and since my return to Washington I have been struck by the number of matters in which you have apparently tried to forestall my judgment by formulating action and merely asking my approval when it was impossible for me to form an independent judgment, because I had not had an opportunity to examine the circumstances with any degree of independence.

I therefore feel that I must frankly take advantage of your kind suggestion that if I should prefer to have another to conduct our foreign affairs you are ready to relieve me of any embarrassment by placing your resignation in my hands, for I must say that it would relieve me of embarrassment, Mr. Secretary, the embarrassment of feeling your reluctance and divergence of judgment, if you would give your present office up and afford me an opportunity to select some one whose mind would more willingly go along with mine.

I need not tell you with what reluctance I take advantage of your suggestion, or that I do so with the kindliest feeling. In matters of transcendent importance like this the only wise course is a course of perfect candor, where personal feeling is as much as possible left out of the reckoning.

10. I Cannot Understand the Difference

To Senator Hitchcock, March 8, 1920

The treaty came up for reconsideration in the second session of the 66th Congress. In February the Senate had passed eight of the fourteen Lodge reservations and it seemed that the treaty might actually be accepted. Republicans and Democrats, knowing that the treaty could be adopted only with the Lodge reservations, were working on a compromise when Wilson sent the following letter. It immediately dissuaded most Democrats from supporting the Lodge reservations and so insured defeat of the treaty. When the vote was taken on March 19, twenty-one out of forty-seven Democrats bolted to the Lodge camp. Had seven more Democrats deserted Wilson, the Lodge resolution would have carried and the United States would have joined the League of Nations.

. . . I THINK, my dear Senator, we can't dismiss from our minds the idea that it is necessary to stipulate, in connection with Article X, the constitutional methods we should use in fulfilling our obligations under it. We gain nothing by such stipulations and secure nothing which is not already secured. It was understood as a matter of concern at the conference in Paris that whatever obligations any Government assumed or whatever duties it undertook under the treaty would of course have to be fulfilled by its usual and constitutional methods of action.

Once or twice in the meetings of the conference, when the treaty was under consideration, "reservations" were made to that effect by the representatives of individual powers, and those "reservations" were invariably received in the way in which men who have met for business and not for talk always receive acts of scrupulous supererogation—listened to with indifferent silence, as such men listen to what is a matter of course and was not necessary to say.

There can be no objection to explaining again what our constitutional method is and that our Congress alone can declare war or determine the causes or occasions for war, and that it alone can authorize the use of the armed forces of the United States on land or on the sea. But to make such a declaration would certainly be a work of supererogation.

I am sorry to say that the reservations that have come under my notice are almost without exception not interpretations of the articles to which it is proposed to attach them but in effect virtual nullifications of those articles.

Any reservation which seeks to deprive the League of Nations of the force of Article X cuts at the very heart and life of Covenant itself. Any league of nations which does not guarantee as a matter of incontestable right the political independence and integrity of each of the members might be hardly more than a futile scrap of paper, as imperfect in operation as the agreement between Belgium and Germany which the Germans violated in 1914. . . .

The choice is between two ideals: on the one hand, the ideal of democracy, which represents the rights of free peoples everywhere to govern themselves and on the other hand the ideal of imperialism which seeks to dominate by force and unjust power, an ideal which is by no means dead and which is earnestly held in many quarters still.

Every imperialistic influence in Europe was hostile to the embodiment of Article X in the Covenant of the League of Nations, and its defeat now would mark the complete consummation of their efforts to nullify the treaty. I hold the doctrine of Article

X as the essence of Americanism. We cannot repudiate it or weaken it without at the same time repudiating our own principles.

The imperialist wants no League of Nations, but if, in response to the universal cry of the masses everywhere, there is to be one, he is interested to secure one suited to his own purposes, one that will permit him to continue the historic game of pawns and peoples—the juggling of provinces, the old balance of power, and the inevitable wars attendant upon these things.

The reservation proposed would perpetuate the old order. Does anyone really want to see the old game played again? Can anyone really venture to take part in reviving the old order? The enemies of a League of Nations have by every true instinct centered their efforts against Article X, for it is undoubtedly the foundation of the whole structure. It is the bulwark and the only bulwark of the rising democracy of the world against the forces of imperialism and reaction.

Either we should enter the League fearlessly, accepting the responsibility and not fearing the role of leadership which we now enjoy, contributing our efforts toward establishing a just and permanent peace, or we should retire as gracefully as possible from the great concert of powers, by which the world was saved. For my own part I am not willing to trust to the counsel of diplomats the working out of any salvation of the world from the things which it has suffered.

I believe that when the full significance of this great question has been generally apprehended obstacles will seem insignificant before the opportunity, a great and glorious opportunity, to contribute our overwhelming moral and material force to the establishment of an international regime in which our own ideals of justice and right may be made to prevail and the nations of the world be allowed a peaceful development under conditions of order and safety hitherto impossible.

I need not say, Senator, that I have given a great deal of thought to the whole matter of reservations proposed in connection with the ratification of the treaty and particularly that portion of the treaty which contains the Covenant of the League of Nations. And I have been struck by the fact that practically every so-called reservation was in effect a rather sweeping nullification of the terms of the treaty itself.

I hear of reservationists and mild-reservationists, but I cannot understand the difference between a nullifier and a mild-nullifier. Our responsibility as a nation in this turning point of history is an overwhelming one, and if I had the opportunity, I would beg every one concerned to consider the matter in the light of what it is possible to accomplish for humanity rather than in the light of special national interests.

If I have been truly informed concerning the desire of some of your colleagues to know my views in this matter, I would be very glad if you should show this letter to them.

11. Mere Instruments of Profit

Article on "The Road Away From Revolution," August, 1923

In the three years of his retirement Wilson *produced only the following article, which appeared in the* Atlantic Monthly *of August, 1923.*

IN THESE doubtful and anxious days, when all the world is at unrest and, look which way you will, the road ahead seems darkened by shadows which portend dangers of many kinds, it is only common prudence that we should look about us and attempt to assess the causes of distress and the most likely means of removing them.

There must be some real ground for the universal unrest and perturbation. It is not to be found in superficial politics or in mere economic blunders. It probably lies deep at the sources of the spiritual life of our time. It leads to revolution; and perhaps if we take the case of the Russian Revolution, the outstanding event of its kind in our age, we may find a good deal of instruction for our judgment of present critical situations and circumstances.

What gave rise to the Russian Revolution? The answer can only be that it was the product of a whole social system. It was not in fact a sudden thing. It had been gathering head for several generations. It was due to the systematic denial to the great body of Russians of the rights and privileges which all normal men desire and must have if they are to be contented and within reach of happiness. The lives of the great mass of the Russian people contained no opportunities, but were hemmed in by barriers against which they were constantly flinging their spirits, only to fall back bruised and dispirited. Only the powerful were suffered to secure their rights or even to gain access to the means of material success.

It is to be noted as a leading fact of our time that it was against "capitalism" that the Russian leaders directed their attack. It was capitalism that made them see red; and it is against capitalism under one name or another that the discontented classes everywhere draw their indictment.

There are thoughtful and well-informed men all over the world who believe, with much apparently sound reason, that the abstract thing, the system, which we call capitalism, is indispensable to the industrial support and development of modern civilization. And yet everyone who has an intelligent knowledge of social forces must know that great and widespread reactions like that which is now unquestionably manifesting itself against capitalism do not occur without cause or provocation; and before we commit ourselves irreconcilably to an attitude of hostility to this movement of the time, we ought frankly to put to ourselves the question, Is the capitalistic system unimpeachable? which is another way of asking, Have capitalists generally used their power for the benefit of the countries in which their capital is employed and for the benefit of their fellow men?

Is it not, on the contrary, too true that capitalists have often seemed to regard the men whom they used as mere instruments of profit, whose physical and mental powers it was legitimate to exploit with as slight cost to themselves as possible, either of money or of sympathy? Have not many fine men who were actuated by the highest principles in every other relationship of life seemed to hold that generosity and humane feeling were not among the imperative mandates of conscience in the conduct of a banking business, or in the development of an industrial or commercial enterprise?

And, if these offenses against high morality and true citizenship have been frequently observable, are we to say that the blame for the present discontent and turbulence is wholly on the side of those who are in revolt against them? Ought we not, rather, to seek a way to remove such offenses and make life itself clean for those who will share honorably and cleanly in it?

The world has been made safe for democracy. There need now be no fear that any such mad design as that entertained by the insolent and ignorant Hohenzollerns and their counselors may prevail against it. But democracy has not yet made the world safe against irrational revolution. That supreme task, which is nothing less than the salvation of civilization, now faces democracy, insistent, imperative. There is no escaping it, unless everything we have built up is presently to fall in ruin about us; and the United States, as the greatest of democracies, must undertake it.

The road that leads away from revolution is clearly marked, for it is defined by the nature of men and of organized society. It therefore behooves us to study very carefully and very candidly the exact nature of the task and the means of its accomplishment.

The nature of men and of organized society dictates the maintenance in every field of action of the highest and purest standards of justice and of right dealing; and it is essential to efficacious thinking in this critical matter that we should not entertain a narrow or technical conception of justice. By justice the lawyer generally means the prompt, fair, and open application of impartial rules; but we call ours a Christian civilization, and a Christian conception of justice must be much higher. It must include sympathy and helpfulness and a willingness to forego self-interest in order to promote the welfare, happiness, and contentment of others and of the community as a whole. This is what our age is blindly feeling after in its reaction against what it deems the too great selfishness of the capitalistic system.

The sum of the whole matter is this, that our civilization cannot survive materially unless it be redeemed spiritually. It can be saved only by becoming permeated with the spirit of Christ and being made free and happy by the practices which spring out of that spirit. Only thus can discontent be driven out and all the shadows lifted from the road ahead.

Here is the final challenge to our churches, to our political organizations, and to our capitalists—to everyone who fears God or loves his country. Shall we not all earnestly cooperate to bring in the new day?

12. Put Self-Interest Away

Address on Peace, November 10, 1923

Wilson read his last address over the radio on the night before Armistice Day. He died less than three months later.

THE ANNIVERSARY of Armistice Day should stir us to great exaltation of spirit because of the proud recollection that it was our day, a day above those early days of that never-to-be-forgotten November which lifted the world to the high levels of vision and achievement upon which the great war for democracy and right was fought and won, although the stimulating memories of that happy triumph are forever marred and embittered for us by the shameful fact that when the victory was won—won, be it remembered, chiefly by the indomitable spirit and ungrudging sacrifices of our own incomparable soldiers—we turned our backs upon our associates and refused to bear any responsible part in the administration of peace, or the firm and permanent establishment of the results of the war—won at so terrible a cost of life and treasure—and withdrew into a sullen and selfish isolation, which is deeply ignoble because manifestly cowardly and dishonorable.

This must always be a source of deep mortification to us and we shall inevitably be forced by the moral obligations of freedom and honor to retrieve that fatal error and assume once more the rôle of courage, self-respect, and helpfulness which every true American must wish to regard as our natural part in the affairs of the world.

That we should have thus done a great wrong to civilization at one of the most critical turning points in the history of the world is the more to be deplored because every anxious year that has followed has made the exceeding need for such service as we might have rendered more and more pressing as demoralizing circumstances which we might have controlled have gone from bad to worse.

And now, as if to furnish a sort of sinister climax, France and Italy between them have made waste paper of the Treaty of Versailles, and the whole field of international relationship is in perilous confusion.

The affairs of the world can be set straight only by the firmest and most determined exhibition of the will to lead and make right prevail.

Happily, the present situation in the world of affairs affords us the opportunity to retrieve the past and to render to mankind the inestimable service of proving that there is at least one great and powerful nation which can turn away from programs of self-interest and devote itself to practicing and establishing the highest ideals of disinterested service and the consistent standards of conscience and of right.

The only way in which we can worthily give proof of our appreciation of the high significance of Armistice Day is by resolving to put self-interest away and once more formulate and act upon the highest ideals and purposes of international policy.

Thus, and only thus, can we return to the true traditions of America.

NOTE ON THE SOURCES

Following are the sources of the documents in the exact order that the Table of Contents lists them.

One. PREPARATION. (1) *Nassau Literary Magazine*, November, 1877. (2) *International Review*, August, 1879. (3) *Daily Princetonian* April 28, 1905. (4) *Princeton Alumni Weekly*, June 12, 1907. (5) *North American Review*, May, 1908. (6) *Woodrow Wilson Papers*. (7) *Pittsburgh Dispatch*, April 17, 1910. (8) *Ray Stannard Baker Collection*. (9) *Princeton Alumni Weekly*, October 26, 1910.

Two. GOVERNOR AND CANDIDATE. (1) *Baker Collection*. (2) *Trenton True American*, July 16, 1910. (3) *Ibid*., August 24, 1910. (4) *Ibid*., September 16, 1910. (5) *Ibid*., October 22, 1910. (6) *Ibid*., October 25, 1910. (7) *Ibid*., December 25, 1910. (8) *Journal of the Senate of New Jersey*, 1911, 58-68. (9) *Trenton True American*, April 22, 1911. (10) *Congressional Record*, vol. 49, 4745-4747. (11) *Trenton True American*, April 12, 1912. (12) 62nd Congress, 2nd session, *Senate Document* 903. (13) John Wells Davidson, *A Crossroads of Freedom*, passim.

Three. NEW FREEDOM. (1) *Cong. Rec*., vol. 50, 2-3. (2) *The New York Times*, March 12, 1913. (3) *Papers Relating to the Foreign Relations of the United States*, 1913, 170-171. (4) *Cong. Rec*., vol. 50, 130, 132. (5) *Ibid*., vol. 50, 2132-2133, 2142-2143. (6) *Wilson Papers*. (7) *Cong. Rec*., vol. 50, 5845-5856. (8) *Ibid*., vol. 51, 1962-1964, 1978-1979. (9) *Ibid*., vol. 51, 6908-6909, 6925. (10) *The New York Times*, July 24, 1914. (11) *Foreign Relations*, 1914, 247-248. (12) *Cong. Rec*., vol. 51, app., 523-524. (13) *The New York Times*, November 8, 1914. (14) *Cong. Rec*., vol. 52, 18-21. (15) *Ibid*., vol. 52, 2481-2482, 2552. (16) *Wilson Papers*.

Four. NEUTRALITY. (1) *Foreign Relations*, 1915, supp., 100-101. (2) *Wilson Papers*. (3) *Foreign Relations*, 1915, supp., 152-156. (4) *Foreign Relations, The Lansing Papers*, 1914-1920, vol. I, 380. (5)

Wilson Papers. (6) *The New York Times,* May 11, 1915. (7) *Foreign Relations,* 1915, supp., 393-396. (8) *Wilson Papers.* (9) *Foreign Relations,* 1915, supp., 436-438. (10) *The New York Times,* June 9, 1915. (11) *Foreign Relations,* 1915, supp., 480-482. (12) *State Department Papers.* (13) *The New York Times,* October 12, 1915. (14) *Wilson Papers.* (15) *Cong. Rec.,* vol. 53, 3318. (16) *Ibid.,* vol. 53, 6421-6422, 6448-6449. (17) *Ibid.,* vol. 53, 7628. (18) *Foreign Relations,* 1916, supp., 263. (19) *Wilson Papers.* (20) *Cong. Rec.,* vol. 53, 1315-1316. (21) *Wilson Papers.* (22) *Cong. Rec.,* vol. 53, 13335-13337, 13361-13363. (23) *Ibid.,* vol. 53, 13656-13659, app., 1984-1987. (24) *Wilson Papers.* (25) *Ibid.* (26) *The New York Times,* January 23, 1917. (27) *Cong. Rec.,* vol. 54, 2550, 2578-2579. (28) *The New York Times,* March 5, 1917.

Five. WAR. (1) 65th Cong., spec. sess., *Senate Document* 2. (2) *Cong. Rec.,* vol. 55, 102-104. (3) *The New York Times,* May 19, 1917. (4) *Wilson Papers.* (5) *Ibid.* (6) *Current History Magazine,* vol. 7, part I, 441-444. (7) *Cong. Rec.,* vol. 56, 680-681. (8) *Wilson Papers.* (9) *Cong. Rec.,* vol. 56, 4747-4748. (10) *Baker Collection.* (11) *Cong. Rec.,* vol. 56, 8671. (12) *Foreign Relations,* 1918, *Russia,* II, 287-290. (13) *Official U.S. Bulletin,* 404, September 5, 1918. (14) *Cong. Rec.,* vol. 56, 10886-10888. (15) *Foreign Relations,* 1918, supp. 1, vol. 1, 358-359. (16) *Ibid.,* 381-383. (17) *Cong. Rec.,* vol. 56, 11494. (18) *Wilson Papers.* (19) *Cong. Rec.,* vol. 56, 11537-11539.

Six. TREATY. (1) *Wilson Papers.* (2) *Ibid.* (3) *The New York Times,* November 19, 1919. (4) *Cong. Rec.,* vol. 57, 3408-3411. (5) *Ibid.,* vol. 57, 4201-4203. (6) *Official U.S. Bulletin, No. 554,* March 6, 1919. (7) *Ibid.,* No. 552, March 4, 1919. (8) 66th Congress, 1st sess., *Senate Doc's* 7, 461. (9) *Wilson Papers.* (10) *The New York Times,* May 11, 1919. (11) *Cong. Rec.,* vol. 58, 40-42. (12) *Ibid.,* vol. 58, 1952-1953.

Seven. TRAGEDY. (1) *Cong. Rec.,* vol. 58, 2336-2339. (2) 66th Cong., 1st sess., *Senate Doc.* 63. (3) *Ibid., Senate Doc.* 76. (4) *Ibid., Senate Doc.* 120. (5) *Cong. Rec.,* vol. 58, 8768. (6) *The New York Times,* December 15, 1919. (7) *Cong. Rec.,* vol. 59, 1249. (8) *Ibid.,* vol. 59, 2882. (9) *Ibid.,* vol. 59, 2883. (10) *Wilson Papers.* (11) *Atlantic Monthly,* August 23, 1923. (12) *The New York Times,* November 11, 1923.

SELECTED BIBLIOGRAPHY

There is now an enormous literature on Wilson. Following are some of the works that proved useful in putting together this book.

Immensely helpful in locating Wilson's public documents is Laura Shearer Turnbull's *Woodrow Wilson, A Selected Bibliography* (Princeton, Princeton University Press, 1948).

The Public Papers of Woodrow Wilson, edited by Ray Stannard Baker and William E. Dodd (6 vols., New York, Harper & Brothers, 1925–27), is the most substantial collection of Wilson's writings that has been published. But it omits much that is important. The publication of Wilson's complete papers by Princeton University is eagerly awaited.

Ray Stannard Baker, in his *Woodrow Wilson, Life and Letters* (8 vols., New York, Doubleday & Co., 1927–39), has written not so much a biography as a chronicle. It is valuable for its extracts from Wilson's personal letters and memoranda on government policies.

The best biography, though still in progress—its latest volume goes up to 1915—is Arthur Stanley Link's *Wilson* (4 vols., Princeton, Princeton University Press, 1947–65). It is exhaustive in detail and finely balanced in judgment. Link has also written *Woodrow Wilson and the Progressive Era* (New York, Harper & Brothers, 1954), which gives an excellent summary account of the New Freedom, of Wilson's Mexican policy and of the progressive legislation of 1916.

Other good biographies are: Herbert C. F. Bell, *Woodrow Wilson and the People* (New York, Doubleday & Co., 1945); John Morton Blum, *Woodrow Wilson and the Politics of Morality* (Boston, Little, Brown & Co., 1956); and James Kerney, *The Political Education of Woodrow Wilson* (New York, The Century Co., 1926).

Works written by or about Wilson's friends and close associates illuminate his political career. Especially important is Edward Mandell House, *The Intimate Papers of Colonel House,* edited by Charles Seymour (4 vols., New York, Houghton, Mifflin & Co., 1926–28). Important, too, are the books by Wilson's wife: Edith Bolling Wilson, *My Memoir* (Indianapolis, Bobbs-Merrill Co., 1939); and by his physician: Cary Travers Grayson, *Woodrow Wilson, An Intimate Memoir* (New York, Holt, Rinehart and Winston, 1960). The intellectual collaboration between Wilson and Brandeis is brought out in Alpheus T. Mason's *Brandeis, A Free Man's Life* (New York, The Viking Press, 1946).

Among the books that concentrate on limited aspects of Wilson's political life the following have proved the most valuable: Ray Stannard Baker, *Woodrow Wilson and World Settlement* (3 vols., New York, Doubleday & Co., 1922–24), which is a straightforward narrative account of the Paris peace conference, the third volume being a documentary supplement; Thomas A. Bailey's two volumes: *Woodrow Wilson and the Lost Peace* (New York, The Macmillan Co., 1944) and *Woodrow Wilson and the Great Betrayal* (New York, The Macmillan Co., 1945), which are sometimes captious, sometimes hasty in judgment, but always provocative; William Diamond, *The Economic Thought of Woodrow Wilson* (Baltimore, Johns Hopkins Press, 1943), which provides a good analysis of Wilson's beliefs, particularly before he became President; and John Wells Davidson, *A Crossroads of Freedom* (New Haven, Yale University Press, 1956), which is the best collection of Wilson's 1912 campaign speeches.

For a general account of the entire period from the turn of the century to the war, see: Harold U. Faulkner, *The Decline of Laissez-Faire, 1897–1917* (New York, Rinehart & Co., 1951); and Mark Sullivan, *Our Times, The United States 1900–1925* (6 vols., New York, Charles Scribner's Sons, 1926–35).